FORGED

Richard Baxell

The Clapton Press

The Clapton Press Limited
38 Thistlewaite Road
London E5 0QQ

www.theclaptonpress.com

ISBN 978-1-913693-33-6

Cover image courtesy of Southworth Collection, Special
Collections & Archives, University of California, San Diego.

Table of Contents

To H, E & PtC

Introduction

The subjects of this new collection of biographies share something unusual: they were all extraordinary people. Extraordinary, because nearly 100 years ago they took the momentous decision to leave their families and friends and risk their lives in a war being fought in a country far from their homes. The country was Spain, and during its bitter and protracted civil war of 1936 to 1939 these individuals would be among some 35,000 men and women from around the world who felt sufficiently enraged that they elected to go. Thousands of them would never return, including more than 500 from Britain.

Despite this, the Spanish Civil War and the involvement of foreign volunteers is often little more than a footnote in British history. This is an oversight, for it was a momentous event in the history of the Twentieth Century, with profound consequences not just for Spain, but for Europe and beyond. The internationalisation of the conflict—the left-wing Republican government was aided by Stalin's Soviet Union while Franco's 'Nationalists' were supported by Hitler and Mussolini—turned what began as a military coup into a 'world war in miniature', to quote the pioneering Spanish Civil War historian, Hugh Thomas. It is also key in any understanding of the western democracies' policy of appeasement towards Hitler and Mussolini. The British Government's dogged determination not to get embroiled led them to push for a policy of 'non-intervention' in the war. This treated the Spanish Government and military rebels equally, depriving what was a democratically elected government of their legal right to obtain arms. Consequently, it forced the Republicans to turn to Stalin's Soviet Union and unscrupulous arms dealers, while doing nothing to stop a flood of troops and military supplies pouring into the country from Nazi Germany and Fascist Italy. The stubborn refusal to abandon non-intervention, despite its manifest failings, revealed to the dictators the lengths that the British Government was prepared

7

to go to maintain peace in Europe.

While the government was determined to 'keep out of it', many people in Britain felt differently. Journalists and reporters flocked to Spain, ensuring that the war received extensive coverage in newspapers and newsreels and became the subject of passionate arguments in homes, workplaces and political meetings across the country. Huge numbers of British men and women joined campaigns, donating time and money. Some went further, helping to rescue Spanish refugees or by joining one of the medical organisations that operated in Spain during the war. Significantly, some 2,500 British men and women were so incensed that they volunteered to join the Spanish Republican armed forces. A handful even fought for Franco.

The majority of those to feature in this collection of biographies were members of the International Brigades, the battalions of foreign volunteers raised by the Communist International (known as the Comintern) to fight for the Republic. However, also included are a number of individuals who served in other roles, such as journalists, functionaries and medics. While the biographies centre on the experiences gained during the war in Spain, they all include an account of the subjects' early lives and backgrounds, to help explain their political development and their choice to become involved in the war. Likewise, the consequences of their participation in the civil war are explored in detail: how they faced up to the defeat of the Spanish Republic and consequent forty years of Franco dictatorship, their involvement (or not) in the Second World War and their attitudes towards the Soviet Union and the Cold War.

The opening chapter is an account of the senior British officer within the English-speaking 15th International Brigade, a Cambridge history and economics graduate called Malcolm Dunbar. Major Dunbar was lauded in parliament by the MP for Ebbw Vale (and later the architect of the National Health Service) Aneurin Bevan as 'the man who threw 150,000 men across the River Ebro'.[1] Despite his importance, the taciturn and enigmatic Dunbar never wrote a memoir, nor did he give interviews and has never previously had a biography written about him. Alongside this 'forgotten warrior' is another

8

prominent British figure in Spain, the senior Political Commissar and *Daily Worker* reporter, Peter Kerrigan. The tough Glaswegian would go on to become a leading figure in the British Communist Party until the 1960s. Dunbar and Kerrigan might be seen to represent the two wings of the British Communist movement in the 1930s: one, middle-class, university educated and a member of the London aesthetic set; the other a tough working-class engineer and Trade Unionist from Glasgow.

Other members of the International Brigades to feature include Clive Branson, a distant cousin of the entrepreneur, Sir Richard Branson. He was a respected artist during the 1920s and 1930s and several of his paintings are held by the Tate Gallery in London. Branson was taken prisoner while fighting in Spain and spent months imprisoned in appalling Francoist jails. Manassah 'Sam' Lesser was one of the earliest British volunteers in Spain, who was wounded in December 1936. He returned to Spain to become a reporter for the Communist *Daily Worker* (later the *Morning Star*), a job that would later give him a ringside seat at many of the most dramatic events of the twentieth century. The surgeon Alexander Tudor Hart also volunteered to go to Spain in the first months of the war, despite a new family and medical practice. His life story has also not appeared in print before, perhaps surprisingly, given that he was at one time married to Edith Suschitzky, one of the most influential Soviet agents to operate in Britain during the twentieth century. His biography is one of several to draw heavily on documents compiled by MI5 and it reveals a great deal about the attitudes of the British Security Services towards former members of the International Brigades. The final veteran of the International Brigades to appear is Alexander Foote. He was one of a number to fight with the British Battalion in Spain who were later involved in espionage. His experiences working for a Soviet spy ring during the Second World War—not to mention his role in an audacious plan to assassinate Hitler—are quite extraordinary.

The remaining biographies feature individuals who served in other roles. They include an account of Stafford Cottman, a young man from Bristol who fought in the POUM alongside George Orwell. Cottman has always been overshadowed by his famous comrade, even if Ken Loach's powerful film set during the Spanish Civil War, *Land and Freedom*, is often assumed to be based on Cottman's life. Also included is Leah Manning, who was the impetus behind bringing 4,000 refugee Basque children to Britain in the summer of 1937. She later served as an MP in Clement Attlee's post-war Labour government, helping to draft and implement legislation raising the school leaving age to 16.

The last chapters include an account of the Haldanes, three members of the same family all of whom volunteered to go to Spain, albeit in very different roles. They were the writer Charlotte Haldane, her husband the illustrious scientist JBS Haldane, and Charlotte's son Ronnie, one of the youngest volunteers for the International Brigades, who was very fortunate to survive the vicious battle alongside the Jarama river in February 1937.

The final biography is an account of the experiences of one of a very small number of Britons to volunteer for Franco's army. On first sight, the inclusion of a Nationalist volunteer might appear at odds with the other biographies; 'why do you want to write about that fascist?' asked one relative of an International Brigader. However, a previously unseen MI5 file throws new light on Peter Kemp and fully justifies his inclusion beyond any theoretical need for 'balance'. Besides, Kemp's experiences during the Second World War were every bit as extraordinary as Alexander Foote's.

The individuals featured in this collection were all, in different ways, forged by their involvement in the Spanish Civil War. It was a pivotal moment, often marking the beginning of a lifelong connection with Spain and its people. It was there, for example, that Sam Lesser was first given the opportunity to learn the craft of a newspaper reporter. The contacts he made, not to mention his mastery of the language, would stand him in good stead in his journalistic career. It was also where he met his wife. While Alex Foote might have been recruited as a spy in Britain, it was in Spain that his years as a Soviet agent began when he was talent-spotted by a superior. Malcolm Dunbar and Clive Branson both discovered hitherto unknown qualities of leadership in Spain. Others were left with more immediate consequences.

Peter Kerrigan's wife Rose strongly believed that he was suffering from post-traumatic stress disorder on his return, a hidden psychological scar to accompany the sudden greying of his hair. And what Stafford Cottman experienced in Spain alongside Orwell tarnished his view of the Communist Party for the rest of his life.

While many of the individuals included in this collection of biographies appear within the literature of British involvement in the Spanish Civil War, few (with the possible exception of JBS Haldane) could be described as 'famous faces of the Spanish Civil War'. Some of them were prominent at the time, but have been all but forgotten, their memoirs now out of print, while others were never particularly well known in the first place. However, all their stories are worth telling and retelling, not least because the release of new archival material has allowed fresh insights into the individuals' lives and the times in which they lived. All fully deserve to be rescued from 'the margins of history', for those who chose to go to Spain during the country's civil war were, by any yardstick, an extraordinary group of men and women.

Chapter One
The Forgotten Warrior: Malcolm Dunbar

In early July 1963, a man's body was discovered washed up on a deserted beach at Milford-on-Sea, near Bournemouth.[1] Police were notified and, as they must do in these circumstances, set about the grisly job of identifying the corpse and establishing the cause of death. Unfortunately, their task was hindered considerably by the discovery that all items of identification had meticulously been removed from the body. There was no wallet, no letters, even the labels in his clothing had been cut out. Only one clue remained, a white pocket handkerchief bearing a small monogram with the initials 'MD'.[2]

Mystified, the police appealed to the Press for help. With the papers dominated by news that a third Soviet agent had been discovered operating high within the British establishment, it was not for three weeks that the puzzle was solved. On 26 July *The Times* featured a brief report identifying the man as 'Ronald Malcolm Loraine Dunbar, aged 51, of Stanhope Gardens, S.W., son of the late Sir Loraine and Lady Dunbar of Whitehall Lodge, Harrogate.'[3] The story of Dunbar's journey from such 'bourgeois' beginnings (to use his own words) to an early, tragic death is one that takes in many key political events and players from the 1930s, including the radical political scene in Cambridge University, the battle against Sir Oswald Mosley's fascists and the Spanish Civil War. It is also, in the end, a whodunit, for rumours persist surrounding the nature of his death. Many people, including members of his family, strongly believed that Dunbar, a Communist and confidant of the notorious Soviet double-agent, Kim Philby, was actually murdered and his death arranged to look like suicide. 'One fact remains to be recorded', noted an account of his death, darkly. 'The coroner's court did not describe his death as suicide. It gave an open verdict.'[4]

Malcolm Dunbar was indeed the son of Sir Loraine Geddes Dunbar, formerly the Secretary and Treasurer of the Bank of Bengal in Calcutta and Lady Liola Violet Dunbar *née*

Cruickshank.[5] His parents had married in 1899 and Malcolm, their fourth and youngest son, was born a leapling, on 29 February 1912 in Paignton, Devon.[6] Educated initially at Clifton House School in Harrogate, in 1922 the young Dunbar was sent to Heddon Court School in New Barnet, just predating the arrival of the poet John Betjeman, who taught there briefly. Three years later, Dunbar moved schools again, joining Repton in Derbyshire, an English public school founded in the sixteenth century on the site of a twelfth-century Augustinian Priory whose headmaster, Geoffrey Fisher, later became the Archbishop of Canterbury.[7] In addition to numerous members of parliament, the school's notable alumni included the gold medallist from the 1924 Olympics, Harold Abrahams (made famous by the film, *Chariots of Fire*), the actor Basil Rathbone and the novelist and playwright, Christopher Isherwood. Unfortunately, little evidence remains of Dunbar's time at Repton; a photograph taken of the pupils is marked frustratingly: 'Dunbar—absent'. What is known is that Dunbar joined the Officers' Training Corps in 1925, gaining the rank of corporal and leaving five years later with a certificate entitling him to an army commission in the event of war.[8] It's also clear that he must have been a good student, for in 1930 Dunbar gained a place at Christ's College, Cambridge, to read economics and history.[9]

With Europe reeling from the consequences of the Wall Street crash and the rise of fascism, the 1930s were a time of economic and political upheaval, casting a shadow even over the university's lofty spires. Increasing numbers of undergraduates were being drawn into left-wing politics and into the Communist Party, disparagingly labelled by Beatrice Webb as 'the mild-mannered desperadoes'.[10] This was, of course, the era of the 'Cambridge spies': Anthony Blunt, who had graduated in 1930, was then a Fellow at Trinity; Kim Philby, Guy Burgess, Donald Maclean and James Klugmann were all contemporaries. Dunbar himself was not, as some historians have alleged, a member of the elite and secretive left-wing Cambridge debating society, the Apostles.[11] Nevertheless he was deeply involved in left-wing activism at the university and would undoubtedly have encountered Communists and 'fellow-travellers' then centred around Kings' and Trinity. A number of the young intellectuals who would go to fight in Spain were part of the set, including the son of a Labour peer, David Haden-Guest who, having returned from studying in Germany in 1931, set about organising the Cambridge branch of the Party. He was joined by Virginia Woolf's nephew, Julian Bell, and the seventeen year old John Cornford, Charles Darwin's great-grandson, who arrived at Cambridge the same year.[12] Cultured and a talented and enthusiastic photographer, Dunbar was a member of what was described as the university's 'advanced aesthetic set'.[13] Yet the distractions of politics and culture do not appear to have unduly diverted Dunbar from his studies, for he left the university in 1933 with a BA (Hons.) in Economics and History.

Following his graduation, Dunbar moved to London, where he began work as a journalist and photographer, working with a number of leading dance companies, such as Ballet Rambert. Here he encountered the sculptor Jason 'Pat' Gurney, who described Dunbar as 'a very elegant and evidently rich member of the local intelligentsia . . . an amusing, if somewhat cynical, character with whom to have a drink.'[14] Like a number of other middle-class intellectual leftists in the mid-1930s, Dunbar made forays outside his comfortable intellectual milieu, becoming interested in and, he claimed, making many friends in 'the working class movement'. While most of these new acquaintances were members of the Communist Party, Dunbar 'was not' he later insisted, 'actually a member of any party.'[15]

However, he was involved in the British Communists' main preoccupation at the time; fighting the rise of fascism across Europe in general and Britain in particular, where Sir Oswald Mosley's British Union of Fascists—the Blackshirts—were physically attacking opponents, particularly Jews. Having previously joined a number of anti-fascist protests in London, in October 1936 Dunbar was working as a reporter for Century Press when he witnessed Sir Oswald Mosley's attempt to march four columns of fascist Blackshirts through the predominantly Jewish area of London's East End.[16] Arrested (probably in error) during the demonstration, Dunbar managed to get himself released, 'almost at once on the production of a press card.'[17] The now infamous 'Battle of Cable Street' clearly made a powerful impression on the young aesthete, for Dunbar later claimed that it was Cable Street that motivated him to volunteer for the International Brigades.[18] This may be true, though Dunbar had, in fact, already purchased a number of rolls of camera film, in preparation for leaving the country the previous month. It's possible that, like John Cornford, he was originally planning to go to Spain to report on the conflict, but later changed his mind and became inspired to fight. Certainly, fully aware of his lack of proletarian credentials, Dunbar may have deliberately cited Cable Street as his epiphany, knowing that it would play well with the Communist leadership of the International Brigades. The precise reasons that lay behind Dunbar's transformation from aesthete to infantryman are not clear; the African-American Political Commissar in Spain, Abe Lewis, later accused Dunbar of being, 'atraído probablemente por la aventura' (drawn by the adventure), while another senior American claimed that he had been informed that Dunbar rather nihilistically 'came to Spain because he did not care about life.'[19]

Whatever lay behind his decision, Jason Gurney described how Dunbar sought out his advice on how to get there:

> The day before I left England he had apparently heard that I had arranged to go to Spain, and he finally ran me down in the old Studio Club over Harris's chemist shop in the King's Road . . . it was just before Christmas and the place was full of people celebrating. I was sharing farewell drinks with all and sundry and I did not take him very seriously, but gave him the information that he wanted and went on my way.[20]

Dunbar left London on 5 January 1937, accompanied by a close friend, John Horner, a publisher's agent from London.[21] They arrived in Spain four days later and signed up for the International Brigades the following day,[22] before being taken southwards to be united with several hundred other British volunteers who were then undergoing training in the small village of Madrigueras, just north of the main International Brigade base at Albacete. Dunbar remained there for four weeks, undergoing what had to pass for basic military training. Most volunteers in Spain at the time would probably have agreed with the Londoner, George Leeson, who considered the training mostly ineffective, though it did at least raise the volunteers' levels of fitness and prevent them from becoming bored and demoralised.[23] Opportunities to practise with live ammunition were severely limited and all too many would later go into battle having fired fewer than half a dozen shots.

Dunbar officially joined the battalion on 28 January 1937,[24] where he ran into an astonished Jason Gurney:

> The Malcolm in Spain was totally different to the one I had known in the King's Road. He . . . had become intensely serious-minded, if still rather cynical in his attitude to life in general. He took his military duties very seriously and rigorously supported the Party line on everything to do with Spain and the army. It sounded very strange to hear the King's Road Malcolm ranting on about the necessity for organization and discipline.[25]

It was not long before Dunbar's new-found skills and confidence would be tested to their limits. His first experience of military action, as it was for the British Battalion itself, was in mid-February 1937, at the Jarama River, thirty kilometres southeast of Madrid. Having failed to capture Madrid over the winter of 1936-1937, Franco had launched an attack designed to encircle the Spanish capital and cut the road linking it to Valencia, seat of the Republican government. Franco could call upon five Nationalist brigades, plus eleven reserve battalions, totalling some 25,000 men.

Having knifed the Republican sentries guarding the bridges over the Jarama River, Rebel forces swept forward onto the high ground occupied by the defending Republican forces. Their aircraft and artillery pounded the Republicans, who held on doggedly. Despite being outnumbered, their desperate attempts to resist eventually ground the Rebels to a standstill. However, it was at great cost, the Republicans losing somewhere in the region of 10,000 soldiers, to Franco's 6,000. Over three days of desperate fighting from 12-14 February, the British Battalion—

which had faced Franco's elite soldiers, battle-hardened from Spain's colonial war in Morocco—was essentially wiped out. Peter Kerrigan, the senior British political commissar in Spain (see Chapter Seven), later described Jarama as 'the bloodiest of all the battles that the British Battalion was involved in.'[26]

Dunbar, serving as a rifleman, was one of very few to survive the three days of bloodbath unscathed. His superior officer reported, in fact, that he 'conducted himself very bravely throughout the Jarama battle', and Dunbar was given a field promotion from lowly *soldado* to section leader, responsible for up to a dozen men.[27] However, Dunbar's period of service as a section leader ended after only three days, when he was badly wounded in the arm. He received treatment in a series of Republican hospitals, before being sent to recuperate in the beautiful Mediterranean seaside town of Benicassim. There, a combination of his newly acquired rank and military-bearing, saw him elected as the political *responsable* of the English-speaking group in the hospital.[28]

After three weeks at the convalescence home, he hitched a lift with the British Battalion Quartermaster, who was picking up a truck load of supplies.[29] He took him back to the Jarama front, where Dunbar found himself surplus to requirements, his section having disappeared in a military reorganisation. However, Dunbar's good French and Spanish led to his appointment as an interpreter, where he quickly made his mark:

> On his return, he presented himself at Battalion Headquarters and found the staff absorbed with a document they did not understand. It was composed in French and read: 'Parole, Stalin; contraparole, ——' (the second clue escapes Capt. Dunbar's memory).
>
> The entry of Stalin upon the Jarama landscape had reduced the staff to bewilderment. Knowing a bit of French, Dunbar was able to figure out that the mysterious document was an instruction for the use of a password, a precaution now introduced for the first time. This achievement put up his reputation several notches.[30]

His obvious intelligence and aptitude led Dunbar, after only three weeks at headquarters, to be one of four British volunteers selected for promotion and sent to the officers' school at Pozo Rubio, near Albacete.[31] After five weeks of instruction, Dunbar left the school with the rank of *Alférez* (Second Lieutenant) and was appointed an instructor at the British base at Madrigueras and the main base at Albacete.[32] When one young London volunteer arrived that May, he found Dunbar able to confidently instruct him and other arrivals on how to dismantle, assemble and fire their rifles. Assuming, of course, that the guns were in sufficient condition to be fired. Many were not. As one new arrival from London discovered, 'some rifles were old Lee Enfields, others from Mexico, some from Czechoslovakia; all were either old or very old.'[33]

New arrivals at the beginning of June 1937 helped further spur Dunbar's advance up the military ladder. However, these newcomers were not volunteers, they were something much rarer: three brand new, state-of-the-art semi-automatic 45mm anti-tank guns from the Soviet Union. As one of the gunners stated proudly, 'the gun was at that time in advance of anything in use in any other army'.[34] Their optical sights and the flat trajectory of the shells made them extremely accurate up to a range of 16km; they were capable of firing both armour-piercing and high explosive shells, ensuring effectiveness against even heavy tanks.[35]

The British were instructed to form a specialised unit to operate the new guns and on 6 June 1937, Dunbar was transferred to join the group. A week later, he was formally promoted to lieutenant and appointed the 15th International Brigade British Anti-Tank Battery's first commander.[36] He and his new assistant, the former International Press journalist Humphrey 'Hugh' Slater, began the task of selecting men for the unit.[37]

Hugh Slater . . . and I made out a list of names, and next morning we left taking with us Jack Black [a miner and Labour Party Chairman from Dover] as second in command. Apart from Black and myself, the men were new recruits from

19

England who had never been to the front.[38]

The men selected tended to be among the better-educated of the British volunteers, for operating the guns, calculating range, precise gun-aiming and the like was felt to require a quick mind.[39] Seen as an elite unit, members of the battery enjoyed perks not available to those in the battalion:

> Each gun-crew was a small team, and at rest—and even sometimes close to action—had certain advantages over the infantryman. For example, because each gun was towed by a lorry, members of the battery were able to stow more material among the ammunition boxes than a 'foot-slogger' could carry—a few books, writing paper, the simplest things which made life more tolerable.[40]

The men were taught how to use the guns by Russian instructors, assisted by an Italian interpreter.[41] Significantly, the instructors instilled in the volunteers' minds the vital importance of the weapons: 'We had a reception at divisional headquarters, and [were] told the guns were of more value than our lives.'[42]

The Anti-Tank Battery was initially attached to a Spanish Republican unit fighting on the Jarama front. Too late to be involved in any of the battle's major actions, the gun crews had to be satisfied with taking the occasional pot-shot at the Rebel lines.[43] Dunbar devised a series of ramps leading to alternate firing positions, so that the guns could fire a few shells before being quickly moved back out of sight.[44] These innovative methods helped earn the anti-tank battery a reputation for being highly effective; Welshman Jim Brewer stated proudly that it was 'the best unit we ever served in.'[45] Even the 'rough and ready' Battalion Commander Fred Copeman, not someone to give out easy praise, admitted that the 'anti-tank company were bloody good . . . and they had plenty of courage'.[46] Accounts by members of the unit make it clear that their reputation owed much to Dunbar's skilful leadership. His intelligence, imagination and military prowess quickly garnered respect not just among his superiors but, crucially, among those serving under him.[47] One

Scottish gunner described him as 'a very, very courageous and dependable soldier, in my opinion probably one of the best of the volunteers that ever went to Spain . . . His ability to deal with all situations, including the times when he was wounded, in a calm, quiet way commanded respect from everybody'.[48]

However, while he was widely respected and admired, few accounts suggest that he was warmly liked.[49] The sensitive, highbrow and intensely private Dunbar seems to have felt uncomfortable in other people's company and 'never got intimate with anyone'. Even Hugh Sloan, who served as Dunbar's *enlace* (runner) and spent a great deal of time with him in Spain, felt he never really got to know him:

> Captain Dunbar, for all the time I knew him, was a very remote, private, uncommunicative person, who always maintained an aloofness and remoteness from the people he associated with. He always remained an enigma to me. I never ever once had any kind of personal talk with him, only through the orders and military requirements he had to give. He kept everybody at their distance.[50]

Dunbar's aloofness, even if due more to social awkwardness than snobbishness, does not seem to have endeared him to his comrades. Always immaculately dressed, six foot tall and blessed with blue eyes and film-star good-looks, Dunbar's university accent and upper-class habit of smoking through a long cigarette holder further set him apart from those from a less privileged background:

> Such men were regarded with suspicion. For years we had sung, and some even believed, that 'The emancipation of the Working Class is the task of the Workers alone' and everyone knew that intellectuals were not workers.[51]

Hugh Sloan was similarly unimpressed when he overheard Dunbar and Slater discussing Socrates' *Dialogues* and he complained that the pair were 'making fun in a rather middle class frivolous way' of workers' unsophisticated understandings of such intellectual and high-minded matters.[52] Dunbar was not the only middle class volunteer to be viewed with incomprehension bordering on distrust, of course; not least Virginia Woolf's nephew, Julian Bell, who had the habit of wandering around in khaki shorts and a pith helmet, loftily remarking that his time of service in Spain 'will sound well when I come to write my memoirs.'[53]

Dunbar's non-Party background didn't help and he was never entirely trusted by his political superiors.[54] He was certainly no 'true believer' and only actually joined the Communist Party in November 1937, after 10 months in Spain.[55] Even as late as July 1938, when he had reached a very senior military rank, Dunbar's political work was still being described as 'weak', despite having been accepted into the Spanish Communist Party at the beginning of the year.[56] He also upset a number of American volunteers by making a rude remark about their tough political commissar, John Gates.[57] While Gates actually thought Dunbar to be militarily 'an excellent officer,' he also accused him of being an intellectual who 'argued for the sake of argument' and needed to develop politically.[58]

However, perhaps what lay behind some of the volunteers' negative reactions towards Dunbar was not distrust of his politics and class, but simple prejudice towards his suspected homosexuality. When Jason Gurney had described Dunbar as being part of the 'advanced aesthetic set' at university it was, of course, a coded reference, which Gurney later made explicitly clear when he described Dunbar as 'a rich homosexual aesthete.'[59] While there was a certain degree of tolerance within some areas of 1930s British society—the worlds of the theatre and the arts, for example—homosexuality was still illegal and widely seen as taboo.[60] The flamboyant Dennis Pratt, better known as Quentin Crisp, recounts regularly being beaten up in London during the time. Even in Spain, among the generally progressive 'volunteers for liberty', prejudice could still be found. In fact, homosexuality was often an issue for Communists, many of whom regarded it not only as socially unacceptable, but politically deviant and associated with fascism and National Socialism.[61] A close, affectionate relationship in Spain between Winston Churchill's nephew, Giles Romilly and Stephen

Spender's ex-lover, Tony Hyndman, very much offended a group of Glasgow volunteers, while a Spaniard who worked in the International Brigades Record Office in Albacete was sent to a punishment battalion after being found 'guilty of homosexual activity'.[62] The battalion commander, Fred Copeman, believing that a number of volunteers were homosexual, later claimed that he deliberately placed them in the Anti-Tank Battery away from the 'roughnecks' in the overwhelmingly working-class infantry companies. 'If you get a good-looking lad among twenty big husky men,' claimed Copeman, 'well, he's going to turn that way whether he likes it or not.'[63]

Certainly Dunbar's attempts to share his aesthetic, highbrow tastes were not always welcomed, or appreciated by his troops, as one recalled:

> I saw Dunbar . . . standing with a group of us in the very large ground floor room, watching a party of ballet dancers performing on an improvised stage. They were from England; more than likely he had himself played a part in their coming to Spain on this supportive visit. Dunbar's face was a study, his obvious pleasure in the performance, the dancers so gracefully whirling away all the dirt and ugliness of war—and the hurt, as he heard the only half-suppressed guffaws and derisory comments from some of the onlookers.[64]

Under fire, however, was a different matter where Dunbar was widely respected and in early July 1937, he and his British anti-tank unit were to be presented with their first real opportunity to demonstrate their abilities, when the 15th International Brigade was readied for a forthcoming action to the west of Madrid. The Brunete offensive, as it became known, was the brainchild of the gifted Republican military tactician, Colonel Vicente Rojo. His plan was to both release the Rebel stranglehold on Madrid while drawing some of the Rebel forces away from the northern Republican zone, where the Basques and Asturian forces' position was becoming increasingly perilous. It was, by some margin, the largest Republican action of the war so far; 'if we cannot succeed with such forces, we will not be able to manage it anywhere,' declared the Republican President, Manuel

Azaña.[65]

Prior to the attack, Dunbar addressed the members of the battery, explaining that they were to be part of the advance and that, despite the weight and cumbersome nature of the guns and the 'vicious nature of the terrain', it was vital that they keep pace with the infantry.[66] Yet they were initially held in reserve, and not used during the battalion's attack on the resolutely well-defended village of Villanueva de la Cañada. As Dunbar recognized, the battery could have played an invaluable role in the assault by picking off enemy machine-gun positions and he later admitted that the Rebels' determined defence had been a 'serious setback'.[67] Nevertheless, over the following days, in soaring temperatures of more than 40 degrees centigrade, they did play an important role supporting the Brigade's infantry units. But, like their compatriots in the battalion itself, their successes came at a heavy price; on 12 July, John 'Jack' Black, the battery's popular second in command, was killed by a shell splinter while trying to rescue ammunition boxes from a fire. And on 25 July, Dunbar was himself wounded on 'Mosquito Ridge' (named after the buzzing sound of thousands of bullets passing overhead), when one bullet passed right through his neck and another hit him in the arm.[68] Dunbar was sent to Elche hospital in Murcia to convalesce, allowing Hugh Slater, described by a subordinate as 'a dilettante in his interests, but an intelligent political man', to take command, while a disciplined young Communist from Reading, Bill Alexander, was promoted to replace Slater as the battery's political commissar.[69]

While Dunbar was recovering in hospital, his anti-tank battery was part of a Republican offensive in the dry plains of Aragón.[70] During the two-day battle for the town of Belchite, the three British anti-tanks guns fired more than 2,700 shells; one was fired at such a rate that its barrel burst and it had to be withdrawn from action.[71] Hailed by Republicans as a triumphant success, the action captured nine hundred square kilometres of territory. However, the offensive had failed to achieve its principal objective, the capture of Zaragoza, and neither had it relieved any of the pressure on the northern front. By the end of the month, Santander was in Nationalist hands; two months later, so was the entire northern Republican zone.

Dunbar finally returned to the front on 22 September 1937. Six days later, he was promoted to captain and joined the brigade staff, the *estado mayor*, as commander of the 3rd section (Operations).[72] His new responsibilities as Officer of the Day—ensuring good general hygiene by improving the dire state of the latrines—must have seemed a long way from his civilised life in England.[73] Nevertheless, Dunbar's military acumen displayed at Brunete was widely acknowledged and in November 1937 he received official recognition when a ceremony was held in honour of three British volunteers nominated for the prestigious Republican Navalperal medal. The first was the leader of the Irish, Frank Ryan, who had helped steady the line at Jarama in February when all seemed lost. The second was to be given to George Buck, 'a thick-set tough guy' from Lancashire, who had boldly torn down the Rebel standard on the summit of Purburrel Hill in Quinto in August.[74] The final medal, for demonstrating 'consistent bravery in action', was awarded to 15th International Brigade Chief of Staff, Ronald Malcolm Lorraine Dunbar.[75]

Dunbar remained with Brigade Staff during the Battle of Teruel that began in December 1937. Having been held back in order to give them time to recover from the losses sustained in Aragón in the autumn, the International Brigades were thrown into the battle on New Year's Eve. They bore the full brunt of a Nationalist attack comprising 80,000 men, backed up with a mass of artillery and the largest air force so far seen in the war. Conditions went far beyond anything the volunteers had so far experienced in Spain. In temperatures that sank to twenty below zero at night, more men died from the cold than were killed in battle.[76] Dunbar was himself hospitalised with 'catarrhal jaundice' remaining out of action until 18 February 1938.[77]

With all the Republican gains at Teruel overturned, there was a brief hiatus in the fighting allowing Dunbar the opportunity to take a brief period of leave in early March. He returned to find the Republican forces facing their most serious challenge of the war. Flushed with the successes at Teruel, Franco launched a colossal offensive against the Republican forces in Aragón. Thirteen divisions, including Italians and the

German Condor Legion, plus a huge number of tanks, artillery and anti-tank guns, backed up with over 900 aircraft, were massed for the push through to the Mediterranean. With Franco's forces outnumbering the defenders by almost five to one, what began as a series of breakthroughs swiftly turned into a rout, as the Republican lines virtually collapsed.[78]

On 14 March, Dunbar joined the British volunteers who were fighting a last-ditch defence of the Aragón town of Caspe, only 40km east of Quinto, in what the tough battalion commander from Manchester, Sam Wild, complained to Dunbar was an impossible position.[79] Despite Wild and Dunbar's efforts to organise the defence, Caspe had to be abandoned the following day. Having been wounded once again during the town's defence, Dunbar was quickly patched up, returning to the front nine days later, only to be wounded once more when the battalion was ambushed by Italian troops outside the small Aragón village of Calaceite on 31 March.[80] Despite his wounds, Dunbar was one of the lucky ones, for apart from the numerous British casualties, more than 100 were captured at Calaceite, ending up in the brutal Francoist prisoner-of-war camp in San Pedro de Cardeña, near Burgos.

Having made a hasty retreat from Calaceite, Dunbar joined up with a group of sixty survivors who were making a defensive stand east of Caspe.[81] By 2 April, the group, with Dunbar in overall command, had swelled to about 200, as troops from a number of Republican units—and a small tank—joined them. In real danger of being overrun, Dunbar elected once again to retreat, wisely choosing a position in a steep cutting a short way south-east of Gandesa, where it was almost impossible to be outflanked. However, as dark began to fall, Dunbar's group was pushed back again, only finding sanctuary on the far side of the powerful River Ebro.

As it became clear that Franco was choosing to consolidate his gains, rather than continue his rapid advance and risk over-extending his lines of communication, the physically and psychologically shattered remnants of the International Brigades were withdrawn for further rest, recuperation and rebuilding. This process was helped considerably by the temporary opening of Spain's border with France between March and May 1938, which allowed new supplies of arms and ammunition to reach the Republic. The volunteers were kept busy with 'training, marching or rifle practice' and 'the procedures for crossing rivers', while at night the former Olympic oarsman, Lewis Clive, clandestinely swam across the swiftly-flowing River Ebro to reconnoitre the Nationalist positions.[82] Safe from the daily risk of death and benefitting from regular food and sleep, some of the British came to see this as one of their most pleasant periods in Spain.[83] Not least for Dunbar, whose impressive coolness and leadership under almost impossible conditions during the retreats, led to a promotion to 15th International Brigade Chief of Staff, placing him in command of the *estado mayor*.[84] However, the peaceful interlude was not to last for long.

On 24 July 1938, Republican forces triumphantly crossed the River Ebro, over which they had been forced to flee only three months earlier. While Dunbar had been closely involved with planning and executing the ambitious offensive, some senior members of the 15th International Brigade were beginning to worry that Dunbar was not the leader he had once been. While his military skills were still *sin reproche*, the American commissar, John Gates, worried that Dunbar was physically and emotionally exhausted. Having endured over eighteen months of bitter fighting, other volunteers were undoubtedly feeling a similar strain. However, morale was boosted by the initial success of the surprise offensive though, within days, the advance ground to a halt in front of the heavily fortified Aragón town of Gandesa. Franco rushed up reinforcements and the Republican leadership braced themselves for Franco's inevitable counter-attack. On 11 August, their fears were realised, as Franco's forces pressed forwards. The International Brigades were subjected to 'eleven days of hell' as a murderous bombardment rained artillery fire on their positions, the explosions creating rock splinters every bit as lethal as the shells themselves. Dunbar was badly hurt when a five-inch Nationalist shell exploded right in front of the Brigade staff's position in the Sierra Caballs. The tough Scottish Communist, Peter Kerrigan, not usually one to give out easy praise, described

Dunbar's bravery with open admiration:

> Dunbar received about 15 fragments in his face, chest and legs, but refuses to be evacuated and carries on. This is the fourth time he has been wounded, or is it the sixth? A good officer Dunbar. He keeps calmly puffing on his cigarette while his wounds are being dressed.[85]

The wounds kept Dunbar out of action for two weeks.[86] By the time he returned, the British, and the other surviving foreigners in the International Brigades, were preparing themselves to be withdrawn from the war. Following one last action on 22-23 September, the Brigades were finally taken out of the line. Their final action had been every bit as devastating as their first at Jarama. In its final forty-eight hours' fighting, some two hundred members of the battalion were killed, wounded or missing.[87] It was a tragic and heart-breaking end to their time in Spain, though, in many ways, a fitting final act. Despite their unquestionable bravery, the men in the British Battalion were simply outnumbered and outgunned. Raw courage and a belief in the essential 'rightness' of their cause 'could not overcome inexperience, poor coordination and superior military force.'[88]

While the slow process of negotiating the volunteers' departure from Spain and re-admission into Britain got under way, a number of ceremonies and parades were held to honour the contribution of the International Brigades on behalf of Spain's democratic republic. On 1 October, a number of officers were presented with certificates at a Brigade lunch in recognition of their 'outstanding work' in Spain. The first to receive his was Malcolm Dunbar. Two weeks later, on 17 October, all the foreign volunteers in the 35th Division (of which the International Brigades were part) were paraded and reviewed in front of the commander of the 15th Army Corps, Lieutenant-Colonel Tagüeña, as well as two leaders of the International Brigades, André Marty and Luigi Longo. To mark the occasion, there were a number of promotions; both Dunbar and the British Battalion's commander, Sam Wild, were promoted to Major.[89]

Despite the earlier concerns about Dunbar's jaded

performance, the vast majority of his fellow International Brigaders had nothing but praise for, as one Scot put it, 'a great man, a good man, an officer, a gentleman'.[90] The *Daily Worker* correspondent in Spain, Sam Lesser (see Chapter Four), who met most of the senior British volunteers at some stage, specifically pointed out that Dunbar was 'a comrade who came from a very upper-middle class family, but who showed remarkable powers of leadership.'[91] As one Welsh volunteer put it simply,

> Dunbar became an officer because he'd proved his mettle as a soldier, in the ranks, in the early days on the Jarama. And him we respected automatically because he was a magnificent soldier.[92]

Dunbar also received fulsome praise from officers in the International Brigades and in the Republican Army itself. Arthur Olorenshaw, in charge of the English Section at the Officers' School between April and August 1937, described Dunbar as 'one of the best C[omra]des to have been in Spain' and Milton Wolff, the Jewish New Yorker in command of the Abraham Lincoln Battalion, thought him one of the two best soldiers in the entire 15th International Brigade.[93] In what Dunbar may have seen as the highest honour, he was one of five British volunteers to receive a signed note from *La Pasionaria*, the legendary Communist orator and Republican talisman.[94]

At the beginning of December 1938, the remaining British volunteers boarded a train to take them out of Spain.[95] Dunbar left with them, though he did not accompany them all the way, mysteriously deciding to disembark the train at Versailles and travel on independently.[96] Hugh Sloan thought it, 'a typical thing for Malcolm to do, because he had the feeling that he was going to be involved in a public way that he wished to avoid.'[97] Dunbar returned home in time to take part in two public meetings held on 9 December to welcome home the veterans, speaking alongside other senior British in Spain and illustrious supporters such as the geneticist JBS Haldane, the left-wing Labour MP, D N Pritt and the Communist Isabel Brown.[98] Dunbar continued to work for the cause, returning to Spain as *Daily Worker* correspondent in January 1939, where he remained until the end of the war.[99]

It was not to be long in coming. At the beginning of 1939, Franco launched a colossal offensive in Catalonia; by 26 January, Barcelona had fallen to the determined Nationalist advance. One month later, on 27 February, with the end of the war seemingly imminent, Britain and France formally recognised Franco's government, an act decried by the British pro-Republican newspaper, the *News Chronicle*, as 'the shameful culmination of one of the blackest chapters in this country's history'. With the Republic abandoned by the western democracies, and the Republican Army of the Ebro in tatters, many felt that defeat was now inevitable. They were proved right, for the Republic essentially fractured, with civil war breaking out between the Communist Party and others determined to continue the fight on one hand, and those who—naively—wished to try and negotiate peace terms with Franco. With rumours swirling that Communists were to be arrested and imprisoned, on 9 March 1939 Dunbar wrote to Harry Pollitt from Valencia, prudently suggesting that, 'I may after all have to get out of here fairly quickly.'[100] A week later, Dunbar was issued with a pass by the General Security Commission, enabling him to leave Spain for good. Within two weeks, a triumphant Franco proclaimed victory for the Nationalists and the end of the civil war.

Back in Britain, Dunbar took on responsibility for the circulation of the *Daily Worker* in the Sheffield area, though he remained living in London.[101] When Chamberlain declared war on Germany on 3 September 1939, it initially seemed to Dunbar that the opportunity to finally overcome fascism in Europe had appeared. However, he and other veterans soon realised that joining the British armed forces might not be as straightforward as they had assumed. Rumours quickly emerged that many veterans of the Spanish war, whether Communist Party members or not, were being prevented from joining the armed forces. In fact, restrictions limiting the admission of Spanish veterans into the armed forces had been put in place in January 1939, shortly after the British Battalion's return from Spain. A secret memorandum stated clearly that 'the presence of such men in the Army would obviously be highly undesirable from the point of morale and discipline.'[102]

Despite the memo, the official policy was not, in fact, to ban all veterans from the armed forces, only those believed to be 'known violent agitators'. And in situations where veterans had been accepted, they were not to be immediately discharged SNLR 'service no longer required', but instead kept under discreet surveillance. In the words of the Cabinet Office Home Defence Committee: 'If they behave themselves the Army welcomes them; if they act subversively they are discharged.' Having briefly returned to his aesthetic world—he was a regular visitor to the Canonbury flat of the poet, Randall Swingler— Dunbar was drafted into the 39th Signals Training Regiment of the Royal Artillery on 18 July 1940.[103] Despite his time in the OTC at Repton, not to mention his military experience and rank of Major in Spain, he was admitted into the British Army as 988732 Private Dunbar.

For the next 3 years and 329 days, Dunbar remained on British shores, as thousands of other former trainees were posted to regiments serving around the world. That he was a good soldier was in no doubt, demonstrated by his distinction in an advanced course at the Signals' School.[104] Nevertheless, during his period of service in the Second World War, Dunbar never received a commission, which many saw as confirmation of discrimination against the Spanish veterans in general and Dunbar in particular.[105] When he was promoted to Corporal in May 1941, it earned a sarcastic piece in the newspaper of the International Brigade Association, the *Volunteer for Liberty*:

Malcolm Dunbar was up on leave last week. He has now reached the dizzy heights of becoming a corporal. Malcolm, as we all know was the very capable Chief of Staff, Fifteenth Brigade, ranking as Major. He served through most of the big battles, and was in Spain for a couple of years. In addition to the military qualifications he has all the other necessary 'qualifications' for an officer in the British Army. He was actually put forward for a commission, but they then learnt that he had been in Spain and nothing further has been heard of it. Of course there is nothing political about that—much.

Politics don't enter into the British Army, my dear fellow. Says you. But didn't Sir Edward Grigg [the joint parliamentary Under-Secretary of State for War] say that it was the policy of the War Office to use to the full the experiences of those who served in Spain. And we can tell Sir Edward that we learnt more than how to blanco gaiters and slope arms in Spain. How about it Sir Edward? Must we, too, put questions in the House before a man's merits can be recognised?[106]

In November 1941, Dunbar was temporarily promoted to sergeant, confirmed as permanent the following August. But that was as high as he ever rose in the British Army. In the House of Commons, the Welsh Labour MP Aneurin Bevan demanded why, given Dunbar's illustrious record in Spain, he was apparently being victimised:

The Prime Minister must realise that in this country there is a taunt on everyone's lips that if Rommel had been in the British Army he would still have been a sergeant. Is that not so? It is a taunt right through the army. There is a man in the British Army—and this shows how we are using our trained men—who flung 150,000 men across the Ebro in Spain: Michael [sic] Dunbar. He is at present a sergeant in an armoured brigade in this country. He was Chief of Staff in Spain; he won the battle of the Ebro, and he is a sergeant in the British Army.[107]

However, in reality, Dunbar's case was not the explicit example of government prejudice that it appeared. As Lord Strabolgi, the Secretary of State for The Colonies, pointed out in a parliamentary reply:

The impression given . . . was that he was prevented from rising in the British Army, prevented from getting commissioned rank. He is not in fact a corporal, but it is true to say he is still a sergeant. It would not, however, be at all true to say that he was not permitted to rise from the ranks. On the contrary, he was in fact recommended for a Commission and recommended for training at an OCTU, for that purpose. But, greatly to Mr. Dunbar's credit, he himself refused to take a

Commission because his unit was mobilized for service overseas and he wished to go with it . . . The military authorities have not prevented him from getting a Commission, which unfortunately was the impression which the noble Lord gave.[108]

Neither was it the case that Dunbar received no decorations while serving in the British Army. In fact, on 21 December 1944, 988732 Sergeant Dunbar, of the 13th Honourable Artillery Company Regiment of the Royal Horse Artillery, was awarded the military medal for a display of 'cool calculating courage in the face of the enemy' during an action in Normandy on 18 July 1944. His commendation, endorsed by Field Marshal Montgomery, described how Dunbar's unit had been part of an advance by the 29th Armoured Brigade, just east of the River Orne outside Caen.[109] Ordered to attack a German strong point, they came under heavy attack from snipers hidden in the ditches, fields and hedges surrounding them. Once again demonstrating the courage and leadership qualities that had impressed his comrades in Spain:

Sgt Dunbar collected his Signallers and raced around the hedges, shooting up and capturing a large number of prisoners, thus preventing the fire of the Battery from being in any way disturbed. By his outstanding presence of mind and grasp of the situation, he inspired his men with complete confidence and averted what might have proved a rather costly minor engagement.[110]

Dunbar remained in service until 8 January 1946 and was released with a glowing testimonial, describing him as an 'exceptional NCO' and, seemingly without irony, as having 'gained rapid promotion.' Describing Dunbar as 'a really high-class soldier having initiative, poise and perfect honesty,' the testimonial belatedly admitted that 'he is an highly efficient and educated man whose qualifications have not been made full use of in the service.'[111]

After demobilisation, Dunbar returned to campaigning for the return of democracy in Spain. He picked up his work for the

International Brigade Association, having been elected vice-chairman the previous year, and worked briefly as Circulation Manager for the *Daily Worker*.[112] However he seems to have struggled to readjust to normal civilian life and professionally, little appears to have inspired Dunbar. He took on a number of jobs, but none seemed to hold his attention for long.

Much of his work involved conducting research for Trade Unions and other Labour organisations. In 1947, he began work for the Association of Scientific Workers in London's Piccadilly, compiling a report on the effects of radiation, investigating the possibility of hereditable genetic mutations. Three years later, he was working for the Labour Research Department in nearby Soho Square, undertaking 'detailed, microscopic research work' alongside Noreen Branson, whose husband Clive (see Chapter Nine) had served with the International Brigades. His colleagues seem to have found him much as his comrades had in Spain: taciturn and withdrawn, dodging committee meetings and never inviting any colleagues back to his flat in Kensington. Other veterans of the war in Spain didn't see much of him either. A letter from the Secretary of the International Brigade Association to a German colleague remarked pointedly that 'though he lives in London we see almost less of him than we do of Sam [Wild],' who despite living in Manchester, made sure to attend the organisation's three-monthly committee meetings.[113] Dunbar remained a member of the Communist Party until 1949, after which he gradually drifted away.[114] Records of his membership of the Clerical and Administrative Workers' Trade Union also tail off at the same time.[115]

Little evidence of Dunbar's life during the late 1950s and early 1960s remains, beyond a brief record in the Labour Research Department archives of his work for the actors' trade union, Equity, investigating the weekly quota of American programmes being shown on British television.[116] His microscopic research led to the publication of an 'erudite little book', brimming with complicated tables, but no mention of his authorship.[117] In 1953, his mother died, ten years after his father, leaving the former major virtually penniless:

At one point, he was reduced to borrowing money from one or two friends and by then his appearance had degenerated from the always smart, always immaculately dressed person into a somewhat gross man with a puffy face and narrow eyes. The good looks were gone; the introversion had become deeper.[118]

Dunbar had apparently become a drinker and a hypochondriac and was unhappy to the point of depression. His close friend, Thérèse Langfield, a dancer who he had met when she was a student at the Ballet Rambert, later revealed that Dunbar's unhappiness had led to an attempt to take his own life. Then in early July 1963, Dunbar abruptly vanished from Langfield's life. It was not until the end of the month that she was able to connect his disappearance with the dead body washed up at Milford, having recognised the description of a handkerchief found in his pocket which she had herself given him. After she went to the police, the body was formally identified. Following an inquest at which all the evidence pointed to him having taken his own life, Dunbar was cremated at Southampton on 30 July 1963.[119]

However, despite his earlier suicide attempt, Thérèse was not so sure. She recounted that for years leading up to his death, Dunbar had been in the habit of visiting her every week, to talk and tend her garden. However, shortly before his disappearance, Dunbar had phoned her in some distress informing her that he could no longer continue. He sounded, she believed, to be at the end of his tether and she was so concerned at his behaviour that, not entirely seriously, she asked him if someone was holding a gun to his head. To the question Dunbar offered no reply. However, he did confess to her that he had met with Kim Philby, shortly before the spy's defection to the Soviet Union. Determined not to let the matter drop, Thérèse consulted one of her neighbours, who she believed to have connections with military intelligence. Having made discreet enquiries, he advised her strongly to 'drop it' and would hear no more discussion of the circumstances surrounding Dunbar's death or, in fact, of Dunbar himself.[120] In a further twist, it later emerged that Dunbar was a close friend of the painter Hal Woolf, who had himself died in mysterious circumstances, while under police surveillance the previous November.[121] The case became a cause célèbre when it emerged that Woolf had connections to Christine Keeler and the Profumo Affair and that his wife had been a friend of the Cambridge spy, Guy Burgess. An investigative piece appeared in *Private Eye* magazine outlining the affair, penned by no other than Claud Cockburn who nearly thirty years earlier, (writing for the *Daily Worker* under the *nom de plume* Frank Pitcairn) had been responsible for the notoriously partisan reporting of the internecine fighting in Barcelona in May 1937.[122] As Cockburn observed darkly, 'From that dark day to the present nobody has been able to find out why this man was held incommunicado during these days, why he was killed or who killed him.' The case remains unsolved to this day, just as rumours of skulduggery surrounding Dunbar's death persist. Over the years, there have been whispers—unconfirmed—that Dunbar was involved in gunrunning. Friends of Thérèse, citing Dunbar's link to Philby, muttered darkly about the involvement of Russian intelligence, or that Dunbar had been murdered by the British secret service. However, no firm evidence to support either suspicion has ever emerged. A recent request to the British Security Services asking whether they held any information on Dunbar was met with a carefully worded denial.[123]

It seems that unless more evidence emerges, the precise nature of Ronald Malcolm Loraine Dunbar's last days will, unfortunately, remain obscure. While suicide appears the most likely explanation, the verdict, like the inquest itself, must remain open. What is beyond doubt is his outstanding record in Spain, particularly given his artistic, non-military background prior to volunteering. The American historian James Hopkin's literary study of the British in the International Brigades elegantly summarises Dunbar's astonishing transformation in Spain from ballet-loving aesthete to inspirational military leader and provides this forgotten warrior with a fitting epitaph: 'For certain individuals . . . circumstances could produce a costume of the moment, and Spain was the greatest theatre in the world.'[124]

Chapter Two
The Niños' Second Mother: Leah Manning

Situated just outside the main entrance to the city library in Southampton lies a small commemorative plaque, dedicated to the dramatic rescue of 4,000 refugee children from Bilbao, during the Spanish Civil War. The plaque was erected in May 2007, to commemorate the seventieth anniversary of what was, and still is to this day, the largest single influx of refugees to this country consisting almost entirely of children.[1] The evacuation of the children from war-torn Spain met with powerful opposition from many in the British government and would probably never have happened at all, had it not been for the determination and tireless efforts of the educationalist, social reformer and Labour Member of Parliament, Dame Elizabeth Leah Manning DBE.[2] While she may not be a household name, Leah Manning continues to generate affection and gratitude among relatives of the rescued Basque children. A plaque commemorating Leah Manning's efforts was presented to the House of Commons in 2002 and a commemorative garden, *Jardines de Mrs Leah Manning*, opened in Bilbao later the same year.[3] In 2019, Stan Newens, the former Labour MP for Epping and for Harlow unveiled a plaque to Leah Manning in Cambridge, saluting her as 'a fighter who committed her life to the betterment of conditions for all.'[4]

Born in Droitwich, Worcestershire, on 14 April 1886, Elizabeth Leah Perrett was one of six children; her father Charles William Perrett was a captain in the Salvation Army, her mother, Hannah Margaret (née Tappin) a former schoolteacher.[5] While Leah was still very young, her parents moved to North America to continue their Salvation Army work, leaving Leah behind to be brought up by her maternal grandfather and his wife in Stamford Hill, north London. Fortunately, her grandfather was very fond of the youngster and though he was a puritanical Methodist, he was also a radical and Liberal and undoubtedly a major influence upon her.[6] Leah was educated at the Misses Thorns' Select

Academy for Ladies in London, run by the Christian socialist, the Reverend Stewart Headlam. Leah later remarked dryly that the headmaster's political ideas had a rather more lasting impact on her than her schooling in drawing, embroidery and the piano.

Having matriculated and left school a year early, Leah took up work as a trainee teacher and began attending St Margaret's church in Westminster. When her grandfather died in 1906, she entered the Homerton Teacher Training College in Cambridge, where she spent three happy and busy years. She was the chair of the debating society, secretary of the Student Christian Union and helped form the College's Socialist League. One of her fellow students was the future Labour Minister Hugh Dalton, who was to become a life-long friend and who thought her 'a fiery orator' and encouraged her to join both the Independent Labour Party and the University Fabian Society.[7] Upon graduation in 1908 she accepted a position at Cambridge's College Practice School, fondly known as the 'Ragged School', for its work with local underprivileged children. The appalling poverty and malnutrition she witnessed at the school undoubtedly contributed to her strong belief in socialism and the value of progressive education.[8]

While working at Cambridge she met and fell for William Henry Manning, an assistant at the university's solar physics observatory. Will was a keen sailor and infected by his enthusiasm, Leah spent many a happy hour with him messing about on the river. The pair were engaged at the beginning of 1913 and they were married in July of the same year.[9] Unfortunately, their marriage did not get off to the best of starts. Leah's hope for a honeymoon in Germany, a country which she loved, was stymied by the deteriorating international situation and an argument between Will's parents resulted in his mother moving in with the newlyweds. She remained with them until her death, fourteen years later.[10]

When the First World War broke out in August, to Leah's horror Will immediately volunteered to fight, but fortunately his services were required instead for secret work on submarines. With Will away in the north of England for weeks on end, Leah continued teaching, benefitting from the pressing needs of wartime which forced the Cambridge Education Authority to drop the marriage bar. Leah also volunteered to work in a local hospital as part of the Voluntary Aid Detachment, despite her strongly held pacifist beliefs which had led her to oppose the war. Her first job was to meet the trains of wounded men arriving from the battlefields. It was grim work: 'the men arrived lousy, their uniforms matted with mud, blood and pus, which the trained nurses had to cut free before wounds could be cleaned up and dressed.[11] Leah lost a nephew and an uncle in the war and while she gave birth to a daughter in the last year of the conflict, tragically the child only survived for three weeks. Leah's response was to pour her time and energy into work and politics.

Clearly a talented teacher, the following year, Leah was appointed head of a new Open Air School for undernourished children in Cambridge, a post she would hold for eleven years. She was also selected as a Justice of the Peace, one of the first women to be so. And yet she still found time for her busy political life, becoming deeply involved in canvassing for the Labour Party, standing for Cambridgeshire County Council and pressing for the unionisation of female workers. In 1924, she was elected to the National Executive Committee of the NUT (National Union of Teachers) and during the General Strike in 1926 she helped set up a strike committee in Cambridge, despite her role as magistrate. Much of her time was also spent abroad; she travelled to Germany soon after the war to establish links with other Socialists and met the revolutionary Rosa Luxemburg shortly before she was murdered by right-wing Freikorps. Meanwhile, Leah's education work took her to Amsterdam, Budapest and Geneva and in 1926 she was awarded a scholarship by the Women's Club of America to visit the United States.

Four years later, in 1930, she was elected President of the NUT, only the fourth woman to hold the post. In her Presidential address, she argued for the raising of the leaving age to 15, believing passionately that the British educational system needed 'a great twentieth century renaissance which will give education an absolute value, because education is life.'[12] In her role as NUT President, she visited the House of Commons to listen to the debate on the second reading of the education bill put forward by

Sir Charles Trevelyan, President for the Board of Education in Ramsay-MacDonald's Labour Government. She was understandably outraged when her male colleagues were ushered to the Distinguished Strangers' Gallery, while she and a female colleague were relegated to the less prestigious Members' Gallery, on the grounds that 'women could not be trusted to keep quiet'. Despite the slight, Leah deeply involved herself in discussions surrounding Trevelyan's bill, but it was defeated in the House of Lords. The disappointment drove Leah to overcome her previous reservations and she agreed to become the first woman to be included in the NUT list of parliamentary candidates.

Selected for the seat of Bristol East, Leah was snubbed once again when the Labour Party Secretary and Treasurer, Arthur Henderson, chose an unknown young lawyer called Stafford Cripps to stand in her stead. Reluctantly, she withdrew, but she never forgave Cripps, accusing him of being a 'sanctimonious' man who 'did his damndest to sow discord, disunity and antagonism towards the Party leadership.'[13] However, in recompense, the following year Leah was selected for the north London seat of Islington East, following the death of the incumbent MP. She successfully won the seat, only to lose it seven months later in the catastrophic 1931 general election when the Labour Party lost over eighty per-cent of their seats, following PM Ramsay MacDonald's decision to resign and join a Conservative-led National Government. After only months as an MP, Leah found herself, like so many others in Britain, out of work. Fortunately, she was offered the position of NUT Assistant Education Officer, a post she would hold for the next twelve years. Leah was also selected to stand for Sunderland in the General Election of November 1935, but, faced by a bitterly hostile press and the loss of the Catholic vote due to her being mistaken for the pro-family planning novelist Ethel Mannin, she was beaten into last place.

However, other concerns were beginning to occupy Leah's mind. Her political activities were becoming increasingly dominated by the struggle against European fascism and its home-grown variant, Oswald Mosley's British Union of Fascists.

She was a member of the Committee for the Relief of the Victims of Fascism and, with John Strachey (then Minister for Food and later the Undersecretary for Air in Attlee's Labour government), co-chaired the Co-ordinating Committee against War and Fascism. She often turned up at Blackshirt meetings in Ridley Road in east London—sometimes with Jewish friends—asking searching questions of the speakers:

> It was very difficult to get answers from such people; indeed we were once involved in a punch-up with the future Lord Haw-Haw, and whenever I heard his hateful voice during the war, I could think with pleasure, 'Well, I once had the satisfaction of smacking his face.'[14]

Her campaigning involved her working alongside and sharing a platform with members of the Communist Party and led some Labour members—who were deeply suspicious of the Party's motives—to consider Leah a 'crypto-Communist', if not actually a clandestine Party member. Certainly, she was on the left of the Labour Party and fully understood the Communist Party's attraction for an increasing number of people:

> It was not surprising that many younger people looked to the Soviet Union as the hope of the world. Our democratic institutions had showed such utter ineptitude in dealing with the crisis of capitalism through which we had passed since the end of the war that we began to wonder if Russia might not have found the solution.[15]

However, Leah always denied joining the Communist Party and despite several visits to Russia, it was Spain that would prove to be the country to which she would donate so much of her time and energy.

Her connection with Spain was prompted by the dramatic events of October 1934, when an abortive general strike in Catalonia and northern Spain descended into a full-scale insurrection in the mining areas of Asturias. The government responded by sending in the army under the command of a young officer called Francisco Franco, who viciously put down the rebellion using tactics learnt in the brutal colonial war in Morocco. Shocking reports received by the Committee against War and Fascism spurred Leah to visit Spain in order to discover the truth. She described the 'unprecedented ferocity of the repression' in her account, *What I Saw in Spain*, published by Victor Gollanz the following year. Franco's brutal suppression of the uprising, in which nearly 2,000 civilians were killed in two weeks, made a deep and lasting impression on her: 'Reverberations of suffering, pain, death, from the mountains of Asturias seemed to fill my ears', she wrote.[16] From that moment on, Spain would be a cause close to Leah's heart.

Two years later, Leah was in Moscow when news of a military uprising in Spain reached her. She promptly cancelled her trip and returned home to throw herself into campaigning for the Spanish Republic. Alongside the gifted and eloquent Communist speaker, Isabel Brown, she travelled around the country speaking on behalf of the Republic and raising funds. As Leah proudly recalled, 'it was quite common to raise £1,000 at a meeting (equivalent to around £70,000 in 2023), besides plates full of rings, bracelets, brooches, watches and jewellery of all kinds.'[17] By August, the committee was in a position to send an entire medical unit to Republican Spain, including an ambulance, four qualified doctors and medical students and a full complement of nurses, assistants, administrators and drivers.[18]

However, not satisfied with just campaigning in Britain, Leah was determined to return to Republican Spain to demonstrate her support. She persuaded some Spanish friends to arrange a meeting with Don Pablo de Azcárate, the Spanish Ambassador in London, who she convinced to support her. Consequently, she left for Paris the following day, flying via Irún to Alicante, where she and a British photographer took an early morning flight to Madrid. There Leah contacted Julio Álvarez del Vayo, the Republican Minister of Foreign Affairs, to offer her help in raising support, food, money and anything else the Republic urgently needed.[19] Del Vayo gratefully accepted but warned her that the Republican Government expected the Spanish capital to imminently fall to the besieging rebel forces and had decided to decamp from Madrid to Valencia. He advised Leah that she would be wise to do the same.

Consequently, Leah set out early the following morning, accompanied by Willie Forrest, a reporter for the British pro-Republican newspaper, the *News Chronicle*. However, about seventy-five kilometres south-east of the capital, they were stopped at a FAI (*Federación Anarquista Ibérica*) road-block. There, 'furious Anarchists' accused them of desertion and ordered them to return to Madrid. Leah later shrugged off the event, stating that 'we suffered no particular hardship, only the disagreeable knowledge that, as soon as transport was available, we would be sent back.' However, they were in fact held for two days, at gunpoint, until news reached the much-relieved Leah that 'Madrid was saved . . . the first contingent of the International Brigades had arrived.'[20] Finally, the Anarchists allowed them to proceed.

When they eventually arrived at Valencia, Leah discovered to her great irritation that del Vayo, fully aware of the potential unpopularity of the government's decision to abandon Madrid, had shrewdly travelled on back roads and arrived unmolested. More frustrating still, del Vayo advised her that he believed she would be more help in Britain where she could make use of her parliamentary contacts. Reluctantly accepting the wisdom of his counsel, Leah and Willie Forrest returned home and within forty-eight hours she had set up an all-party meeting in the House of Commons. At the meeting, Forrest speaking 'quietly and unemotionally, but with consummate force' reported his own observations on Spain. Impressed, the meeting proposed that a delegation, led by Dai Grenfell, the Welsh MP for Gower, should go to Madrid. Probably of more long-term significance, however, was the suggestion by another member of the delegation, the Radical Liberal MP Wilfrid Roberts, that a National Joint Committee for Spain should be formed. 'This' wrote Leah Manning proudly, 'was the *real* genesis of the Aid Spain Committee, which did such magnificent work throughout the war.'[21] The Joint Committee, formed in January 1937, became the largest of the British Aid to Spain organisations, raising as much as two million pounds (equivalent to more than one hundred and sixty million pounds in 2023) for the Spanish Republic.

Despite del Vayo's advice, Leah would be back in Spain in only three months. With Franco's forces advancing ominously through the Basque Country in northern Spain, British newspaper reports of the bombing of Bilbao and the starving population created considerable sympathy. The government maintained that, due to a Nationalist blockade, the Royal Navy could not protect British shipping carrying supplies to Republican Spain.[22] However, the safe arrival of a number of British merchant ships in northern Spanish ports, most famously the Welsh 'Seven Seas Spray' on 20 April, rather undermined the government's position. While historian Tom Buchanan generously argued that 'the British Government was bamboozled by the illegal blockade', less charitable observers might question how enthusiastic they ever were to challenge it. *Times* journalist George Steer was convinced that 'the blockade existed only in the "hopes" of the Nationalist capital Salamanca and the "imagination" of Whitehall'.[23]

In the spring of 1937, Leah was approached by 'a Spanish gentleman' (actually a member of a Basque delegation to London) who pleaded with her to go to Bilbao to help evacuate thousands of Basque children:

> He outlined his plans so reasonably, with no idea that I might refuse to go and live in a beleaguered city, bombed and starving, and undertake such a terrifying responsibility as the evacuation of its children, that it never occurred to me to say 'No'.[24]

So she set off once again for Spain, flying to Bilbao via St Jean de Luz in order to avoid the 'blockade'. She landed a day earlier than she had expected, consequently nobody was at the airport to meet her. Using her initiative, she took a taxi to the British Consulate, where the Consul, Sir Ralph Clarmont Skrine Stevenson (later British Ambassador to China and Egypt), made it abundantly clear that he was not pleased to see her. Coldly, he instructed her to forget her mission and return home, rudely informing her that: 'I can't accept responsibility for you. I've had enough trouble over the Romillys with Churchill demanding they be got out.'[25] However, when Leah stubbornly refused to return, insisting that she was in Bilbao at the request of the Basque government, he reluctantly agreed to take her to meet the Basque President, José Antonio Aguirre.

While the Consul may not have been pleased to see her, the Basques certainly were; gathered to meet Leah was a huge crowd of dignitaries including the President, several Ministers and a number of officials from the *departamento de asistencia social*. But they had a surprise in store for her. Leah had been led to believe that she was arranging the evacuation of between 250 and 500 refugees but was taken aback to discover that the President wanted to evacuate some 4,000 children, accompanied by 300 adult helpers: 'My first coherent thought was that perhaps the Basque Government had chartered an ocean liner ... but since I had lost the power of speech I said nothing.'[26]

Two days later, on 26 April 1937, following a morning of negotiations with staff of the *departamento*, Leah Manning joined George Steer of *The Times* and Philip Jordan of the *News Chronicle* for an afternoon drink in a Bilbao bar. Having chosen to sit outside in the sun, they suddenly heard the sound of aircraft approaching and, fearing an imminent raid on the city, Jordan prudently suggested decamping to the air-raid shelter. When Leah fearlessly refused to move, they watched 'wave upon wave' of German Heinkels and Junkers fly overhead, heading inland. Horrified locals immediately guessed that they must be heading for the ancient market town of Guernica, home of the famous oak tree and symbol of Basque liberty. They watched on, horrified, as the bombers rained down incendiary and high explosive bombs on the defenceless wooden town. When the bombing finally ended at 8pm, the three set off to witness the devastation for themselves:

We drove over that night, to find such a scene of utter devastation as will be printed for ever on our minds. It cannot be described in words; only Picasso's 'Guernica' can depict its stark horror. If this raid was intended to destroy the morale of the people it utterly failed in its purpose. Bitter hatred against the Germans, who were responsible, and against non-intervention controls, which were to operate from the end of that month, filled the hearts of the people with a cold fury. Morale stiffened and, for the time being at least, this led to a heart-warming spurt in the rebuilding of defences, a task in which all might take part.[27]

Understandably, the bombing of Guernica also had a profound effect on the three English visitors. Philip Jordan had already written a number of important pieces on the defence of Madrid during the winter of 1936-37 and would continue to report for the *News Chronicle* during the Second World War. George Steer, until then known principally for his critical reports of Mussolini's invasion of Abyssinia, would write an account of the bombing for *The Times*, undoubtedly one of the most powerful pieces of journalism to come out of the civil war.[28] For Leah Manning, already deeply immersed in her efforts to evacuate Basque children to Britain, the horrifying atrocity would encourage her to work with renewed determination.

Leah made a number of impassioned radio appeals and sent off urgent telegrams from Spain to the Archbishops of Canterbury and Westminster, the former Liberal Prime Minister Lloyd George and TUC General Secretary, Sir Walter Citrine, begging them to intercede.[29] Her efforts were assisted by an appeal from the Basque President calling for the evacuation of children to safety abroad. However, valiant though Leah Manning's efforts undoubtedly were, it was the publication of George Steer's report in *The Times* on 28 April that was the decisive factor in pressing the British Government to drop their opposition to the evacuation.[30] It also stirred Walter Citrine to instigate discussions between Basque government representatives in Britain, Labour Party politicians, and members of the National Joint Committee. These led to the foundation of the National Committee for the Care of Basque Children (usually known as the Basque Children's Committee), with the 'Red' Duchess of Atholl (the maverick Conservative MP for Kinloss and West Perthshire, Kathleen Marjory Stewart-Murray) as Chair

46

and the 'MP for Spain', Wilfrid Roberts as Secretary.[31]

Four days later, Leah sent a telegram to Labour leader Clement Attlee, confirming that arrangements were proceeding for the evacuation of 2,300 children to France, but that there was an urgent need to rescue thousands more. In response, the Duchess of Atholl wrote to the British Prime Minister, Stanley Baldwin, asking that the British Government contribute financially to the evacuation. However, as Manning recounted furiously, 'the Basques received no sympathy from either the Home Office or the Foreign Office who both regarded the whole thing as a nuisance and myself as an officious busy-body.'[32] Consequently, on 14 May, Leah sent a frantic telegram to TUC General Secretary Walter Citrine, beseeching him '[in the] name [of] civilization and humanity' to obtain immediate authorisation from the Foreign Office for the evacuation of the Basque children to Britain.[33] The following day, fearing another Guernica, official permission was finally granted for the evacuation of 2,000 Basque children. However, the Basque Government had already chartered a ship to take 4,000 children to Britain, so on 17 May, the Pro-Consul telegraphed the Foreign Office advising that the number of refugee children had doubled. Under substantial pressure, and having already agreed to accept some refugees, the Government had little choice but to accede.[34] The government's decision to support the evacuation (albeit reluctantly) flew in the face of almost all the expert advice they had received.'[35] However, as a condition of their support, the government insisted that the cost of the evacuation must be met by the organisers and that the children had to be returned to Spain as quickly as was practicable. Furthermore, they stipulated that children under eight years old or over fourteen would not be eligible. This would inevitably have resulted in the breaking up of families, something Leah was determined not to do. So, once again, she appealed to influential figures in Britain for support, including the Archbishop of Canterbury. However, the British Government prevaricated, suggesting that British Consul Stevenson should decide. He, to Leah's intense frustration, supported the government's position. In desperation, Leah turned to Philip Jordan, who was about to accompany Stevenson aboard a British submarine to St Jean de Luz for a celebration in honour of the coronation of King George VI and Queen Elizabeth. Jordan shrewdly suggested that, while Stevenson was away, she should instead approach the Basque pro-Consul and persuade him to telegram London agreeing to her arrangement for the children. He agreed and 'from then on, things began to move very quickly,' Leah declared with relief.[36] The evacuees were allocated in strict proportion to the electoral composition of the Basque government including, as the British Government had stipulated, children from Franco-supporting families. Leah immediately agreed, maintaining that, 'to us there were neither Anarchists nor Nationalists—only people in danger of their lives asking for safety.'[37] Two doctors arrived from Britain to help prepare the children for evacuation aboard the SS Habana, an ageing liner designed to carry only 800 passengers:

> At last, the night of departure arrived. The quay was a thick, black mass of parents, defying bombs as the children, some happy and excited, some in tears, were taken aboard in orderly companies. Head to tail the *señoritas* laid out our precious cargo—on the bulkheads, in the swimming pool, in the state rooms and along the alley ways, for all the world like the little *sardinas* about which they were always singing; and out there, in the grey waters, two ships of the British Navy stood by to guard our going.[38]

The *Habana* set off from Bilbao for Southampton at 6.40am on Friday 21 May 1937. Unfortunately, the weather in the Bay of Biscay was typically atrocious. As one of the two British doctors on board recounted, 'four thousand wretchedly seasick children crowded into an old boat whose very latrines are apt to regurgitate in sympathy are not a pretty sight.'[39] Leah recalled with horror how she 'slipped and slithered from one pool of diarrhoea and vomit to another.'[40] The bedraggled and thoroughly seasick young passengers eventually arrived early on the morning of 23 May, to find that the Duchess of Atholl, *News Chronicle* editorial director Sir Walter and Lady Layton and Sir Walter and Lady Citrine had all turned out to welcome them.[41]

Following a Catholic mass held by a local priest, the children were taken to an emergency camp at the village of Stoneham, a few miles north of Southampton. Initially taken aback at living out of tents 'like Gypsies', as one young girl put it,[42] most of the children adjusted quickly and were relatively happy there, even if Leah could see that the Spanish war had left its ugly mark:

> It was impossible to make the children believe that the food would not run out: there was never a meal when we did not see them surreptitiously hiding some part of it in their pockets or tucked up in their jerseys. To those who have starved for months, the threat of hunger is always there.[43]

Over the next few months, the children were gradually dispersed around the country, to schools, private homes and houses, known as 'colonies'. Leah herself took charge of one group of children who were initially quartered in the village of Pampisford south of Cambridge before moving to a house owned by Jesus College.[44] Another colony was located in a large house in Theydon Bois, Essex, known for a time as Leah Manning House.[45] Despite their experiences, it was a happy time for many children, one describing it as 'like a fairy story':

> In my own home, we used to have baths in a large pail, but when I arrived at this colony, I was shown to a bathroom with towels and sponge bags for all of us, containing soap, toothbrush, toothpaste and eau de cologne. And then there was the bedroom: four beds for the little girls, with eiderdowns and curtains. I've often wondered how we could have been so lucky, after the hard times we had the misfortune to live through in Spain during the war.[46]

Though the initial plan had been for the children to be away from their families 'only for three months', the changing nature of the situation in Spain—and in Europe—meant that many stayed considerably longer. While the process of returning the children did begin in November 1937, there were still 1,000 stranded in Britain when war was declared in September 1939. Almost 500 were still in Britain at the end of the war, with many refusing to return to Franco's Spain.[47]

The rescue of the Basque children would not mark the end of Leah Manning's efforts on behalf of the Spanish Republic. In October 1937, four months after the arrival of the *niños*, as Franco's forces were over-running the last of the Republican forces in northern Spain, Leah Manning travelled to Catalonia on behalf of the Joint Committee. There she observed the desperate plight of Republican refugees who were arriving in Catalonia at the rate of 8,000 per day:

> I saw exactly the same conditions among these little children which I observed in Germany in relief work which I did among children there in 1919. Stick-like limbs, abnormally swollen abdomens, vacant eyes and pallid complexions. The undernourishment is terrible. Most of the children have had no milk more than once or twice a week for a long time.[48]

She made an urgent appeal for 'milk, flour, beans, sugar, cocoa, cod-liver oil and malt', for blankets and 100,000 pairs of children's shoes. She also suggested that, rather than well-meaning knitting groups making clothes for the refugees, it might be more practical to send the wool to Spain so that 'the women could knit clothes and give them direct to the children as soon as they are made'.[49]

Manning returned to Spain the following summer, hitching a lift on a lorry carrying supplies to Vich hospital in Gerona, where there had been an outbreak of typhoid. She was intent on visiting a German refugee called Doctor Glaser, who had been placed in charge of the hospital, and of whose son Kurt she was a trustee.[50] Her report, written on 26 July 1938, demonstrates her huge contribution to British medical aid. In addition to ironing out tiresome administrative and bureaucratic issues, she ensured that the medical unit was supplied with necessary supplies and equipment, having seen for herself the catastrophic impact of a lack of equipment:

> You remember [Dr. González] Aguiló with whom we have been working since the first days at [the first British hospital in] Grañén, he has now been at the front for 20 months and has been recalled to his own civil hospital in Barcelona. He is one

of the finest surgeons in Spain, so you can imagine his horror when he discovered that there was absolutely nothing in the operating theatre with which to do surgical work, although the results of bombardment were filling his wards. I have seen the theatre myself—there are 19 surgical instruments only, and everyone is broken. A little boy was brought in while I was in the hospital with a scalp injury and fractured skull. They could do nothing for him as they had not the proper instruments—and so he just died.[51]

She showed considerable sympathy and understanding for the almost impossible demands placed upon the medical teams:

I cannot close this second report without saying how deeply I admire the courage, the patience, the cheerfulness under extremely adverse conditions and professional skill of the surgeons and nurses we met on this tour of the front line hospitals.[52]

On Sunday 31 July, Leah set off on a tour of the hospitals lying north of Barcelona, accompanied by the British Medical Unit's administrator, Rose Davson (known as Rosita), and Winifred Bates, the Spanish Medical Aid Committee's liaison officer.[53] At the large hospital at Mataró, lying 30km north of Barcelona, Leah was stunned by the pioneering medical skills of the English surgeon, Alex Tudor Hart (see Chapter Ten):

[One thing] which seems to me extraordinarily interesting was a synthetic thumb, which he was growing out of the man's stomach. He had taken a piece of bone out of his leg somewhere, put it in his stomach, and there it was growing out just like an ordinary thumb with Hart cogitating how he could make a nail grow later on when he had grafted the thumb on to the man's hand![54]

Leah also visited a Republican hospital just outside the little Catalonian village of La Bisbal de Falset, half-way between the River Ebro and Tarragona. It was, Leah discovered, in a unique location:

An enormous natural cave in the mountain side . . . had been cleverly blasted to make a great ward for sixty beds, a triage, an operating theatre and a kitchen. I suppose that in all the history of modern warfare there has never been such a hospital. It is the safest place in Spain, beautifully wired for electric lights and with every kind of modern equipment.[55]

While Leah had planned to return to Barcelona that night, a Spanish surgeon persuaded her to stay and sit with a Welsh volunteer who had been wounded in the abdomen:

The hours dragged by. Sometimes [the English nurse] Faith came to bring me a black coffee and look at her unconscious patient.[56] At about four o'clock, the boy opened his eyes. He stared at me. In a voice of astonished wonder he said, 'Leah Manning!' Then smiling quietly, 'You see I made it, comrade.' He closed his eyes again and I went to fetch Faith. It was the end of one boy's heroism and tragedy which had begun in a quiet Welsh mining village a few years earlier.[57]

Leah had previously met the volunteer, a young miner from the Rhondda called Harry Dobson, at an anti-Mosley demonstration in south Wales, where he had invited her back to his family's house for tea. There Dobson had told her of his determination to join the International Brigades and had quizzed her on how he might go about it. According to Leah, she told him that she thought he was too young (though this seems strange, as Dobson was born in 1907), but he nevertheless successfully joined the International Brigades in June 1937. When Leah met him, Dobson had been in Spain for a year, having risen to the rank of Company Political Commissar. Leah sat with him for fifteen hours, during which time he was given several emergency blood transfusions. 'We did everything possible for him', reported a distraught Leah Manning, 'but without avail.'[58] Clearly deeply upset by Dobson's death, she wrote a personal letter of condolence to his sister.[59]

With their hospital tour approaching its end, Leah returned to Barcelona with Rosita Davson, briefly visiting a hospital in

Gerona *en route*, before heading north for the French border, travelling on roads that were already becoming flooded with desperate refugees. Over the following months, their plight, and their shameful treatment by the French government, would increasingly preoccupy Leah. However, back in Britain, her immediate task was to present a detailed report to the Joint Committee on the state of the British medical services in Republican Spain.[60] Much of her report dealt with the practical needs of the unit, such as the necessity of compiling an up-to-date list of all the British medical personnel in Spain and making clear the 'serious difficulties' that were caused by medical staff overstaying leave. Of particular interest to Leah was the impressive work of the Blood Transfusion Unit run by the Reading GP, Reginald Saxton, which, she was proudly informed, was taking blood from two hundred donors every day to provide the vital supplies for badly wounded soldiers such as Dobson.[61]

The trip had also embroiled Leah in ongoing disputes between a number of the British working in Spanish hospitals. The doctors, nurses and support staff came from a diverse range of backgrounds and bitter arguments had erupted on several occasions. Inevitably, many of the arguments were fuelled by the phenomenal stresses of working in wartime: short periods of working flat out for days on end, interspersed with long idle periods in which there was little to do. Some of the disputes arose over politics, but many were personal and based on petty jealousies. Of particular concern to Leah was a simmering row that had developed between her two travelling companions, Rosita Davson and Winifred Bates.

Bates had accused Davson of having 'bourgeois tendencies' and implied that she was not 'politically reliable'.[62] Bates' criticisms were supported by Bill Rust, a Senior British Communist in Spain, who claimed that Davson had been responsible for the arrest of two medical aid volunteers, which he interpreted as deliberate sabotage. In her report, Leah admitted that other colleagues had remarked upon Davson's bluntness and lack of tact.[63] However, she pointed out that the 'tough [and] resilient,' Davson had worked for the Spanish Medical Aid Committee (SMAC) 'for over two years . . . without receiving a penny piece in payment' and that 'it appears to be impossible to take responsibility without incurring someone's displeasure.'[64] Leah concluded that while personal feelings lay behind many of the arguments, politics also played a part. Davson was regarded with particular suspicion by senior British Communists, as she had previously worked for the British Embassy and Diplomatic Corps.[65] Leah noted pointedly that 'all the complaints come from people who have formerly worked, or are now working with, what is familiarly known in the committee as the 35th Division.'[66] As the Division included all the Communist dominated International Brigades, the implication was clear: that all the complainants were members of the Communist Party and that many of the criticisms were politically motivated. By the end of 1938, Leah's ability to work alongside members of the Communist Party appeared to be coming under strain.

Three months later, Franco's declaration of victory plunged Leah into a profound depression. However, having devoted superhuman efforts to the Republican cause, she wasn't prepared to give up on the cause of democratic Spain. A month later she was involved in another rescue mission, though the refugees were trapped not in fascist Spain, but in democratic France. Following the fall of Barcelona in February 1939, nearly half a million desperate Spanish Republicans 'a mass of broken unhappy people, all their illusions destroyed', had headed north for the security of the French border.[67] On arrival, however, they were not welcomed, but thrown instead into primitive internment camps established on the beaches of seaside towns such as Argelès-sur-Mer and Saint-Cyprien. Enclosed by barbed wire and lacking any form of shelter, conditions in the camps were brutal, heavily overcrowded and insanitary. Leah was horrified:

> What did they expect, these people, when they reached the border? Friends, a warm welcome, relief from hunger, cold, weariness, and the bitterness of defeat? Instead they found the barricades, harsh resentment and the inhospitable waste of Les Boules.[68]

She became involved following the disappearance of her friend from the Vich hospital, Doctor Glaser. His wife was desperate to find him and, suspecting that he had been interned in one of the camps, wrote to Leah for help. She, in turn, contacted Rosita Davson, recently returned to London, who set off to find him. After days of searching, Davson eventually found him 'at the point of death' in the French camp at Argelès.[69] Fortunately for Glaser, Rosita's access to 'food and drugs, transport and money' enabled her to get him released and transported to Paris, where he was safely reunited with his wife. Inspired by having secured the release of her friend, Leah determined to help rescue other refugees imprisoned in the camps.

With other members of the Joint Committee, she set about raising funds to help charter a ship to carry refugees to Mexico (the seat of the Republican government in exile), where they could start new lives. A French ship, the SS Sinaia, had been chartered by Wogan Philipps, the Second Baron Milford, who had served as an ambulance driver in Spain. The ship was to transport 1,800 refugees, looked after by a complement of medical staff. The former administrator in Spain, Nan Green, would also be on board, organising the care of the very young children.[70] Leah hoped that the story of the refugees' journey might help publicise the appalling plight of the Republican refugees interned in the French camps:

> The British Committee for Refugees from Spain are very anxious to make a film of the journey from Port Vendres in the 'Sinaia' and also if possible a Mexican film . . . to give an idea of the terrible conditions from which our Spanish comrades are going and the new conditions which we hope await them in Mexico. We would use these films at our meetings as the basis for the campaign to raise the next £20,000 in order to send a further ship to Mexico.[71]

The SS Sinaia left Sète in southern France on 23 May 1939, having been given a rousing send-off by the Duchess of Atholl and a huge crowd, and arrived at Vera Cruz in Mexico almost a month later.[72] Leah got her wish for publicity when photographs of the refugees taken by 'Chim' were published in *Life* Magazine.[73]

Meanwhile, Leah's work on behalf of the defeated Spanish Republicans continued. Two months later, she was a member of a British commission at an international conference in Paris on the Spanish Republican refugees. Her primary concern, once again, was children, of whom there were estimated to be some 20,000 still imprisoned within the French camps: 'all are undernourished and the majority are suffering from scabies and other skin diseases.' It was, argued the Commission, a matter of urgency that the children be rescued and placed safely in 'colonies' in countries such as Britain or America. Here, the work of the Basque Children's Committee in Britain during 1937 was cited as a good example. But, as had been the case with the *niños*, Leah was concerned that the children's precarious legal position as potential orphans might lead to Franco laying claim to them. 'The only safe line to take', she argued, 'is to assume that *none* of the children is an orphan, which, in view of the difficulty of proving the death of missing parents, would appear to be a fair assumption.[74] The delegates returned home, determined to press the British Government to do more. Unfortunately, on 1 September 1939 the plight of the refugees was overshadowed by other events.

After Britain's declaration of war on Germany two days later, Leah's efforts were obviously limited to Britain. Yet, like many who had been involved in supporting the Spanish Republic, she was determined to carry on the fight against fascism. She had been appalled by the Hitler-Stalin pact, and was bitterly disappointed by Communists' opposition to what they argued was an imperialist war: 'The Communist Party, which had shared to the full our hatred of fascism, quit the field on orders from the high command in Paris,' she wrote indignantly.[75] With her husband Will transported to the safety of Canada to work on industrial and scientific research, Leah volunteered for the London Ambulance Service, but soon discovered that during the 'phoney war' there was little to do. So, following a call from the NUT General Secretary, Sir Frederick Mander, she resigned and lent her efforts instead to the national evacuation programme.[76] She worked with children in London, visiting them prior to and after their relocation, which involved travelling across the country. As she quickly discovered, the nation's terror of spies meant this was no easy task:

> There were no signposts, no cheerful lights from cottage windows, and to ask for directions was to court the inevitable reply, 'Sorry I'm a stranger hereabouts myself'.[77]

Nevertheless, she found the work hugely enjoyable and satisfying and she was constantly impressed by the dedication of those involved:

> Many alarmist stories were written at that time about the disgusting habits of some town children and many perhaps were true, but above all and glorifying all was the infinite patience of the reception officers responsible for fitting evacuee children into strange homes, and the wonderful kindness of those who received the children.[78]

Leah continued to work for the NUT throughout the war and in 1944 was promoted to Head of Organisation at the London Office. This led her to become closely involved in implementing the 1944 Education Act, which recommended raising the school leaving age to 15 and dividing the elementary education sector into primary and secondary schools and splitting the latter into grammar, secondary modern and technical schools. It also proposed abolishing fees and providing free school meals for secondary schoolchildren. Leah was appointed a joint-secretary of the Teachers' Registry, set up to ensure that, once the war was ended, all boroughs would be allocated good teachers, not just those fortunate enough to be unscathed by five years of Nazi bombing.

Following the end of the war in Europe, Leah returned to the political arena, standing in the safe Tory seat of Epping in the general election of July 1945.[79] 'This Election,' she wrote in her election material, 'is probably the most important in British history.'[80] At public meetings held across the constituency, the Labour Candidate promised 'food, work and homes,' were she and her Party to be elected. Her election material contained a passionate denunciation of Conservative policies between the wars: 'Believe me, the Tories have nothing to offer you,' she argued, 'War is their only remedy for unemployment. You should say "NEVER AGAIN."'[81] It was a hard-fought campaign, for the Conservatives were determined to hang on to the seat, which had been Winston Churchill's before the war. When the result was declared, Leah discovered that she had won by less than a thousand votes. Not that the margin mattered, of course, what counted was that she was to be an MP once more. 'What a glorious victory it was!' she exclaimed triumphantly, summarising the euphoric feelings of Labour supporters across the country after their remarkable landslide victory:

> Five solid years at least, in which a Labour Government, independent of any other Party and in no coalition, could begin to build the Socialist Britain of which we had dreamed for so long.[82]

Throwing herself into her new job as a Member of Parliament, Leah dedicated a huge amount of time and effort to her particular area of expertise: education. Yet she also involved herself in other issues of Attlee's government, including nationalisation and Beveridge's plans for a national health service. She campaigned for family planning provision and supported a Conservative bill which aimed to provide analgesia for women in childbirth. She was a strong supporter of the creation of new towns around London, taking a particular interest in Harlow, just to the north of her Epping constituency.

Yet, despite the demands of her new office, Leah still found time to continue campaigning for a democratic Spain. In October 1946, she and Nan Green, now Secretary of the International Brigade Association, were part of a delegation organised by the Emergency Committee for Democratic Spain which visited Ventas prison in Madrid, where 7,000 female political prisoners were being held.[83] Their visit was made all the more urgent by a letter the International Women's Day Committee had received from the *Unión de Mujeres Españolas*, which claimed that several women held in the prison had been badly tortured. One prisoner had allegedly been driven insane by the brutal treatment she had received.[84]

Initially, both Leah and Nan were refused visas to travel to Spain. This was no great surprise, for Leah had previously been warned that she would be arrested if she ever tried to enter Franco's Spain. However, following pressure from the British Foreign Office, who coolly pointed out that Leah Manning was an elected member of Her Majesty's Parliament, the Spanish Embassy agreed to issue visas to the members of the delegation.[85] Accompanied by a representative of the International Women's Day Committee and a social worker, the delegation visited the prison in order to establish for themselves the conditions in which women were being held.[86] During the visit, prison officials took the delegates on a carefully orchestrated tour, clearly designed to prevent them from seeing anything untoward. However, by deliberately dragging her heels, Leah allowed Nan the opportunity to forge ahead and speak freely, if briefly, to prisoners. They confirmed the reports of torture.

There is no doubt that the visit helped publicise the women's plight and it probably played a role in the commutation of a death sentence that had been imposed on one of the prisoners. However, the dispiriting experience of visiting Franco's Spain was not one Leah wished to repeat: 'Except for poignant memories,' she wrote, 'the Spanish chapter is closed for me.'[87] Yet she still did not entirely abandon the cause. In November, she spoke at an anti-Franco demonstration, held to mark the tenth anniversary of the defence of Madrid.[88] And the following year, the American veteran's association, ALBA, invited her to tour the US speaking in support of Spanish refugee orphans in France and Belgium and in support of ALBA's protest against American economic aid to Franco's Spain. It was an ambitious, yet surprisingly successful trip; she spoke at major venues such as New York's Madison Square Gardens and was even granted the honour of a meeting with Eleanor Roosevelt. It also had an unexpected consequence: on her return to Britain, Leah began a campaign against the import of 'horror comics' which she had encountered in America and she strongly believed were 'vicious drugs for the child mind.'[89] In a parliamentary debate in March 1947 she asked her old friend Hugh Dalton, then Chancellor of the Exchequer, how many comics were imported from the United States; 'I have no idea,' he responded, pithily. Thinking his reply disrespectful, she complained, leading Dalton to retort, 'I thought it was a much better answer than the customary, "The information required by my Hon. Friend is not available"' at which the House erupted with laughter.[90] Leah had the last laugh though, for her campaign eventually led to the 1954 Children and Young Persons (Harmful Publications) Act.

While Leah's Spanish chapter may have come to an end, her involvement in other left-wing causes certainly had not. She authored a Labour Party pamphlet on 'maternity and child welfare, day nurseries and nursery schools, school meals and milk, and family allowances.'[91] She was horrified by the apparently unstoppable drift from world war to cold war and its passive acceptance by many in the British political establishment. This led to giving perhaps the most famous speech of her career, during a debate on civil defence in March 1948. She witheringly accused the former Chancellor of the Exchequer, Sir John Anderson, of downplaying the damage likely to be caused by a nuclear war; 'trying to persuade us that a few layers of brown paper were a good protection.'[92] She was appalled that another potential conflict was being openly considered after the ravages of six years of world war:

The iron curtain, which we are told exists between East and West, has today given way to a kind of sheet in a shadow play, across which both sides see a phantasmagoria of distorted, horrible grotesque people passing. Someone ought to tear down that sheet and show people on both sides; we are all ordinary human beings, hating war and longing for peace.[93]

Leah tried to help 'tear down the sheet' by personally visiting countries behind the Iron Curtain. On a tour to Yugoslavia in

1948, she met General Tito, who she believed she had met in Paris during the Spanish Civil War.[94] She also visited Stalin's Soviet Union the following year. 'You may see anything you want to see,' she was assured and, despite her initial reservations, she returned impressed by much of what she saw, particularly their educational system. However, many of her constituents were outraged at what they saw as pro-Soviet treachery. They would soon have an opportunity to express their fury.[95]

The general election campaign of 1951 was a bitterly fought affair: an effigy of Leah was burnt in her constituency and during the count two female Conservative supporters spat in her face. Leah was in no doubt that Nye Bevan's notoriously offensive description of the Tories damaged her personally in Chingford, where meetings were packed with angry constituents defiantly sporting 'vermin' badges. While Leah actually increased her personal share of the vote, it was not enough and she lost to the Conservative candidate, Sir Graeme Bell Finlay, by almost 4,000 votes.[96]

Leah's friend and Labour Councillor, Lady Patricia Gibberd, was at the count, which she found 'an awful experience. Leah was so hurt and disappointed.'[97] Reflecting on her defeat, Leah believed that three main issues had made the difference: opposition to nationalisation (especially the coal industry); enduring price controls and rationing; and slow progress with the provision of housing. She also noted a new trend in voting behaviour, which was to occupy the thoughts of many future leaders of the Labour movement:

Canvassing in the narrow little streets adjacent to Walthamstow, one became aware of a phenomenon which is part of our changing society. Voters born and brought up in solid working-class Labour homes suddenly change when they buy or rent a house in what they consider a more middle class milieu . . . one was driven to the conclusion that a Tory bill in the window was for them an outward and visible sign of that inward grace which had transferred them into 'middle class' respectability.[98]

1952 was 'a black year' for Leah Manning. 'I had lost my

seat, my husband [Will, who she had not lived with for some time, died in January, aged 68] and my enchanting cat Mimi— and only those who are owned by a Siamese cat can know what that meant to me.'[99] Consequently Leah kept herself busy in local issues, supporting the Harlow Labour Party's campaign to convert all local secondary schools to comprehensives. She passionately believed that, '[the eleven plus] was one catastrophic examination taken on one catastrophic day in the life of an immature child.' But when she failed to retake Epping in the 1955 election, Leah decided to retire fully from political office. Not that this stopped her from campaigning and she spoke out passionately against Eden's involvement in Suez in 1956 and in support of Britain's entry into the EEC in the 1960s. She dedicated much of her time and energy to local issues, helping set up a controversial family planning clinic in the new town of Harlow in 1964, which provided contraception to unmarried couples.

But, freed from the demands of political office, she was able to return to her first love, taking up a teaching post in an independent primary school, working with children from all backgrounds, focussing on those with personality disorders. She eventually retired to a thatched cottage in the little Essex village of Hatfield Broad Oak, near Bishop's Stortford, where she devoted her remaining energies to the affairs of the local Parish Church. Her final years were spent in an NUT home for retired teachers in Elstree, where she died in 1977, aged 91.

Leah Manning's long and distinguished life has received a number of tributes over the years, including the erection of several memorials. A photograph of her hangs in the National Portrait Gallery and she was made a Dame of the British Empire in 1966 honouring a lifetime of political service. She appears in much of the literature surrounding British involvement in the Spanish Civil War, has published two memoirs (now out of print) and in 1991 was the subject of an admiring biography by two fellow Labour Party activists, the local historian, Ron Bill and the Euro MP, Stan Newens (also out of print).[100] Yet despite all of this, it is hard not to feel that the name of Leah Manning is not as widely recognised as it should be, for it was a life 'as remarkable as it was long and busy.'[101]

Why this should be the case is hard to say with any certainty, though during the cold war Leah, like many others who had lent their support to the cause of the Spanish Republic, were often seen, or portrayed, as 'crypto-Communists'. However, as Harry Pollitt had recognised as far back as the 1930s, Leah Manning was ultimately too independent-minded to join—or be accepted—into the disciplined Communist movement.[102] Her socialism was based on humanitarianism, rather than dogma.[103] For example, while she opposed the invasion of Egypt in 1956 over Nasser's nationalisation of the Suez Canal, she fully supported the UN action on Korea.[104] In fact, Leah Manning followed a similar trajectory to a number of other non-Communist supporters of the Spanish Republic: feeling betrayed by the Hitler-Stalin pact, outraged by Communists' refusal to condemn the Soviet Union's invasion of Finland and baffled by the Party line on the Second World War that, until June 1941, portrayed it as an imperialist rather than anti-fascist war. While she supported 'Aid for Russia' during the war and was a prominent member of the 'Second Front Now' campaign, her autobiography makes clear that, as early as the 1940s, she was no longer an uncritical admirer of Stalin's Soviet Union; '[the] treatment of Poland and the betrayal of the heroic victims of the Warsaw rising stuck in my throat.[105]

In Ron Bill and Stan Newens' biography, they argue that 'she was in some respects inconsistent and she allowed her personal likes and dislikes to take precedence over what might have been a more considered judgement.'[106] That's probably a fair assessment. A good example was her personal animosity towards Sir Stafford Cripps, who she never forgave for taking her seat in 1930 and who subsequently could do no right in her eyes. No respecter of protocol, Leah's tactlessness and impatience could sometimes cause ruffled feathers and bruised egos. Her high-handed demand in 1937 that 'the Basque Government in London should charter two ships for the purpose of evacuating children' was greatly resented by the Basque Government's representative in London, who acidly pointed out that 'he was not employed by Mrs Manning but by the Basque Government, and any instructions to him should come from his Government.'[107]

Yet, had she not been single-minded and tenacious, she might never have overcome the British government's opposition to the evacuation. It is certainly true, though, that Leah Manning did not achieve the children's rescue single-handed; she readily admitted that she would not have succeeded without the help of Philip Jordan and the Basque pro-Consul. She also was at pains to point out that, despite rumours to the contrary, the work of the Basque government was highly effective, particularly their efforts to persuade the local population that evacuation was the best option available for the children. The evacuation was strongly opposed by the Foreign Office and many influential organisations and 'Leah Manning's success,' as the historian Tom Buchanan pointed out, 'was a rare triumph for emotive political pressure over expert opinion.'[108] Leah undoubtedly dedicated enormous time and energy to the cause of the Basque refugee children and it is something for which they and their relatives remain extremely grateful. A letter, signed by a number of the Spanish children and teachers at Stoneham camp in the summer of 1937, emotionally voiced their gratitude, and it is appropriate that the final words should come from those whose lives Leah Manning touched most profoundly: 'we have been given shelter by a second mother, this second mother we do not know how to thank for her attentions and kindnesses shown to us.[109]

Chapter Three
The Cambridge Rebel: Peter Kemp

On 12 January 1932, a strange report dropped onto the desk of Colonel Sir Vernon Kell, the head of British intelligence, MI5. It concerned a letter apparently written by a determined left-wing revolutionary living in in the south of England, which had been sent to the headquarters of the Communist Party in Covent Garden.[1] MI5, which routinely kept a close surveillance on post and telephone calls to and from the Party's King Street offices, had intercepted the letter from 'a certain Andrew WHITE'. He claimed to have lived in India for some years, where he had witnessed for himself 'British tyranny at its vilest.' Accompanying the letter was an article White had written on 'The Indian Scandal' for the Communist newspaper, the *Daily Worker*. The piece attacked the 'vacillating, cowardly and sanctimonious hypocrite' Mahatma Gandhi and his policy of passive resistance and called on the Indian leader and his Congress Party to be 'swept aside and utterly destroyed so that the workers and their real leaders can replace it.'

Having read White's letter and the diatribe against British imperialism, Sir Vernon sent a concerned letter of enquiry to Lieutenant-Colonel Ormerod, the Chief Constable of East Sussex Police.[2] A police sergeant was duly dispatched to make discreet enquiries about White at the address given in the letter, in the genteel seaside town of Bexhill-on-Sea. However, questioning the neighbours revealed that no individual of that name was to be found at the address. Nor, for that matter, did the residence appear to be the likely site of a Communist revolutionary cell. Living at the address was a Miss Burrows, 'a Councillor of the Bexhill Corporation and the principal of the largest and most aristocratic ladies' school in the town.' Bemused, the Sergeant approached Miss Burrows directly for assistance about the whereabouts of 'Mr White'. A mortified Miss Burrows confessed that her 16-year-old nephew might, perhaps, know something about the letter.

Further enquiries revealed that, rather than a Marxist revolutionary, the teenager was in fact a member of the Anti-Communist League, run by the Conservative MP for Birmingham Handsworth and founder of the British Blueshirts, Sir Oliver Stillingfleet Locker-Lampson. Furthermore, Miss Burrows confessed that her nephew had once casually mentioned to her that he was contemplating posing as a member of the Communist Party in order to obtain sensitive information which he could then pass on to the government. Anxious about the potential impact of her nephew's antics on his father, a retired High Court judge in India, Miss Burrows confirmed that, yes, she would most certainly treat the matter as confidential.

The sergeant delivered his report to the local superintendent at Lewes police station, who passed it on to the Chief Constable's Office. The highly amused Chief Constable forwarded the report to Sir Vernon, noting, 'it rather looks as if this lad is, or would like to be in your line of business!' To the relief of Miss Burrows, Sir Vernon, secure in the knowledge that armed revolt was not likely to erupt in Sussex just yet, agreed that the incident could be put down to youthful high jinks and that 'no further action of any kind will be necessary.'[3]

The name of this premature anti-Communist and would be double-agent was Peter Mant MacIntyre Kemp. Born in Bombay on 19 August 1915, he was the son of Olivia Maria Martin and Sir Norman Kemp, who had indeed been a High Court judge in the Indian Colonial Service.[4] Kemp had initially been educated at a Hastings preparatory school before attending the private Wellington College from 1929 to 1933.[5] While Kemp excelled at cross-country running and fencing and was a Sergeant in the OTC, he was hardly a diligent student, with one of his teachers remarking sarcastically that '[Kemp] gives no trouble and takes none.'[6] Nevertheless, perhaps due to skills honed in debates with fellow Wellingtonians Esmond and Giles Romilly (who both fought in Spain on the Republican side), he managed to secure a place at Trinity College, Cambridge. When he graduated in 1936, having scraped a third-class degree in classics and law, the twenty-one year old found that he was 'at a crossroads in his life and had been somewhat of a disappointment to his family.'[7]

Under pressure to take up a profession, Kemp reluctantly studied for the Bar, just about managing to pass his preliminary exams, but never got around to taking his finals. Instead, bored of the law and desperate for adventure, Peter Kemp decided to volunteer to fight for the military rebels in the war in Spain. While he considered himself a 'radical Tory', his main political motivation was the 'deep-seated hatred and fear of Communism' that had come to the attention of Sir Vernon Kell five years earlier:

> I had been active in politics in Cambridge, where my traditionalist, Tory opinions caused me to view both communism and fascism with equal loathing. But of the two, I believed that communism presented the greater danger to Europe.[8]

Drawing on his extensive family and society connections, Kemp secured a meeting with the Marqués del Moral, who ran the Spanish Nationalist Agency in London. He provided Kemp with a letter of introduction to officers based at Franco's headquarters at Burgos. Meanwhile, a friend from Cambridge provided him with cover as a journalist for the *Sunday Dispatch*, to help him evade non-intervention officers, who were attempting to prevent foreign volunteers from entering Spain.[9] Kemp departed from Newhaven on a cold, wet day in mid-November 1936; five days later he was in Burgos. One of the first people Kemp encountered there was the English amateur pilot and bull-fighting aficionado, Rupert Bellville, who had enlisted in a military unit of the Spanish *Falange* (the Fascist Party) but had found them frighteningly blood-thirsty. Despite Bellville having been considered 'too conservative for the Conservative Association' at Cambridge, Kemp heeded his advice, rejecting the *Falange* for the ultra-conservative, Carlist *Requetés* from Navarre. Placed initially in a cavalry unit, Kemp soon found life too dull for his tastes, particularly when the victims of his first cavalry charge turned out to be a panic-stricken herd of goats.[10] He was also tormented by an inability to get to sleep, due chiefly to the unpleasant nocturnal consequences of a diet consisting mainly of beans.[11]

Impatient to confront something more challenging than goats, at the end of December Kemp transferred to an infantry unit then fighting on the south-western outskirts of Madrid. This, Kemp immediately realised, was an entirely different proposition; as dangerous as the cavalry had been boring. Marooned on a Nationalist salient with enemy soldiers as close as ten metres away, all conversations had to be carried out at a whisper. His only route to safety was by crawling silently through an underground passage; 'even the dead had to be sent out through the tunnel, for there was nowhere we could bury them.'[12] At the end of the year, shortly after Kemp's unit had been withdrawn to the Madrid suburb of Getafe for a rest, the position was destroyed by a mine, killing an entire company of soldiers.

Early in the new year, Kemp received the devastating news that his father was dying and he was given permission to return home. He rushed back to London, only to arrive the day after his father's funeral. Honouring the commitment he had given to his unit before leaving, Kemp returned to Spain, arriving on 9 February. Mirroring the experiences of some of his compatriots fighting in the International Brigades, Kemp was to see action in the bloody battle of Jarama to the south-west of Madrid. Posted to a position overlooking the valley of the Manzanares river, Kemp and his fellow *Requetés* were on the receiving end of a huge Republican counter-offensive. During the bitter two-day battle, Kemp's outfit lost one hundred men, a third of their strength. Kemp later vividly described the chaos and terror of the fighting:

My throat was dry, my face hot and my hands shaking as I feverishly loaded and fired my rifle. With a great effort I pulled myself together and began to fire more slowly, checking my sights, resting my elbows on the parapet and talking careful, aimed shots. This had a steadying effect on me and I began to feel much better. I began, too, to feel a kind of pity for my enemies, exposed in the open to this murderous fire; so that, as I aligned my sights on one of them and pressed the trigger with a slow steady pressure as I had been taught, I found myself praying that my bullet might put him out of action, but not maim him grievously for life . . . Many fell; some lay down where they were and fired back at us, others turned and ran in all directions, looking for cover, not realizing that this was the most certain way of being killed . . . The bombardment intensified as a new wave of attackers surged forward, in much greater strength than the first . . . Our ears were throbbing with the explosions, our eyes almost blinded with dust; not so blinded, however, that we could not see that the enemy was getting closer, finding his way surely round to our left flank. Bullets from his light machine-guns were slapping against the parapets and whistling by our heads. Sometimes a Requeté, carried away by excitement, would clamber up on the parapet, half out of the trench, to get a better shot; in a moment he would slump back, torn with bullets, or fall forward over the parapet to roll a few yards down the slope in front.[13]

Fortunate to have emerged from the battle unscathed, Kemp briefly returned home in the spring to help his mother resolve legal issues arising out of his father's death. His return to Spain was arranged by another well-connected friend, Pablo Merry del Val, the son of the former Spanish ambassador in London, who even organised a lift for him to Seville with a 'distinguished looking' Spanish diplomat. Kemp returned on 21 April and while awaiting orders he ran into the leader of the Irish Blueshirts, General Eoin O'Duffy, whose unit was awaiting repatriation following a less than glorious contribution to the Nationalist war effort. In their first action at Jarama, several of the members of the unit had been killed, having mistakenly got into a firefight with Falangist troops from their own side and at a subsequent action to the south of Jarama, O'Duffy had refused to order his troops to advance. The unimpressed commander of the Spanish Foreign Legion, General Yagüe, recommended the Irish unit's dissolution and his proposal was soon echoed by a disillusioned O'Duffy.[14] Kemp was as unimpressed as Yagüe with the 'portly' General O'Duffy and his Irish Bandera:

The 'Brigade' was in fact equal in strength to a battalion, but O'Duffy was granted the honorary rank of General in the Spanish Army. Few generals can have had so little responsibility in proportion to their rank, or so little sense of it. Whatever the ostensible purpose of the Irish Brigade, O'Duffy never lost sight of its real object, which was to strengthen his own political position. He therefore gave the most responsible appointments to his own political supporters, regardless of their military experience; one of the most important he gave to an ex-liftman from Jury's Hotel in Dublin, a man who knew nothing of soldiering and was prepared to learn nothing. In favour of such men as this he declined the services of experienced ex-officers who did not happen to belong to his party . . . To his men he was known as 'General O'Scruffy' or 'Old John Bollocks'.[15]

Like many of the foreigners serving in Spain, Kemp was afflicted by a number of health issues, a consequence of the alien food and poor hygiene and sanitation. Having fallen ill with jaundice, Kemp's condition and consequent 'weakness and depression' improved no end following visits from 'friends in Vitoria' among whom, Kemp recounted grandly, was the Duchess of Lécera. Following his recuperation, Kemp persuaded Merry del Val to talk to General Millán Astray, the commander of the Foreign Legion, about a possible transfer. Renowned as the toughest unit in the Spanish army, Kemp's desire to join them displayed considerable courage. The Legion, explained Kemp, 'were deployed, like the International Brigades on the other side, as "shock troops" in situations of the most critical importance or the greatest danger.' The unit had a well-founded reputation for brutality as much as for military prowess and fearless bravery, much of which was due to the savagery inflicted upon Legionnaires at any sign of disobedience:

There was a grimmer side to the discipline, which reminded me how far I was from the OTC. The day after my arrival two troopers reported for duty incapably drunk; apparently they were old offenders. The following evening [their Catalan officer] Llancia formed the whole Squadron in a hollow square in the main barrack-room. Calling out the two defaulters in front of us, he shouted, 'There has been enough drunkenness in this Squadron. I will have no more of it, as you are going to see.' Thereupon he drove his fist into the face of one of them, knocking out most of his front teeth and sending him spinning across the room to crash through two ranks of men and collapse on the floor. Turning on the other he beat him across the face with a riding crop until the man dropped half senseless to the ground. He returned to his first victim, yanked him to his feet and laid open his face with the crop, disregarding his screams, until he fell inert beside his companion. Then he turned to us: 'You have seen, I will not tolerate a single drunkard in this Squadron.' The two culprits were hauled, sobbing, to their feet to have a half-pint of castor oil forced down their throats. They were on duty next day, but I never saw either of them drunk again.[16]

As Frank Thomas, a Welsh volunteer for Franco's Rebels remarked, 'The Spanish Legion must be one of the few military forces where men are drilled by the use of whips.'[17] Insubordination was routinely punished by death and Kemp, promoted to platoon commander, was himself severely reprimanded for merely court-martialling a soldier rather than shooting him outright.[18]

At the end of October 1937, Kemp was accepted into the 14th Bandera of the Spanish Foreign Legion. Any optimism on his part was soon disabused by the discovery that the Spanish officers in the Legion did not welcome foreigners and treated him with distrust and contempt. 'I shit on Englishmen,' Kemp's Company commander informed him coldly.[19] The awful conditions in which the Legion was fighting at Teruel in the winter of 1937 only made matters worse. In one of the most severe Spanish winters for years, temperatures plummeted to minus twenty Celsius:

[It was] a very savage winter. Our casualties were due to frost-bite more than the enemy and we had to lie down to sleep, we had to lie down in the snow and we didn't have any greatcoats because they never arrived. No fires were allowed. There used to be five or six people every night who, when we woke up in the morning, they were as stiff as boards. I'd have to comb the frost out of my hair and get the icicles out of my nose. I spent

71

most of the night walking around. The people who were stupid and didn't wake up were the people who took half a bottle of brandy—and that was the killer.[20]

Nevertheless, the situation was even worse for the Republican forces, who were soon cut off and unable to bring up adequate supplies and reinforcements. Fighting in snowdrifts up to their waists, the Republicans were slowly driven out of Teruel. In the huge Nationalist offensive that followed in March 1938, Kemp was involved in an attack on Republican defences in the Aragón town of Belchite, where he discovered a sack-load of mail destined for American and Canadian International Brigaders:

Some of the letters I had to examine were tragically moving; letters from sweethearts, wives and even, in one or two cases, children. It was horrible to feel that many of these men, who spoke my own language and who had come even further from home to fight for a cause in which they believed as deeply as I believed in ours, would never return to enjoy the love that glowed so warmly from the pages I was reading.[21]

To his horror, Kemp discovered that the determined resistance put up by the Republican defenders had earned a vicious response from the victorious Legionnaries, who were 'shooting the wounded as they gasped for water.' As Kemp knew, Republican prisoners were all too frequently summarily executed; he had himself seen a Spanish lieutenant of the *Caribineros* who was trying to surrender shot through the head. The attitude of many senior Nationalist officers towards their enemies was made explicitly clear by his superior officer, after Kemp had approached him begging that a captured British member of the International Brigades could be treated with mercy:

I found Colonel Peñaredonda sitting cross-legged with a plate of fried eggs on his knee. He greeted me amiably enough as I stepped forward and saluted; I had taken care to leave the prisoner well out of earshot . . . 'I have the fellow here, sir,' I concluded, 'in case you wish to ask him any questions.' The

Colonel did not look up from his plate: 'No, Peter,' he said casually, his mouth full of egg, 'I don't want to ask him anything. Just take him away and shoot him.'

Kemp stared at Peñaredonda, aghast. Furiously the officer snarled at him, 'You heard what I said. I warn you, I intend to see that this order is carried out.' Despairing, Kemp returned to the prisoner to break the news that he was going to be shot. To ensure that Kemp followed his order, the colonel sent two Moroccan soldiers with him, instructing them to execute Kemp if he disobeyed.

It was almost more than I could bear to face the prisoner, where he stood between my two runners. As I approached they dropped back a few paces, leaving us alone; they were good men and understood what I was feeling. I forced myself to look at him. I am sure he knew what I was going to say.
'I've got to shoot you.'
A barely audible 'Oh my God!' escaped him.
Briefly I told him how I had tried to save him. I asked him if he wanted a priest, or a few minutes by himself, and if there were any messages he wanted me to deliver.
'Nothing,' he whispered, 'please make it quick.'
'That I can promise you. Turn round and start walking straight ahead.'
He held out his hand and looked me in the eyes, saying only: 'Thank you.'
'God bless you!' I murmured.
As he turned his back and walked away I said to my two runners: 'I beg you to aim true. He must not feel anything.' They nodded, and raised their rifles. I looked away. The two shots exploded simultaneously.[22]

Despite his disgust, Kemp stayed with the Tercio and, a few days later, was part of a desperate fight for a strategic position overlooking the town of Caspe, 70km east of Belchite, which Republican forces had captured the previous autumn. During the fighting, Kemp was hit in the throat by a bullet and in the arm by grenade fragments. Ironically, the injuries probably saved his life:

> The day after we were wounded, Caspe fell to an assault from three directions by overwhelming Nationalist forces. The International Brigades, particularly the 14th (British), had fought a gallant and determined action, inflicting terrible casualties on the 16th Bandera and ourselves; our own company had barely twenty men left, out of the hundred and ten with which we had started the battle.[23]

Whilst convalescing at a hospital in Zaragoza, Kemp encountered the English nurse, Priscilla Scott-Ellis, known as 'Pip', who had been serving as a nurse with the Nationalists since the previous October.[24] Kemp was quite taken with the daughter of the eighth Lord Howard de Walden and fourth Lord Seaford, describing her as 'a cheerful girl with a great sense of humour' and a 'sympathetic drinking and dining companion.'[25] Scott-Ellis appears to have been equally enamoured, describing him to a friend as 'the good-looking Englishman I once saw in Salamanca.' They stayed up drinking into the early hours, at which point Kemp confessed to her about the shooting of the British International Brigader. Pip sympathised, admitting that it was 'a nasty thing to have to do.' However, in a comment which described the Nationalist Rebels rather more accurately than she perhaps realised, she continued, 'Having power, especially over human lives, seems to go to people's heads and make them horrible almost always.'[26]

Once back on his feet, Kemp returned to serve with the Bandera until, on 23 July 1938, he was wounded again, on this occasion by a grenade which exploded immediately in front of him, nearly blowing off his jaw:

> I barely heard the explosion: I was conscious of it only as a roaring in my ears, a hammer blow on the left side of my face and a sickening dizziness as I fell to the floor. My mouth seemed to fill with a sea of pebbles; as it fell open, the sea resolved itself into a deluge of blood and the pebbles into fragments of my back teeth; twice more the flood welled up into my mouth to pour in a widening pool across the floor. I

watched with a detached bewilderment, changing to near-panic. 'Oh God!' I prayed, 'don't let me die now, like this, in terror!' I took a grip on myself, remembering how someone had once said to me, 'You're never dead till you think you are'.[27]

Initially, doctors didn't expect Kemp to survive, but he was extremely fortunate to be treated by two of the best surgeons in Nationalist Spain.[28] However, Kemp would take no further part in the fighting. After a long, slow period of recovery, the pain of his injuries leading him to self-medicate with brandy, Kemp was sent home to Britain in October, having been granted two months' convalescence leave. By the time he returned to Spain, the civil war was over.

When Franco held a victory parade in Madrid on 19 May 1939 to celebrate his victory, Kemp was in the crowd, accompanied by Pip Scott-Ellis and by Major Hugh Pollard, the MI6 agent who had helped organise Franco's flight from Gran Canaria to Morocco during the initial uprising in July 1936.[29] In July, Kemp was honoured with an audience with Franco, in recognition of his service for the Nationalist cause. Kemp was not much impressed with the Caudillo, describing him as 'a small tubby figure, dwarfed by the broad scarlet sash and pendulant gold tassels of a full general.' Nevertheless, he listened politely while Franco lectured him on the perils facing the western world due to Communism, loftily assuring Kemp that a world war was absolutely out of the question.[30]

Two months later, Britain declared war on Germany. Kemp, still recovering from the wounds sustained in Spain, was declared temporarily unfit for military service. Reluctantly, he settled for what he considered to be an 'uninspiring' job in the press section of the Postal censorship office, working on material from Spain and Latin America.[31] However, once he had recovered, Kemp once again turned to his seemingly inexhaustible contacts and obtained an interview with 'a rather secretive section of the British forces':

Returning home from work one evening, I ran into Douglas

Dodds-Parker (the Head of Military Intelligence Research), whom I had met in Spain during the summer; because he had also been in Prague at the time of the Sudetan crisis, I suspected that he was connected with intelligence. My spirits rose when he asked me, 'Would you like me to give your name to my people at the War Office?'[32]

In due course, Kemp received a letter from the War Office asking him to come for an interview. There, a Staff Captain asked him detailed questions about Spain, before casually advising Kemp 'that he might be of use at some stage'. Typically, as he was leaving, Kemp was spotted by a friend from Cambridge, who introduced him to his companion, Lieutenant-Colonel (later Major-General) Colin Gubbins. The officer further quizzed Kemp on his time in Spain, letting him know that they had a friend in common: Pip Scott-Ellis. Kemp was reassured to discover that the senior British Army officer 'didn't seem to disapprove of the side I had chosen.'[33] This chance encounter was to prove highly significant in determining Kemp's wartime experiences.

Discreet enquires about Kemp's family and military background determined that he was of 'the right sort'; in fact, one of Kemp's referees took great umbrage at the impertinence of the request:

I can assure you, that if you want to give a commission to a fighting man, you have here someone with 3 years' more experience of war than most of you have at the War Office, and it is even absurd that you have asked for a reference. It seems to me absolutely indecent that you should ask a man like Peter Kemp for credentials as if he were going out as a Commercial traveller to sell stockings.[34]

Consequently, in December 1939, Kemp received a letter from the War Office confirming that he was to be commissioned into the army as a Second Lieutenant and on 19 January 1940 he joined the 110th (Horsed Cavalry) Officer Training Cadet Unit, based at Weedon in Northamptonshire.[35] Kemp enjoyed the soldiering, particularly the horse work, but was unimpressed with his training:

Our theoretical training might have been of use to cavalrymen in or before 1919. We heard lectures in tactics from an earnest young officer in the Inns of Court Regiment who took his chief illustration from an accident in the First Battle of Mons; lectures on animal management from the Veterinary Officer, who was inaudible; lectures on Military Law, which was incomprehensible, and lectures on the light machine-gun (Hotchkiss 1913 model).[36]

Nevertheless, after five months' training, Kemp was ordered to report back to the War Office in London for his posting. A rather more interesting type of military service beckoned.

Kemp had been selected for 'Operation Knife', a clandestine operation run by MI(R), the War Office department conducting research into guerrilla warfare. The mission would involve Kemp and five other officers being smuggled into Norway by submarine, in order to blow up the main train line from Oslo to Bergen. Appointed the group's Bren Gun instructor, Kemp was promoted overnight to Captain.[37] Their send-off speech was almost beyond parody: 'I say, you know,' said the head of MI(R), 'it's frightfully nice of you chaps to go on this show.'[38] The saboteurs set sail for Norway in April 1940, but their mission was brought to an abrupt halt when their ship was torpedoed by a German submarine. The frustrated would-be saboteurs returned to Britain, fully expecting to make a second attempt, but the withdrawal of Allied troops from Norway in May made the mission redundant. Instead, the following month, Kemp was posted to Inverailort House, a remote mansion near Lochailort, forty kilometres west of Fort William in the Scottish Highlands, to be part of a new training school. Trainees were instructed in the techniques of guerrilla and irregular warfare, ominously informed that 'hardship shall be your mistress, danger your constant companion.' It was to become the first of a number of special training schools across the world and its illustrious alumni included the Hollywood actor David Niven and David Stirling, founder of the Special Air Service. Under the instruction of Lord Lovat, the centre's senior fieldcraft instructor, Kemp believed he learnt more of the art of concealed movement in a month 'than I could have learned elsewhere in a year.'[39]

For Kemp, the year of 1941 had begun with personal tragedy when his elder brother Neil was killed in a Stuka attack on the *HMS Illustrious*.[40] Kemp was visiting his bereaved sister-in-law in Dorset when he received a telegram from MI(R) recalling him to London. There, he was informed that he was to be enrolled into a new ultra-secret force, referred to by the purposefully bland name of the Inter-Services Research Bureau, but which was to become famous as the Special Operations Executive. More usually known by its initials, SOE, the organisation had been founded in 1940 by Colin Gubbins, Pip Scott-Ellis's mutual friend, who Kemp had been introduced to at the War Office. The organisation had been charged by Winston Churchill personally to promote subversion in enemy-occupied territory. Often acting completely independently from conventional military forces, the covert unit made use of all kinds of military personnel from around the world armed with a variety of non-standard weaponry, from captured German and Italian *materiél*, to booby-trapped rats and exploding cow-pats.

In February 1941, Kemp was recruited for a covert mission to travel to Spain to help resist a potential Nazi invasion, though enquires by MI5 about Kemp's temperament suggested that he might not be the most appropriate candidate. J N Kennedy of MIR described Kemp as 'an exceedingly nice fellow,' but admitted that '[he] drinks a little too much for his own good and cannot be guaranteed to be completely reliable.'[41] Concerns had also arisen relating to Kemp's association with right-wing Spaniards, particularly his friend D José Brugada who worked at the Spanish Embassy, raising the possibility that Kemp might unwittingly provide information which could end up with their German allies:

> In these circumstances you may think it worthwhile warning KEMP to steer clear of his Spanish friends, but I should be grateful if you would refrain from telling him that we have anything specific against the Embassy personnel.[42]

Nevertheless, Kemp was admitted once more to Lochailort,

where he encountered a number of Spanish Republicans training on Loch Morar. They were, thought Kemp 'a villainous group of assassins' apparently interested in little but foraging for food.[43] Wisely keeping his distance, Kemp underwent three weeks of intensive training in demolition and the use of small arms, before being sent by ship to Gibraltar. However, on arrival at the British overseas territory, Kemp was informed that Sir Samuel Hoare, the British Ambassador to Spain, had categorically forbidden any SOE activity in the country, forcing the mission to be abandoned. Kemp returned to Britain for yet more training, principally in the skills necessary for work behind enemy lines: parachuting, sabotage and other undercover tactics. Though brave and hard-working, Kemp clearly did not endear himself to his training officer, whose report noted, 'Not once, not twice, but three times have I seen this officer punctual.'[44]

His training completed, Kemp spent two months kicking his heels in London. In March 1942, he joined a new commando-type outfit called the Small Scale Raiding Force (SSRF), led by two highly experienced veterans of Dunkirk, the intrepid Major Gustavus Henry 'Gus' March-Phillipps and his more methodical assistant, Captain John Geoffrey Appleyard.[45] Kemp discovered that the unit was a haven for mavericks too independent-minded and undisciplined for conventional forces, such as Anders 'Andy' Lassen, 'a cheerful lithe young Dane with a passion for killing Germans' that won him a Victoria Cross.[46] Lassen, a 'cross between a marauding Viking and James Bond', hailed from a very wealthy Danish family; when visiting London before the war, his father was in the habit of summoning his Rolls Royce from the steps of the Hyde Park Hotel with a hunting horn. If anything, Andy Lassen was even more unconventional than his father, typically going in to combat bristling with unorthodox weaponry such as a 10-inch knife and a crossbow. While his troops revered him, Lassen drove his superiors to despair with an utter disdain for military protocol; one operational report submitted following his unit's advance into Italy remarked simply: 'Landed, killed Germans, fucked off.'[47]

Though the Small Scale Raiding Force was officially labelled No. 62 Commando, and its members all wore the Marines' green beret, they were essentially autonomous and encouraged to wear civilian clothes when off duty, in keeping with March-Phillipps' notion of 'Elizabethan gentlemen adventurers': 'we were to be gangsters, with the knowledge of gangsters', explained one SOE recruit, 'but with the behaviour, if possible, of gentlemen.'[48] Kemp, newly married to Hilda Phillips, the twenty-four year old daughter of a South African born army Captain, joined the small elite group which, during the summer of 1942, launched a number of daring raids on German coastal defences across the English Channel.[49] The SSRF's formidable reputation was to be sealed by 'Operation Dryad', an attack during the night of 2 September 1942 on the German garrison based in the Casquets lighthouse, which lay on a group of rocks 13 kilometres northwest of Alderney in the Channel Islands.

The mission's objective was to disable a German transmitter in the lighthouse and grab anything of interest. Kemp was instructed to kill or capture any German soldiers they encountered, before they could use the radio. Like his fellow 'gangsters', Kemp was laden down with equipment and weaponry:

> I was carrying a tommy-gun and seven magazines, each with twenty rounds, a pair of wire-cutters, two Mills grenades, a fighting knife, a clasp knife, a torch, emergency rations, and two half-pound explosive charges for the destruction of the radio transmitter.[50]

Having left their base in Portland at 9pm the commando unit sailed to the Channel Islands aboard a motor-torpedo boat fondly nicknamed 'The Little Pisser', before switching to rowing boats for the final assault.[51] Landing in silence just after midnight, the force made their way cautiously up a 25m cliff before launching their surprise attack on the lighthouse. They caught the seven strong German garrison completely by surprise, though not without incident: Kemp was accidentally wounded in the leg by one of his fellow commandos and Appleyard badly sprained his ankle. The force returned to Portland at 4am, bringing with them important intelligence, including codebooks, diaries and letters. Information gleaned from the terrified prisoners—still dressed in their pyjamas—also proved invaluable.

Ironically, Kemp and Appleyard were fortunate to have been injured, for they missed the raiding party's next action, Operation Aquatint, which was a disaster. Ambushed during an attack on the Cherbourg Peninsula, the group were all taken prisoner, with the exception of March-Phillipps, who was killed attempting to swim to safety. 'It was,' admitted Kemp, 'a crippling calamity which nearly put an end to our activities.'[52] It was also a personal tragedy for Kemp, who clearly admired his commander: 'His magnificent ideals and his personal charm and kindliness made him one of the finest men I have ever had the privilege of knowing and I am proud to have served under him,' he wrote in a heartfelt letter to Marjorie, Gus March-Phillipps' widow. 'Please do not think of answering this,' Kemp added, considerately.[53]

Despite the setback, Appleyard managed to rebuild the force, Kemp helping to train troops seconded from the Royal Marine Commandos. In October 1942, they successfully completed a dangerous reconnaissance operation on the Channel Island of Sark, capturing two more German soldiers in the process. However, the raid had a significant, unforeseen consequence. During the action, four bound German prisoners had been shot trying to escape. In response, an outraged Hitler issued the *kommandobefehl* on 18 October, ordering that all captured commandos in uniform were to be executed without trial, while any caught out of uniform were to be handed over to the Security Services to be brutally interrogated, before they were themselves put to death.

Nevertheless, the raids continued for a time. On 11 November, Kemp commanded a landing party which attacked a German semaphore station on Point de Plouezec, on the Brittany coast. However, the German forces were now on high alert and the mission was unable to capture any prisoners. Kemp's report of the action, which outlined how the operation had at least given the German forces a major fright, was shown to Churchill. 'Good', responded the Prime Minster succinctly.[54] However, this was to be the final raid. In early 1943, the unit was transferred to

North Africa and renamed the Second Special Air Service Regiment. A number of Kemp's comrades in the SSRF were killed later fighting in special-forces operations in Italy. One of these was 'the marauding Viking', Andy Lassen. Brave to the point of recklessness, he was killed on 8 April 1945 at Lake Comacchio, 140km south of Venice, in the very last weeks of the Italian Campaign.[55]

Kemp did not go with the SSRF group to North Africa but, instead, left the unit to return to parachute training, where his lack of punctuality had gone down badly the previous year. Determined to make a better second impression, Kemp was rewarded with a report which grudgingly admitted that 'he is not entirely the irresponsible officer that he appears on first sight.' Kemp was posted to the SOE section responsible for operations in Greece, Yugoslavia and Albania, the transfer coming, as ever, through his inexhaustible contacts:

One morning in the middle of May 1943, I was sitting in an office in Baker Street, talking to Lieutenant-Colonel James Pearson, who had been in my troop at Weedon [where Kemp had received his basic military training] . . . 'We're looking for officers', he told me, 'who would be prepared to parachute into Greece or Jugoslavia to work with the guerrilla forces there. Would that interest you? If so, which country would you prefer?'[56]

Knowing little of either country, Kemp plumped for Yugoslavia and was sent to Cairo to await a parachute drop into the country. However, while waiting for a plane, Kemp discovered that Yugoslavia would be an extremely dangerous posting, for the country was not just at war with Germany, but also embroiled in a bitter civil war between Tito's mainly Communist partisans and General Mihajlovic's Chetnik guerrillas. Persuaded of the potential difficulties and anyway unable to secure a flight, Kemp agreed to go to Albania instead. He was parachuted in on 10 August 1943, where he joined the SOE's resident commander, twenty-five year old Lieutenant-Colonel Neil 'Billy' McLean.[57] The Eton and Sandhurst educated officer immediately impressed Kemp, who found him, 'gifted with outstanding qualities of imagination, leadership, courage and endurance'. McLean, observed Kemp shrewdly, 'hid beneath a nonchalant and charming personality a shrewd and ruthless mind.'[58] McLean was assisted by former cavalry officer and commando, Major David Smiley and by Captain Julian Amery (later a Conservative Minister), who had known McLean at Eton.[59] However, Kemp was utterly unimpressed with the 'infinitely ambitious' Albanian Communist liaison officer, Frederick Nosi. In Kemp's view, Nosi, the nephew of an influential political figure in Albania, 'trampled ruthlessly on all who impeded his progress, allowing no conditions of friendship to stand in his way. He terrorized his subordinates, fawned on his superiors and spied on his comrades.'[60] As a rule, Kemp didn't think much of the partisans:

> They were a thoroughly dishonest, unscrupulous and murderous collection. They were not very brave in action. Their two leaders were Enver Hoxha, who promoted himself shortly afterwards to Colonel-General, and Memet Shehu, who was a gunman and a thug, who claimed [in fact, accurately] to have fought with the International Brigades in Spain.[61]

During Hoxha's 40 year rule as Communist dictator of Albania, thousands were ex-judicially killed or perished in forced labour camps. Kemp nursed a particular loathing for the Albanian Communist dictator; on hearing of Hoxha's death in 1985, Kemp got to his feet and let loose a loud cheer. Raising his glass of beer, Kemp exclaimed, 'Stoke well . . . the furnaces of Hell!'[62] Kemp liked his sidekick Shehu little better: 'a sour taciturn man of ruthless ambition, outstanding courage and sickening ferocity,' who was believed to have recently cut the throats of seventy Italian prisoners. 'I took care', Kemp remarked, 'that he shouldn't discover I had been on the other side [in Spain].'[63]

To Kemp's relief, McLean handled most of the meetings with the partisans, while Smiley looked on with barely-disguised disgust: 'the interminable discussions . . . never really got anywhere,' Kemp recalled, 'because they were usually an excuse for the partisans to complain that we had been helping some other resistance group.'[64] While McLean did his best to explain to Kemp the labyrinthine complexities of Albanian politics, Kemp summarised the situation very simply:

> The tactic of the Communists . . . once they were strong enough, was to attack any groups belonging to the other resistance movements and to complain to us that those groups had attacked them.[65]

Despite the challenges, the British mission's orders were to train up the Albanian partisans in guerrilla warfare, coordinating ambushes and attacks on enemy outposts, while mediating disputes between rival warlords. In addition to the inevitable personal dangers, their work was made substantially more difficult by the knowledge that while they and the partisans could hope to escape from danger into the hills, the Germans would not hesitate to take harsh reprisals against the local villagers.

Kemp's outfit were initially based in a small mountain village called Shtyllë, lying near the Greek border, from which they launched small-scale ambushes on Italian military outposts or on staff cars spotted travelling without escorts on Albania's remote, mountainous roads.[66] However, only ten days after Kemp's arrival, they were ambushed by Italian soldiers and had to abandon the base. Kemp later discovered that it had been rumoured that he had been killed in the retreat and consequently drafted a brief message to his superiors in London: 'Still alive [stop] please refrain from wishful thinking.'[67]

Two weeks later, on 9 September 1943, the Italians' surrender to the Allies brought their military action in Albania to an end. With winter approaching, Kemp was transferred to Kosovo, to help Serbian Irredentists, who were bitterly opposed to the Axis' forced incorporation of Kosovo into Albania. Now promoted to Major, Kemp worked alongside Albanians living in Kosovo, relying on Hasan Beg, a rich influential landowner and farmer. Sympathetic to the Allies, Beg claimed to be on good terms with all the Kosovan political groups; even the Communists. However, in January 1944, following complaints by

Hoxha of Kemp's 'treachery' (meaning attempts to bring together the factions, rather than support the Communists), attempts to coordinate the various forces were abandoned. Kemp was furious:

> So we are to ditch Gani Beg, the one man in this part of Albania who really means to fight the Germans and has got the guns and ability to do it; the one man who can rouse the Kossovars to fight; a man who has just suffered two years of imprisonment for his loyalty to the British—just to please Hoxha and his bunch of scheming thugs who hate the British anyway![68]

His mission now impossible, Kemp was withdrawn from Albania, never to return. Within a year, Hoxha's Communist-dominated partisans had crushed their rivals and taken control. Those who had worked with the British were regarded as traitors and many of them, including those who Kemp had fought alongside, were murdered.

Kemp flew back to London, arriving in the spring of 1944, just too late to join the preparations for D-Day. Instead, he joined a six-strong team of SOE agents, as part of an operation in support of the Polish Resistance movement.[69] The unit was commanded by Lieutenant Colonel 'Bill' Hudson, who had been a leading agent in Yugoslavia and Colonel Harold Perkins, the head of SOE's Polish section. The perilous nature of the mission became all too clear when Kemp's kit was issued:

> We were also supplied, in an atmosphere of grim and silent sympathy, a small supply of 'L-tablets', each containing enough cyanide to kill a man in half an hour if swallowed, in a few seconds if chewed.

Unfortunately, the cyanide tablets got mixed up with their supplies of aspirin, so the agents prudently decided to destroy the lot.[70]

Initially, the British Foreign Office had opposed the operation, aware that Stalin objected to any involvement in support of Polish 'bandits'. The Soviet leader had, after all, watched on as the uprising in the Warsaw Ghetto was brutally crushed by the Nazis, even going as far as to deny the Allies permission to use Russian airfields for aircraft involved in dropping supplies to the desperate Poles. Kemp was incensed, accusing the British Foreign Secretary, Anthony Eden, of 'an obsessive admiration for Stalin.'[71] However, Churchill's determined support for the SOE eventually held sway and the Foreign Office was overruled.

The operatives' journey to Poland began in October 1944, with a parachute drop into Italy. The mission could not have had a more inauspicious start:

> The sortie was marked by an ugly incident caused by the inexperience of the dispatcher. While hooking up one of the agents to the wire strong point in the aircraft he somehow passed the static line through one of the straps that held the man's parachute to the man's back; when the agent jumped, the static line, instead of pulling open his parachute, held him swinging in the slip stream. Although the aircrew tried desperately to pull him back, the slip stream was too powerful; he remained hanging in space until he froze to death.[72]

Forced to return, the group sat on their heels, drinking and reading the newspaper of the British forces in the Central Mediterranean, the *Union Jack*. The paper was notorious for its fun-poking and double-entendres; one headline memorably recounted how 'Soviet Push Bottles Up One Hundred Thousand Nazis In Lower Balkans.' Finally, after two months of waiting around, the weather improved sufficiently to undertake the final section of their journey. On Boxing Day 1944, after a six-hour flight in an unheated Liberator, Kemp's unit was dropped near Radomsko in southern Poland. Unfortunately, the Polish aircrew, perhaps over-excited at returning to their native country, flew not at 800 feet, but at 300, so their parachutes barely had time to open. When the team landed on the frozen farmland, all the agents were injured: Kemp couldn't walk for days and his chief, Bill Hudson, was seriously concussed.

Their mission's instructions were very clear: they should keep a low profile and not under any circumstances become involved in a firefight with the Germans. However, after less than a week in Poland, they ran out of luck and were discovered hiding in a farmhouse. Under attack from German tanks and infantry, they had little choice but to flee, abandoning much of their equipment, including their vital radio. Ironically, having evaded capture by the Germans, two weeks later saw them hiding from Russian soldiers, as the Red Army offensive swept across Poland. As Kemp discovered, while the Poles hated the Germans, they dreaded the Russians. Soviet occupation, they explained to Kemp, 'meant extinction for both their country and their class.'[73] Kemp, of course, felt exactly the same and had no wish to have anything to do with the Russian forces.

Unfortunately, notice of the SOE group's presence in the area had been passed to the British Military Mission in Moscow and then onto the Russian political and military authorities. Consequently, Hudson's group was ordered to turn themselves over to the nearest Russian divisional headquarters. Praying that, as allies, they would at least be given a friendly reception, Kemp's worst fears were realised when they were all promptly handed over to the NKVD.[74] The six 'guests' (four British officers and their two Polish liaisons) were locked up in an unpleasant, filthy prison, which only 48 hours earlier had been under the charge of the Gestapo. The conditions were abominable; the prisoners were fed on stale rye bread, accompanied by a thin soup of warm water and grains of barley. There was filthy vermin-infested straw for bedding, assuming that anyone could sleep, for a bare light bulb blazed out overhead day and night.

The men were put through long and exhausting interrogations, but all indignantly refused to answer any questions. Suffering 'humiliation, discomfort and near starvation' and 'the ever-present threat of a firing squad or a labour camp,' there were moments when Kemp and his fellow captives wondered if they would ever be released. Their sanity was only preserved by two packs of playing cards that their captors had overlooked, with which the men played Bridge solidly for days on end. 'I've never played Bridge since', Kemp later admitted. It was three weeks before the group was finally released; the day after the Yalta conference they were put on a train to Moscow and the safety of the British Military Mission.[75] The imprisonment and brutal treatment did nothing to endear the veteran anti-Communist to Stalin's murderous regime. As Kemp later discovered, his worst fears while a prisoner were fully justified: 'I learned after the war, that SOE parties taken by the Russians in Hungary had been liquidated on the spot.'[76]

After a frustrating two months in Moscow nervously waiting for permission to leave, Kemp was flown, via Tehran and Cairo, to Britain. Back home, he was given two weeks leave to recuperate, which he spent with relatives in Ireland. Unfortunately, his hosts' generous hospitality (and extensive drinks cabinet) proved rather counter-productive:

On my return to London, feeling distinctly shaky, I approached my doctor for a prescription to restore my health. He wrote one out for me, which read simply, 'Say "No, thank you", three times daily.'[77]

One month later, the war in Europe was over. Yet Kemp, utterly embittered by his recent experiences, was unable to greet the Allied victory with any enthusiasm, feeling that 'the wine of victory had turned to vinegar.' It was 'a hideous peace' Kemp felt, for while people danced joyously in the fountains in London's Trafalgar Square, singing the praises of good old Uncle Joe, 'Russian soldiers raped and murdered in Vienna, Prague and Budapest.'[78] Thoroughly dispirited and with his private life 'an ugly mess' following the recent collapse of his marriage, Kemp had little reason to remain sitting on his hands in Britain. So he volunteered to link up with his former SOE commander in Albania, David Smiley, who was involved in setting up a guerrilla force to counter Japanese forces in south-east Asia.

Consequently, in July 1945, Kemp was parachuted into north-east Thailand. In addition to a wireless operator and a demolitions expert, Kemp was accompanied by Rowland 'Roly' Winn, the 4th Baron St Oswald, who Kemp had met in Spain when Winn was a correspondent for the *Daily Telegraph*. The group's principal task was to rescue French refugees who were being imprisoned and murdered by the Japanese.[79] They were also ordered to provide support to the small number of French officers fighting alongside Laotian irregulars against Communist Annamites, the Viet Minh. Despite falling severely ill with malaria and dysentery, Kemp managed to organise the smuggling of arms across the Laotian border, while successfully avoiding detection by both the Japanese and Viet Minh.

When the Japanese formally surrendered on 2 September 1945, Smiley and Winn were recalled to England, leaving Kemp in sole command of an area of some 50,000 square miles. Given the rank of 'Local Lieutenant-Colonel', his task was to help maintain the peace between the different forces and interests in the region: locals, French, independence movements such as the Viet Minh, plus the first Americans to be sent to Vietnam. It was an almost impossible task and he had limited success. In one frightening stand-off with a band of Vietnamese Communist soldiers, a French officer friend of Kemp's was shot and killed.[80] To his disgust, an American OSS officer watched on, having been given strict orders forbidding him from becoming involved. As Smiley confirmed from London, Kemp's efforts were not popular with the Viet Minh command:

'By the way, Peter, you're not to go to Thakhek again. The Vietnamese are after your blood and they've put a price on your head.'

'How much?'

'I can't quite make it out. It's either five hundred pounds or half a crown, depending on the rate of exchange.'[81]

The exchange of gallows humour made light of what was, in fact, an extremely dangerous situation. And in early 1946, Kemp's luck very nearly ran out. Having spent a long evening drinking and playing cards with a young Australian Captain from the War Graves Commission, Kemp decided to take a short stroll. Sometime later, he awoke to find himself lying on the floor of a very dirty hut, accompanied by a blinding headache, but no trousers. As his senses slowly returned, Kemp realised that he must have been bushwhacked and that his trousers had been removed to discourage him from escaping. When a villager entered the hut, but made no effort to help him, Kemp panicked, realising that he must have been captured by the Viet-Minh:

> Nothing so concentrates a man's mind, observed Dr. Johnson, as the knowledge that he is going to be hanged. My own mind instantly became clear: I must get away from this hut, and quickly. Shivering with disgust I snatched up a piece of the sacking I had been lying on, and wrapped it around my middle. I padded across the earthen floor to the doorway and peered cautiously outside. There was no sign of a guard.[82]

Quaking with fear, Kemp fled, hiding out in the jungle to prevent any pursuit. More by luck than anything else, the concussed and trouser-less Kemp eventually made it back safely to his barracks. There, the disbelief at his story was only exceeded by the hilarity at his appearance. The real truth of the matter, all agreed, was that Kemp had actually lost his trousers in a brothel.

When a peace treaty was signed between Britain and Thailand on 1 January 1946, Kemp was given a period of leave in Bangkok, 'a startling contrast of extravagance and poverty, squalor and splendour.'[83] Finally enjoying a run of good fortune, (temporary Major) 107025 Peter Mant MacIntyre Kemp was awarded a Distinguished Service Order, citing his 'great gallantry', 'resourcefulness', 'initiative and personal courage', before being presented with 'the most marvellous job the army has ever given anyone; I had to liberate and then govern the island of Bali.'[84]

Arriving on the archipelago in February 1946, Kemp looked forward to enjoying a tropical idyll. Unfortunately, despite the surrender, the Japanese garrisons on the islands had not yet laid down their arms and Kemp was ordered to discover their intentions. As his commanding officer put it charmingly, 'if they cut your throats we'll know we'll have to launch a full-scale invasion.'[85] In the event, the Japanese surrendered without a fight, but Kemp soon realised that the former Dutch East Indies were now home to a growing nationalist movement, encouraged by Japanese propaganda. On the island of Java, 'a melancholy spectacle of neglected paddy-fields and derelict plantations', the situation was particularly tense, and occupying Allied troops were ordered to carry arms at all times.[86] During the day, Batavia (now Jakarta) was relatively safe, but during the hours of darkness the situation was very different:

> The nights were full of danger for the foolhardy; almost every morning patrols would retrieve from the drainage canals the dismembered bodies of British or Indian soldiers who had defied the curfew in search of liquor or women.[87]

Outside the city, the situation was even more perilous. Transport could be undertaken only in heavily armed convoys which, even then, frequently ran into ambushes. To be captured meant almost certain death, hacked to pieces by machetes.

Kemp was instructed to lead a small reconnaissance party into the adjacent islands of Bali and Lombok, in preparation for the arrival of Dutch forces, who were determined to regain their pre-war colonial empire. On 2 March 1946, 2,500 Dutch soldiers cautiously landed on Bali, while Kemp and his Japanese liaison watched on to ensure security. The landing passed without mishap, so Kemp moved on to Lombok where the Dutch hoped for a similar outcome. Initially, Kemp received a warm welcome by the local population, though he had been warned not to take anything on trust: 'the Balinese warned us to be very wary of the Sasak leader; the Sasaks advised us to have no dealings with the Balinese. The Eurasians urged us to trust no one.'[88] However, any realistic possibility of armed opposition was foiled by the preventative arrest of 30 suspects, two of whom turned out to be members of the Japanese garrison. On 27 March, a larger Dutch force landed under the watchful eyes of the world's press. The successful occupation of Bali and Lombok by Dutch forces brought Kemp's work in south-east Asia to an end, so he bid the beautiful islands a reluctant goodbye. By June, he was back in Britain; four months later, he was demobilised from the British army.[89] Having spent most of his previous ten years at war, Kemp had to ask himself an important question: 'How I should make out in peace?'[90]

Initially, it was to be a calm, even conventional peace for the ex-soldier. In November, he got married for the second time and landed a steady job as a salesman with Miles Aircraft based in Reading.[91] In the spring of 1947, they sent him to a conference in Rome, though he was unlucky enough to fall ill with pulmonary tuberculosis. It was serious enough for him to be hospitalised in Switzerland for six months, and he wasn't well enough to return home until February of the following year. In November he had a relapse, necessitating another six months in hospital and a further year convalescing at Roly Winn's house in southern Spain.[92] In September 1951, now fully recovered, Kemp returned to London, where he rented a flat in South Kensington and took up selling insurance for Canadian Imperial Life Insurance, based in nearby St James' Square. He clearly enjoyed the work, for Kemp remained with the company until his retirement in 1980. This is not to say that he found the work entirely fulfilling, for the first of many travelling adventures was not to be long in coming. As ever, Kemp's visceral loathing of Soviet Communism was to act as his motivation.

The popular uprising against the Soviet-backed Hungarian government in October 1956 was applauded by the long-standing anti-Communist. Kemp had a particular loathing for the Hungarian Communist regime, arguing that, 'for the previous eleven years the countries of Eastern Europe had endured a repression crueller and more thorough than any since the rule of the Mongols.'[93] He reserved a special hatred for Erno Gerö, 'Krushchev's tool' who had led Hungary from July 1956 until the uprising. Consequently, Kemp decided to personally go to Hungary 'to do what I could to help there' and Imperial Life, clearly a very understanding employer, made no objection. Having secured temporary employment—or cover—as a reporter for the Catholic newspaper, *The Tablet*, Kemp flew to Vienna, hitching a lift with a British journalist across the border into Hungary. There, while ostensibly reporting on the uprising, he covertly helped smuggle students across the border into Austria. However, the Hungarian Security Services suspected that Kemp was rather more than a newspaper correspondent and ordered him to leave the country by the end of the day. Kemp protested vainly that the nearest border was nearly 200km away, that it was snowing heavily and that he had no transport. 'That's your problem,' they informed him. 'But heaven help you, Mr Kemp, if you are still in this country after midnight.'[94] No doubt mindful of his experiences in an NKVD jail, Kemp prudently took the decision to leave. Fortunately for him, British Embassy staff were sympathetic to his plight and provided him with a Land Rover and driver. After a hair-raising drive across Hungary, Kemp escaped into Austria with fifteen minutes to spare.

Back in Britain, Kemp's second attempt to return to a peaceful civilian life was soon brought to a similar premature conclusion. After twelve years of marriage, he and Cynthia parted, mainly, he admitted, due to his 'excessive fondness for alcohol.'[95] Once again freed from any reason to remain in the UK, a combination of wanderlust combined with anti-Communism led him to actively seek out conflicts and hot-spots around the world.

In 1961, he spent six 'disagreeable' months in the Belgian Congo (now the Democratic Republic of the Congo or DRC), which had gained independence the previous year. Kemp found it extremely dangerous, with members of the Congolese National Army prone to stopping Europeans and robbing them of money and valuables. Four years later, Kemp returned to South-East Asia as a correspondent for the *News of the World*, commissioned to write 12 articles on 'communist penetration and subversion in the region.' He revisited Java and Bali, finding that they had changed dramatically since independence, with President Sukarno's Indonesian regime having put in place 'oppressive and puritanical' restrictions on the islanders' freedom. Conditions for the populace were dreadful, he reported: 'poverty, misery, near starvation and a pervading sense of hopeless and purposeless stagnation among the peasants and workers.' Utterly depressed, Kemp returned to Singapore, before flying into Saigon in southern Vietnam, in August. He joined an American bombing mission near the Cambodian border, which annihilated an allegedly pro-Vietcong village, before electing to visit an American military camp at Duc Co, south of the de-militarised zone established in 1956 that separated North and

South Vietnam. It was a hazardous trip, for the base had been under siege for more than six weeks and on a number of occasions it had almost been overrun by the North Vietnamese Army. Despite rumours that another attack was imminent, Kemp was flown into the camp in an American helicopter, skimming the treetops to avoid enemy machine-gun fire. At the camp he was introduced to a number of soldiers from special forces, at least one of whom had fought with the British Army in the Second World War. After twenty-four hours of intermittent machine-gun and mortar fire, Kemp prudently made his escape and returned to the safety of the Vietnamese 2nd Army Corps headquarters. Seemingly, the helicopter ride wasn't exciting and dangerous enough for Kemp, for a couple of days later he boarded a flimsy reconnaissance plane, which was engaged in the hazardous task of seeking out bombing targets. As the aeroplane came under fire from the ground, Kemp's main concern was not the enemy fire, but airsickness, as the pilot threw the plane into sharp twists and turns. Safely back at base two hours later, the pilot congratulated the ex-soldier on his composure under fire: 'That wasn't a dangerous flight, surely?' Kemp asked, nonchalantly. 'But you're an *old man*, Mr Kemp,' responded the pilot, to the fifty-year old's chagrin.

Following brief stops in Vietnam's former capital of Hue and the large US military base at Danang, Kemp flew home. Soon after his return, he fell seriously ill once again, spending most of the next two years in poor health, before finally admitting the cause of his problems: 'I was drinking too much and had been for too long. I was drinking now without even enjoying it.' After spending a week in hospital, his doctor prescribed a complete abstinence from alcohol, which Kemp took on board, for a while, at least.

In the early 1970s, Kemp made two further trips to South-East Asia, probably the area of the world he knew and loved the most, despite his loathing of the Communist regimes of Vietnam and Cambodia. He also travelled to South America to report for *The Spectator* on left-wing guerrillas operating in Uruguay, who had just kidnapped the British ambassador in Montevideo. Having interviewed a number of defectors holed up in Paraguay,

Kemp pieced together tales of Russian infiltration and attempts to hijack left-wing nationalist movements. For Kemp 'the lesson was that Moscow would not tolerate a left-wing guerrilla movement it couldn't control', adding that '[someone] who had to learn this the hard way was Che Guevara.'[96]

Kemp retired officially from Imperial Life in 1980, aged 65, though he remained with the Company on a part-time basis, allowing plenty more opportunities for travel and writing. In 1982, two years into retirement, Kemp visited Mexico and Central America to write a number of articles for the *Spectator* and *Daily Telegraph*. While in Nicaragua, he sought out the US supported right-wing Contras, keen to show his support in their fight against the Sandinista government. His appearance reminded one journalist of a character from a Graham Greene novel:

Deep in the rain forests of Central America, where Nicaraguan Contras are making war on their own Marxist government, one is likely to meet these days an incongruous figure, a tall, stooped Englishman, now entering his seventies, wearing a well-tailored safari suit, with a shoulder bag full of essential kit, such as maps, a pipe and tobacco, a bottle or two of beer, and a paperback copy of *Right Ho, Jeeves*.[97]

Fifty years after the outbreak of the civil war, Kemp returned to Spain to report for the *Daily Telegraph*. While Franco was dead and buried and the country had gone through a surprisingly peaceful transition to democracy, Kemp was still surprised at how much Spain had changed:

The Civil War and its aftermath had left most Spaniards deeply mistrustful of extremist parties and political philosophies, either of the left or right, and thanks partly to the enlightened leadership of King Juan Carlos, partly to a new understanding of popular political responsibility, the transition to a democratic system had been completed . . . I found everywhere a wish to forget the Civil War and put aside the old antagonisms and bitterness.[98]

Kemp revisited Hungary the same year and found it too, very different. It was, he accepted, less repressive, with western goods on sale in the Budapest shops, even if the prices were beyond the reach of most Hungarians. Perhaps signalling some small *glasnost* of his own, Kemp reluctantly conceded that the improvements owed much to the efforts of János Kádár, the reformist General Secretary of the Hungarian Communist Party.[99]

When Peter Kemp died on 30 October 1993, he received a generous obituary in *The Independent*: 'He acknowledged many of his own mistakes and never said a word of his calm, gentle, unfailing courage', wrote the expert on SOE and MI9, MRD Foot.[100] That's perhaps a generous assessment, but not far from the truth. Kemp left behind several memoirs and an autobiography, all well-written, engaging and frequently amusing, for Kemp undoubtedly knew how to tell a story.[101] As Foot states, his accounts are often self-effacing, even if Kemp could never resist dropping the names of his powerful connections. As one recent study remarked:

> Unknowingly, Kemp divides the world into two unequal halves: fellows that one might have met at Cambridge or at an embassy reception with their sisters and wives on one hand; and on the other the vast majority of humankind who are not out of the top drawer.[102]

The memoirs do, however, often feel dated, even though *The Thorns of Memory* was actually published in 1990. Peter Kemp was, in many ways, old-fashioned in his attitudes—particularly towards women—and he did not always appear in a hurry to change.[103] For example, despite the passing of the years, Kemp personally had little time for, or understanding of, the defeated in Spain, continuing to see them through the Francoist anti-Communist prism of his time as a Nationalist volunteer. The world, Kemp maintained, had unfairly misjudged Franco, losing 'all memory of the Communist threat he had defeated.'[104] Despite the mass of evidence to the contrary, Kemp, like Franco's English biographer, Brian Crozier, continued to deny that the

Nationalists were responsible for the bombing of Guernica.[105]

Peter Kemp spent a great deal of his life as a soldier and travelling to various hotspots around the world. Despite this, he always disputed an accusation that appeared in the *Spectator* that he was 'lured by the sound of guns':

> I have spent a large part of my life engaged, like many others, in the struggle between the two most dangerous evils of this century, fascism and communism. My own small rôle in this contest, taking part in or observing conflicts all over the world, has involved me in plenty of shooting. But I have never enjoyed it.[106]

Kemp argued that he was simply attracted to travelling; it was just that there were many places in the world where people were shooting at each other. But Kemp was hardly a neutral bystander. While a Foreign Office official described Kemp in 1965 as holding 'romantic right-wing political views,' it's difficult not to see this as a somewhat generous interpretation.[107] Given his terrible experiences in Albania and Poland during the Second World War, it's not that surprising that Kemp was a passionate and convinced anti-Communist. His rage over what he saw as 'the misdirected sympathy of the Liberals and the left' in America and Europe towards Communist dictatorships and regimes across the world, was also understandable.[108] Many regimes were fully deserving of his disgust. Yet Kemp's refusal to acknowledge the worst excesses of the Franco dictatorship, his overt support for the Contras in Nicaragua, suggest that Simon Courtauld's description of Kemp in *The Spectator* as a man 'fighting for common decency' is disingenuous at best. In truth, Kemp clearly leant more to the right than to the romantic and when it came to seeking out the shooting, Kemp rarely had far to travel. After all, as Kemp willingly admitted, on a number of occasions, the person doing the shooting was himself.

Captain Malcolm Dunbar.
Bishopsgate Institute

Captain Malcolm Dunbar.
Bishopsgate Institute

L to R: Macolm Dunbar, British *Daily Worker* correspondent Bill Rust, Major Vladimir Ĉopić, the Yugoslavian Commander of the 15th International Brigade and Hugh Slater, Dunbar's Number Two in the British Anti-Tank Battery, who joined Dunbar on the Brigade Staff. *Bishopsgate Institute*

Leah Manning visiting the pioneering Blood Transfusion Unit in Spain.
Marx Memorial Library

Basque refugee children at the Stoneham refugee camp, near
Southampton, in 1937. *Marx Memorial Library.*

Peter Kemp (centre, with dark jacket) alongside SOE's Major Alan Hare (L) and Major Richard Riddell (R) and locals, Albania, 1943. *The National Archives*

Former Independent Labour Party volunteers at the Party's summer school in Letchworth, August 1937. L to R: John McNair, Douglas Moyle, Stafford Cottman, George Orwell and Jock Braithwaite. *Orwell Archive, University College London*

Sam Lesser (front) with Margaret Powell (r) and British Battalion
Commander, Sam Wild (back right, behind Margaret Powell)
Marx Memorial Library

Sam Lesser and Che Guevara in November 1962.
Photographer unknown

Chapter Four
Their Man in Havana: Sam Lesser

One of the benefits of writing historical fiction must be that the author is free to place their protagonist within any dramatic event or epoch that they wish. Or any number of them. George MacDonald Fraser's re-imagining of Tom Brown's schoolboy tormentor, Harry Flashman, sets the unlikely hero at the Siege of Jalalabad, the Crimean war, General Custer's defeat at Little Bighorn and the opium wars with China, among many others. More recently, William Boyd's *Any Human Heart* recounts Logan Mountstuart's long and full life, reporting on the Spanish Civil War, working in Naval Intelligence alongside Ian Fleming, hanging out with Jackson Pollock in 1960s New York, teaching in Nigeria during the Biafran War and, perhaps most bizarrely of all, becoming the Baader-Meinhoff Group's prize newspaper seller. Such vivid storylines are not normally the realm of the historian, for the likelihood of one individual participating in so many internationally seismic events seems far-fetched. However, the real-life experiences of the subject of this chapter really were every bit as full and vivid as those of Flashman and Mountstuart. As Foreign Correspondent for the Communist *Daily Worker*, Manny or Sam Lesser (known for years by his *nom de plume*, Sam Russell) was witness to many of the most famous—and infamous—events of the twentieth century.

Manassah Lesser was born on 19 March 1915 in London's East End. The eldest of eight children born to Polish immigrants, Lesser was raised as an orthodox Jew. He grew up speaking Yiddish, took Hebrew lessons and was sent to a Jewish seminary in Whitechapel as preparation for training to become a rabbi.[1] Having just missed out on passing the eleven plus, he attended a local elementary school until he was fourteen, when he transferred to a co-educational Grammar school in Poplar called George Green's. There Lesser discovered a talent for languages and developed a love of history and politics, partly due to the efforts of his female history teacher who, rather than spoon-feeding students tales of British imperial greatness, introduced them to progressive and radical interpretations of the past.[2] Yet, while an ardent reader, the young student was not lost in books. Impressed by the arguments of the British Communist intellectual, Raj Palme Dutt, he became a keen school debater and made regular Sunday forays to 'Speaker's Corner' in Hackney's Victoria Park, renowned for its political meetings and demonstrations. Besides, growing up in London's East End, the Jewish shopkeeper's son could see for himself the devastating inequality and the realities of unemployment in a society without welfare. He also witnessed the government's heavy-handed reaction to dissent when Victoria Park was closed to provide billets for troops charged with guarding local electricity sub-stations during the General Strike of 1926. And several years later, during the 'hungry thirties', Manny experienced personally the rise of fascism and its scapegoating of Jews, following Sir Oswald Mosley's foundation of the British Union of Fascists in October 1932:

> The Fascist threat in Britain was no joke. The Blackshirts held marches in the East End of London and I went with some other students to a couple of their rallies—particularly the ones in the Albert Hall and at Olympia—where there was quite a punch up . . . there was a strong anti-Semitic element to their propaganda, in which Mosley in person played a strong part. Coming from a Jewish family myself, I was suddenly alerted to what was going on—and now it wasn't just something that was happening solely in Germany. It was happening here, on our own doorstep.[3]

In 1933, the eighteen-year-old Lesser won a scholarship to read history at University College in London, though as his grant was not sufficient to provide for accommodation, he remained living at home with his parents.[4] They prized education and were very supportive, but he was still expected to help out in their busy Hackney grocery store, opening up every day at seven o' clock in the morning. He was also expected to attend Hebrew school five evenings a week. Nevertheless, he found time at university to hone his debating skills and was spotted by the

Communist Party's National Student Organiser, Jack Cohen, who persuaded him to join the Party.[5] More surprisingly perhaps, Lesser and a student friend called Brian Pearce decided to join the OTC, the Officers' Training Corps. The decision baffled many fellow students who, scarred by the slaughter in the Great War, were vehemently opposed to militarism and stood with the infamous Oxford Union motion of 1933, which vowed to refuse to fight for King and Country. The Communist Party also opposed their membership of the OTC, but the two students artfully justified their decision by invoking Lenin's dictum that 'a working class which doesn't learn the use of arms deserves to be slaves.'[6] In fact, the young undergraduates found life in the OTC enjoyable and instructive, picking up military tactics from their Grenadier and Coldstream Guards' instructors, while learning to shoot Lewis and Maxim machine-guns at a firing range in Princes Risborough. Lesser qualified with Certificate 'A', placing him on the supplementary reserve of officers entitled to a commission in the event of war. However, he considered the chance of actually being called up extremely remote. 'Nobody', he thought, 'would be so stupid as to have another war.'[7]

In the summer of 1936, having switched from history to archaeology, Lesser was looking forward to going to Egypt to work on an archaeological site run by the distinguished head of the department, Professor Flinders Petrie.[8] However, events outside academia were becoming an increasing distraction for Sam, particularly in Spain, with newspapers reporting that there had been a military coup. Incensed that another democratically elected government in Europe was under attack, he determined to do what he could to help raise support for the Spanish Republicans.

Initially, Lesser envisaged becoming involved in fund-raising, attending meetings, knocking on doors—the bread and butter of political campaigning. However, he was approached by Jack Cohen, who explained that the Spanish government was in desperate need of people with military training. Despite his keen support for the Republican cause, Sam was unconvinced, believing that Spain urgently needed arms, not volunteers. So, to help persuade him, Cohen took Sam to the Communist Party's head office in King Street, in London's Covent Garden, where he introduced him to the Party's General Secretary, Harry Pollitt, and to a very intense young man who had just returned from Spain, called John Cornford. Though Sam initially found the young student 'toffee-nosed' and a little patronising, Cornford's fervour convinced Sam that he was needed. Cornford—a brilliant Cambridge scholar—was to become both a good friend of Sam and an iconic symbol of British volunteers in the Spanish Civil War.

Following a process that would be shadowed by nearly two and a half thousand other volunteers from Britain and Ireland, Sam went to see R W Robson, familiarly known as 'Robbie', who was in charge of recruiting volunteers. Robson warned Sam of the dangers of volunteering, but persuaded that the young student was determined, gave him a contact address in Paris with strict instructions not to say anything about volunteering, even to his parents. However, while he said nothing to his father, he did tell his mother, who was appalled. She tried her utmost to persuade him not to go and was distraught when he set off in late September.[9]

Underneath his clothes Lesser wore his OTC uniform, arguing that he 'might as well use it for something real, rather than just parading around' and he was equipped with £10 in cash and a British army gas-mask, bought for him by friends in the university's Communist Party group.[10] Having taken a train to Newhaven then the ferry to Dieppe, Sam continued on to Paris, where he discreetly sought out the secure address in a working class district (the French Communist Party's office in Place du Combat) given to him by 'Robbie':

[We] were told to keep our purpose very, very secret. But none of it seemed very secret to me—everybody was going around shouting 'Les avions pour l'Espagne' . . . it seemed to me that everybody was going to Spain to fight.[11]

After a brief stay in the French capital, Lesser joined up with an international group of volunteers bound for Perpignan, just north of the Franco-Spanish frontier. There he was reminded once again of the importance of secrecy and instructed to pretend to be a local and, if asked, to say his name was 'Raimundo Casado'. He followed the instructions, though believing the pretence to be a 'bit of a farce', not least because he was carrying his British passport. Fortunately, his identity was never checked and he and the group of mainly French and German volunteers were simply driven over the border under cover of night. They were then transported to the town of Figueras, some 20km south of the frontier, where they were billeted in the dilapidated castle of San Fernando. There he and the other volunteers hung around, awaiting instructions.

As Lesser was discovering, the situation in the early months of the civil war was extremely chaotic. There were not sufficient weapons or uniforms, nor was any military training provided for the new arrivals, so some frustrated volunteers took matters into their own hands and began to train themselves. However, there were other obstacles:

> We immediately ran into the problem—a core problem for the International Brigades—which was, quite simply, the language. Here you had people from different countries, different nationalities speaking their own languages.[12]

Fortunately for Lesser, who had studied French at school, his group was placed in the French Commune de Paris Battalion of the 11th International Brigade.[13] Sent initially to the heady, revolutionary city of Barcelona, the volunteers were then forwarded to the distinctly less thrilling city of Albacete, which had been chosen as the main base for international volunteers. There Sam was united with a number of compatriots and, the following day, some 20 English volunteers were transferred to a small, poverty-stricken village, 35km north-west of the Albacete base, called La Roda. Finally, military training began in earnest. Unfortunately, Sam quickly realised that the standard of military calibre of his group was very poor, even compared to the university OTC. While H Fred Jones, the leader of the English group, and a few others had military experience, most did not: 'it was just a collection of odds and sods,' Sam acknowledged ruefully.[14] They were, at least, provided with uniforms and weaponry, though blue overalls and ancient rifles from the Franco-Prussian war were not exactly what they had imagined. The ammunition, they discovered, was even worse; it was in a terrible state and Sam was convinced that it 'posed a greater danger to us than the enemy.'[15] Having initially been allocated some essentially useless Spanish machine-guns, the group wisely traded them for a complement of Lewis guns, which were far superior and more familiar to those with British military experience. A number of dependable Maxim machine guns, supplied by the Soviet Union, arrived in late October.

Nonetheless, the rapid advance of Franco's forces on Madrid meant that the international volunteers, no matter how inexperienced and poorly equipped, were urgently needed. Consequently, Sam's unit was rushed to the front in early November, following a triumphant parade along the Gran Vía in Madrid's city centre and an inspiring speech by the famous Republican orator, Dolores Ibárruri, known as *La Pasionaria*. On 9 November 1936 they joined an attack on Franco's forces occupying Casa de Campo, the large park to the west of the Spanish capital. It was easily repulsed by the Rebels and the English group were taught a harsh lesson about the reality of the situation that faced them, when three members of their section were killed. While nobody lost their lives in a follow-up assault two days later to the north of the city, the attack fared no better.

Transferred a week later to the Philosophy and Letters building in Madrid's newly constructed, and still partly unfinished University City, Sam and his comrades attempted to adjust themselves to the typical experience of soldiers during warfare: hours of boredom interspersed with moments of terror. Holed up in the university buildings, they sniped out of the windows at enemy soldiers who were occupying the adjacent block, while taking shelter behind barricades constructed from library books. They discovered that the piles of dense volumes of Indian metaphysics and early nineteenth-century German philosophy gave highly effective protection against enemy small arms fire. The irony was not lost on the group, which included a poet, several writers and a future Professor of Hellenic Studies.[16]

During the skirmishing both Lesser and John Cornford were wounded, though neither seriously and the exhausted members of the group were given a week's leave.[17] Sam went sight-seeing in Madrid's famous Puerta del Sol, accompanied by a young Scot called 'Jock' Cunningham, a veteran of the Argyll and Sutherland Highlanders. There they bumped into the renowned *Daily Express* reporter, Sefton Delmer, who they initially viewed with great suspicion, given his paper's Francoist sympathies. However, Delmer charmed them over lunch and introduced them to the *News Chronicle* correspondent, Geoffrey Cox, later the head of Yorkshire Television. Sam and Jock happily recounted to him the story of their unit, the first report of a British unit in Spain to appear in a newspaper, which Cox also included in his vivid eye-witness account, *Defence of Madrid*.[18]

When the bloody hand-to-hand fighting in University City finally came to a standstill on 23 November, it marked the failure of Franco's attempt to mount a direct attack on the Spanish capital. Relieved and triumphant to have thrown back the attackers, the victory had come at great cost to the defenders, particularly to the Internationals, who had been used as shock-troops, thrown into battle where it was fiercest. Only five of Sam's initial group of 28 English remained; hundreds of the 2,100 Brigaders who had left Albacete five weeks beforehand were dead or wounded. On 7 December, the survivors of Sam's group, too few in numbers to form an independent section, returned to Albacete and were absorbed into other units. Lesser, whose military aptitude had led to his promotion to Second Lieutenant, joined the first fully English-speaking Company to be formed, as part of the French (La Marseillaise) Battalion of the 14th International Brigade.[19] There he resumed the military training which had been cut short at the start of the month.

On Christmas Eve 1936, following news that Franco's troops had broken through the Andalusian front in southern Spain, the English-speaking Number One Company was rushed down to Andújar, 70km east of the historic city of Córdoba. Attacked from the air the moment they arrived, the Republican troops advanced towards the nearby Nationalist-held village of Lopera, launching an assault early on Christmas Day. Dangerously exposed on olive tree-capped ridges, the Internationals made several attempts to capture the village, but were thwarted by the Rebels' greater numbers and, crucially, their absolute air superiority. A further attempt three days later was repulsed with very heavy casualties. Among those killed were the unit's popular commissar and senior figure in the British Communist Party, the Magdalen scholar Ralph Fox. Worse was to come with the news that John Cornford had also lost his life. It was a cruel blow which Sam, who was himself badly wounded in the leg and back—probably by friendly fire—never forgot.

Rescued from the battlefield at great personal risk by Jock Cunningham, Lesser was ferried to safety on a foul-smelling manure cart, before being taken by lorry to a hospital in the city of Linares in Jaén, famous for its lead and silver mines. There he and the other wounded were nursed by nuns from the Catholic Sisters of Mercy and visited by grateful locals who plied the *extranjeros* with gifts, including some of their meagre stocks of food. 'It moved some of us to tears,' Sam admitted.[20] He was less impressed when he heard rumours that the local Honorary British Consul was believed to be a clandestine Franco supporter. Still reliant on crutches, Lesser hobbled off to confront him and though the Consul strongly refuted Lesser's accusations, his denials were somewhat undermined by the portrait of Benito Mussolini hanging on his office wall.[21]

Despite a serious lack of medical supplies including such simple things as bandages, Sam's wounds gradually improved until, in late January, he was deemed well enough to be discharged. However, Sam continued to walk with a pronounced limp and as his wound needed regular dressing changes, he was allocated administrative duties in the Albacete office, under the command of Peter Kerrigan, a senior Scottish Communist and the International Brigade base's Political Commissar (see Chapter Seven).

In mid-February, news reached Lesser and Kerrigan in Albacete that the newly-formed British Battalion, which included a number of veterans of Lopera, had been involved in a fierce battle in the Jarama Valley, 25km south-east of Madrid. News was hazy, but it soon became clear that this had been no minor skirmish. When Sam received a list of the casualties sustained, he was 'absolutely horrified'.[22] During three days of heavy fighting between 12 and 14 February 1937, the battalion had been virtually wiped out and dozens of men that Lesser and Kerrigan had known personally had been killed. Aghast, Kerrigan and Lesser worried how to get the shocking news to the families back home. The answer lay with Lesser, whose leg was stubbornly refusing to heal and clearly needed expert treatment. So, in late February, Sam headed home, taking with him the awful list of casualties.[23] Back in London, he passed it to Communist Party General Secretary, Harry Pollitt, who wrote a personal letter of condolence to all the families of the fallen volunteers.

Lesser's dismal task completed, arrangements were made for him to see Lord Horder, one of Harley Street's top orthopaedic surgeons. Though the wound responded to treatment, it was still some time before Sam was pain free. Nonetheless, Sam was determined to return to Spain and soon declared himself ready and willing to rejoin the fight. However, much to his frustration, he was overruled and ordered to take a safe job behind the lines. Consequently, on 1 June 1937, Sam travelled to Paris to work on what was known as 'the pipeline', liaising with international volunteers as they arrived in the French capital, on their way to or from Spain.[24] His work was not always glamorous and all too often involved rescuing compatriots who had been arrested for drunkenness, before sending them on their way.

Still determined to get back to Spain, in July Lesser was eventually given permission to help a group of nurses who were on their way to the country but had got trapped in Perpignan. Unwilling to put them through a gruelling fourteen-hour climb over the Pyrenees—and in no condition to undertake the trek himself—Lesser arranged for a fishing boat to smuggle them into Spain. They set sail from the small village of Agde (just over 20km east of Béziers), careful to keep out of sight of Nationalist and Royal Navy patrols. Once into Spain, Sam bid a fond farewell to the nurses, particularly to a young Polish-born Jewish woman from Palestine called Dora Bienbach, who he had befriended on the voyage.[25]

Sam continued on to Barcelona, still hoping to rejoin the International Brigades, but was bitterly disappointed to be told, just as he had been in London, that his injury rendered him ineligible for military service. Instead, Lesser was informed that he would be providing assistance to Bill Rust, the *Daily Worker* correspondent and the British Communist Party's *responsable* in Spain and should prepare himself to give short-wave radio broadcasts in English for Radio Barcelona. That Lesser had never given a broadcast, had never worked as a journalist, was no matter; he was issued a desk and a typewriter, handed his predecessor's notes and told to prepare for his first broadcast that evening. The key phrase to include, he was told, was, 'Save Spain, Save Peace, Save Britain.' Advised to disguise his identity, Sam simply reversed his surname, so on 15 July 1937, Manassah Lesser became Sam Russell and began his work.[26] He was soon broadcasting every day for both Catalan and Spanish radio stations, toiling diligently late into the night. The work, he admitted ruefully, 'turned out to be a job unlike any before or since.' Having been broadcasting every day for several weeks, Lesser was having a relaxed conversation with the sound engineer one evening over a glass of cognac. The engineer, apparently feeling sorry for him, let slip in some embarrassment that not a single word had actually been broadcast, for as soon as Sam started speaking, he switched the transmitters off. The sound engineer explained that he was acting on the instructions of the POUM, the organisation that secretly controlled the transmitter, which had been banned on 16 June, following the fighting in Barcelona in May 1937.

Though Lesser hadn't been in Spain when the dramatic events played out in Barcelona and he hadn't returned to Spain until two months afterwards, the issue with the POUM's transmitter was not the only consequence of the May Day events to embroil the former volunteer. In late May, or early June 1937, a former member of the ILP militia called Frank Frankford had been arrested in Barcelona for being unable to produce identity papers. Suspected of being involved in the theft of artworks from museums and churches, he was thrown into jail. According to Frankford, he was rescued from jail by Sam Lesser in late August

1937, who warned him that he would be wise to leave Spain as quickly as possible. Frankford later wrote a letter, reprinted in the *Daily Worker*, falsely accusing his ILP comrades of fraternising with the enemy.[27] Many years later, in his biography of Orwell, Gordon Bowker claimed that in order to get out of jail, Frankford had been 'induced by the *Daily Worker* correspondent Sam Lesser to sign a document confirming that the POUM were dealing with the Fascists.'[28] However, Lesser always disputed that he had been the person who was involved in Frankford's release and denied having written the reports for the *Daily Worker*.[29] By the time he was interviewed (in 1976) he was expressing 'serious doubts' about the suppression of the POUM and Andreu Nin's 'disappearance', even if he still felt that the POUM's support for pursuing revolution during the war was misguided.[30] It's difficult to establish the truth of the matter, not least because Frankford changed his story over the years, later admitting that the charges against him and his comrade hadn't been trumped up; the pair had indeed been trying to sell stolen paintings.[31] Yet Frankford always stuck to the story that he had been released by Lesser.[32]

On top of his broadcasting, due primarily to his decent French and Spanish, Lesser began helping Bill Rust with his daily reports for the *Daily Worker* and did the same for Peter Kerrigan when Rust was recalled to London. And when Kerrigan himself returned to Britain later in the year, Lesser took on both his journalistic and political responsibilities, becoming the British Communist Party's representative in Republican Spain. Having been granted accreditation with the Foreign Press Department, Lesser (or Russell) was soon hobnobbing with his journalistic colleagues, many of whom were writing very knowledgeably and movingly about the Spanish war: Geoffrey Cox of the *News Chronicle* and his successor Willie Forrest, Henry Buckley of the *Daily Telegraph* and Herbert Matthews of the *New York Times*. Lesser also renewed his acquaintance with Sefton Delmer of the *Daily Express*, dubbed 'Seldom Defter' by his journalistic colleagues for the canny ability to sneak out stories under the nose of the fearsome Republican Press Censor, Constancia de la Mora.[33] As a cub reporter, Sam was always grateful to his colleagues for their help, particularly Forrest and Buckley.

Lesser's first major assignment was to report on the Republican Ebro offensive launched in July 1938. The bold operation involved soldiers, including Lesser's compatriots in the International Brigades, crossing the dramatic Ebro River and attacking deep into Nationalist-held territory. Based just behind the front line, Lesser watched on in frustration as Republican forces launched attack upon attack against the Francoist held town of Gandesa but were repeatedly thrown back by the defenders. After their initial successes, Republican troops were slowly pushed back over the following two months, bitterly contesting every metre. By September, the Spanish Prime Minister, Juan Negrín, had accepted that the shattered remnants of the International Brigades were no longer an effective fighting force and ordered their withdrawal in the vain hope that Franco would respond by withdrawing Germans and Italian soldiers. The following month, on 28 October, Sam watched from the balcony of the Foreign Ministry in Barcelona as the departing volunteers were given a huge farewell parade, which has become forever associated with the famous speech by the Communist Deputy for Asturias, Dolores Ibárruri, *La Pasionaria*:

> You can go proudly. You are history. You are legend. You are the heroic example of democracy's solidarity and universality. And when the olive tree of peace puts forth its leaves again, entwined with the laurels of the Spanish Republic's victory— come back! Come back to us. With us, those of you who have no country will find one, those of you who have to live deprived of friendship, will find friends.[34]

Lesser spent the following weeks shuttling between Barcelona and the small town of Ripoll in the foothills of the Spanish Pyrenees, where the remaining British volunteers were waiting in the cold and rain for permission to return home. Following permission being finally granted, Sam watched as the former soldiers put on a moving, final parade:

> As the first streaks of dawn crept across the Northern Spanish sky, the Battalion paraded in the square and the Roll was

113

called. One after the other the men reply to the last rollcall of the British Battalion in Spain. The scene in the graying [sic] dawn brought back vivid memories of past roll calls of the Battalion. Of that first roll call after Jarama when so many could not reply. Of that roll call at Mora de Ebro after the fighting retreat in Aragón. Today every man replies. 500 there are who never more will reply as the names ring out, and one could see that every man was silently determining that those whose bodies lie beneath every one of Spain's battlefields, shall not be forgotten.[35]

Despite the Internationals' departure, the Spanish Republic struggled on, determined to resist for as long as possible, Premier Negrín still vainly hoping that France and Britain might come to their aid. Lesser also stuck to his task; on 11 November 1938 he reported the final end of the Republican Ebro offensive, launched so optimistically several months earlier: 'On Tuesday night, after nearly four months of heroic resistance on the right bank, the Army of the Ebro, under the orders of Higher Command, withdrew to its positions on the left bank of the river.'[36]

As Nationalist troops continued to advance, Sam returned to Barcelona, recounting sadly how 'the war continued and the suffering got worse.' He wrote a number of reports telling of the horrific bombing of civilians, including two vicious attacks by Italian bombers on New Year's Eve, 1938. Over one hundred civilians were killed and many more were wounded.[37]

They bombed our area of Barcelona and I shall never forget the smell there when I went outside. There was one wonderful row of lime trees; a beautiful scent when they're in flower. But people had come out . . . from their shelter, strolling around and more bombs had been dropped. The gutter was literally flowing with blood and the smell of the blood of those poor people mixed with the smell of the lime trees.[38]

Given the devastation that had been wreaked on the Basque town of Guernica the previous year, Lesser's conclusion was understandable: 'the truth is that no military objective is being sought. The world is faced by a deliberate attempt to terrorise the people of Spain by bombing every tiny village and hamlet.'[39] After the bombing on New Year's Eve had finally ended and the all-clear sounded, Lesser discovered bomb fragments lying in a crater in a Barcelona street, bearing the words *Rheinische Stahlwerke 1937*. It was stark evidence of what the Spanish Republic faced: 'Franco's war, Mussolini's planes, Hitler's bombs.'

With Nationalist troops bearing down on the Catalan capital, on 23 January 1939 Sam wrote defiantly that 'Barcelona is showing that she can equal if not surpass the heroism of Madrid and Valencia. This morning not a shop is open in Barcelona. 15,000 of Barcelona's civil population, old men, women and children have gone to fortify the town.'[40] However, under no illusions about the desperate situation facing the Republic and terrified of being trapped and captured by the Francoists, Sam urgently prepared himself to leave. Before departing, he assisted Alonso 'Lon' Elliott, a senior British Party figure based at the headquarters of the political commissars in Madrid, to box up the records of the International Brigades. They were sent to Russia for safekeeping, where they remained in a Moscow archive for fifty years, locked away from prying eyes.[41]

Two days later, Lesser was driven to the frontier by another volunteer-turned-journalist, Keith Scott Watson of the *Daily Herald*. In a foretaste of what would soon be re-enacted across Europe, the road was crammed with a flood of desperate refugees, predominantly women and children. Many were carrying their lives on their back; all were frantically trying to hide from the murderous shelling by Nationalist warships lying off the coast. Unable to get past the mass of refugees, the two journalists were forced to abandon their car and make for the frontier on foot. However, when they finally arrived at the border, they found it closed and guarded by Senegalese guards, many of whom didn't speak French, let alone Spanish or English. Only when a French officer recognised them as English journalists were the pair allowed to pass. As they crossed over into France, Lesser saw for himself how the Spanish refugees were being greeted:

Women and children are being concentrated in the area around Le Boulou [10km north of the border] and Argelès[-sur-Mer] in conditions that belie description. In the open fields without shelter, without even a blanket, with the bitter wind of the Pyrenees sweeping down upon them, and with a guard of French troops with fixed bayonets, the Spanish refugees are dying of hunger and exposure. Herded together worse than cattle, with no sanitary arrangements, this is the hospitality which France is giving to those who have held up the advance of the Italian army on the French frontier for 2½ years.[42]

The following day, the battered Catalan capital finally surrendered to Franco's forces, leading Sam to file a despondent report admitting that 'the epic resistance of the Army of Catalonia has come to an end.'[43] He appealed for the sympathetic and humane treatment of Republican refugees, particularly for 'the thousands of wounded who at the moment have been for days without attention. The women and children above all must be placed in good homes and cared for.'[44] His words fell on deaf ears, for refugees and former Republican soldiers were incarcerated in what were essentially concentration camps in southern France. For the next week Lesser travelled backwards and forwards across the frontier but was in Spain to witness Juan Negrín's final speech in the San Fernando Castle in Figueras on 2 February 1939, just before the Republican government fled the country. The fortress was in Nationalist hands less than two weeks later. Distraught, Sam Lesser filed his final report from Cerbère, just over the frontier, on 12 February 1939. He would not return to Spain for more than thirty years.

With the Spanish Republic in its death throes, Lesser returned to London, joining the *Daily Worker* staff at Cayton Street, just north of London's Shoreditch. After the briefest of rests, he was posted to Paris to work for the New York *Daily Worker* and the English-language section of the French news agency, *Agence France-Monde*.[45] As a veteran of the war in Spain, Sam was treated with great respect by the French comrades, who even organised a welcome party for him. However, Lesser was shocked to find that the welcoming celebration was held in a brothel, full of practically naked women. When a colleague hinted that if he were attracted to one of the women he could go off with her, the embarrassed and scandalized young journalist hurriedly left the party. 'I knew such places existed', he remarked later, 'but it was another matter to be introduced to them by those I thought were the moral leaders of a new world.'[46]

Though the Spanish Civil War was over, much of Sam's work in Paris was still concerned with the country, particularly the plight of the refugees languishing in French internment camps. In a piece for the *Daily Worker* during the summer of 1939, Sam bitterly criticised the treatment of Spanish Republicans, leading to a summons to the French Foreign Ministry where he was given a formal reprimand. His furious question, 'Was what I wrote untrue?' was coolly ignored. It was while Lesser was in Paris that, on 23 August 1939, news leaked out about the Nazi-Soviet pact. Like many loyal Communists, while Lesser was stunned by the agreement, he dutifully accepted it. Unlike some International Brigade veterans, Sam fully accepted the Communist Party line that the war against Nazi Germany was not a continuation of the war had fought in Spain. As he explained to his university friend, Brian Pearce:

Can you tell me what the war in Spain had in common with the present? I can't see it. From every point of view they are totally different in character and in the conditions in which they were and are being fought . . . How could anyone for a moment have fallen into [the] error of thinking that this war had even the remotest chance of being a war against fascism?[47]

As Russia was not involved, Sam argued that it was clearly an imperialist war. 'We are for peace', he wrote, 'but not for a peace which will certainly result in the formation of a new anti-Comintern bloc, headed by the Daladier Govt.' The British establishment's attitudes he felt, had been fully laid bare at a dinner he had recently attended, held by the British Military Attaché in Paris. 'The war against the Boche was all very well and as it should be,' argued the attaché, 'but let it not be forgotten that these "*Sales Russes*" had to be squashed, and we'd do it, by heck.'[48]

On 27 September 1939, Édouard Daladier's government outlawed the French Communist Party, forcing Lesser to flee to Belgium. However, in a stroke of good fortune, his enforced exile provided a journalistic coup when Sam was granted an interview with the leader of the French Party, Maurice Thorez, who was also hiding out in Belgium.[49] Sam's report appeared in the *Daily Worker* on 4 November 1939 and was read with great interest by members of the British Security Services.[50] It also attracted the attention of the Belgian police, who were urgently trying to track down the French Party leader. Sam was picked up and questioned, before he was put under close police surveillance. With little alternative, Lesser prudently returned to Britain in the spring of 1940.[51]

On his return, Lesser was interrogated by Special Branch but, determined not to give the officials any excuse for arresting him, categorically denied that he'd participated in any fighting in Spain. He claimed, with some truth, that he was returning to Britain because his age group (single men under 25 years of age) were in the process of being called up and he didn't want to be regarded as a deserter. Consequently, and in spite of his personal antipathy towards the 'imperialist war', Sam registered for the armed forces and passed the medical board as A1 fit, despite the wound sustained in Spain. He heard nothing, until a letter finally arrived informing him that he had been removed from the list of Royal Scots Guards reserve officers. Sam's claim that he didn't want to be seen as a deserter had been dismissed as a Communist ruse by the Security Services, who regarded Lesser as a 'dangerous civilian Communist,' whose 'presence in the army would be a serious menace to morale and discipline.'[52] Indeed, MI5 alleged that '[the] CP propose to employ him as a Communist agent and propagandist in Forces.'[53] Consequently, it was ordered that he was not to be allowed to join any of HM Forces and, furthermore, steps were also taken to ensure that 'LESSER is not granted an exit permit to go abroad again as correspondent of the Daily Worker.'[54]

Lesser was furious and complained to the Party, to see if something could be done. However, Harry Pollitt tactfully suggested that the Spanish veteran had already seen his fair share of fighting and, pulling on the Party's contacts, found him work in a reserved occupation as a trainee inspector at D Napier & Son Ltd, an arms factory in Acton. The firm had a strong Trade Union and Communist Party presence and already employed a number of former International Brigaders, including Peter Kerrigan.

Sam started at Napiers on 9 October 1940 and was soon appointed a shop-steward in the Amalgamated Engineering Union.[55] Following Hitler's launch of Operation Barbarossa in June 1941, and the Communist Party's consequent abrupt shift to supporting the war, Sam enthusiastically supported the Party's efforts to boost productivity, promoting them in Napier's monthly magazine, *New Propeller*. He was also active in the campaign for a Second Front to take pressure off the Soviet Union, publishing articles anonymously in pro-Party publications such as the *British Worker*, *The New Year Clarion*, *The Workers' Gazette* and *The Worker's News*. At the same time he continued to work against the Franco regime, joining the editorial board of the *Volunteer for Liberty*, the newsletter of the Spanish veterans' organisation, the International Brigade Association (IBA), and attending its national conference in London.[56] There, the plight of former International Brigaders fighting with the Allies and those recently released from or still incarcerated in internment camps were raised. The IBA campaigned for those still trapped in the camps, which garnered much support and soon raised more than £2,500.00.[57] Lesser also joined the Home Guard, a role he took very seriously, and from May 1942 worked for the BBC at Bush House in a department of the Political Warfare Executive run by the future Labour Minister, Dick Crossman (which also employed Sefton Delmer), giving broadcasts in French about work and life in a British armaments factory.

Sam remained working at the Napiers factory in Acton until October 1942, when he was involved in an unfortunate incident:

I was severely censured in 1942 because as a result of carelessness on my part an aero-engine which I had passed as

119

OK failed on test as some bolts pinning a gear wheel to a shaft, had been signed by me as having been correctly nutted and split-pinned, when in fact they were not.[58]

Though Lesser vehemently denied that he would ever be so careless as to sign off faulty equipment, he was nevertheless reprimanded by his employers. He was also rebuked by the Party 'for sabotaging the war effort' and initially threatened with expulsion, though the support of Bill Rust and Peter Kerrigan kept him in the Party. However, having been transferred to the company's sister plant in Aldenham, Lesser was subsequently involved in another incident. When returning from his lunchbreak, Sam was taken aside and curtly informed that an engine he had signed off was defective. He was sacked on the spot. He was outraged, not least because he was certain that he had not made a mistake. For the rest of his life, Lesser remained convinced that the incident had been a set-up to get rid of him.[59]

After his dismissal from Napiers, Sam found work with the Soviet news agency TASS and with the ban on the Communist daily having been lifted on 26 August 1942, he returned to the *Daily Worker* in 1944 under his nom-de-plume. One of his many roles was to report on the impact of Nazi bombing, though his coverage of the appalling damage caused by a V2 rocket in November earned the paper a sharp reprimand from the Ministry of Information: there could be no mention of German rockets, nor where or when one had fallen, nor could there be any report of a crater. While the official explanation was that no information could be published that might be useful to the enemy, Lesser suspected that the real reason was a patronising view among the governmental class that the general public could not be trusted to react maturely to such issues.[60]

When the war in Europe ended in May 1945, Lesser was given a major assignment for the *Daily Worker*: to go to the Channel Islands, the only part of the British Isles to have been under Nazi occupation. There he made contact with the Jersey Democratic Movement, a broadly leftist coalition which had been set up during the war to oppose the German occupation. Following the islands' liberation and amid fears of a return to the political system that had existed before the war, the movement began pushing for social and industrial reforms. Sam wrote up his reports as a pamphlet, *Spotlight on the Channel Islands*, which laid out the details of the population's resistance and the authorities' collaboration. The pamphlet portrayed Jersey as 'seething with discontent', and strongly attacked its leaders, accusing them of having acted anything but heroically during the occupation:

> They are the same men who discouraged even such minor manifestations of resistance as the showing of the V sign, the cutting of telephone wires and the keeping of radio sets. They are the same men who assisted the Germans in the mobilisation of the Island's manpower and who used all their police forces to round up the English inhabitants of the Island for deportation to Germany.[61]

Realising that the British government was determined not to prosecute the island's political leaders for collaboration, nor for their assistance in the roundups of Jews, Sam wrote a bitter denunciation in the *Daily Worker*: 'War Office Whitewashes Jersey Authorities.'[62] The inclusion of a photograph showing Alexander Coutanche, the Bailiff of Jersey, greeting the German commander as he arrived by plane, suggested what might have happened had a Nazi invasion of Britain succeeded, especially given that Coutanche claimed he was acting under instructions from the British government.[63] The piece provoked fury from the British War Office, not least because MI5 believed that Sam was being passed secret Government documents by a typist working at the Board of Trade.[64] Yet despite Lesser's efforts, the Labour Government refused to criticise the islands' leaders, several of whom were later actually decorated for their service.

Five years later, in the summer of 1950, Lesser was appointed the paper's Diplomatic Correspondent. His first task was to go to Czechoslovakia to report on the trial of the Socialist politician and former member of the resistance movement Dr Milada Horáková. She had resigned from the government following the Communist coup in February 1948 and had subsequently been arrested and charged with conspiracy and treason against the country's new regime. Despite petitions from supporters around the world, including Winston Churchill, Eleanor Roosevelt and Albert Einstein, Horáková and three co-defendants were found guilty; she was hanged in June 1950 and the others spent years in prison. Though the trial was little more than a sham and despite accusations that Horáková had been physically and psychologically tortured, Lesser faithfully assured his readers that 'the conduct of this trial could not have been fairer.'[65] Years later, he ruefully acknowledged that 'he must have been incredibly naïve not to have seen what was going on', but pointed out that there were other journalists in the courtroom—not all of them Communists—who were similarly taken in.

Perhaps Lesser's attention was elsewhere, for his personal life was in the midst of upheaval. During the war, Sam had been staying with his younger brother Frank (who had also fought in Spain) and Frank's wife, Mira.[66] Lodging with them was a switchboard operator at the *Daily Worker* called Nell, the widow of H Fred Jones, who had been killed while commanding Sam's unit in Spain. Though she was twenty years his senior, Sam and Nell found that they had much in common and the two had fallen for each other. They were married just after the war and lived together in Hampstead, where they were both members of the local Party.[67] However, by 1950 Sam and Nell had grown apart and Sam had developed a growing affection for a young Welsh nurse he had met in Spain, called Margaret Powell. A former midwife, she had worked as part of a surgical trauma team in Spain and, though young, gained respect as a 'sincere, disciplined and hard-working' nurse.[68] Like Sam, she left Spain in 1939 but, lacking the credentials provided by Lesser's occupation, ended up in a French internment camp at Argelès-sur-Mer alongside thousands of other Republican refugees, in abominable conditions, without food, water or shelter. She was only released following pressure from a team of Quakers who'd been alerted to her plight.[69] Sam and Margaret had lost touch after Spain and during the Second World War Margaret worked as an ARP nurse and later served in Egypt and Germany, before becoming a health visitor in some of the poorest areas of north London.[70]

However, Sam and Margaret were able to renew their friendship, for Margaret's sister worked in the same factory as Sam. The pair 'saw more and more of each other' and following Sam and Nell's divorce, they were married. The newly-wedded couple moved into semi-furnished rooms in north London and a daughter, Ruth, was born on 12 October 1951.

Not long after his wedding, Lesser travelled to Poland to cover another show trial, known as the 'Trial of the Generals' of July and August 1951, which saw a number of senior Polish military figures accused of espionage. Some of them had fought with the British forces during the Second World War, some had fought with the Red Army and others had been part of the Polish resistance. Yet all were accused of spying on behalf of Britain and the US and despite a lack of evidence, all were sentenced to life imprisonment. The following year, Lesser returned to Czechoslovakia, to report on what was to become the most infamous of all the show trials, the prosecution of Rudlolf Slánský and 13 other senior Czech Communists. Among the defendants were several who had been in Spain: the Deputy Prime Minister, Artur London, and Otto Sling, the Party Secretary in Brno who was a close friend of the British Communist, John Gollan. Also on trial was the former Comintern propagandist, Otto Katz (the model for Humphrey Bogart's character, Victor Lazlo, in *Casablanca*) who Lesser knew personally. Just like the Polish Generals, the group of Party figures were accused of spying for the West and the evidence against them—much of it derived from torture—was clearly concocted. Yet at the end of a week-long trial, they too were found guilty. Eight of the defendants, including Slánský, Katz and Sling were hanged, their bodies cremated and the ashes scattered on a Prague roadside.

While Lesser might have been prepared to accept the evidence put forward in previous trials, MI5 believed that on this occasion he harboured serious doubts:

[Lesser] said that he was personally acquainted with two of the prisoners (who had been sentenced to death) and was amazed at the confessions made. He found it extremely difficult to believe that they admitted so many crimes.[71]

Sam was not the only senior British Communist to feel uneasy. Gollan probably had doubts as certainly did Harry Pollitt, who later confessed, 'You know Sam, I knew Rudolf Slánský, and I will never believe that Slánský was a traitor.'[72] There was also a strong suggestion of anti-Semitism, for eleven of the fourteen defendants were Jewish. However, when Lesser interviewed the Chief Rabbi of Prague, Dr Gustav Sichl, he insisted that anti-Semitism had not been an issue and that the trial had been fair. While Sam accepted his word, his wife Margaret was not convinced and many others in the British Communist Party weren't either. Yet despite their strong misgivings, neither Lesser, Gollan nor Pollitt made their doubts public. For Lesser, his silence would later become a source of great personal regret, particularly following the publication of Artur London's dramatic and terrifying account of the trial in 1968.

The resignation of the *Daily Worker*'s Foreign Editor, Derek Kartun in the wake of the Slánský trial led to Lesser's appointment as Moscow correspondent, a post he was to hold for nearly four years. Initially, he was positive about his new role, for since the death of Stalin two years earlier, there was a sense that Russia was changing, slowly perhaps, but changing nonetheless. This feeling was confirmed when, less than a year after his arrival, Lesser was tipped off by a Russian journalist that in a secret session on 25 February 1956 the new Russian Premier, Nikita Khrushchev had sensationally denounced Stalin's crimes and the cult of personality to a stunned audience. Lesser was determined to report what was clearly a major international story, but the Soviet authorities categorically refused to allow him to mention the secret speech. Clearly some things had not changed. Lesser was personally warned off reporting the story by Yuri Zhukov, an assistant editor at *Pravda*: 'Comrade Russell, it doesn't mean to say, because you are a friend, that you have the right to look into our cupboard.' Furiously, Lesser shot back:

If that's the case, there's nothing more that you and I have got to say to each other. All I want to say is this: unfortunately for you and for us foreign communists, this cupboard of yours is full of skeletons and one day it's going to burst wide open and what you call 'bourgeois' correspondents will be there, and we will have to clear up the dirty mess that comes out of this cupboard.[73]

Any further attempts to talk to members of the Soviet authorities met with a stone wall of denials. When Lesser did finally manage to phone a detailed twelve-page report to London, it had already been broken by a Reuters' journalist. An incandescent Lesser was only too aware that he had missed out on the journalistic scoop of a lifetime.[74]

Lesser's fury was slightly ameliorated by the arrival of his family in the spring. Margaret had planned to join him once he had found a flat, but Ruth had been ill, preventing her mother from working and leaving the pair in a precarious financial position. She had 'poured out her troubles' to Peter Kerrigan, begging him for £50.00 to buy clothes in preparation for their departure. Aware that her unhappiness could affect Sam's work in Moscow, Kerrigan arranged for her to be simply given the money.[75] So, on 18 May 1956, Margaret and Ruth sailed for Moscow onboard the 'Viatcheslav Molotov'. The family were found a pleasant new flat in Moscow and a grateful Lesser telephoned Kerrigan in London to report that his wife was settling in and had even managed to find part-time work translating for Moscow News.[76] Adjusting to Moscow life was made easier by a friendship that had developed with fellow Englishman Mark Petrovich Fraser, better known as Donald Maclean, the Cambridge spy who had defected to the Soviet Union in 1951 (Guy Burgess was also in Russia, but kept himself apart). The two English Communists and their families developed a close friendship, both having daughters of a similar age.

However, Sam had scant time to indulge in a comfortable family life, for his job required him to travel across the Soviet Union searching out stories to illustrate the successes of the Communist regime. He dutifully described in glowing terms

Soviet efforts to reform and modernise all aspects of Russian culture and society from agriculture to industry; from technology to labour relations; and from education to divorce. He recounted how great advances in productivity were bringing benefits to a cheerful and grateful Russian populace.[77] 'Soviet Siberia', he wrote 'is a man-made miracle where Soviet power plus technique, mechanisation and the sweat of Siberian settlers is producing results never dreamed of before.'[78]

> The scientific industrial and engineering triumphs represented by such Soviet achievements as the world's first earth satellite, the world's first atomic power station, the world's first regular passenger jet service, to the world's first atomic ice breaker and many other world firsts are only a small part of these triumphs . . . But backing up these headline hitters are a host of new ideas, new inventions, new machines in all fields and to such an extent that no scientist or technician whatever his [sic] speciality can afford any longer to ignore Soviet experience.[79]

He extolled the technological genius behind the Soviets' nuclear weapons and the Sputnik programme. In the arts too, he reported, Russia excelled and Sam was genuinely a great admirer of the Bolshoi which, he argued, was 'recognised today not only at the heart of Russian musical culture but as one of the greatest centres of world art.'[80]

However, despite these fawning reports, it would be a mistake to see Sam Lesser simply as a caricature of a Soviet apparatchik. The British Security Services certainly saw him as very much more independent-minded than many of his contemporaries. While one unnamed MI6 source went as far as to say that he 'found it hard to believe that he was a real Communist', more subtle minds recognised that it was possible to be critical of Soviet Communism on one hand, while on the other remain loyal to Communism as an ideology.[81] In an astute piece of analysis, one Foreign Office mandarin concluded that:

> Perhaps the most interesting thing about my lunch with Mr Russell was to see the impact of Soviet Russia upon this intelligent life-long Communist. He adopts towards the Soviet

system a completely detached and cynical approach. He looks down on the Russian just as any other East End cockney might, or any other western correspondent. He speaks of the Soviet system and the Soviet leaders with a complete lack of respect or appearance of loyalty. Yet I felt he was probably a firmer Communist than when he went to Russia. The discrediting of Stalin provides the perfect scapegoat . . . in short, the Soviet revolution seems in his view to have a decisive turning, and one which is wholly in the right direction.[82]

Lesser's independence could only go so far however and 1956 would see him loyally defend a Soviet action that would cause many Communists to leave the Party in disgust.[83]

On 23 October 1956, a student protest against the Soviet-backed Hungarian government's inability to tackle serious food and fuel shortages rapidly escalated into a full-scale national revolution. Initially, the Soviets appeared willing to negotiate, but on 4 November Russian forces invaded the country and instituted a brutal crack-down.[84] Ordered to report on the uprising for the *Daily Worker*, Lesser was flown to Hungary in a Soviet military plane and driven to his Budapest hotel in an armoured car. When he arrived in the Hungarian capital he was taken aback to discover that his predecessor, Peter Fryer, had rebelled against the Communist paper's pro-Soviet line and resigned from his post on the *Worker*. Having hailed the Hungarian 'people's revolution' Fryer had taken refuge in the British Embassy. He was, unsurprisingly, later expelled from the Communist Party.

However, despite Fryer's resignation, Lesser still accepted the official Soviet line that the 'counter-revolution' was an attempt to overthrow the People's democratic Republic; 'New Hungarian Govt acted to save world peace,' he wrote. In fact, he justified the clamp-down, convinced that the protestors were essentially reactionaries—or worse—spurred on by former members of the Hungarian SS and CIA propaganda.[85] 'Members of the Hungarian fascist Crossed Arrow organisation produced arms and forced workers to participate in the demonstrations,' he claimed.[86] His reports told of more than 50 killed and another 100 wounded; 'the over-whelming majority had received wounds in the back from the fire of the fascists behind them.' Lesser argued that peace had only been restored when, 'at the request of the Hungarian government, Soviet tanks arrived' and that the Russians would quit Budapest once peace was fully restored. However, while Lesser's pro-Soviet reporting of the Russian invasion and clampdown earned the approval of senior Communists, many members of the British Party opposed it, albeit quietly and ineffectively.[87] There was, in fact, great sympathy among many in Britain for the Hungarians' stand against the Soviet Red Army, which created feelings of solidarity not seen since the civil war in Spain. As the former International Brigader, George Leeson, admitted, 'the final blow, of course, was Hungary . . . I just would not accept the version put forward on Hungary at all.'[88]

By January 1957, with Soviet control in Hungary fully re-established, Sam was able to return to Moscow. That summer he and Margaret came to the reluctant conclusion that seven-year-old Ruth should return to the UK for her education. For the Party leaders in London this meant that the family's precarious finances could once again become an issue. It was clear that either permission would be needed from the Russians for Sam to convert some of the millions of (essentially useless) roubles he had been paid into sterling, or the British Communist Party would need to find the money. Despite Margaret's long-standing Party membership, her track record of work on behalf of the Spanish Republic, not to mention her sacrifices for Sam's career, the Security Services believed that not all at King Street were as sympathetic to her plight as they might have been: '[*Daily Worker* Editor, JR] CAMPBELL thought the trouble was that his wife hadn't got much Party spirit, and she was fickle and he wouldn't be surprised that her coming back was due to some tension between them.'[89] However, others, including John Gollan, the Party's General Secretary, were more supportive, arguing that Ruth's schooling was a perfectly legitimate reason for their return. Nevertheless, the question was raised whether it might simply be better for all concerned if Sam, for whom they clearly had a great deal of respect, simply returned home with his family.

In fact, a return to London might not have been wholly unwelcome for Sam. Having rashly bought a car in Moscow, he was heavily in debt. Furthermore, his friendship with Donald Maclean had cooled, for he had become tired of the renegade's maudlin drinking and homesickness.[90] Sam confessed to Peter Kerrigan that life in Moscow was not what he had been told: 'In the past, the Party had tried to give the impression that it was a bloody paradise, which it most certainly was not.' A lack of decent housing was causing hardship and it was by no means the only problem: 'it cost a month's pay to buy a suit of clothes,' he complained.[91] However, it would not be money, but politics which lay at the root of Sam's departure from Moscow.

During the summer of 1957, rumours had been flying around Moscow that the defence Minister, Marshall Zhukov, a Soviet Second World War hero, was rumoured to be in line for a big promotion. Zhukov had played a key role in defeating an internal power play within the Politburo, which had aimed to depose Khrushchev as Premier. However, in October, Khrushchev, concerned that Zhukov might be becoming too powerful, appointed a rival in his place while Zhukov was out of the country. While official statements continued to push the story that Zhukov was a 'Hero of the Soviet Union', Sam winkled out the truth from a Russian journalist friend and his account duly appeared in the *Daily Worker*. 'Then the trouble started,' Lesser remembered. Rumours reached him of enquiries being made into his activities and who he was meeting. Sam suspected that his telephone had been tapped and Margaret became convinced that that she was being followed and was understandably frightened and upset.[92] Confirmation that Lesser had indeed fallen out of favour came following Harry Pollitt's visit to Moscow in November and the British Party Secretary was informed by the Russians that, due to Lesser's reporting of the Zhukov story, the journalist had to be replaced. The row got as far as a meeting with Khrushchev, but when both Pollitt and Gollan vigorously defended Lesser, the Russians relented and, for the moment, he was allowed to remain.[93]

As Sam wryly observed, while Khrushchev's 'thaw' had seen the removal of some of the excesses of the Stalin period, a large number of dangerous icebergs still remained. Russian society was still highly restricted and anyone perceived as a dissident could experience heavy censure. Though Alexander Solzhenitsyn had been freed from prison, Dmitri Shostakovich was still suffering persecution and, as Sam discovered for himself, Boris Pasternak was coming under heavy criticism for his 1957 novel, *Doctor Zhivago*, even though the book was almost impossible to obtain in the Soviet Union. Though he had not read the book, Sam was ordered to interview Pasternak, with the aim of getting the author to accept that the work was anti-Soviet. However, after having met with Pasternak and learning that the author's father had suffered censorship under the Tsar, to his credit Lesser refused to write a piece pillorying the author.

However, Lesser's determined independence of spirit was not universally admired. When Harry Pollitt arrived in Moscow in early 1959, Lesser got the distinct impression that the British Party leader was avoiding him. When the pair did actually meet, Lesser found his old friend to be cold and distant and Pollitt eventually admitted that the Russians were still furious about Sam's article on the fall of Marshall Zhukov. Aware that Lesser was entirely likely to obtain further damaging scoops, the Russians had informed Pollitt that he was no longer welcome. As Pollitt reluctantly admitted to Lesser, the British Party had finally given way and Pollitt informed Lesser that he was to be withdrawn.[94]

So, in June 1959, Sam was reunited with Margaret and Ruth in a warm, dry and sunny London.[95] A letter from the British Embassy in Moscow to the Foreign Office News Department in London noted his replacement by the former *Challenge* Moscow correspondent, Denis Ogden. As with much of the Foreign Office material regarding Lesser, it's clear that while some may have found his politics reprehensible, there was more than a sneaking regard for him both personally and professionally:

Our relations with Russell have been somewhat exceptional. On the whole we should find it rather distasteful to establish such close relations with a more or less permanent Communist expatriate, who is no doubt working directly for the Russians.[96]

Lesser's return was of great interest to the British Security Services, who wondered if he might have fallen out of favour, and questions were raised about potentially making an approach. However, a top-secret memorandum bluntly laid out the risks of doing so:

> RUSSELL is a dyed-in-the-wool long-term Party member who has been through all the hoops, including the Hungarian one. I think that he is similar to GOLLAN in that he is a "British" rather than an "International" communist, but if anything this should make his relationship with the leadership of the Party warmer and easier. It would, therefore, in my view be a mistake to believe that RUSSELL would respond to any approaches from revisionist elements in this or any other country.[97]

That Lesser was not being frozen out became clear when he replaced Bill Carritt as the *Daily Worker*'s Foreign Editor later that year.[98] The appointment—combined with his experience gained reporting on the war in Spain—was to offer Lesser a unique opportunity, when he was sent to Cuba during the infamous missile crisis, 'when the world held its breath.'[99] The crisis had begun the previous year, when American deployments of missiles in Italy and Turkey had been countered by the Soviets placing their own in Cuba. On 22 October 1962, the US instituted a naval blockade around the Caribbean island to prevent further warheads being deployed. Following a terrifying standoff as Soviet ships headed towards the island, urgent diplomatic negotiations between Kennedy and Khrushchev led to an agreement that both sides would withdraw their missiles and on 20 November 1962 the US lifted their blockade.

Articles in the *Daily Worker* made very clear who had been responsible for the crisis: 'President Kennedy's threats of nuclear war against the seven million people of tiny Cuba, with the danger of starting World War III, are the culmination of events which began on January 1, 1959 [the date Castro came to power in Cuba],' Lesser argued.[100] In mid-November, Lesser was instructed to fly to Cuba (taking the longer but cheaper route via

Prague, Ireland and Newfoundland) where he would be reporting the fallout from the crisis. He was the only British journalist to be given permission to report from Cuba and he duly filed several flattering articles lauding Castro's revolutionary regime and the heroic Cuban people.[101] While the positive reportage was no doubt appreciated, it was the Spanish Lesser had picked up during the civil war that helped him score a journalistic coup when, to his astonishment, Lesser was granted a personal interview with Ernesto 'Che' Guevara.

Though it was hardly a conventional interview, Lesser found it to be an utterly unforgettable encounter, not least because Che started talking at 10.30pm and was still talking five hours later.[102] Lesser was genuinely impressed by the charismatic revolutionary, but also came away with the distinct suspicion that Guevara was, in Lesser's words, 'a bit off his rocker'. This feeling was further compounded by Che's furious remark about what he would have done, had the Cubans, rather than the Russians, been in charge of the missiles:

Unfortunately they were not under our control, but if they had been under our control and if the Americans had lifted a little finger, we would have fired every one of them off, on New York and Chicago, on Washington and Ohio![103]

'Well', said Lesser to himself, 'thank Christ they weren't!'

However, when Lesser submitted his piece to the *Daily Worker*, the paper's editor, George Matthews, prudently excised Che's explosive declaration. In fact, the only part of the interview to make it into the paper at all was Guevara's infamous criticism of the reformist strategies being pursued by Communist Parties in South America: *'los partidos comunistas de América Latina son una mierda'* (the communist parties of Latin America are shit). Sam was furious at Matthews' editorial decision, but there wasn't much he could do about it, for he had no text of the interview, having unwisely entrusted the original to a departing correspondent from the New York *Daily Worker* whom he had known in Spain. Ironically, while Lesser's interview didn't appear in the British *Daily Worker*, it did appear in newspapers around the world, for Lesser's report was intercepted by the CIA and leaked to the US news agency, United Press. They then accused the British Communist Party of having censored Sam's report. Which, of course, was exactly what they had done.

Six years later and twelve years after witnessing the Hungarian uprising, Lesser was sent to another eastern-bloc country in the throes of popular protest. The country was, of course, Czechoslovakia, which was in the midst of the 'Prague Spring'. Unrest had begun in 1967 when students began peacefully demonstrating against the regime, which had led to the replacement of the pro-Soviet President Antonín Novotný by the reformist First Secretary of the Party, Alexander Dubček. However, the new President's attempts to introduce a more liberal, democratic and open regime, 'socialism with a human face,' did not meet with the approval of the Soviet Communist leadership. In August, they responded with a show of force, sending in 250,000 troops. Dubček was arrested and a pro-Soviet President, Gustav Husak, was installed who quickly reversed Dubček's reforms. In September, Lesser arrived in Czechoslovakia to report on the uprising.

While he had very much followed the Party line in Hungary, by 1968 Sam's confidence in the Soviet regime and its foreign policy was beginning to waver. His doubts hardened after witnessing the brutal crushing of what was essentially a peaceful revolt. Talking to Czech workers and people in the street, he found that nobody—not even his official interpreter —supported the Soviet invasion. Yet what really shook him was the discovery of papers and records in the Department of the Interior revealing that the organisation of Czech veterans of the International Brigade had been listed as a suspect organisation equivalent to fascists. As Sam was beginning to realise, Stalin had regarded those who had survived Spain, particularly those from Eastern Europe who had spent time incarcerated in French internment camps, as tainted and suspect.[104]

Appalled, Lesser declared himself to be 'absolutely in support of the British Party's condemnation of the invasion.'[105] His pro-reformist reports for the *Morning Star* (as the *Daily Worker* was renamed in 1966) were picked up by the CIA-backed radio Free Europe, infuriating the Soviets.[106] While many in the British Party (and beyond) still saw him as a 'dyed-in-the-wool Stalinist', Sam later explained his fury at the crushing of the Prague Spring and argued that many had misunderstood him:

> A lot of people think I was a party 'yes man' all along, whatever the party line did . . . an absolute out-and-out Stalinist. The thing is, I always made and continued to try and make a distinction between Hungary and Czechoslovakia . . . Czechoslovakia was a country which had this strong working-class and communist tradition from before the war, whereas Hungary . . . was a stronghold of fascists in one form or another . . . Therefore I justified the Soviet action in Hungary, whereas I didn't for a moment in Czechoslovakia.[107]

As he later explained, 'Czechoslovakia was a defining moment for me politically,' for it led him to the realisation that the only realistic future for the British Communist Party was a complete break with the Soviet Union.

However, disillusionment with the Soviet regime did not signify any softening of Lesser's criticisms of western-style capitalism and imperialism. His antipathy to the US, in particular, was reinforced by a trip to war-torn Vietnam in 1970. Lesser was one of very few western reporters to be given permission to visit North Vietnam and he was shocked by the devastation caused by US planes dropping high explosives and napalm. Such was the scale of the damage that he came to believe privately that the North could never achieve complete victory. On a visit to Dong Ha, the northernmost city in South Vietnam, he found it to be littered with anti-personnel mines, which were wreaking havoc on the civilian population. Sam was introduced to an 11-year-old boy who had innocently picked up one of the devices and lost his right hand and right eye in the ensuing explosion. 'The US were bastards in Asia,' he wrote in disgust. He would soon be equally disgusted by American involvement in another continent on the opposite side of the world: Latin America.

On 3 November 1970, a left-wing government was narrowly

elected in Chile, which pursued a programme of reforms and nationalisations. In a situation that echoed Spain in the 1930s, President Salvador Allende's policies were initially very popular on the left, though perhaps fuelling unrealistic expectations. Meanwhile, many on the right bitterly opposed the changes. During the next three years the situation became increasingly fractious, with widespread civil unrest and strikes. In the autumn of 1973, with rumours abounding of a possible CIA-backed plot to overthrow the government, Sam took a flight with the Soviet airline, Aeroflot, to Santiago, via Moscow. He arrived late in the evening of 10 September and took a room in the Carrero Hilton where the BBC's John Humphrys was also a guest. As Lesser was about to turn in for some sorely needed sleep, the hotel was rocked by a huge explosion. Peering cautiously out of his hotel window, Sam watched, aghast, as the Chilean army and air force attacked the presidential palace. Rumours soon began passing among the hotel guests that President Allende had been killed. Over the course of the night, the sound of gunfire provided a chilling soundtrack and the following morning Sam could see for himself the grim consequences of the shootings, for dead bodies littered the streets.

When General Pinochet's victorious junta held a conference for the world's press, Sam was impressed by Humphrys' interrogation of a Chilean military officer with the aggressiveness for which he became famous. However, as the foreign correspondent for the *Morning Star*, Lesser wisely refrained from asking any questions. As a well-known Communist Party member with a return ticket to Moscow in his pocket, Sam later admitted that he feared for his life: 'I could do nothing other than pick up stories and try to do so without endangering anyone who talked to me.' Fortunately, his passport was in his real name rather than his professional *nom-de-plume*, so when the military lifted the curfew three days later he was able to pose as an engineer and escape the country. Only once he'd left did Sam feel safe to report what he had seen, under the compelling headline: 'I saw democracy murdered.'[108]

Lesser was, of course, only too aware of the parallels between the military coups in Chile in 1970 and Spain in 1936.

The Iberian country remained close to Sam's heart and over the years he had written numerous articles denouncing the Franco dictatorship. The brutal torture and execution of Julián Grimau, a member of the central committee of the Spanish Communist Party in 1962, had spurred Sam to write a pamphlet, *Murder in Madrid*, which sold over five thousand copies.[109] Like many veterans, for years Lesser refused to set foot in Franco's Spain, yet in the spring of 1972, with the dictator becoming increasingly frail, he returned for the first time since the civil war. There Lesser saw for himself the violent suppression of student protests and the vicious attacks launched by members of the Francoist secret police upon often innocent bystanders. His visit led to a spate of furious articles in the *Morning Star*, lambasting the regime's 'savagery' and publicising the plight of jailed Trade Unionists and students who had been boycotting their studies, but were being forced to sit their examinations at gunpoint. 'Franco' Sam declared, 'was a dictator whose regime began amid blood and continued in the same way.'[110]

When Franco died in November 1975 and Spain began its transition to democracy—which included the legalisation of the Communist Party—it was met with elation by Lesser and other supporters of the former Spanish Republic. Yet it was tinged with sadness that so many had died fighting for democracy in Spain, both during the war itself and during the nearly forty years of Franco's dictatorship. As Sam's friend and fellow veteran Jack Jones declared, 'the price was very heavy, very heavy indeed.'[111] However, Spain had not forgotten the sacrifices made: in 1976 Margaret's efforts were honoured by her being made a Dame of the Order of Loyalty to the Spanish Republic by the government in exile.[112] In 1977, there were free elections and five years later, the newly-elected socialist government of Felipe González declared its intention to confer Spanish citizenship on all the surviving veterans of the International Brigades.

However, some of the political upheavals to occur during the 1980s were less welcome. As Lesser approached retirement, his professional and political lives were thrown into turmoil as the Communist Party of Great Britain was riven by splits between the increasingly dominant Eurocommunists and the more traditional pro-Soviet wing. The battles between the 'Euros' and the 'Stalinists' spread to the *Morning Star*, where Sam, who was the NUJ's father of the chapel, supported the Eurocommunists in defiance of Tony Chater, George Matthews's successor as editor. He took a similar position within the Party itself and, following his retirement in 1984, wrote articles for *Seven Days*, the Party's new weekly newspaper. At the beginning of the following decade, when the CPGB was finally dissolved, Sam decided to join the Labour Party.[113] The following year, the former Communist supported the west's invasion of Iraq, to the surprise—and often disapproval—of many of his friends on the left. The revelation in 1991 that, like other western parties, the British Communist Party—contrary to what it had always maintained, and unknown to all but a very few of the top leadership—had received money from the Soviet party from 1958 until 1979, 'just rubbed salt in the wound'.

As the twentieth century drew to a close, the rank of veterans of the Spanish Civil War was becoming increasingly depleted. In 2000, Bill Alexander, who had ruled the International Brigade Association as President for many years, died and a new organisation was formed, combining the old veterans' association with a group made up of family, friends and supporters. Sam Lesser was an enthusiastic founder-member of what was to become the International Brigade Memorial Trust and he took up a position on the Trust's executive committee. Now in his mid-eighties, Lesser worked hard to keep alive the memory of those who volunteered to fight in Spain, helping to organise lectures, exhibitions and publish books. The IBMT continued the IBA's tradition of hosting an annual commemoration at the national memorial to the International Brigades on London's South Bank and Lesser was a frequent and popular speaker. Having given a well-received speech at the *Homenaje*, the huge, unforgettable reunion in Madrid in 1996, Lesser became a regular visitor to Spain. He was one of five veterans to attend an unveiling of a memorial in La Bisbal de Falset in Catalonia in November 2001. One of Sam's enduring hopes was to see the installation of a memorial in Britain to the men and women from Cambridge, particularly to his friend John

Cornford who had been killed in Spain at a very young age. So far, despite the presence of a memorial to the Oxford volunteers, his wish has not yet been fulfilled.

In 2006, following the retirement of his predecessor, Jack Jones, Lesser was elected Chair of the IBMT. While he might have occasionally rested his eyes during long committee meetings, he was an effective chair, commanding respect from the other members of the Executive Committee. He could, occasionally, show flashes of impatience, banging the floor with his walking stick to bring order, though he was just as likely to succumb to humour, his body vigorously shaking with laughter. On 9 June 2009, he was one of seven surviving veterans to be invited to the Spanish Embassy in London to be awarded passports, symbols of the country's wish to grant the aging men and women with honorary nationality. At the ceremony, Lesser gave an eloquent speech on behalf of himself and his companions, delivered in fluent Spanish. 'Hemos tardado un poco', he remarked with a wry grin, 'pero creo que hoy podemos decir que hemos llegado a casa.' ('We are a little late, but I believe that today we can say that we have come home.') As his life entered its final years, Sam gave up his Brixton flat, with its voluminous bookshelves and abstract Terry Frost prints, for a Jewish residential home in nearby Clapham called Nightingale House, where his father had died of cancer in 1942. An interest was reignited in some of the orthodox Jewish beliefs of his childhood and he specifically requested that Kaddish should be said at his funeral. When the 95-year-old died on 2 October 2010, his ashes were scattered near the International Brigade memorial at Montjuïc in Barcelona in accordance with his wishes.

Like many veterans of the Spanish Civil War, Lesser had been interviewed many times during his long life. Most significantly, two friends and colleagues from the Morning Star, Colin Chambers and Chris Myant, recorded a wealth of his reminiscences, which have recently been published.[114] Many of Lesser's other interviews can be accessed online, including a long account for the Imperial War Museum recorded in 1986 and a piece in The Guardian's anniversary supplement in 2000 (which included a portrait by the acclaimed photographer, Eamonn McCabe). Most interviewers found Sam to be a rewarding subject, for in addition to possessing several languages and an encyclopaedic memory, he was a skilled raconteur, delivering well-honed anecdotes with practised charm. He was also honest and self-reflective about his role in the Communist Party, expressing regret for 'perpetrating a lie about Stalin's Russia.'[115] He accepted that he should have seen the awful crimes that were being committed in the name of Soviet Communism, but insisted that although he might have been naïve, he had never knowingly or cynically perpetuated lies (though he acknowledged that senior figures in the Party undoubtedly had).

Nevertheless, while Lesser was generally happy to be interviewed and generous with his time and knowledge, it's probably fair to say that his time in the Communist Party instilled a certain sense of discretion. For many years he remained unwilling to write his memoirs and, in a typical flash of self-deprecating humour, he explained why to Harry Pollitt's biographer, Kevin Morgan: 'One of the main things, apart from sheer laziness, why I haven't done this is that I've always felt that if I write all this down, even if I find a publisher and get it published, the feeling that [former *Morning Star* editor] George Matthews will sit there reading it, and Bill Wainwright [his assistant editor], laughing away and thinking, "Heh, heh, heh, he doesn't know the half of it."'[116]

Chapter Five
A Family Goes to War: The Haldanes

When the Pulitzer Prize-winning author, Adam Hochschild, wrote his account of Americans in the Spanish Civil War, he shrewdly took as a major theme the involvement of romantic couples.[1] His most illustrious pair, the writer Ernest Hemingway and the journalist Martha Gelhorn, were famously committed to the Republican cause while clandestinely to each other. Though his book concentrates on Americans, the work also includes Britons such as the International Brigader Jason 'Pat' Gurney, who had a liaison with the American nurse, Toby Jensky. In fact, there were several couples from Britain who Hochschild might have included, most obviously George Orwell and Eileen O'Shaughnessy, but also the author Ralph Bates and his wife Winifred, both of whom gained important positions in Republican Spain. There was also Nan Green, the efficient administrator at a Republican hospital in Valdeganga, north-west of Albacete, whose husband, George, was killed on the International Brigades' last day of action in September 1938.[2] There are many other examples. However, there is only one case of an entire family volunteering to go to Spain; they were the journalist, writer and feminist, Charlotte Haldane, her teenage son Ronnie and her (second) husband, the distinguished geneticist and scientist, Professor JBS Haldane. 'The Republican cause,' as one of JBS's biographers acknowledged, 'consumed the family wholesale.'[3]

Charlotte Haldane was born Charlotte Franken on 27 April 1894 in London, daughter of the American-born Matilda Saarbach and Joseph Franken, a prosperous German-born fur dealer.[4] Cultured, politically radical and a Freemason, Charlotte's father donated large sums of money to charity and was, wrote Charlotte, 'a man of deep religious feeling, but of little faith'.[5] Both Charlotte's parents were Jewish and haunted by anti-Semitism, something with which Charlotte became familiar, long before she knew the facts of life. Its widespread, covert and malign existence had gained dramatic exposure at the end of the nineteenth century by the shameful Dreyfus affair in France, which her father followed with horrified fascination.[6]

Charlotte and her younger sister Elizabeth were raised mainly by an English nanny, though they spoke German at home. The girls were initially home educated by a German governess, but in 1901, Charlotte was sent to South Hampstead High School, where she thrived. However, she was forced to leave after five years much against her wishes when the family moved to Antwerp.[7] Thereafter, she was taught in French and German, instilling in her, Charlotte confessed, a love of the former very much at the expense of the latter. On the family's return to London, the sixteen-year-old Charlotte, who had already decided that she wanted to become a writer, was destined for further education. However, the collapse of the family business in 1910, rumoured to be the result of a swindle by Charlotte's uncle, scuppered the plans and forced her into what she complained was the tedious mundanity of secretarial college.

When the First World War broke out four years later, Charlotte's father was initially interned as an enemy alien, though after a year he and Charlotte's mother were allowed to emigrate to America. Charlotte, however, chose to remain in London, where she met and fell in love with 'a charming and penniless young man' called John 'Jack' McLeod Burghes. Despite her parents' reservations, the two were married in 1918 and a son, Ronald John, known as Ronnie, was born the following year.[8] With Jack severely incapacitated by a wound sustained during the Great War, Charlotte was forced to be the bread-winner, a role she undertook by writing short stories on the role of women and hawking them to newspapers. A sale to the *Daily Express* led to the offer of a job as 'Social Editor', despite a complete lack of experience of journalism. However, she managed to bluff her way through for three years, so successfully, in fact, that she was promoted to the staff as a reporter, a feat almost unheard of for a woman at the time. Her writings displayed Charlotte's intelligence and wide-ranging interests: politics, feminism, even utopian science-fiction and the potential impact of developments in science and technology.

Having read a piece on genetics in an American magazine, Charlotte was inspired to read *Daedalus*, the text of a lecture given at the University of Cambridge in 1923, which discussed the potential impacts of genetics. She immediately decided to approach the author for help, an eminent academic by the name of JBS Haldane.

John Burdon Sanderson Haldane (known as Jack or JBS) was a scientist and polymath, famous for his ground-breaking work on genetics and evolution.[9] Born on Guy Fawkes' Night in 1892, he was the son of the physiologist John Scott Haldane and Louisa Kathleen Coutts Trotter, a Conservative aristocrat. A nephew of the former Secretary of State for War, the First Viscount Haldane, JBS later claimed he could trace his ancestry back to Robert the Bruce.[10] Gifted with a prodigious memory and intellect, by the age of four JBS was reading newspaper reports of the British Association for the Advancement of Science. A life-long fascination with genetics began when he was eight, having been taken by his father to a lecture at the Oxford University Junior Scientific Club. He gained a scholarship to Eton in 1904 and to New College, Oxford seven years later. Initially a student of maths and biology, he switched to *Literae Humaniores* in order, he insisted, to develop a broader education.[11] However, his education had to be paused when war was declared in August 1914.

Haldane immediately volunteered for the British Army and was commissioned into the Black Watch as a Second Lieutenant, rising to the rank of Captain.[12] Once described by Field Marshall Haig as 'the bravest and dirtiest officer in the army', Haldane seems to have relished his wartime experiences, setting about the exercise of killing with grim determination.[13] He later wrote a powerful and evocative description of being on the receiving end of a German artillery bombardment:

> Imagine the loudest bang you have ever heard, say a clap of thunder from a house struck in your immediate neighbourhood. Now imagine this prolonged indefinitely, a solid bang without intermission. And behind this, like the drone of a bagpipes behind the individual notes, a sound as of

devil-driven tramcars taking a sharp corner.[14]

While Haldane admitted that he had been terrified during earlier, much smaller bombardments, he somehow found this 'novel sound' completely intoxicating. Until, that is, he was hit by a shell and wounded in his left side and right arm and had to walk three miles to get medical help.[15] Wounded on a second occasion, Haldane was transferred to India, where he remained for eighteen months, before being sent home for intelligence training, prior to being briefly posted to Aden. When the war ended, Haldane was appointed a Fellow of New College Oxford, researching into genetics and physiology, moving five years later to Trinity College Cambridge as Reader in Biochemistry. There, during the following summer, he encountered the young journalist, Charlotte Burghes.

Charlotte was, she confessed, 'completely over-awed by the largeness of the man and nearly scorched by the blaze of his intellect.' The gifted Haldane undeniably cut an impressive figure; he was almost two metres tall and weighed in at nearly 110 kilogrammes. He always sported a large bushy moustache— apart from a brief period at the start of the Second World War when he trimmed it so extremely it resembled Hitler's. Wisely, he let it return to its full grandeur, declaring 'If I have to look like a dictator, I prefer to look like the Russian one.'[16] The poet Stephen Spender would later describe JBS as 'a man of great abilities, of which perhaps humility is the least outstanding.'[17] While Haldane possessed an overbearing personality to match his physical size and could be highly insensitive if not downright rude, he could also be supremely charming, as Charlotte was to discover.

Initially scolding her that the last reporter to interview him 'had made a complete hash of the story', JBS promised to take Charlotte to lunch, 'if you haven't made an equal mess of yours.'[18] To JBS's surprise she didn't: 'the resulting paragraph in the *Daily Express* not only kept to the facts', he admitted, 'but, as had been stipulated, did not mention my name.'[19] Their lunch was to be the first of many, as JBS adopted the role of Charlotte's personal tutor. At first, both seemed to have been entirely comfortable and happy in their roles: 'teaching was JBS's supreme hobby,' Charlotte declared, 'as learning was mine.' However, their intellectual relationship soon developed into a physical one and with Charlotte's marriage to Jack essentially moribund, JBS proposed that they should get married. This proved difficult for, despite their estrangement, Jack was not prepared to countenance a divorce. Ignoring his vehement objections, Charlotte secured a divorce by the timeworn charade of arranging for a private detective to witness her and JBS overnighting in a London hotel. Unfortunately, the divorce became a national scandal, leading to Haldane's dismissal from his university posts for 'gross immorality' (though he was reinstated following a robust appeal, supported by such notables as GK Chesterton and Bertrand Russell).[20] Nevertheless, the masquerade achieved its objective and on 20 October 1925, Jack Burghes obtained a divorce from Charlotte on the grounds of adultery. As co-respondent, JBS was ordered to pay £1,000 damages.

JBS and Charlotte were married the following May and moved in together in the ancient Fen village of Old Chesterton, near Cambridge. That year Charlotte wrote her feminist dystopian novel, *Man's World*, set in a world where a male scientific elite uses sex selection to restrict the number of girls born.[21] She also continued her education in scientific methodology and plant genetics, while devouring poetry, history and psychology and enjoying the variety of classical concerts available in the city. To help with the bills, they took in lodgers, one of whom—a young biochemistry student called Martin Case—seems to have become very close to Charlotte.[22] Whether Case was actually Charlotte's lover is not clear, though Charlotte later confided to her daughter-in-law that JBS, a heavy smoker and drinker, was impotent.[23] The couple never had children and JBS does not appear to have been overly interested in them; certainly Charlotte's son Ronnie felt that JBS didn't take much interest in him. Apart, that is, from doing his utmost to ensure that his stepson never beat him at anything (bar badminton, at which Ronnie was an accomplished player).

Still, despite any personal problems the couple may have

been having, when they were offered the opportunity to visit the Soviet Union in May 1928, the pair eagerly accepted. Both were keen and seasoned travellers and conscious of what they felt was the dangerous propensity of academics and intellectuals to 'shut themselves up in their pleasant ivory towers.' They were also both fascinated by 'the Russian system' and while neither at this stage were members of the Communist Party, they were both certainly sympathetic to Socialism.[24] During their brief visit they were, of course, carefully chaperoned by their Russian hosts, particularly by the notable Russian geneticist, Nicolai Ivanovich Vavilov, who they both came to greatly like and admire. JBS in particular enthused about Stalin's Russia and its enthusiasm for scientific progress, though Charlotte later claimed that she found the tortuous bureaucracy and constant police surveillance dispiriting.

Like many who turned to the left in the 1920s and '30s, their sympathy for socialism in general and the Soviet Union in particular was driven by a loathing of the fascist movements on the rise across Europe. While JBS's involvement in activism was limited by the demands of his research, Charlotte held regular political discussions at her home with Cambridge students.[25] Given her Jewish heritage and good knowledge of German, it's not surprising that she personally became involved in the fight against Hitler's regime:

> The rise of the Nazis, the persecution of innocent Jews, the rabid attack on all forms of culture precious to a civilised person, the horrors of the concentration camps, were responsible, as these dreadful events unfolded themselves, for driving me further and further leftward.[26]

While Georgi Dimitrov's spirited defence at his show-trial over the Reichstag fire made a fool out of Hermann Goering, it made a disciple out of her. The Nazis' torching of books led her to enthusiastically accept the role of Honorary Organiser of an organisation established to raise awareness of the burnings: the 'Library of Burned Books'. However, what Charlotte didn't know was that the instigators of the scheme were German members of the Communist International, the Comintern, who had infiltrated Britain as refugees. One of them, a young German Jew who she described only as her 'protégé', convinced her to become more closely involved in the Communist movement and the fight against fascism.

Despite Charlotte's personal association with Germany, it was actually the travails of another vulnerable European democracy that were to occupy her thoughts. In the spring of 1933, she accompanied JBS (who had been promoted from Reader to Professor the previous year) to a week-long conference in Madrid, chaired by the Nobel prize winning scientist, Marie Curie.[27] On a trip to Toledo, Charlotte seems to have fallen in love with Spain, its culture and people, even, she admitted guiltily, becoming an admirer of bull-fighting. She began learning the language and when she returned to Spain later that year, she was able to communicate reasonably confidently. Her second trip was more extensive, taking in Barcelona, Tarragona, Zaragoza and Madrid once again, before travelling down to Andalusia in southern Spain. There, like millions of other tourists before and since, Charlotte became enchanted by the city of Córdoba. Yet her feelings were tempered by seeing the appalling conditions in which many people lived:

The poverty in Andalusia was tragic. It was bad in Córdoba, worse in Granada, almost universal in Seville. The peasants were starving everywhere; they squatted in miserable huts of wattle and straw, in rags, barefoot. The town workers were even worse off, for they had neither work nor food. Everywhere was economic, mental and physical depression.[28]

Charlotte strongly supported the efforts of the country's new Republican government to limit the power of the three pillars of the Spanish establishment: the landowners, the Catholic Church and the army. These efforts were, unsurprisingly, being strongly resisted by the powerful troika and their supporters on the Spanish Right, including the new fascist party, the *Falange*. Many Spaniards had never supported the Republic and were determined to overthrow it, if not democratically, then by the manner with a long history in Spain, the *pronunciamiento*, or military coup. So, when a fascist-backed military uprising was launched in Spain in July 1936, Charlotte was appalled and determined to do what she could for the beleaguered Republic. Based on an article she wrote on Spain for the *New Statesman*, Charlotte was approached by Republican supporters and she immediately agreed to help, despite having no experience of public speaking.[29] She soon discovered, with conflicting emotions, that she was not the only member of her family to be committed to anti-fascism and the cause in Spain.

Her teenage son Ronnie had recently joined the Young Communist League, having seen for himself 'the envenomed anti-Semitism of the speakers' at a British Union of Fascists meeting on Hampstead Heath.[30] In November 1936, the sixteen-year-old revealed to his aghast mother that he had volunteered to go to fight in Spain. Caught between admiring his sense of self-sacrifice and terrified at the prospect of him being killed, Charlotte considered revealing to the Communist Party recruiters that he was underage. She went to see the Party's General Secretary, Harry Pollitt, but perhaps put off by his gruff manner, or stung by his shrewd assumption that she had come to try and prevent Ronnie from going, she backed down. Her only insistence, based on the recommendation of JBS—who was an international authority on gas and had invented an early type of respirator during the First World War—was that Ronnie must not leave without a gasmask.

On 6 December 1936, Special Branch, who routinely kept watch on anyone suspected of going to Spain, recorded that Ronald JM Burghes had left Dover (without gas mask) aboard the Dunkirk ferry. They correctly ascertained that he was on his way to Spain as part of a large group of volunteers for the International Brigades.[31] Burghes continued on from Dunkirk to Paris, making good use of two things the majority of his working-class comrades lacked; fluent French and a passport. Within less than a week he had arrived in Spain and joined the first entirely 'British' unit of the International Brigades: Number One Company of the French Battalion of the 14th International Brigade.[32]

Following a brief period of training, Ronnie fought at the Battle of Lopera in Andalusia, which his mother had found so enchanting several years before. For Ronnie and his comrades, it was anything but, as they found themselves virtually defenceless against sustained Nationalist air attacks. Utterly overwhelmed, only the cool-thinking and commanding presence of their commander, the former British army officer George Nathan, enabled Ronnie and his fellow volunteers to retreat in some semblance of fighting order. After the battle, which had been a disaster for the Republican forces, the French commander of the International Brigades, André Marty, and Peter Kerrigan (see Chapter Seven), a senior British Communist Party representative in Spain, launched an investigation into the debacle. As a fluent French-speaker, Ronnie acted as interpreter for Kerrigan during the consequent trial of the Battalion's Commander, Lieutenant-Colonel Delasalle. The unfortunate Frenchman was convicted (almost certainly erroneously) of sabotage and summarily shot.[33]

Ronnie went on to join the British Battalion itself when it was formed at the end of the year as part of the new English-speaking 15th International Brigade. When it first went into action at Jarama, to the south of Madrid, on 12 February 1937, Ronnie was serving as a runner for the battalion command, a notoriously dangerous role. His captain remembered him clearly as 'very young and with dark irresponsible eyes that were usually full of amusement.'[34] Despite his young age, Ronnie was a brave and dedicated soldier, ferrying messages to the front line under enemy fire. Like the majority of those who served at Jarama, Ronnie was wounded; a bullet passed clean through his left arm, causing 'two neat holes', but without leaving any permanent injury.[35] He was one of the lucky ones, for one hundred and fifty-two men, a quarter of the entire battalion, were killed during the battle. Following several months of convalescence and sustained pressure from his mother, who argued convincingly that he had 'done his bit', Ronnie was repatriated in September 1937.

While Ronnie was serving in Spain, the initial conversation between Charlotte and Harry Pollitt (about Ronnie wanting to volunteer) had led to a meeting between JBS and the Communist leader to discuss the dangerous prospect of gas attacks in Spain.

This would encourage the scientist to make the first of three wartime visits to Republican Spain for, like his wife and stepson, JBS was a determined anti-fascist and supporter of the Spanish Republic.

JBS's first trip was made in December 1936, dressed rather curiously in a black leather jacket, breeches and a motorcycle cap.[36] He was put up in a flat sequestered by Dr Norman Bethune's Canadian Blood Transfusion Unit, whose members helped him try out gas masks. He also ran into a young English medical student called Archie Cochrane, who had volunteered for the Republican medical services. Later to be a distinguished epidemiologist, Cochrane sarcastically described the eminent Professor as 'JBS Haldane, who had failed to teach me chemistry at Cambridge.'[37] The International Brigade command provided Haldane with a pass allowing him to travel around Republican Spain and recommending him as an expert in protection against gas warfare.[38] So, despite the war-time restrictions, Haldane was able to hitch-hike around the country. *En route,* he checked in on his stepson Ronnie, who was by then working as Kerrigan's interpreter, before writing to let Charlotte know that he was well.[39] JBS also visited Alicante, travelling in a third-class carriage, surrounded by desperate refugees. Back in Madrid, JBS made a number of propaganda broadcasts in English for a local Republican short-wave radio station.[40] He visited the front line where he horrified the American writer and journalist Victoria Cowles with his perilously cavalier attitude to safety, sauntering around No Man's Land in full view of Nationalist snipers.[41] Nevertheless, Haldane survived to return home in January 1937, leaving behind his warm pyjamas for the South African film maker, Vera Elken, who he had rescued from a freezing hostel. Unfortunately, the pyjamas were big enough to wrap around her three times.[42]

Back home, JBS made a number of speeches in support of the Republic and the British volunteers in Spain, all carefully recorded by Special Branch.[43] He also became a fully paid-up, if clandestine, member of the Communist Party, though Special Branch suspected that he had long been a member in all but name.[44] He returned to Spain two months later, aiming to assess the quality and quantity of Republican air-raid shelter provision.[45] Dressed on this occasion in bourgeois flannels, the eccentric professor was at one stage arrested on suspicion of spying. Fortunately, he had a letter from Harry Pollitt confirming his loyalty and reliability: 'Haldane', Pollitt wrote, 'is one of the most distinguished scientists in Britian (*sic*), and an expert on all forms of combatting gas warfare.'[46] Once the unfortunate misunderstanding had been cleared up and he had been released with fulsome apologies, JBS prudently decided to dress in more acceptable, proletarian corduroy.

Having visited Bethune's transfusion unit in Madrid, where he agreed to donate blood, Haldane took the opportunity to spend several days with the British and American battalions in the trenches at Jarama. Haldane was alarmed to find that the fortifications had been constructed in the most primitive and dangerous manner, in 'long straight sections . . . so that a single shell could easily kill a dozen men.'[47] His alarm was not assuaged by an encounter with Walter Greenhalgh, a painter and decorator from Manchester, whose accommodation he was to share. Greenhalgh made up a bed for JBS in the billet in Morata de Tajuna he shared with his Dutch commander, Piet Jansen. On entering their quarters, JBS was disturbed to find it stacked with what looked suspiciously like artillery shells. Greenhalgh casually explained that Jansen had a habit of collecting unexploded Nationalist shells, in the firm belief that the large number of duds were a result of deliberate sabotage by Republican supporters in Nationalist arms factories. Jansen's intention, Greenhalgh explained to an increasingly horrified JBS, was to open one up to see if he could find a note expressing solidarity. 'You must be stark raving mad!' exclaimed the apoplectic scientist. 'There's enough explosive in there to blow the town to pieces!' 'We never saw him again,' confessed Greenhalgh.[48]

Given this experience, it's perhaps unsurprising that JBS was initially not greatly impressed with the quality of the British volunteers, 'most of whom had never fired a rifle, and some of whom thought that because they were volunteers they need not obey orders.' However, he was sufficiently understanding to realise that 'they were terribly exhausted ... [having] held the line for longer than any battalion.'[49] One London volunteer, a former waiter, recalled JBS scolding them about 'the merits and demerits of how we looked after ourselves and all about the health and welfare of people.'[50] It's difficult to imagine that the exhausted volunteers took much notice of the criticisms, nor of his advice on what to do in the event of a gas attack: 'He told us to piss on our hankies and put them over our mouths,' complained one disgusted Scottish volunteer.[51] The battalion's commander, the rough and ready Fred Copeman, certainly wasn't very flattering about Haldane:

He was a big fat fella, who wore a little leather jacket with only one button on. I don't think he ever changed his bloody shirt in four months, you know. And the button used to meet on his big fat old belly and it kind of stuck out. And he had funny, dirty old trousers.[52]

In fact, Copeman was not at all convinced that Haldane's presence at the front was helpful:

Old Haldane was there. More bloody nuisance than it was worth . . . he insisted on being on the front line when there was that and he had a little tiny revolver . . . He would hop on the step and hold this bloody thing and I would go up and every time I would say, 'What bloody good do you think you are? First of all you're taking two blokes' room, two blokes could sit where your fat arse is, so get down and get back to bloody . . .' I'm being told politically that JBS Haldane must not get killed, he's too valuable. Keep him out of the line. He was all the time in the bloody line. After about three months of it, I had a long talk with him. I said, 'Look, you've done enough bloody talking old fat man,' I said, 'you've got to go home. You've got to go home.'[53]

To be fair, JBS felt much the same way: 'Many hundreds of Englishmen have come out to Spain to help the cause of democracy since July 1936,' he wrote. 'Many have given their lives, others have shed their blood. Few or none can have been as useless as myself.' Suitably crestfallen, Haldane returned home in mid-April 1937.[54]

While Haldane was being plagued by existential doubts over his relevance to the struggle, the very much down-to-earth Charlotte was suffering from no such misgivings. In November 1936, she had fallen ill with pleurisy, perhaps brought on by the demands of her new foray into public speaking, though more likely due to a long evening's drinking with JBS following Ronnie's decision to go to Spain. As soon as she had recovered, she threw herself into work on behalf of the Spanish Republicans' cause, speaking at numerous meetings and helping raise money for the Dependents' Aid Committee Fund.[55] Like her husband, she also quietly joined the Communist Party.[56] In December, she wrote a piece for the Communist newspaper, the *Daily Worker*, admitting that she worried for her 'two men' in Spain, but begging for more support for Spain and the International Brigades: 'Everybody should talk, talk, talk of the Brigade,' she pleaded.[57]

The following spring Charlotte who, like Ronnie, was a fluent French-speaker, was approached by a representative of the Comintern (the Communist International) asking her to go to Paris to work as their representative. Based in a workers' café, in Place du Combat (now Place du Colonel Fabien) in the French capital's staunch left-wing district, Charlotte was to act as the point of contact for British volunteers arriving in the city. As volunteering was illegal and to avoid the attention of the gendarmes, Charlotte used the pseudonym 'Rita' and potential volunteers were instructed to ask the café staff for 'black lentils'. Unfortunately, this cunning subterfuge was rather undermined by the fact that the café was often crammed full of men, many of them kitted out in identical clothing, chatting away loudly in a babble of languages.[58] One of Charlotte's most challenging tasks was to try and keep the potential volunteers out of trouble and away from the familiar soldiers' haunts:

In order to avert the danger that any of the volunteers should get drunk, start brawls or become involved in them, or be lured into the neighbouring brothels, the leadership had decided that, on arrival, their spare cash should be confiscated, and that each man should receive no more than ten francs daily pocket money, to provide him with a packet of French cigarettes and a couple of *bocks*. Food and lodging they received free. The 'responsable' had to carry out these instructions, and also to give the men lectures—on the routine to be followed, and on the dangers of venereal disease.[59]

Many volunteers were deeply offended by her explicit lectures: 'I never heard a woman talk like that in my life, never,' exclaimed one horrified Scot.[60] Charlotte was fully aware of the men's discomfort, but had no time for those who 'were apt to gape or be embarrassed when given a solemn lecture, by a woman, on the dangers of the "gay city" and of venereal disease.'[61] Some of the more judgmental volunteers responded by spreading gossip, insinuating that she was having an affair with an American *responsable*. As she makes clear in her autobiography, the rumours were not without basis, for she had fallen head-over-heels for a young American activist, who she refers to as 'Jack':

He was young, in his thirties, but looked like a man who knew exactly what he was doing, where he was going, and for what purpose. His dark hair was brushed back from a high intellectual forehead, his eyes were dark, too, and large, the nose straight and small, the mouth beautiful, sensitive and obstinate. Our eyes met, as I opened the door, with one of those lightning flashes of recognition, as of a man and a woman who had waited for this precise moment all their lives.[62]

The rumours, together with her stormy and unconventional relationship with JBS and her scandalous divorce from Jack Burghes, led some narrow-minded bigots to sneeringly refer to her as 'Charlotte the harlot.'

However, disapprovals of Charlotte's role in Paris went beyond the prurient criticisms of Charlotte's personal life. Many volunteers were angered by her instructions that everyone must leave their luggage in Paris, despite assurances that it would be forwarded on to them. As many suspected, this was not a promise she was in a position to keep: 'We never saw our luggage again,' complained one Nottinghamshire volunteer, bitterly.[63] To make matters worse, Charlotte had been instructed to confiscate their passports, which were, as she knew, 'the only instrument which would make their legal return home possible.'[64] Ironically, when her own son was repatriated from Spain, Ronnie's journey was made considerably easier by his prudent refusal to surrender his passport.

Despite the criticisms, Charlotte remained in Paris for two months, returning home in May 1937. Back in London, she took up work for the International Brigades' Dependents' Aid Committee, visiting the homes of those in need such as Sally Maskey, whose husband Bert had been killed fighting at Jarama but had only received one solitary payment of five shillings.[65] Charlotte did what she could to help with families' claims for financial support, but the organisation always struggled to raise sufficient funds.[66] Fundraising rallies helped of course, and in July she helped organise a huge demonstration to mark a year since the outbreak of the civil war. Speakers included a number of former British volunteers, the Labour MP (and Basque refugee organiser) Leah Manning (see Chapter Two), and the popular Communist orator, Isabel Brown.[67] Also on the platform, doing his bit, was Charlotte's husband. The Spanish Republican cause was, of course, every much as important to him as it was to Charlotte. Consequently, after several months of travelling around Britain giving speeches in support, JBS decided to return to Spain for the third time. He left on 15 December 1937 and was given a big send-off from colleagues and students at University College, London. Mindful of the unfortunate misunderstanding on his previous visit, they helpfully presented the professor with a suitably innocuous corduroy jacket and trousers.[68]

The purpose of Haldane's third visit, he declared, was to examine Republican *refugios* (bomb-shelters) 'with a view to humbly (or not so humbly) suggesting that London might have as good ones as Valencia'. Just prior to his departure, JBS was approached by a Foreign Office official, asking whether he would be willing to pass on any of his observations and conclusions to the British government. This he declared he was quite prepared to do, though there is no evidence that the request was ever actually followed up. Accompanying JBS was Harry Pollitt, who was determined to pay his respects to the British Battalion.[69] Consequently, one week before Christmas, the duo arrived at the British reserve positions in the little village of Mas de las Matas, lying in a pleasant valley just over 100km south-east of Zaragoza.[70] Their visit was a very welcome surprise, not least because Pollitt was accompanied by cigarettes and more than 500 letters from home. 'God bless him,' wrote one grateful soldier.[71] To welcome their eminent guests, the British laid on an impromptu concert with sketches and music and the Manchester boxer Joe Norman performed a traditional Russian folk song, despite the groans of his comrades in the battalion.[72]

On Christmas Eve, a farewell parade was held for Pollitt and Haldane prior to their departure for the convalescence hospital in Benicassim, on the Mediterranean coast. At the hospital they were greeted by the London volunteer George Watkins who, having falsely told his recruiters that he was 22 rather than 16, had been badly wounded the previous August.[73] Wishing Watkins a speedy recovery (he was eventually repatriated in July 1938), Pollitt and Haldane returned to Mas de las Matas, arriving on Christmas Day. They watched on proudly as their compatriots handed out presents to local children, before they were asked to be the battalion's guests for Christmas dinner. 'So ended Christmas Day, 1937,' wrote Pollitt. 'Victory will have been won for Republican Spain long before Christmas, 1938,' he predicted confidently.[74]

Watching the members of the British Battalion on parade and in training, JBS was impressed at how far they had come since his previous visit, having transformed themselves from 'a group of extremely brave, but untrained men, into a unit which would be a credit to any professional army.'[75] They would need to be, for they were about to join other Republican forces fighting in the mountains surrounding the remote provincial capital of Teruel, captured by Republican forces on 8 January 1938. In a typical hyperbolic flourish, Pollitt proclaimed that the capture of the remote provincial capital 'will have the same significance as Waterloo, Sedan and the decisive battles on the Western Front in the last world war.'[76] It was, in fact, nothing of the kind. In the coldest Spanish winter for many years, snow lay waist deep and soldiers were more likely to be killed by cold than by enemy fire. Despite Pollitt's bullish confidence, the British fighters and the Republican army were powerless to prevent Franco's forces from counter-attacking and recapturing Teruel.

Having spent 12 days in Spain, Pollitt and Haldane returned home on 6 January 1938.[77] Shortly after his return, JBS wrote an introduction to a Dependents' Aid Committee leaflet, telling of the appalling carnage being inflicted by the Nationalists' bombing of civilians. He railed against Francoist propaganda which, he believed, was being blindly reproduced in 'the British reactionary press' and duping the British people into believing the canard 'that loyal Spain is the scene of massacres, governmental terrorism and unspeakable orgies.'[78] He concluded with an impassioned plea, astutely situating the war in Spain within a wider context:

These men are fighting, not only for Spain, but for Abyssinia, for China, for the rights of British merchant shipping. We appeal for their support, not merely to democrats of all parties and of none, but to all men and women to whom the unprovoked slaughter of defenceless people and the open defiance of international law is hateful.[79]

Following a desperate personal request from Sam Wild and Bob Cooney, the military and political commanders of the British Battalion, JBS redoubled his efforts, delivering some 100 lectures over the following twelve months.[80] Nevertheless, he still managed to find the time and energy to join the *Daily Worker* as their Science Correspondent. He would hold the position for 13 years, producing over 300 articles that gave extremely lucid explanations of complex scientific issues.[81] Whether he found any time for a personal life is difficult to know. Besides, Charlotte was equally dedicated and just as JBS was returning from Spain, Charlotte was herself preparing to go. She had agreed to act as guide and interpreter for the famous American baritone singer (and Communist), Paul Robeson, and his wife Essie, a fellow-activist and anthropologist. As ever, the trio's departure for Spain via Dunkirk on 21 January 1938 was carefully recorded by Special Branch.[82]

On their arrival in Spain, the world-famous Robesons were honoured by the provision of a large Buick in which to travel, along with a young Republican officer as *aide-de-camp*. Charlotte accompanied them on their visit to Barcelona, where she managed a snatched conversation with her American 'Jack'. They would never meet again, for she later discovered that he had been killed fighting in Spain.[83] After Barcelona, the trio continued on to Valencia and Madrid, staying in what luxury and comfort the war-torn Republic was still able to provide. However, Charlotte felt very uncomfortable enjoying these hotel comforts, while the population of Madrid faced starvation and the constant prospect of death from the devastating Nationalist bombing. Evidence of the destruction was particularly apparent in the city's new University district, which had been the scene of bitter fighting in November 1936:

> The sight of these fine, well-built apartment houses, now blasted and shredded, of still furnished rooms hanging drunkenly by a few girders, of broken toys and children's picture-books lying forlornly in the gutters, of the new University buildings, now hopelessly wrecked, brought home vividly the beastliness, the sordid wickedness of modern aerial warfare on defenceless civilians.[84]

Charlotte left the devastated Spanish capital behind her, accompanying the Robesons on a visit to the British volunteers' training base at Tarazona de la Mancha, near the Brigades' main headquarters in Albacete. Just as Harry Pollitt had done, they took along items guaranteed to endear them to the Britons fighting in Spain: letters from home, plus 'several pounds of chocolate and eight thousand cigarettes.' Their packages safely delivered to the grateful volunteers, they continued to follow Pollitt and JBS's footsteps, visiting the convalescence hospital on the Mediterranean coast at Benicassim, before returning to Barcelona. When the Robesons flew home, Charlotte remained in

Republican Spain, accompanying the senior British Communist, Bill Rust, on a trip to see Fred Copeman, who was in hospital having fallen ill with appendicitis. They eventually tracked him down in Alcañiz (some twenty kilometres north of Mas de las Matas) where, despite the 'indescribable physical conditions' the tough and resilient Copeman was slowly recuperating. He was repatriated that April, still suffering from complications associated with his illness.[85]

Perhaps aware that her husband had paid visits to the front, Charlotte was determined to do likewise. She headed to Teruel, and cajoled Vladimir Čopić, the Bulgarian commander of the 15th International Brigade, into allowing her to visit the British positions on a cliffside overlooking a valley outside Teruel. There she encountered a number of volunteers she had met in Paris the previous spring and delivered a heartfelt speech, demonstrating her support for their sacrifices. The soldiers were clearly moved, for they gave her a standing ovation and, before she left, members of the Machine-Gun Company presented her with an empty cartridge case. Placed carefully inside was a small piece of paper personally inscribed by all 32 members of the unit.[86]

With their cheers ringing in her ears, Charlotte set off for Barcelona, where she hoped to meet with Dolores Ibárruri, *La Pasionaria* (the passionflower), the legendary Republican orator and Communist deputy for Asturias who had become the personification of Spanish democracy's struggle against fascism. After several days' wait, Charlotte was finally granted an audience with the Republican talisman. In person, Ibárruri was evidently every bit as impressive as her reputation: 'She had' wrote Charlotte, 'a matronly but magnificent figure . . . [and] bore herself with unselfconscious nobility and dignity'. A somewhat overawed Charlotte was highly flattered when Ibárruri congratulated her on her proficiency in Spanish. The audience with *La Pasionaria* was the highlight of Charlotte's trip, which had already strongly bolstered her emotional link with the life-or-death struggle of the Spanish Republic. The sacrifices of the foreign volunteers, the murderous bombing of civilians, the desperate shortages of food and medical supplies, were all things she would never forget. When she finally crossed the border,

Charlotte was devastated to see huge quantities of food trapped on the French side of the border.[87]

She returned home energised and more determined than ever and was therefore distraught when Harry Pollitt pressured her, very much against her wishes, to relinquish her role as organiser in the Dependents' Aid Committee. Pollitt had decided that Fred Copeman, who had just returned from Spain, would be a more effective front-person. Swallowing her disappointment, she continued her fund-raising efforts. Though she and JBS were becoming increasingly estranged, unlikely to have been helped by the long absences, Charlotte suggested to the Party leadership that the two should write a book together recounting their experiences of aerial bombardment in Spain. This led to the publication of *ARP*, a trenchant criticism of the British Government's woeful lack of air-raid provision.[88] As JBS declared in the preface and in a number of talks and meetings held around the country, it was his hope that 'the people of Britain will never see what I have seen in Spain.'[89] His vigorous campaigning for better air-raid shelters led to an exasperated report by a representative of the Ministry of Supply, complaining that Haldane was 'stirring up trouble . . . he could do far more valuable work for the proletariat as a co-operator,' he argued, 'rather than by riding his "hobby-horse" to death, and antagonising the authorities.' The Ministry's fundamental problem, however, as he privately admitted, was that Haldane was 'very clever, and quite often perfectly right.'[90]

Meanwhile, freed up from her aid-Spain committee responsibilities, Charlotte agreed to be a delegate to the Comintern's Congress against War and Fascism in Marseilles. There she delivered a barnstorming speech applauding the 'heroism and stoicism' of the women of Spain. This so inspired a Chinese delegate that she asked if Charlotte might be prepared to offer her country similar support, following the Japanese invasion of Manchuria the previous summer. Charlotte agreed immediately, convinced that 'the British Labour movement was in strong sympathy with China's heroic and desperate struggle against Japanese aggression.'[91] She was one of many Spanish Republican supporters to take up the Chinese cause, though in fact support actually came from across the political spectrum in Britain, where public opinion tended to be less divided than it had been over Spain.[92] With Mao Zedong's Communists and Chiang Kai Shek's Nationalists fighting alongside each other to repel the Japanese invaders, the conflict appeared to be less a fractured civil war, than a straightforward national struggle for survival.[93]

Consequently, in October 1938, while the International Brigades were waiting to be withdrawn from Spain, Charlotte joined a Comintern-sponsored delegation visit to China. Provided with accreditation by the Labour-supporting *Daily Herald*, her mission gained the support of both the Labour leader, Clement Attlee, and the Liberal chief, Sir Archibald Sinclair. However, when she arrived in China, it was quickly made apparent to Charlotte that she would not be free to travel around with impunity, visiting the front line, as she had been able to do in Spain. Other things, however, were not so different, not least the shocking conditions in which much of the population existed. China, Charlotte observed, was still essentially a feudal country, with millions of farmers and peasants living in 'primitive conditions; for the most part illiterate, underfed and under-privileged, whose hardest struggles during the past centuries were waged against the inimical forces of nature on a scale unimagined in Europe.'[94] The country faced acute public health issues: measles was widespread and there was a fifty per cent infant mortality rate derived mainly from tetanus, itself a result of the widespread practice of cutting the umbilical cord with an unsterilised knife.

Two months of giving speeches across the country, travelling by all manner of transport, left Charlotte thoroughly exhausted. Consequently, rather than going on to Canada and America to deliver more speeches as the Comintern representative wanted, Charlotte decided to return home to recuperate, arriving in London in the icy winter of 1938. Initially, Charlotte hoped to raise awareness of the Chinese people's plight, but she quickly realised that 'China was too far away' and most Britons were preoccupied with the precarious situation in Europe, where the Munich agreement had clearly made a European war more, rather than less likely. Besides, Charlotte's laudable aspirations were anyway dashed by health problems. While she had remained remarkably healthy during her trip to the tropics, the return to a freezing, wintry London hit her hard and she fell successively ill with tracheitis (a severe infection of the windpipe), German measles and two separate bouts of influenza. Her personal life was no healthier and she had got to the point of contemplating divorce. Unwisely, she made the mistake of confiding in Bill Rust, who sanctimoniously informed her that 'the Party would not for one minute tolerate a divorce between two comrades whose partnership, in addition to the usefulness of their individual services, was of immense propaganda value.'[95] Reluctantly, Charlotte 'dropped the subject', though she and JBS effectively separated.

Besides, other matters dwarfed her personal problems. In January 1939, with Barcelona having fallen to Franco's Nationalist forces, it was clear that the Spanish Republic's defeat was inevitable. Franco's triumphant declaration of victory on 1 April united the Haldane family in misery. Four months later, the signing of a non-aggression pact between Hitler and Stalin seemed to go against everything that they had believed in Spain. So when Harry Pollitt responded to the declaration of war in September by announcing that the Communist Party would support the war against Nazi Germany, it came as a huge relief. As Charlotte put it, 'all those who had fought in Spain, or taken part in the anti-Nazi struggle in any way, responded with enthusiasm to Pollitt's declaration. I know I did.'[96] But this relief quickly turned to bitter disappointment when, following Moscow's instructions, the British Party decreed that the conflict was an imperialist, not anti-fascist war, and that Communists must oppose it. Incensed, Charlotte began to question the authority of the Communist Party, seeing it as an agent of Soviet power, rather than a defender of 'liberty, freedom [and] democracy'. However, having already contemplated one painful separation in her life, she was not yet ready to consider another.

She was not the only member of the family trying to accommodate contradictory viewpoints. As a loyal and disciplined Communist, JBS had written a long letter in defence of the Nazi-Soviet pact to the *New Statesman*. He was a relentless critic of the British Government, forcefully expressing himself via the pages of the *Daily Worker*. However, within two weeks of the declaration of war, he was also working for the British Government's Ministry of Information, and by the end of the year he was an advisor to the Air Ministry's top secret Air Intelligence. This highly secretive work developed from Haldane's involvement in an investigation into a disastrous accident on *HMS Thetis* on 1 June 1939, in which ninety-nine men aboard the submarine lost their lives. JBS had been approached by the Amalgamated Engineers' Union, who had lost 19 members in the accident, to investigate the potential causes and provide expert evidence at the official inquiry.[97] He worked *pro bono*, donating £65.00 of his fee to the International Brigade Association and the remaining £40.00 to the ARP Coordinating Committee.[98]

To assist his research, JBS recruited a number of the former International Brigaders, including Bill Alexander, a Chemistry graduate from Reading University who had both commanded the British Battalion and served as a political commissar. The three other veterans were the Irish Communist, Patrick Duff, George Ives (who had trained as a radio operator in Moscow) and another former political commissar, Donald Renton.[99] However, the principal subject for the experiments was JBS's long-standing guinea pig: himself. Haldane's seemingly irresponsible practice was partly a means of avoiding the bureaucracy associated with testing on animals, though it was also a consequence of his experiences working alongside his father, John Scott Haldane who, in keeping with the family motto 'Suffer', had done exactly the same when conducting his own experiments.[100]

The main purpose of JBS's research was to prevent another disaster by examining individuals' reactions to atmospheric pressure and carbon dioxide and to establish the most effective way to escape from a sunken submarine. His experiment involved sealing the volunteers into a chamber containing a high level of CO_2, which was then further increased. As George Ives recounted, within an hour of beginning the experiment, all the

162

subjects were 'gasping for breath, panting and perspiring.'[101] It was especially gruelling and dangerous for Paddy Duff, who was still convalescing from wounds he had received in Spain.[102] It was most unpleasant work:

I was on one occasion immersed in melting ice for thirty-five minutes, breathing air containing 6½ per cent of carbon dioxide, and during the latter part of the period also under ten atmospheres' pressure. One of our subjects has burst a lung, but is recovering; six have been unconscious on one or more occasions; one has had convulsions.[103]

JBS himself suffered seizures from hypoxia on a number of occasions and one of his teeth exploded when he compressed too quickly.[104] Worse still, a helium bubble trapped in his spinal cord resulted in a back injury that plagued JBS for the rest of his life.[105] While Haldane took most of the serious risks, all of the participants endangered their lives, just as they had in Spain. As Haldane explained, 'I chose these men as colleagues because I had no doubt of their courage and devotion.'[106]

At the official enquiry in the summer of 1939, Charlotte was asked by a *Daily Sketch* journalist if she were being brave by not worrying unduly over JBS's experiments. Her reply was typically no-nonsense: 'Why should I worry about him? He knows extremely well what he is doing. I'm just confident—not brave.'[107] How much her blasé apparent lack of concern was a response to the collapse of her unhappy marriage is not clear. Certainly, Harry Pollitt was aware of Charlotte's miserable home life and he encouraged her to get involved in political work as a diversion. In May, she joined the local Air Raid Precautions Emergency Committee though, as she frankly admitted, her acceptance was probably due more to the reputation of her husband's expertise than hers. Nevertheless, Charlotte threw herself into the work with typical determination, quickly grasping the huge task they faced: how to provide bomb shelters for the 177,000 residents of St Pancras.

Having seen the effects of bombing in Spain, Charlotte was well aware of the devastation and suffering it could wreak. Yet she was honest enough to admit that she personally found the danger intensely thrilling. During air-raids on London, she would often remain above stairs, coolly playing the piano in her drawing-room. On some nights she would even wander outside:

> A friend and myself made our way down to the Embankment. A large paint factory on the South Bank was ablaze. It was a night of full moon. The river fire service was directing sparkling streams of white and pluming water on to the crimson and golden furnace on the bank; the indifferent and serene heavens poured silver moonlight on the scene. We were so enthralled by its beauty that not until a bomb dropped so close behind that we were sprayed by a shower of broken glass from an adjacent lamp-post did I realise it might possibly be better to refrain from such foolhardy sight-seeing.[108]

JBS entertained no such irresponsible foolery, taking shelter in the basement once the bombs began to fall. This would have reassured Admiral Sir Max Horton, Commander of the Royal Navy's Submarine Service, for whom the eminent scientist was engaged in top-secret work. In August 1940, Haldane and his Cambridge colleague, the biochemist Martin Case (their former lodger who JBS successfully fought to keep from being conscripted as an officer), began work in Plymouth investigating how an individual could exit and re-enter a submarine while remaining undetected under the surface. Experimenting mainly on himself, Case and Helen Spurway, a former biology student, JBS also drew once again on his Spanish Civil War connections. The former guinea-pig, Patrick Duff, was joined by three other Irish veterans: John Larmour, a sailor, who had been wounded at Lopera in December 1936; a company political commissar, Jim Prendergast and another former British Battalion commander, Patrick 'Paddy' O'Daire.[109] Others to join his work included the former premier of the Spanish Republic, Juan Negrín, and Hans Kahle, a German veteran of the International Brigades.[110]

The work was every bit as dangerous and unpleasant as the earlier Thetis experiments had been. Cramped into a five-foot square tank, with condensation dripping from the walls and ceiling, Haldane and Case were submerged at the bottom of

Plymouth harbour. In addition to the dangers of asphyxia and hypoxia, Haldane and his team subjected themselves to the extremes of cold that unfortunate submariners could be exposed to in an emergency. The miserable combination frequently led to them slipping into unconsciousness. However, the experiments were to prove invaluable, demonstrating that by using oxygen and soda lime to absorb carbon dioxide, it was possible for individuals to remain in the mini-submarines for up to three days with no serious effects. This proved key in enabling underwater attacks such as that on the *Tirpitz* (the sister ship of the *Bismarck*) in September 1943 and in the clearing of underwater mines in Normandy ports before the D-Day landings.[111]

While JBS was, literally, immersed in his secret work for the Admiralty, Charlotte continued her work for the Air-Raid Precaution Committee until the dramatic Nazi invasion of the Soviet Union in June 1941. This was, of course, a seismic and transformative event for Communists, for it promptly brought to an end Moscow's opposition to the war. It also had a significant personal consequence for Charlotte, for it offered an opportunity to pick up her journalistic career. The editor of the *Daily Sketch*, Sydney Carroll, offered her a job as Britain's first female war correspondent. It was a shrewd decision, for Charlotte's Party contacts proved invaluable, allowing her to obtain a visa to permit her to travel to Moscow several days ahead of journalists working for rival national newspapers.

Consequently, having endured a long, dangerous trip by ship to Archangel on the northern Russian coast, Charlotte made her way overland to Moscow, where she was housed in the upmarket National Hotel. Eager to report on the heroic defence of the Russian Motherland, Charlotte quickly found herself frustrated, not just by the infamous Soviet bureaucracy and obsessive secrecy, but by an important cultural difference of opinion over what exactly constituted 'news'. Charlotte encountered nothing resembling her notions of journalistic practice:

All the correspondents . . . were frenziedly trying to obtain the sort of news their papers wanted, and by which they all understood the same things—facts, figures, interviews, information obtained directly from the Army leaders, without censorship or intervention from the political commissars. Every endeavour was made to see that they did not obtain it.[112]

Yet, despite the official intransigence, Charlotte still displayed an 'unshakeable enthusiasm and utterly uncritical attitude' towards Stalin's Russia, which infuriated her colleagues. However, her zealous enthusiasm was to suffer a number of nasty shocks. The first came when she attempted to reconnect with the geneticist, Nikolai Vavilov, who had hosted Charlotte and JBS during their visit to Russia in 1928. She could find no trace of him and enquiries only led to warnings that she should not ask too many questions, that there had been 'many changes' since her previous visit.[113] Her unease increased when she encountered a young Soviet pilot who had fought in Spain, who revealed to her that all veterans had been warned not to discuss their experiences. Worse was to come during a visit to the small village of Dorogobuzh, 50km east of Smolensk. The Russian village had recently been bombed by German aircraft, but it was not the devastation inflicted by Hitler's Luftwaffe that she found so disturbing, it was the shuffling lines of miserable, destitute peasants, clutching their pathetic rations of bread:

> The scene I had just witnessed, more tragic and powerful than any engraving to Dante's Inferno by Doré or Blake, seemed to mock my facile and naïve optimism, my wishful dreaming, and to accuse me of bearing false witness to my own people.[114]

Observing the scene, a Russian Red Army Officer admitted to a shocked Charlotte that, contrary to the relentlessly upbeat reports in the British *Daily Worker*, many Russian peasants were not enthusiastic about Stalin's collectivisation of their smallholdings. In October, with her faith in Stalin's regime now plagued by doubts and with German forces bearing down on Moscow, Charlotte decided that it was time for her to leave. Having secured a flight to Archangel, she found herself trapped by a heavy blizzard and only the help of the British Ambassador, Sir Stafford Cripps (who she knew from their mutual work for the Spanish Republic) managed to secure her a place on a train to Kuibyishev (now called Samara), 800km east of Moscow. There the final vestiges of her belief in the Soviet system received their coup de grace when she witnessed a young woman 'carrying her child, dead from starvation, to the graveyard'. Utterly disgusted, Charlotte vowed that:

> Never again would I get on any platform, anywhere, at any time, to use my oratorical or persuasive gifts to convince an audience of working-class men, women, and children, that the Soviet Union was the hope of the toilers of the world.[115]

Despite this Damascene conversion, Charlotte avoided any overt criticisms of the regime in her article in *Russian Newsreel*, convinced that it was 'neither the time nor the place to furnish the Nazis with gratuitous material for anti-Soviet propaganda.' However, her determination to sever her connections with the Party remained undimmed, even if it led to contradictory emotions. On the one hand, she was relieved to be free from the binding constraints of the Party line, yet, on the other, there was both a lingering guilt at having 'abandoned the cause' for which she had dedicated several years of her life, together with a sense of disloyalty to the people she'd known who had fought and died in Spain. With this guilt came bitterness and great anger towards the leaders of the Communist Party, the 'paid agitators and propagandists' who, she was now convinced, had persuaded British workers to submit 'to a modern form of Oriental despotism'. Nursing her guilt and anger, she returned home on a British destroyer, arriving in Glasgow on 22 November 1941.

Back home, she revealed to JBS what she had seen in Russia and in China: the disappearances of their friends, the grinding poverty, the lack of education and persecution of much of the population, and the resentment of the peasantry towards the enforced collectivisation of their landholdings. Yet despite having declared that he was 'anxiously awaiting the return of his wife from Russia so that he could learn something of what Soviet life was in war time', JBS simply did not believe her.[116] It marked the final end of their tortuous relationship. They separated 'without acrimony' in 1942 and were divorced on 26 November 1945. The Professor and his colleague and former student, Helen Spurway, were married quietly shortly afterwards.[117]

Word of Charlotte's political disillusionment soon spread. She received an extremely frosty phone call from Bill Rust, 'suggesting' that she should come into the *Daily Worker* offices to 'discuss the situation'. During their meeting, he accused Charlotte of having been 'got at'. She laughed out loud at the idea, realising that there was no way she would be able to explain her newfound revulsion for the Soviet regime. Trying to limit any potential fallout, Rust asked her if she planned to write an account of her time in Stalin's Russia and, if so, would she accept Party collaboration in her book? She politely declined. 'And that', she declared, 'was the end of my connection with the Communist Party of Great Britain.'[118]

The Party's response was typically brutal. Immediately depicted as a traitor and a renegade, Charlotte was accused of Trotskyism and shunned by former friends and comrades. A nasty smear revived the 'Charlotte the harlot' slur, snidely insinuating that her anger was due to sexual frustration, having been unable to find a lover during her Russian visit. More significantly, she was dismissed from her position at the *Daily Sketch* and found herself unable to find work as a journalist. While radical newspaper owners rejected her due to her dramatic political transformation, many Conservatives were unconvinced by her new-found anti-Stalinism, suspicious that it might be some form of Communist ruse. After some time she managed to find some freelance work for 'a small woman's paper,' writing articles 'in the simplest style, dealing with world and current affairs' though she did later replace George Orwell as Talks Producer on the BBC's Eastern Service.[119]

Conversely, Charlotte's split from the Party seemed to only encourage JBS to become more dedicated. During the Communist Party's national conference in London in May 1942, he announced that he had at long last formally joined the Party, though he later admitted that he had been a member in all but name since the Spanish Civil War.[120] He continued to be involved with the veterans and their association, speaking at an IBA

(International Brigade Association) rally in Manchester in November 1942, where he continued to blame the British Government's policy of non-intervention for the Spanish Republic's defeat.[121] Unfortunately, JBS's new role as 'one of the most active members of the Communist Party', in the words of one Special Branch report, offered an opportunity for those in the Admiralty and Security Services who were unhappy at his use of Spanish Civil War veterans—and Communists—in secret work.[122]

On first sight, it appears strange that someone of his political views was ever allowed to work within some of the government's most secretive departments. However, JBS was no fool and his advocates in the intelligence community and government were fully aware of that and confident that he possessed enough integrity and discretion to not to give away secrets.[123] Whether their trust was misplaced is a matter of debate. Recent research on the secret messages exchanged between Soviet embassies and consulates and Moscow, known as the VENONA intercepts, suggest that Haldane passed the Russians a copy of his secret report for the Admiralty relating to the length of time a man could stay underwater.[124] It's also clear that MI5 had learnt, via a wiretap, that Bill Rust was aware that JBS was working with midget submarines and had discussed it with Harry Pollitt.[125] Concerns were such that, during a secret meeting held in November 1943, his critics argued that Haldane's work had become a 'hindrance to the programme of work by military personnel.' Despite a number of supporting letters arguing that his research was an invaluable contribution to the war effort, it was decided that 'the personality of Professor Haldane and the presence of his assistants . . . compromises the smooth working of the Admiralty Experimental Diving Unit.' The volunteers were dismissed and Haldane's secret work was summarily curtailed.[126]

However, by the end of the war, at the same time that JBS was publicly expressing loyalty to the Party, in private he was having serious doubts and actually got as far as drafting a letter of resignation. Certainly, senior members of the Party were concerned at Haldane's increasing tendency to make 'anti-

Russian remarks', that is to criticise the Soviet geneticist Trofim Lysenko, whose theories chimed with Communist ideology, but that Haldane knew were manifestly false.[127] By criticising Lysenko's theories as 'illogical, contradictory and unscientific' Haldane was deviating fundamentally from the Communist line and stretching to breaking point any tolerance towards aberrant ideas.[128] When, in early 1949, Haldane claimed to be too busy to visit the Soviet Academy of Science in Moscow, a furious Harry Pollitt banned him from undertaking any Party work, apart from his articles on science for the *Daily Worker*.[129] While Haldane's prestige meant that the Party allowed him a degree of latitude, there were limits.

By the end of 1949, JBS had decided to leave the Party but was determined to do so without creating a huge furore. In December of that year, furious that his articles were being edited without permission, Haldane complained vehemently that he was not being allowed to make 'a balanced case' on Lysenko. Fully aware that his views were out of step with the Party line, he resigned his position as Chairman of the Editorial Board of the *Daily Worker*. His final article for the Communist paper, a criticism of eugenics, appeared in August 1950.[130] The same year, he resigned from the Medical Research Council, after the Admiralty refused to allow them to see important and highly secret details (necessary for underwater physiology research projects), while Haldane was a member. Some recompense came a few years later, with the award of the Huxley Memorial Medal of the Royal Anthropological Institute in 1956. The following year, Haldane decided to emigrate to India, ostensibly as a protest over Suez, though he had, in fact, been thinking of retiring there for several years. The British climate undoubtedly played its part: 'Sixty years in socks is enough', he grumbled.[131] After several years working in India, in late 1963 JBS was diagnosed with cancer of the colon and he died on 1 December the following year. Charlotte survived him, though by 1968 a degenerative eye condition had left her almost blind, unable to read or write or enjoy the view from her St John's Wood flat.[132] A life-long smoker, Charlotte Haldane died of pneumonia on 16 March, 1969, aged 74.

During the last few years, interest in the work and life of Professor JBS Haldane has experienced a resurgence. The geneticist Krishna Dronamaraju, who worked with Haldane in India, published a new biography of the famous geneticist, to complement Ronald Clark's, which was published shortly after the Professor's death. A new exposé by Gavan Tredoux was published in 2018, followed shortly afterwards by Samanth Subramanian's 2020 study. The Genetics Society and the John Innes Centre in Norwich, a research centre for plants and microbial sciences, both hold annual lectures in JBS's honour. And Haldane's prolific contributions to the fields of genetics, population research and abiogenesis (the origins of life), stand on their own merits. He remains eminently quotable, whether quipping about 'God's inordinate fondness for beetles', or his dismissal of religion's distrust of scientific advances: 'There is no great invention,' he argued, 'from fire to flying, which has not been hailed as an insult to some god.'[133]

Yet, one insightful biography published in 1998 aside, very little has been published about Charlotte Haldane. 'For all her accomplishment, she has been remembered as the talented, but conceited, abrasive and cocksure wife of JBS Haldane,' complained her biographer.[134] Among the many interviews and memoirs of the volunteers in Spain, she all too regularly appears either as 'Rita' or under her insulting nickname. The description by Tony MacLean, the political censor in Spain, is one of the more positive, but hardly flattering: '[an] enormous, tough, highly-sexed, good-looking, middle-aged, Don's wife.'[135] In fairness, MacLean did acknowledge that she was 'very capable.' It's worth pointing out that Charlotte and her journalistic and literary talents lay behind much of JBS's success as a populariser of science.

Their relationship was as stormy as it was unconventional for the time. British Battalion commander Fred Copeman always saw their relationship as 'free and easy' but was careful to point out that 'they were two very good people, you know.' [136] Whatever the problems that existed between them, they both wanted to help make the world a better place. And while tying their colours to Stalin's mast was something they later came to regret, their enthusiasm for the Republican cause remained untarnished. Neither Charlotte nor JBS lived to see Spain's (mostly) peaceful transition to democracy, though Charlotte's son Ronnie did. After his return from Spain, he spoke at meetings in support of Spain organised by the Dependents' Aid Committee and was on the board of the Young Communist magazine, *Challenge*.[137] Having enlisted in the Territorial Army in October 1939, Ronnie was commissioned into the British Army in July 1940. He served as a Second Lieutenant in the Wiltshire Regiment and saw active service in Normandy in 1944, until he was wounded in the lung during the Battle for Caen.[138] Married during the war, he and his wife Betty had two children: John Ronald, born in 1943 and daughter Louie, born six years later. Ronnie remained a supporter of the cause he had fought for in Spain for the rest of his life, regularly attending commemorations of the International Brigade Association.[139] When he died in May 1997, Bill Alexander, the IBA's Secretary, warmly praised Ronnie's long and dedicated contribution to Spain and the anti-fascist cause.[140] It was a deserving tribute—and one that could equally have been said about his mother and his step-father, the pioneering feminist writer, Charlotte Franken and her ex-husband the eminent scientist and polymath, Professor JBS Haldane.

Chapter Six
Out of Orwell's Shadow: Stafford Cottman

Sitting within the Orwell archive in University College London lies a photograph of the celebrated author captured shortly after his return from fighting in the civil war in Spain. Entitled 'On the lawn at Letchworth', the image was taken in August 1937 at the summer camp of the Independent Labour Party (ILP), a radical party to the left of the Labour Party which had been formed at the end of the nineteenth century. Standing alongside George Orwell are four other members of the ILP who volunteered to go to Spain: the Party's organiser, John McNair, two Scottish former militiamen, Douglas Moyle and Jock Braithwaite (or Branthwaite) and, immediately to Orwell's right, a young man from Bath called Stafford Cottman. More informally dressed than his companions, with cigarette in hand, he is by far the shortest of the group, dwarfed by Orwell, and in the author's shadow. It's a glaring metaphor for the relative influence that the pair and their accounts of fighting in the Spanish Civil War have had on knowledge of, and attitudes to, the conflict.

Years after the end of the civil war, when Cottman was interviewed for the Imperial War Museum's Sound Archive, he remarked mildly that, though he had been a Trade Unionist and member of the Labour Party all his life, almost all interviewers were interested not so much in him, but his famous comrade.[1] But if Cottman lived his life in the author's shadow, he was not the only one. This is probably true of all the British volunteers in the Spanish Civil War, for Orwell's *Homage to Catalonia* has come to be, by some margin, the most widely read book in English on the civil war. Consequently, it has become the prism through which many people view the Spanish conflict. This is unfortunate, for despite the memoir's undoubted merits, it shouldn't be seen as a history of the Spanish Civil War, nor as representative of the experiences of most of the volunteers in Spain.[2] The majority of volunteers from Britain served in the International Brigades, of course, but Cottman was one of around forty to serve with the ILP section who fought alongside the Spanish POUM militia.

Over the years, there have been several articles and books on the ILP volunteers, notably by the historian Chris Hall, all of which make some reference to Cottman.[3] Nevertheless and despite the existence of an interview in the Imperial War Museum, very few people know much about the young ILP volunteer, nor about his experiences in Spain. His story deserves wider recognition, partly because he was one of the youngest volunteers from Britain—the ILP leader Fenner Brockway affectionately referred to him as 'a boy with the heart of a giant'— but also because there are so few accounts by ILP volunteers.[4]

Born in Southampton on 6 March 1918, Stafford Leslie Charles Cottman was lucky to survive infancy at all, for he almost perished in the infamous flu pandemic, which saw more than 50 million deaths across the globe and could be particularly lethal to young children.[5] To his parents' huge relief Stafford survived to grow up in the Hampshire city, then one of the country's largest and busiest commercial ports and 'gateway to the empire'. Cottman came from a family of mariners: his grandfather and great-grandfather had been sailors and his brothers Neville and Peter both followed in the tradition. So too had his father, who had appalled his middle-class family by marrying the parlour maid before running off to sea to become the captain of a Russian oil tanker.[6] When Stafford's father died in a motor accident on the docks, his mother raised the three boys in what a family friend described as 'an atmosphere of artistic endeavour.'[7]

In 1926, the year of the General Strike, Stafford's family moved from Southampton to Barking in east London. The East End was then a hive of political and religious non-conformism and the eight-year-old Cottman joined the Socialist Sunday School, which followed the teachings of Keir Hardie, Karl Marx and William Morris. The young students were taught 'the ten precepts', essentially a socialist version of the ten commandments, earnestly reciting that 'we desire to be just and loving to all our fellow men and women, to work together as brothers and sisters and so help to form a new society with justice as its foundation and love its law.' Pious as it may sound to a modern, more cynical audience, it appealed strongly to the young Cottman, who thought 'it seemed a very worthwhile thing to believe in.'[8] Alongside Sunday School, Cottman joined the Guild of Youth, the Independent Labour Party's junior wing. Though Cottman later derided it as 'almost monastic', the Guild of Youth, like the Young Communist League, was very much geared towards providing enjoyable activities for young people, while gently preparing them for—and guiding them towards— joining the adult organisation. Fun though it could be, the organisation was decidedly political and, during the 1930s, many members were involved in noisy and sometimes violent protests against Sir Oswald Mosley's fascists.

At the age of fourteen, Cottman's personal anti-fascism was crystallised by his presence at a meeting at Kingsway Hall in central London, then the base of the West London Mission of the Methodist Church, where (later Lord) Donald Soper was Minister. During the meeting, a number of German refugees recounted sickening stories of the brutality being meted out to Jews, Communists, Trade Unionists and others not seen as worthy of membership of Hitler's Third Reich. Nazi instruments of torture such as steel whips and rubber truncheons were revealed to a horrified audience. Stafford Cripps, the leader of the Socialist League, and 'Red' Ellen Wilkinson, the Labour MP for Jarrow, gave passionate warnings of the dangers of European fascism. Cottman left the meeting convinced that this was something he could not ignore: 'Here was something going on that was manifestly inhuman and that any human being worth his salt would seek to put a stop to it.'[9]

In 1932, the family moved to Bristol, where Cottman joined a religious endowed school called St Mary Redcliffe's. It was, by all accounts, a good school, and Cottman was forever grateful for their help improving his mathematics. As there was no ILP Guild of Youth in Bristol, Cottman joined the Young Communist League, inspired by the USSR's role as 'the first Socialist country' and the British Communist Party's reputation for anti-fascism and political militancy. The Communists, felt Cottman, were 'more purposeful' and a welcome change from the Guild of Youth's 'do-gooding, pie in the sky' atmosphere. He joined up with other young Communists who were active anti-fascists, heckling meetings and physically confronting Blackshirt members. Cottman was one of a number to infiltrate a British Union of Fascists meeting held in Bristol's Colston Hall, where the speakers included the fascist movement's leader, Oswald Mosley, and William Joyce, later to achieve notoriety during the Second World War as Lord Haw-Haw. As each of Cottman's group of young protesters stood up to heckle, they were jumped on by Blackshirt stewards, who physically threw them out of the hall and down the outside stairs.[10]

In 1934, aged 16, Cottman left school hoping to be a journalist, but with Britain's economy in slump, there was no work of the kind to be found. So he reluctantly took what he hoped would be a temporary clerical job, managing the accounts for a Bristol tailors. Two years later, bored stiff with his work at the tailors and still a YCL activist, he heard news of the military coup in Spain which had been launched against the country's democratically elected government. While he knew very little of the country, Cottman had plenty of experience of fascism at home, and had not forgotten what he had heard in Kingsway Hall. So when he discovered that the British government was refusing to support a fellow democracy, he was outraged:

I felt a personal disgust that Franco should get military aid from Hitler and Mussolini, while Britain and France agreed on a 'non-intervention policy' which starved the rightful government of Spain of arms and meant Spanish workers bled to death.[11]

Later admitting that his politics were 'more instinctive than analytical', Cottman was convinced at the time that 'there were few problems that couldn't be solved by planting a few bombs in the right place,' so was determined to go and 'fight for democracy' in Spain.[12] He contacted both the Independent Labour Party and the Communist Party about volunteering. The ILP responded first, so he immediately headed down to its head office in London's St Bride Street for an interview.

Unlike the Communist Party, with its 10,000 members and

robust structure of local branches, the ILP was, as Don Bateman (later the Party's National Treasurer) admitted, 'a small party sadly in debt and without any kind of financial reserves.'[13] Nevertheless, when the civil war in Spain broke out, the ILP had been contacted by the leadership of the POUM, 'the Workers' Party of Marxist Unity', the ILP's sister organisation in Spain. Consequently, the Party's National Administrative Council agreed to send John McNair, a leading Party figure, businessman and a good linguist, to Spain on a fact-finding mission. There he made contact with the POUM leadership, who asked McNair whether the ILP might be able to help by sending medical supplies. Persuaded by their requests, McNair returned to Britain on 7 September, submitting a report that portrayed the war as a straightforward fight between two opposing forces. One side was made up of 'not only all the reactionary and Fascist forces of Spain, but of Europe too.' Pitted against them were the 'Spanish workers—badly armed and ill-equipped—defending the pitiful conditions of existence they have already managed to secure.'[14] McNair stressed the role of ordinary working people in combatting the rising, rather than the efforts of the armed forces and central government. 'The workers,' argued McNair, are not fighting merely to save some vague Liberal Democratic Republic; they are fighting to crush fascism first and then to construct a Socialist state.'[15]

The ILP agreed to hold a number of public meetings to publicise the Spanish Republic's plight and run appeals in its paper, *The New Leader*, to help raise funds. Despite the Party's small size, so successful were the appeals that by the end of the month they were able to send a fully equipped ambulance unit to Spain. One of the drivers, W B Martin, who had military experience, remained in Spain to fight with the POUM militia, while the other, Bob Edwards, who had been the ILP candidate for Chorley in the 1935 General Election, returned home, determined to persuade the ILP to send a military contingent to fight in Catalonia.[16] However, the leadership of the Party, scarred by the slaughter of the First World War, had long been resolutely pacifist and were strongly opposed to the idea.[17] Younger members of the organisation, however, such as Bob Smillie, the

Guild of Youth's Chair and grandson of a famous Scottish miners' leader, and the former Cambridge student Ted Fletcher (later Labour MP for Darlington) saw things differently and supported Edwards.[18] For Smillie and Fletcher, the conflict in Spain was part of an international revolutionary struggle against fascism and they were determined to fight alongside their comrades in the POUM. Swayed by the manifestly urgent need to defend the socialist cause in Spain, at the end of 1936 the ILP leadership gave the go-ahead and requests for volunteers for what Bob Edwards referred to as 'The ILP Brigade' appeared in *The New Leader* in December and January of the following year.[19]

So, when Stafford Cottman arrived at the ILP head office in St Bride Street in late 1936, he was welcomed with open arms, despite being only seventeen years of age, 165cm tall and a member of a rival political organisation.[20] He was interviewed by Edwards, John McNair and Fenner Brockway (the former Labour Party MP for Leyton), who were weeding out adventurers and undesirables.[21] They warned him that volunteering for the Spanish war was not to be taken lightly, though precise details were scarce and there was no mention of the possibility of being killed. The interviewers also asked him about his military experience, probably more in hope than expectation.[22] As other volunteers discovered when volunteering at the Communist Party headquarters in King Street, political experience was frequently taken as an acceptable surrogate for military knowhow. Which was just as well, because, like the majority of ILP volunteers, Cottman knew nothing of soldiering. He later confessed that the only time he'd ever fired a gun was at a fairground.[23] Nevertheless, convinced of his trustworthiness and seriousness, Cottman was accepted by the ILP leadership. He was to become one of the youngest of all of the British volunteers in Spain, known affectionately to his comrades as 'the boy'.[24] Along with 25 other volunteers, Cottman was placed under the command of Bob Edwards, who was later accused by one member of the group of knowing 'nothing about military affairs,' adding dismissively, 'he might make a good Salvation Army officer.'[25]

In accordance with the British Government's policy of non-intervention in the Spanish war, the Security Services paid close attention to the ILP volunteers. The police made several rather ineffective efforts to prevent them leaving for Spain, including sending an anonymous warning that the border between France and Spain had been closed. Undeterred, the group set off from Victoria Station on 10 January 1937.[26] Cottman had managed to hurriedly secure a passport the previous day, but the majority of the group had bought weekend return tickets to Paris, in a vain attempt to conceal their real destination.[27] They were watched carefully by Special Branch as they departed Newhaven by ferry to Dieppe.[28] They then made their way down through France via Paris to Perpignan, where they were given a good lunch before being bussed across the border and into Figueras in northern Spain. There Cottman had his first experience of Spanish food when he was fed sardines, artichokes, and French bread. He later remembered it as the best meal he had in Spain.

From Figueras, the volunteers headed south, arriving at Barcelona's Estació de França on 12 January 1937.[29] 'The atmosphere in Barcelona,' remembered one of Cottman's comrades, 'was terrific.'[30] The volunteers were overwhelmed by the enthusiastic welcome they received, with a brass band playing suitably inspiring music such as *La Marseillaise*, the *Internationale* and the Spanish libertarian anthem, *Hijos del Pueblo*.[31] Cottman was utterly captivated by the intoxicating atmosphere, famously described by Orwell as a city where 'the working class were in the saddle.' The city was decked out in red and black flags, with loudspeakers blaring out rousing music. Pro-Communist and Anarchist graffiti and posters were everywhere, and an unfortunate dog had been branded with the initials POUM. 'It was the only Marxist dog I've ever seen,' Cottman laughed. All transport and restaurants had been collectivised and many people had prudently chosen to forego their bourgeois dress for the safety of the proletarian blue overall, the *mono*. Orwell summed up the feelings of many of the English group when he wrote, 'there was much in it that I did not understand, in some ways I did not even like it, but I recognized it immediately as a state of affairs worth fighting for.'[32]

Accompanied by the brass band and cheering locals, the

dumbfounded new arrivals were marched off to their billet, the 'clean but pretty basic' Hotel Falcon at the southern end of Barcelona's famous thoroughfare, La Rambla. They were then escorted in small groups to the Lenin Barracks, a huge area formed from several colonial buildings, situated on the Gran Vía between the city centre and L'Hospitalet to the west. There the new recruits were fed before being issued with basic uniforms consisting of corduroy trousers, puttees, donkey jackets, low boots and the occasional forage cap. The outfits, Cottman admitted 'were not very smart looking and we must have looked a pretty rough old crowd.'[33] More seriously, the arms that they were given were also very battered; Cottman was issued a German Mauser rifle, not a bad gun in itself, but rendered almost useless by its age, having been constructed at the end of the previous century. Nonetheless, they began their military training.[34] To his alarm, it quickly became clear to Cottman that, while one or two had some military experience, the majority obviously didn't and were, in fact, rather 'more booksy and political' than soldierly.[35] Sadly, there was little time to correct these deficiencies, for the Spanish Republic was very much on the back foot. Consequently, training was brief and hurried, lasting less than two weeks in total.[36] It consisted mainly, Cottman discovered, of 'rifle instruction, drill and square-bashing . . . obeying commands and walking up and down.'[37] As Cottman would come to realise, both their weaponry and their training were to prove woefully inadequate.

On 20 January 1937, Cottman and the other members of the group—now joined by the ILP youth leader, Bob Smillie, who had deserted his job in the Party's Barcelona office—were transferred to the POUM headquarters at Lérida, before being sent to the front at the Black Mountain, near Alcubierre, a small village lying on the Aragón front, 30 kilometres north-east of Zaragoza. Cottman was greatly affected by the appalling hardship of village life in Spain he saw there. As Orwell described, the village was little more than 'a mass of mean little houses of mud and stone huddling round the church . . . it did not possess and never had possessed such a thing as a lavatory or a drain of any kind.'[38] The village squalor was avoided by sleeping in caves, with light provided by oil lamps made from old sardine tins. At 500 metres above sea level, the men found the climate surprisingly cold, but they were at least able to keep dry.

At the front, the thirty English volunteers formed part of a Centuria of 100 men, under the command of Georges Kopp, a portly 45-year-old Russian-born Belgian. Kopp's involvement in the war had begun, so he claimed, by the smuggling of arms into Spain, though he was one of many foreigners in Spain to possess a carefully crafted back-story.[39] The Centuria was organised on democratic militia lines; there were no signs of rank, no titles, no badges, no saluting; and military orders were agreed by discussion among all ranks.[40] Bob Edwards was awarded the rank of captain and remained in charge of the English ILP section, but he never grew to be a popular or respected commander. One volunteer remarked scathingly that 'they were happy when Edwards returned to Britain in March and happier still when he stayed there.'[41]

Edwards would be replaced as commander by one of the unit's *cabos* (corporals), 'a fine type of Englishman, 6ft. 3in. in height, a good shot, a cool customer, completely without fear.'[42] A former colonial policeman, the corporal possessed a 'cut-glass Eton accent'. This was, of course, Eric Blair, author of *Burmese Days*, *Down and Out in Paris and London* and *The Road to Wigan Pier*, already well known by his pen name.[43] A number of the ILP group did not take to the author, who spent a considerable amount of his time reading and writing, 'scribbling' as Bob Edwards dismissively put it.[44] Frank Frankford, a volunteer from Hackney in east London, confessed that he disliked the 'supercilious bastard' on sight, adding scornfully that 'I rather think that he fancied himself as another Bernard Shaw . . . "a parlour pink".'[45] However, Cottman liked him greatly and felt that Orwell's detractors were suffering from 'a wrongly applied class prejudice.'[46] On the contrary, he believed, Orwell's background and his experience as a schoolteacher 'gave him an air of authority . . . he was a natural leader.'[47] Cottman also admired Orwell's sometimes self-deprecating sense of humour, though he also remembered that Orwell took his politics very seriously and could get extremely heated and acerbic in discussions. Orwell explained to Cottman that his particular bugbear was Spaniards' treatment of animals and he would often step in to prevent cruelty. He believed that animals were often treated badly in Catholic countries, compounding the people's major sin of habitually siding with the oppressors, rather than the oppressed. Consequently, he explained to Cottman, while the sight of burned-out churches saddened him, it didn't shock or even surprise him.[48]

While Orwell might have disapproved of their attitude to animal welfare, he and the other ILP volunteers very much admired the Spaniards' courage on the battlefield. Unfortunately, this bravery could sometimes become reckless bravado, with soldiers standing up in full view of the enemy. Initially, Spanish soldiers laughed at the English habit of taking cover and lying prone to shoot, but following high casualty rates, a propaganda campaign was launched to encourage Spanish militiamen to follow the example of the *extranjeros* (foreigners).[49]

While some of the officers possessed pistols befitting their rank and the POUM possessed a number of machine-guns, there was a crucial lack of firearms and what they did possess was of doubtful quality.[50] Certainly, unlike his compatriots fighting in the overwhelmingly Communist International Brigades, Cottman never saw any Russian arms in Spain.[51] In fact, the ILP militia were totally ill-equipped:

> [There were] no hats, no bayonets, hardly any revolvers or pistols . . . no maps or charts . . . no range-finders, no telescopes, no field-glasses . . . no flares, or Very lights, no wire-cutters, no armourers' tools, hardly even any cleaning materials . . . there was not even any gun oil.[52]

To make matter worse, resupplies could take weeks to reach the Aragón front, if they arrived at all. 'I think that neither the discipline, training, weaponry nor clothing improved during my time in Spain,' Cottman remarked, ruefully.[53]

Clearly, in the circumstances, any major offensive action would be suicidal, and all they could realistically hope to do, as the East-Ender, Frank Frankford, admitted, 'was to hold the line.'54 The trenches, Cottman discovered, were often rudimentary and rarely deep enough, showing little improvement from the previous August, when the young English student, John Cornford, had dismissed Aragón as 'a quiet sector of a quiet front.'55 Georges Kopp agreed, describing the front as 'a comic opera war where people occasionally got killed.'56 The enemy lines were over 700 metres away, high up on an adjacent hillside, much too far away to be able to shoot at accurately. In fact, the most effective weapon was probably the megaphone, which the Spanish soldiers used to harangue their counterparts in the Nationalist trenches, explaining that they were fighting men of their own class and pleading with them to desert.

With neither side possessing sufficient resources to launch an attack, there was effectively a stalemate and Cottman saw very little actual action. While the risk of death from snipers or shellfire was small, conditions were nonetheless extremely unpleasant, with freezing cold weather and the irritations of rats and lice. With no washing facilities beyond a communal open-air laundry, the volunteers' uniforms quickly became dirty, louse-infested and threadbare. Like the British volunteers in the International Brigades then fighting on the Jarama front, the ILP group suffered from dreadful infestations, which multiplied much more quickly than they could be killed. Consequently, much of the time was taken up with the prosaic needs of soldiering: trying to keep warm, dry and fed, while eking out their minimal supplies of tobacco. Most of the Republican soldiers in Spain found the food, where they could get it, hard to adjust to and Cottman was no different. 'The food was not very good,' he admitted, 'it consisted of a thin soup, artichokes, rice and sardines. I left Spain hating rice, sardines and olive oil.57

Fortunately, supplies could occasionally be supplemented by food parcels from home. Missing his home comforts and having discovered that the chocolate available in Barcelona was not to his taste, Cottman asked his friends in the Barking Guild of Youth to send him a bar. Post was notoriously slow and unreliable in Spain so, having sent off his request, he promptly forgot all about it. Several months later, the ILP unit's administrator, John McNair, sought Cottman out to tell him a delivery had arrived, but that it would need to be collected in person, as it needed an import licence. A bemused Cottman accompanied McNair to the import office to discover nine large packing cases, all crammed full of bars of chocolate. His young ILP friends had pounded the streets of Barking collecting money and had been overwhelmed by support. They proudly crated up the results of their efforts and sent it off to Spain. Dumbfounded by the mountain of chocolate and with no means of lugging it back to the trenches, McNair and Cottman helped themselves to a couple of bars, before charitably donating the remainder to a local children's hospital.[58]

In late February, Cottman's group was transferred to a new position facing La Granja, on flat, arable land overlooking the road between Huesca to Zaragoza, about 50 km north of Alcubierre.[59] This was a much more dangerous proposition than their previous posting, subjecting the volunteers to the terrifying daily experience of artillery barrages and bombing by Italian planes, whose camouflage rendered them almost invisible from below. There was also sporadic shelling from enemy mortars, but much more dangerous were the isolated exchanges from rifles and machine guns. The ILP volunteers' only really serious action occurred on 13 April, when they took part in a daring night attack on enemy trenches just to the south-east of Huesca, graphically described by Orwell in *Homage to Catalonia*.[60] They initially secured an enemy position at Ermita Salas, though the imminent danger of being overrun by a Nationalist counter-attack soon forced them to withdraw. The fighting at one point descended into hand-to-hand combat, a terrifying experience for the inexperienced volunteer soldiers. Cottman, however, remained unharmed, principally because the eighteen-year-old was protected by his older comrades, who ensured that he had a junior role in the action. The youngster, in fact, never took part in any serious combat, confessing to firing fewer than 30 shots during his entire time in Spain. Not that his comrades' experiences were greatly different, given both the scarcity of ammunition and the constant terror of an ancient rifle blowing up in one's face.

By April, after four months at the front, the inability to break the deadlock had become a source of intense frustration to some members of the group, including Cottman: 'It became a joke that we looked forward to the day when we would capture the town [Huesca] and drink coffee at our leisure,' he complained.[61] He, Orwell and several others argued that they had come to Spain to fight fascists, not to be shot by a stray bullet. Cottman explained that Madrid was taking the brunt of it, where the Communist-dominated International Brigades were defending the Spanish capital:

> [Madrid] . . . was the place under attack and we had a comradely duty to help. Here we were on the Aragon front with very little happening, you saw the enemy miles over there as a little moving dot on the landscape. You didn't really feel as though you were making a useful contribution to the Spanish Civil War.[62]

For Cottman, the issue was more about defending Madrid than joining the International Brigades, but many of Cottman's comrades, wary of the growing influence of the Communist Party in Republican Spain, were horrified.[63] However, Cottman felt strongly that 'we had the moral, or comradely responsibility, to do our best to help them' and he and Orwell decided to investigate the prospect of leaving the ILP militia to join the Brigades.

So when the ILP group was pulled out of the line on 25 April to go on leave, Orwell approached 'a Communist friend, attached to the Spanish Medical Aid' in Barcelona to enquire whether he could join the International Brigades.[64] Five days later, both Orwell and Cottman spoke to Walter Tapsell, a senior Communist in Barcelona, who would later be killed in Spain while serving as a political commissar with the British Battalion. Tapsell sent a report to London, reporting that some members of the ILP militia had become disaffected. However, an outbreak of violent internecine street-fighting in early May dashed any ideas that the disgruntled ILP volunteers had of joining the International Brigades.

Tensions between Anarchists on one hand and the Madrid

government on the other had long been simmering. Partly they had root in long-standing philosophical differences, but these had been brought into stark focus by the pressures and demands of the war. When the ILP volunteers returned to Barcelona on leave at the end of April 1937, they found the city much changed. A year of war and its consequences for the city's population— overcrowding, food-shortages, inflation and bombing—had left the city in tatters. There was a febrile atmosphere and a marked tension, with propaganda for the new Republican Popular Army replacing that for the militias. Trade Union cards, which had previously operated as *salvo conductos*, had been replaced with official government passes. Cottman's British passport, which had been viewed with scorn in January—one official spat on the passport when he saw British Foreign Secretary Anthony Eden's name—was now looked upon with respect by the new authorities, certainly more so than his identity card issued by the Anarchist trade union, the CNT (*Confederación Nacional del Trabajo*).

Government attempts to restore in the Republican zone the kind of centralised authority which had virtually collapsed following the military rising the year before were receiving strong support from the Communist Party, who had their own reasons for wanting to limit the power of the Anarchists and their militias. Moves had already been made against the POUM, which had earned the enmity of Stalin by the Party's condemnation of the Moscow show trials in August 1936 and the expression of solidarity with Trotsky made by their leader, Andreu Nin. Stalin was determined that Spain should not become a breeding ground for Trotskyists and other 'deviationists' critical of the Soviet Union; if he had any agenda in Spain beyond keeping Hitler embroiled in a war for as long as possible, it was to eradicate all forms of perceived Trotskyism.[65] During April, many of the POUM's newspapers had been closed down, and a number of members had been expelled from factory committees. With tensions rising, the May Day parades in Barcelona had been cancelled to prevent disorder.

The simmering violence was brought to the boil on 3 May by the government's attempt to take over the Telefónica (the Barcelona telephone exchange) held by members of the CNT.

186

Having infuriated government officials by eavesdropping on official phone calls, the occupiers had refused to admit three lorry loads of Assault Guards sent by the local police chief to remove them. Shots were exchanged and Anarchists across Barcelona, supported by members of the POUM who believed that the government was attempting to roll back their revolutionary gains, erected barricades and prepared to defend themselves. Meanwhile, Communists seized their opportunity and accused the POUM of being 'Trotskyists' and agents of Franco.

Amid rumours of battles between Republican police and Anarchists over control of the Barcelona telephone exchange, Cottman, Orwell and other members of the ILP militia in Barcelona were ordered to protect the headquarters of the POUM's military committee in the Hotel Falcon at 30 La Rambla. There were not enough rifles to go around, so Cottman was issued with two phosphorous grenades. He wisely treated them with great care for, as he knew, they could be 'much more of a hazard to the user than the recipient.' Cottman took up a position on the roof, remaining there for three nights, watching as hundreds lost their lives in the street-fighting, and many more were arrested.[66] The clashes only ended when six thousand Republican Assault Guards arrived in the city on 6-7 May and the barricades began to be dismantled.

Clearly, despite Cottman's impression that Walter Tapsell seemed to be 'an honest Communist', the street-fighting had ruled out any notion of joining the Communist-dominated International Brigades. Tapsell's attempts to persuade them were summarily rejected by the ILP volunteers, who were incensed by Communist portrayals of the POUM as Trotskyists and fascist agents, correctly surmising that they would be seen as politically unreliable within the International Brigades.[67] Not surprisingly, morale among the group plummeted after the fighting and a number decided that they wanted no more of the war and made moves to return home. Cottman and Orwell agreed to return to the Huesca front on 10 May, but Cottman soon fell ill with suspected tuberculosis and was sent to the Sanatorium Maurín, a POUM-run convalescent hospital located in the north-west suburbs of Barcelona, near Tibidabo.[68] Unfortunately, while Cottman was convalescing, the situation in Barcelona was deteriorating rapidly. On 16 June, the POUM was officially banned and leading members were rounded up and arrested, including the group's commander, Georges Kopp. Cottman was very fortunate not to be picked up himself when the hospital was raided by the police on the hunt for POUM sympathisers. Several patients were arrested, including one POUMista who was only twelve years of age.[69]

Having surreptitiously discharged himself from the hospital, Cottman laid low in a lodging near Plaça de Macià. To his great alarm, he discovered that Bob Smillie had been arrested while trying to cross the border into France.[70] More frightening still, rumours were circling that Andreu Nin, the leader of the POUM, had disappeared and was believed to have been shot. Fortunately for Cottman, help arrived in the form of John McNair, who was determined to do what he could to get the ILP members safely out of the country. Having already been interrogated by the police, McNair had been tipped off that he, George Orwell, his wife Eileen O'Shaughnessy (who worked in the POUM Barcelona office) and Stafford Cottman were all on a list of suspects and that warrants had been issued for their arrest.[71] The sense of alarm and distrust was palpable; Orwell vividly described it as 'an atmosphere of suspicion, fear, uncertainty and veiled hatred.'[72]

Aware that police were waiting to arrest him at his hotel, McNair joined Cottman at his lodgings. However, he was woken up in the middle of the night by police banging on his hotel room door. McNair was interrogated, but having flushed any incriminating papers down the toilet, he managed to talk his way out of trouble. Once the police had left, he quickly woke up Cottman and told him what had just happened. At first light, they crept out of the hotel and laid low in a café owned by a sympathetic Spaniard. A by now seriously alarmed McNair asked Cottman to warn other foreign POUM volunteers that they were in danger of arrest or worse. Understandably anxious to leave Spain as quickly as possible, on 21 June, Cottman and Orwell sought help from the British Consulate in Barcelona but were informed that arranging the necessary paperwork would take several days. Terrified of being arrested, the pair spent the day trying to avoid the attentions of the police by posing as prosperous English businessmen. Unwilling to risk booking into a hostel, they were forced to spend a very unpleasant night hidden among long grass at the edge of a derelict building site.[73]

The following afternoon, Cottman, McNair and George Orwell nervously returned to the British consulate and collected their papers. The three then made their way to the railway station, to discover to their horror that the train to Port Bou had already left. At a loss, the group of fugitives were very lucky to find a hostel whose owner was a sympathetic CNT member and who reassured them that he would not notify the police (as he was legally required to do). Next day, 23 June 1937, they cautiously returned to the station and boarded the train they fervently hoped would carry them safely across the border. To appear as respectable as possible, they sat in the dining car. Orwell read and 'scribbled', while McNair read a collection of Wordsworth poems and Cottman made a valiant, though probably unconvincing effort to appear lost in a volume by the Poet Laureate, John Masefield.[74] Crossing the border was nerve-rackingly slow and the group anxiously endured two sets of passport checks before, to their relief, they were let across without any problems. Once over the frontier, the Orwells left for the restful calm of the nearby seaside village of Banyuls, while McNair and Cottman continued on to Paris and then the safety of home.

When Orwell returned to England a few days later, having failed miserably to enjoy his time by the sea, he was still raging about the Communist Party's role in scapegoating the POUM. He wrote a furious article for the *New Statesman*, disputing the lies told about his comrades, but the editor, Kingsley Martin, refused to publish it.[75] Yet, despite his trenchant criticisms of Soviet Communism, Orwell remained a committed advocate of both the Spanish Republican cause and democratic socialism. So too did Cottman, despite his disillusionment at the internecine fighting in Barcelona and his anger over the liquidation of the POUM and the arrest and imprisonment of friends and comrades.

Cottman threw himself into working for the 'Aid-Spain movement'; he attended campaign meetings, took part in door-to-door collections and helped out Spanish refugees. He paid a number of visits to a Basque refugee hostel, known as a 'colony', which had been established in Street, just south of Glastonbury in Somerset.[76] Cottman joined the Orwells and McNair's efforts to secure the release of Georges Kopp, their commander in Spain, who was still incarcerated in a Republican prison. Kopp was eventually released on 7 December 1938, when he made his way to England and, unwell and emaciated after several months in jail, convalesced under the watchful eyes of Eileen's brother and his wife.[77]

However, while Kopp's release was the cause of much celebration, Cottman's life was being made very difficult by the Communist Party, which was continuing the attacks on ILP members that had begun in Spain. On 2 July 1937, Cottman was expelled from the Young Communist League, with the organisation's National Secretary, John Gollan, taking the trouble to travel to Bristol to do it personally. In fact, the Communist Party had a particular beef with Cottman due to an account of the Barcelona uprising that he had written. The article, entitled 'Unity in the Trenches', very much put across the ILP and POUM's side of the story, criticising the Communists' slanders against the POUM, yet still proclaiming faith in the Communist Movement and in the idea of left unity. It appeared in the *News Chronicle*, the *Socialist Leader* and the *Bristol Labour Weekly*. Unsurprisingly, the YCL's paper, *Challenge*, refused to run it.[78]

Cottman's expulsion from the YCL was justified by the claim that he and the other ILP volunteers had been 'in the pay of Franco' and that Cottman was therefore, 'an enemy of the working class.' Despite the utterly mendacious nature of the accusation and the ILP's furious denials, many of Cottman's former friends in the Communist Party believed it and turned against him.[79] His mother's home was picketed by Party members, who intimidated visitors and paraded waving placards proclaiming, 'Stafford Cottman is shooting policemen in Spain' and 'Stafford Cottman receives Franco's gold.' Hounded out of

Bristol, Cottman fled to London, finding a job with the ILP, where he could at least be among friends.[80] Orwell, who was also receiving the Communists' ire, was very supportive, joining friends and supporters at a protest meeting.

> I heard that the Cottman's house had been shadowed by members of the YCL who attempt to question everyone who comes in and out. What a show! To think that we started off as heroic defenders of democracy and only six months later were Trotsky-Fascists sneaking over the border with the police on our heels.[81]

The attacks only tailed off when Orwell complained to the publisher Victor Gollancz, threatening libel action.

During August 1937, Cottman, Orwell and other former members of the ILP group in Spain were guests of honour at the Party's summer school in Letchworth where the group shot of Cottman, Orwell and the three other ILP volunteers was taken.[82] A report of the summer school in *The New Leader* lauded Cottman as 'very young, frail in body and yet with a spirit of steel.'[83] Both Cottman and Orwell spoke briefly, though Orwell could hardly be heard, as his voice box had still not recovered from the wound sustained in a Spanish trench, three months earlier. While Orwell was exhausting himself writing numerous letters and articles about Spain—including his searing personal memoir, *Homage to Catalonia*—his former comrade Frank Frankford's account, accusing the ILP and POUM of collaborating with the fascists, appeared in the *Daily Worker* in September 1937. Orwell wrote an apoplectic letter to the ILP paper, *The New Leader*, denouncing Frankford and his attacks on his former comrades, which was signed by fourteen of his comrades from Spain, including Cottman.[84] In October 1938, five months after the publication of Orwell's account, the trial of the POUMistas in Spain further strengthened the ILP volunteers' version of events, when the defendants' confessions were shown to have been obtained under duress and accusations of espionage against those who it was accepted were 'sincere anti-fascists', were dismissed.[85]

However, any feelings of vindication were outweighed by the growing realisation that the Republic was facing defeat. By early 1939, with infighting once again plaguing the uneasy Republican coalition, John McNair reported that 'Barcelona Has Fallen' in the *New Leader* on 3 February. The final defeat in March suggested to many that a wider war with fascism now looked more likely than ever. Articles in *The New Leader* discussing Spain were increasingly replaced by articles denouncing the forthcoming war and opposing conscription.[86]

When the Second World War broke out in September 1939, despite the ILP's participation in the war in Spain, the Party stuck to its position that the war was a capitalist enterprise and that the working class should stay out of it.[87] This very much chimed with Cottman's view, for he remained deeply embittered by the British Government's policies of non-intervention in Spain and appeasement of the dictators, which had effectively seen the sacrifice of the Spanish Republic in a vain attempt to preserve wider European peace. He also admitted to feeling little personal sympathy for the plight of the Poles, seeing their regime as quasi-fascist. Consequently, as other ILP members such as Fenner Brockway had already done, Cottman registered as a Conscientious Objector on political grounds.[88] Called in front of a tribunal chaired by the Liberal historian, H A L Fisher, Cottman admitted that he had fought in Spain, but argued that the current war with Germany was nothing but the creation of elderly, wealthy statesmen. He explained angrily that he saw absolutely no reason why the nation's young working-class men should sacrifice their lives to repair the damage inflicted by those famously described by Michael Foot as 'the guilty men'. When he was asked by an army officer on the panel why, given his previous experience of combatting fascism, he wasn't signing up, Cottman furiously responded, 'Well, I was fighting in Spain, when you bastards were not doing anything. Why would I sign up now?' Had the western democracies stood up to the dictators earlier, particularly in Spain, he argued trenchantly, the war could have been avoided.

However, the terrifyingly swift fall of France to the Wehrmacht's blitzkrieg in June 1940 caused Cottman reconsider.

Now convinced of the need to do whatever it took to resist the Nazis, on 29 August he volunteered to join the RAF. Admitted as an Aircraftman Second Class, on 11 October 1376681 AC2 Cottman was posted to the 20 Operational Training Unit, which had been formed at RAF Lossiemouth in May 1940 to train night bomber crews.[89] His training completed, on 4 January 1941, Cottman was posted to Number 10 Squadron, based at Leeming near Northallerton, which flew twin-engined Armstrong Whitworth Whitley bombers. There he served as a 'tail-end Charlie', a notoriously dangerous job with an appallingly high mortality rate; few rear-gunners survived more than five sorties. Cottman was very lucky: having survived a number of bombing raids over enemy-occupied Europe, his period of active service was brought to a close by a burst eardrum. How lucky he was became only too clear when, the day after his accident, his former aircraft was shot down. There were no survivors.[90]

Following his discharge from the RAF's hospital at Kirkham, Lancashire (now a Category D Men's prison) on 15 April 1941, Cottman was permanently invalided out of flight crew and retrained as an airfield controller. During his time with the 60th Operational Training Unit, Cottman was promoted to Leading Aircraftman in August 1941 and again to (Temporary) Sergeant the following month.[91] Eventually posted to Limavady airfield in Northern Ireland, Cottman gained a reputation for irreverent and mischievous humour, regularly waking up the aircrew by playing Rossini's stirring *The Thieving Magpie*. Sadly, though Cottman was generally well-liked by his fellow aircrew, not all shared his taste in music—nor his sense of humour.[92]

It was while he was based in Northern Ireland that Cottman met the woman who would become his wife. During 1943, he was returning from a period of leave in Ulster, when he saw a young WAAF in first class being pestered by a drunken officer. Having paid the guard to upgrade his ticket, Cottman gallantly came to her assistance. There was clearly a strong and immediate mutual attraction, though they were very different in temperament; while Stafford was passionate and full of energy, Stella was calm and measured, 'a towering stable presence.' Perhaps the uncertainty of wartime added a sense of urgency, for Stafford

Cottman and Stella Enfield were married only a few months after meeting and their daughter, Barbara, was born in March 1945, just before the end of the war in Europe.[93] Having had to put up with his release being postponed for six months, Cottman was finally released from military service on 8 November 1946, though he remained in the RAF Reserve for another thirteen years.[94]

During the war, Cottman had remained in the ILP, not particularly because he was a dedicated member but because, as he admitted, 'I didn't see any point in leaving it.' Besides, he remained very grateful that '[the ILP] told the truth about Spain at a time when other people weren't telling the truth.'[95] However, after the war, caught up in the peacetime euphoria, he followed the lead of Fenner Brockway, now a close friend, who had joined the Labour Party. Nonetheless, he remained on very good terms with former members of the ILP, particularly Orwell, who had written him a very friendly letter in the spring, when Cottman was still in the RAF. Letting him know that he had 'run into [their former ILP comrade] Paddy Donovan in the Edgware Road', Orwell confessed that, having written three articles a week for the previous two years, he was sick of journalism and was taking a break. He invited Cottman to visit him at his flat in London, advising him that he was giving up his Hertfordshire cottage to move to the island of Jura in the Hebrides.[96] Cottman later took him up on his offer, visiting Orwell in Scotland, just before the author's death in January 1950.

The following year, Cottman joined BOAC, the British Overseas Airways Corporation. This brought to an end a miserable period during which—due to a desperate lack of housing available after the war and, the couple believed, a prejudice against families with children—the family had been unable to live together permanently. With the help of BOAC's housing association, Cottman at last managed to secure a home in Ruislip, in north-west London, where the family settled down and remained for 35 years. Based in air traffic control at London's Heathrow airport, Cottman put his efforts into trade union activism, becoming the Treasurer of the Clerical and Administrative Workers' Union at BOAC, then Apex (the

Association of Professional, Executive, Clerical and Computer Staff, now part of the GMB). He remained an ardent socialist and a passionate anti-capitalist, eschewing unnecessary consumption. He would habitually remind listeners (not least his wife) that he only owned one shirt, 'because I can only wear one.' He was also a dedicated internationalist; both he and Stella travelled to Czechoslovakia to attend Alexander Dubček's May Day parade during the Prague Spring of 1968 and he was incensed when the Russians invaded. He also remained a determined anti-fascist, later leading him to support the British war against Argentina over the Falkland Islands in 1982, which he saw as a war against a fascist dictatorship, despite strong reservations about Prime Minister Margaret Thatcher's cynical militarism.

Unlike many veterans of the Communist-dominated International Brigades who boycotted the Franco regime, Cottman did return to Spain during the dictatorship. The first occasion was for a family summer holiday at the beginning of the 1960s, during the country's meteoric rise in tourism. The second trip, in 1983, was with a BBC Arena film unit, which was making a five-part documentary about Orwell.[97] Despite the programme makers being much more interested in Orwell's experiences in Spain than his, Cottman was a generous guide, dedicating a great deal of time and effort to ensure that the documentary provided an accurate account of Orwell's time in Spain. The ILP veteran was particularly overjoyed to be back in the former revolutionary city of Barcelona. Once again it was an exhilarating time to be in the Catalan capital, for Spain was still celebrating the result of the previous year's election, when Felipe González's Socialist Party, the PSOE, had been swept into power. However, as Cottman was walking around the city, attempting to recapture the atmosphere he remembered so keenly, his wallet was snatched. In a taxi on the way to the police station to report the incident, the driver commiserated with Cottman, raging over the city's thieves: *'Són uns fills de puta! Uns cabrons! Em cago en la mare que els ha parit!'* the driver exploded in earthy Catalan. Instantly Cottman sat up, excitedly. 'That's it!' he exclaimed, 'That's it! That's what the POUM used to say at the front!'[98]

In 1986, the Workers' Educational Association held an event

in Bristol's Transport House to mark fifty years since the outbreak of the civil war. Many of Cottman's old comrades from the YCL attended, including those who had taken part in victimising him when he returned from Spain: 'All were very contrite, friendly and affable,' observed Cottman's friend, Don Bateman, now a Head of Department at Brunel College of Technology. 'If there are such things as national characteristics, this was a very English event,' he observed with some amusement.[99] It was not only Cottman's former enemies in the Communist Party who were mellowing. The late 1980s saw a marked change in attitude towards the Spanish war and the veterans who had fought for the Spanish Republic, due in part to Russian President Gorbachev's policy of perestroika. With cold war attitudes beginning to thaw, the Bristol event marked the beginning of a resurgence of interest in the veterans' stories. In 1987, Cottman was interviewed by a local newspaper, keen to hear his story of the tumultuous events in Catalonia 50 years earlier.[100] The reporter, no doubt hoping for exciting tales of derring-do, must have been a little disappointed to hear Cottman's view that his 30 strong contingent 'made not the slightest military difference to the war.'[101] Repeating his former commander Georges Kopp's phrase that it was 'a comic opera war', the short, balding and bespectacled veteran (Cottman self-effacingly described himself as 'the very image of a Soviet bureaucrat') insisted that his greatest danger came from shooting himself with his own rifle. While admitting that Orwell's 'cut-glass Eton accent' had not endeared him to all the ILP volunteers, Cottman nevertheless insisted with typical generosity that the author was 'absolutely straight' and was the sort of comrade 'you could rely on.' He also continued to defend the ILP view of the conflict, arguing that the Communists were wrong to believe that 'you should forget about the revolution and concentrate on the defence of Madrid. The revolution had already happened,' he continued with conviction, 'and people weren't going to give it up.' It was a theme to which he would regularly return over the coming years.

During the late 1980s, the Cottmans left Ruislip for Bath, where the 70-year-old stood for a seat in the local council, helping to almost unseat a Conservative councillor who had been thought to have an unassailable majority. He remained a committed socialist and Trade Unionist, 'flinging himself into every argument and activity on the side of the labour movement', as one admiring interviewer put it.[102] Yet, perhaps surprisingly, given his involvement in Spain and a lifetime in the Labour Party and Trade Union movement, he did not give the impression of an evangelist 'bursting with politics.'[103] A devotee of cricket and classical music, Cottman regularly visited his brother Peter and his family in New Zealand, where they had emigrated to in the mid-1950s. It was a country Stafford came to love and see as a second home.[104]

Cottman's involvement with *Land and Freedom*, Ken Loach's powerful and evocative film set during the Spanish Civil War, arose completely by chance. One of Cottman's friends in Bath was a children's piano teacher, who happened to also be the tutor to Ken Loach's children. It was only when the director mentioned that he was making a film about the civil war that the piano teacher thought to mention that she had a friend called 'Staffy', who had fought in Spain. Loach immediately realised that this must be the young Stafford Cottman mentioned by Orwell in *Homage to Catalonia*. She put the two in touch and Loach gave Cottman an early draft of Jim Allen's script. Cottman made a number of useful suggestions to the script and confirmed to Loach—much to the director's relief—that 'it was a fair description of his experiences.'[105] However, Don Bateman's later remark in *The Guardian* that Cottman accompanied Ken Loach around the battlefields in Spain is not actually the case.[106] The notion that the film is based on Cottman's experiences is also false, though it is certainly true that Ian Hart's portrayal of the Liverpudlian volunteer, David Carr, has effectively brought Cottman's story to the foreground. At a private screening of the film organised in 1995 by Loach for the increasingly frail veteran, Cottman declared that 'George Orwell always said, "The truth about what happened to the Republican cause in Spain will never be told." But now it has.'[107]

However, not all were as taken as Cottman with Loach's interpretation. At an early screening of the film in Madrid, a number of International Brigade veterans, furious at the portrayal of the shooting of POUMistas by an American International Brigader, walked out of the cinema. Arguments still rage over the portrayal of the Spanish Civil War by Orwell and Ken Loach, which have led to many believing that it was Stalin and the Communist Party which were responsible for the Republic's defeat, rather than British and French appeasement which did nothing to stem German and Italian intervention. As Orwell himself wrote, 'the outcome of the Spanish war was settled in London, Paris, Rome, Berlin—at any rate not in Spain.'[108] Yet, while disagreements over the film persist, few would doubt the film's emotional intensity and dedication to those like Cottman who went to Spain to fight to save the country's democracy.

To this day, Ken Loach remains grateful to the contribution by the 'modest, informative and very helpful' Cottman. Many others who met the veteran feel the same way. One former member of the Labour Party's Young Socialists encountered Cottman when the Spanish veteran was the Party's Youth Officer in Ruislip. Many of the younger members of the Party were members of the Militant Tendency, with whom Stafford disagreed and argued strongly against. 'It was a great delight to get to know this man who was very fiery, but really, really liked young people,' remembered the young socialist.[109] Though passionate and forthright, Cottman was always patient and courteous and was consequently hugely admired and respected. He was also extremely modest, rarely talking about his time in Spain with Orwell, 'you had to prise it out of him . . . he never bragged about it.' Cottman was, thought the former activist, 'a thoroughly decent man' and his impression chimes with many who came to know Cottman over the years. After he was interviewed by the historian Chris Hall in 1993 for a book on the ILP veterans, the pair remained in touch. Several years later, Hall recounted admiringly how he had found Cottman to be: 'a lovely, warm and generous man, and someone I wish I had known for more years.'[110]

When he died of pneumonia on 19 September 1999 in the Circus Nursing Home in Bath, Stafford Cottman was the last of the group who fought alongside Orwell in Spain.[111] Unlike the British volunteers for the International Brigades, who have memorials scattered around Britain and Spain, for many years there was no memorial to the volunteers from the Independent Labour Party. However, in 2001 a commemorative plaque was finally unveiled at the Working Class Movement Library in Salford.[112] Cottman's death was followed, just under twenty years later, by the last of the British volunteers in Spain, a former worker at the Vauxhall car factory called Geoffrey Servante who had served in the International Brigades. Two years later, on 25 May 2021, the Spanish Press carried the story that 101-year-old Josep Almudéver, the very last of all the 35,000 foreign volunteers in Spain, had also succumbed to old age.[113]

Yet while all the foreign volunteers in the Spanish Civil War may now be gone, they have certainly not been forgotten. The Spanish government's granting of nationality to veterans was a powerful reminder of the enduring gratitude felt towards the foreign volunteers. In Britain too, their legacy lives on, partly due to the work of historians and organisations such as the International Brigades Memorial Trust, but also to the volunteers' role as a touchstone when the issue of British volunteers—whether fighting in the Balkans, the Middle East or, as is the case currently, in Ukraine—comes under the media spotlight. Above all, though, in Britain, the war in Spain is mainly remembered through George Orwell's memoir and Ken Loach's film, both of which, in different ways, tell the story of Stafford Leslie Charles Cottman. Perhaps now the youngest of the ILP volunteers can finally step out of Orwell's shadow.

Charlotte Haldane with Ronnie Burgess (on her right), Paul Robeson (far right of photo) and members of the 15th International Brigade in Spain. *Marx Memorial Library*

L to R: Unknown (possibly Lieutenant Edwin Bee Commander of 15th International Brigade Cartography), JBS Haldane and Malcolm Dunbar. *Bishopsgate Institute.*

JBS Haldane with International Brigade veteran volunteers for the Thetis experiments in 1939. L to R: Bill Alexander, Donald Renton, JBS, Paddy Duff and George Ives. *Marx Memorial Library*

On the banks of the Ebro, July 1938. Peter Kerrigan (L) with American *Daily Worker* correspondent, Joe North. *Marx Memorial Library*

Accompanying distinguished visitors to the Spanish Republic in the summer of 1938. L to R: Krishna Menon, Unknown, General Enrique Líster, Peter Kerrigan and the future Prime Minister of India, Pandit Jawaharlal Nehru. *Marx Memorial Library*

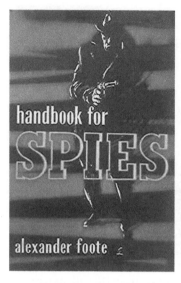

Handbook for Spies.
1953 edition.

Alexander Foote.
Photographer unknown.

Self-portrait by Clive Branson.
Rosa Branson.

Clive Branson's portrait of his wife
Noreen (née Browne) and
daughter Rosa. *Rosa Branson.*

British doctors Alex Tudor Hart (centre) and 'one of the grandfathers of evidence-based medicine' Archie Cochrane (L) in Spain, with unidentified colleague (R), 1937. *Marx Memorial Library*

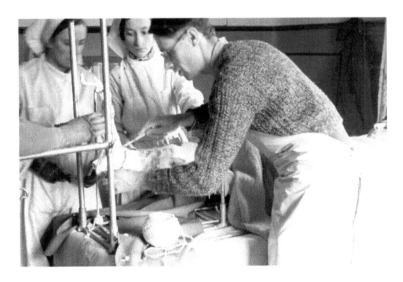

Alex Tudor Hart conducting an operation in Spain, assisted by British nurse Thora Silverthorne (centre). *Marx Memorial Library.*

Chapter Seven
The Truculent Scotsman: Peter Kerrigan

A number of the British men and women who volunteered to serve in the Spanish Civil War have become widely known, including the writers George Orwell and Laurie Lee; the Trade Unionist Jack Jones; Tom Wintringham, the founder of the Home Guard; Thatcherite political analyst Sir Alfred Sherman and Doctor in the House actor, James Robertson Justice. Yet few of the volunteers who gained outstanding reputations in Spain experienced the same level of recognition after their return. Sam Wild, the popular and reputedly the best of the Commanders of the British Battalion is a case in point. His rebellious and undisciplined temperament probably contributed to being denied an important role in the British Communist Party and 'he spent the rest of his life in and out of work, never ever finding something that interested him.'[1] Wild was not alone in this: most people would be hard-pressed to name the senior British military and political commanders in Spain, though both survived the war and went on to lead full lives. The story of the most senior British military officer in Spain, Malcolm Dunbar, appears elsewhere in this book (see Chapter One); this chapter is an account of a man whose importance in Spain equalled, if not surpassed, Dunbar's: the Scottish Political Commissar and *Daily Worker* correspondent, 'Big Peter' Kerrigan. His name is probably unfamiliar to many twenty-first century readers, yet Kerrigan was an important and influential figure in the labour movement and one of five key leading figures in the Communist Party from the 1930s to the 1960s, reflected in a huge, meticulous file put together by MI5 and Special Branch officers.[2] From the late 1920s onwards, Kerrigan, believed to be one of the Party's 'most active and dangerous men', was kept under close observation by Special Branch and all his travels recorded, particularly overseas, his daily activities were noted, his correspondence opened and a telecheck placed on his home telephone.[3] His file includes an evocative description of the man as 'a truculent Scotsman and convinced Communist.'[4]

> A burly Scot; 6' 1" in height; fresh complexion; grey eyes; thick fair hair, combed back without a parting; has an aggressive manner and talks loudly with a distinctive Scots accent; usually wears tweed jacket and grey flannel trousers or a light coloured suit, white shirt and pullover instead of a waistcoat; does not drink to excess and is not known to be fond of women.[5]

Peter Kerrigan was born on 26 June 1899 in Hutcheson-town, part of the deprived working-class area of Glasgow known as the Gorbals. Kerrigan was one of six children born to firmly working-class parents: his mother was a weaver and his father was a life-long Trade Unionist and founding member of the Transport and General Workers' Union in Glasgow.[6] Kerrigan went to a local school in the Gorbals before moving to Elmvale School in Springburn, in the north of the city. A keen sportsman, he took up boxing and played football for his local team, Bridgeton Waverley.

When he left school at 15, Kerrigan began an apprenticeship in the railways, but it was cut short by Britain's declaration of war on 4 August 1914. Initially, Kerrigan was not conscripted, so he avoided the fate of the many who were slaughtered on the Somme and at Ypres. Instead, he joined the Amalgamated Society of Engineers in Clydeside as an apprentice member.[7] However, in the last few months of the Great War, Kerrigan was called up into the Royal Scots and posted to Egypt and the Middle East. Too late to take part in the fighting, Kerrigan learned how to drive lorries while honing his boxing skills, becoming Regimental Champion.[8] His love of boxing continued after his demobilisation in April 1920 and 'Kid Kerrigan' established a formidable reputation in Glasgow. He found work as an apprentice turner, but with the economy sliding and unemployment on the rise, Kerrigan was laid off in 1921 after only five months.[9] Angry and bitter at being cast off, he joined the Socialist Labour Party in Glasgow and the National Unemployed Workers' Movement, an organisation set up by the Communist Party to highlight the plight of those unable to find work. The following year, he joined the local branch of the Communist Party in Springburn, Glasgow.[10]

He briefly found work at the Emshott Forge in Glasgow, where he was elected an AEU shop steward.[11] Helped by tough negotiating skills and his role as a member of the Central Strike Committee in the infamous Engineers' Lock Out of 1922, Kerrigan quickly earned a reputation for strong militancy. It didn't seem to help his employment prospects, however, for after two years Kerrigan was 'paid off' by his employers and, following a number of temporary jobs, ended up in Brown and Poulson's, the Paisley cornflour manufacturer. In 1924, Kerrigan made the first of many trips to Russia, as a delegate at the Congress of the RILU (the Red International of Labour Unions), an organisation in the inter-war period formed to spread international communism.[12] The following year, he was appointed the Communist Party's delegate to the Trades and Labour Council and elected vice-chairman of the Glasgow Trades Union and Labour Council and he chaired the Strike Co-ordinating Committee in Glasgow during the General Strike. He was distraught and incensed when the strike failed, believing that it had been sold out by its leaders.[13]

More happily, 1926 saw him married to a fellow Glasgow Trades Council delegate called Rose Klasko, who he had met while hiking with members of the Minority Movement, an organisation set up by the Communist Party to infiltrate and radicalise the Trade Unions. Born in Dublin in 1903, Rose was the daughter of Russian Jewish immigrants, who had moved to Glasgow when she was three.[14] A veteran of the Glasgow rent strikes in 1915, Rose was every much as dedicated to the Party as her husband, even if she never achieved his prominence. Nevertheless, as an MI5 memorandum noted, Rose had 'considerable influence with her husband on political matters, with the result that her likes and dislikes among Party members is of some importance.'[15]

Kerrigan's personal political trajectory within the Communist Party and labour movement continued. He was selected as the AEU delegate to attend the 1927 Labour Party Annual Conference and as the Communist Party's Candidate for the Cowlairs Ward in Springburn, inner city Glasgow, in the 1928 municipal elections.[16] While his campaign was ultimately unsuccessful, his admission to the highest ranks of the British Communist party was confirmed by his selection in October 1929 to undertake 'a special course of Marxist-Leninist training' at the International Lenin School in Moscow. This essentially acted as the Party's finishing school, instructing cadres from around the world in Communist political theory and organisational tactics. Kerrigan was to be one of more than twenty-five senior British Communists who would attend the school and serve in the Spanish Civil War.[17] While in Moscow, where he was instructed to remain incognito and adopted the pseudonym 'John Curry', Kerrigan had his first meeting with an individual who would have a singular role to play in his life: the General Secretary of the Communist Party of the Soviet Union, Joseph Vissarionovich Stalin.

Initially, Kerrigan expected to remain at the Lenin school for two years, but he was forced to return to Scotland prematurely in 1930 when a major textile strike broke out. Back in Britain, he was appointed Secretary of the Communist Party's Scottish District and he soon became a regular speaker at Glasgow Party meetings, campaigning against capitalism and arguing for stronger labour organisation.[18] His efforts soon caught the eyes of Raj Palme Dutt, a member of the Executive Committee of the CPGB and the Party's leading intellectual:

> Kerrigan, the new organiser, Lenin School trained, is definitely good, has something fresh about him, and though he is a little of the CI [Communist International] official, even as to a characteristic intonation of speaking, he does make an impression of having sense, knowing what is required, not antagonising other people and being ready to work.[19]

Kerrigan's first major task as Scottish Secretary was to organise an election campaign for the former Communist MP for Battersea, Shapurji Saklatvala, who was standing in the 1930 by-election for the Shettleston Division of Glasgow's East End. It was a hugely ambitious task, for Labour had gained over 60 per cent of the vote in the previous election. Despite Kerrigan's best efforts, Saklatvala only managed fourth place with less than 1,500 votes, compared to over 10,000 for the Labour candidate, John McGovern. Yet Kerrigan's dedicated work had not gone unnoticed and the following April he was himself selected as a candidate in the Glasgow St Rollox by-election. Unfortunately, Kerrigan's hopes were soon dashed when he proved unable to raise the £150.00 deposit and could not be put forward. His precarious financial situation was not helped by being fined £5.00 for obstruction at a May Day parade and ordered to either pay within a month or serve 30 days' imprisonment.[20] When Kerrigan was unable to pay, the Glasgow District Party Committee had to step in to cover the fine.[21]

During the early 1930s, Kerrigan became involved in organising demonstrations against unemployment and the hated Means Test, which intrusively assessed families' entitlement to financial assistance. In January 1934, he joined a group of almost 400 men marching from New Cumnock in Ayrshire to London, a distance of over 350 miles. Officially, Kerrigan was acting as the *Daily Worker* correspondent, though MI5 believed that he was actually 'responsible for all political moves in connection with the Scottish marchers.'[22] Those on the march remembered the tough Glaswegian activist working his way back and forth through the ranks, searching out anyone who was exhausted, or whose boots weren't in good condition, finding them a temporary ride in a lorry: 'Your Peter walked more than once to London,' one admiring Scot remarked to his wife, Rose.[23] The long trek completed, Kerrigan returned to London in June for a demonstration against the British Union of Fascists' rally at Olympia, before he went on to speak at a number of anti-Blackshirt rallies across Britain. The rise of fascism was to be the central theme of Kerrigan's campaign when he was adopted once again as a Communist Party candidate in the Glasgow municipal elections of November 1934. He spoke passionately about the situation in Asturias, in northern Spain, where an armed uprising had been launched against the right-wing government. The insurrection was viciously suppressed by troops of the elite Army of Africa, using terror techniques developed in Spanish

Morocco; some 1,500 were killed, with many thousands thrown into prison. However, Kerrigan's appeals on behalf of the Asturian miners seem to have fallen primarily on deaf ears, for he polled only 485 votes, a tenth of the number for the Labour candidate.

His second attempt to enter parliamentary politics thwarted, in May 1935, accompanied by his wife, Kerrigan returned to Moscow as the British Party delegate to the Seventh World Congress of the Communist International (known as the Comintern).[24] The Congress marked a significant moment for the international Communist movement, for it saw the abandonment of the disastrous policy of 'class against class', which had portrayed reformist and social-democratic parties as 'social fascists'. Instead, the leader of the Comintern, the Bulgarian Communist Georgi Dimitrov, announced a move towards working with other parties of the left in a policy of collective security against fascism, known as People's or Popular Fronts. Dramatic though the volte-face clearly was, Kerrigan blithely played down its significance, portraying the move away from sectarianism merely as 'a shift' to 'acting along similar lines to them, or with them for certain common objectives.'[25]

Prepared for a long stay in the Soviet Union, Kerrigan set about learning Russian, until news arrived that a general election had been called in Britain for November 1935. Considered vital to the campaigns of both Harry Pollitt in the Rhondda and Willie Gallagher in West Fife, Kerrigan was once again recalled prematurely. He arrived at Croydon Airport on 7 November and by the following day he was back at work in Glasgow.[26] However, within weeks Kerrigan had to return to Moscow, when he and Pollitt were personally summoned to meet with Stalin. The Soviet leader emphasised to Kerrigan how important he considered Gallagher's election campaign to be and instructed him to become his election agent. After a campaign in which issues of unemployment and the role of the League of Nations figured heavily, the Conservative-led National Government was returned to power, though Clement Attlee's Labour Party regained many of the seats lost in the disastrous election in 1931. One seat they didn't gain, however, was Fife, for in a remarkable triumph for the Communist Party, Willie Gallagher was successfully elected, beating the Labour candidate 13,462 votes to 12,869.[27]

His reputation burnished by Gallagher's victory, in May 1936 Kerrigan was promoted to Scottish District Organiser of the Communist Party. He quickly cemented his reputation as a strict enforcer of the Party line and even experienced, hardened activists could find him intimidating. The Communist Party Organiser in Aberdeen, Bob Cooney, who later served with distinction as a Political Commissar in Spain, admitted that 'I was terrified of him. When I heard he was coming to Aberdeen I used to want to hide . . . there was always something that he could find that you hadn't done well enough.'[28] Kerrigan had a reputation for not accepting any deviation from the Party line and anyone falling foul of him could swiftly find themselves being threatened with expulsion from the Party.[29] In the case of one young Scottish Party member who did stand up to Kerrigan, it was to have serious, almost fatal, consequences. Alec Marcovich, a leading organiser in the Young Communist League (YCL) and Trade Union movement in Glasgow, initially crossed swords with Kerrigan after criticising Stalin's persecution of Russian Jews in the early 1930s. As Marcovich later recalled, the Party's response was typically unequivocal:

> Peter Kerrigan came down to present on behalf of the central committee a report on the justification for the trials and so forth. And the justification simply was that it had been decided in accordance with the Russian law that these people were guilty, that they had received a fair trial and what the charges were and they had been dealt with, you know, and that you've got to take this in your faith.[30]

Marcovich was not satisfied with Kerrigan's response, pointing out that many people were simply not prepared to accept that just because 'Joe Stalin says they're guilty, they're guilty.' Kerrigan's reaction, Marcovich claimed, was to threaten to throw him down the stairs. Marcovich complained bitterly to other Party members, accusing Kerrigan of being 'a bully, an arrogant bloody big man'.[31] How big a man Kerrigan actually was, Marcovich would find out to his cost, when the two encountered each other again in Spain.[32]

When the civil war broke out in Spain in July 1936, Kerrigan was on a camping holiday with his wife on the Isle of Arran.[33] He was immediately determined to go, having 'welcomed the February election victory of the popular front government' in February 1936 and not forgotten the military's brutal actions in Asturias two years earlier.[34] However, as the principal organiser of what would be the final march of the National Unemployed Workers' Movement (NUWM), Kerrigan was told by the Communist Party leadership that he had more important matters to attend to at home. Larger, though less well known than the famous Jarrow Crusade, the NUWM's march set off from Glasgow in October 1936 and Kerrigan, as the principal organiser, was responsible for planning the march and drumming up support. Some 500 activists joined him on the month-long walk to London, where they were welcomed by a huge crowd in Hyde Park, including the NUWM leader, Wal Hannington.[35]

The march completed, the Party released Kerrigan to go to Spain. Rose was expecting a second child and didn't want him to go, but as the Party had asked him and she was a strong supporter of the Republican cause, she chose not to stand in his way.[36] Her decision was taken in the knowledge that while her husband was away, she and their children would have to survive on a pitifully small allowance from the International Brigade Dependents' Aid Committee, set up by the Communist Party to provide for the families of those fighting in Spain. The payments provided very little to live on, but with her brother unemployed, it was her only source of income.[37]

On 21 December, an article in the *Daily Worker* confirmed that Kerrigan had left for Spain with 70 volunteers (Kerrigan later claimed it was nearer 120), 'the biggest single grouping of volunteers that ever left Britain at one time.'[38] Kerrigan already held a British passport so, unlike the vast majority of the party, he didn't need to engage in the deception of buying a weekend return ticket to Paris. The group followed what would become a well-trodden route: the ferry from Dover to Dieppe, then a train to the central recruiting office for the international volunteers at the French Communist Party headquarters in Place du Combat (now Place du Colonel Fabien) in Paris. From there they were put on a train to Perpignan, where they were split up into small groups and billeted with sympathetic locals. All were instructed to be discreet and not to walk around in large groups in order to avoid the attention of the gendarmes. After two or three pleasant days in the town lazing in the autumn sunshine, the group was bussed over the frontier into Spain during the night. The volunteers were then mustered in the Castle of San Fernando in Figueras, before being forwarded to the main headquarters of the International Brigades in the city of Albacete, where Kerrigan took a moment to write the first of many reassuring letters home to his wife.

Despite his lack of combat experience, Kerrigan's seniority within the Communist Party led André Marty, the French commander of the International Brigades, to appoint the Scottish Trade Unionist as an officer. As the Political Commissar for all English-speaking volunteers at the International Brigade base, Kerrigan became the senior ranking British political officer in Spain. His charge included not just the volunteer soldiers, but also the political officers, known as commissars. All units, from brigade down to company level, were allocated commissars who were, theoretically at least, expected to represent the Popular Front composition of the Brigades, where soldiers in uniform were not allowed to wear political emblems and political meetings were forbidden without the express permission of the Ministry of War.[39] It was a laudable policy, if somewhat undermined by the fact that most commissars were experienced Party cadres, many of whom, like Kerrigan, had been educated at the Lenin School in Moscow.[40]

Officially, the job of the political commissar was to keep up morale and ensure that the battalion of volunteers knew why they were fighting and remained committed to the fight. Frequent speeches, meetings, and cultural and sports activities were all part of a process of fostering a sense of political unity. The Commissars' slogan, '*¡El primero en avanzar, el último en* *retroceder!'* (the first to advance, the last to retreat!) was not entirely rhetorical: three British Battalion commissars and several company commissars were killed in Spain. However, significantly, their responsibilities also included keeping watch for, and on, malcontents, political dissidents, and potential spies and traitors.'[41] Kerrigan's claim that all volunteers, 'even the liberal and labour people', welcomed commissars is not entirely true. Even some dedicated Party members found some of the commissars' 'pious' rhetoric patronising or irrelevant and consequently ridiculed them as 'comic stars'.[42] 'The political commissar is a comrade whose job is to promise everything you ask for,' complained one battalion member, 'and to blame it on Albacete when he doesn't get it for you.'[43]

One of Kerrigan's first responsibilities as Commissar was to attend the funeral of a young Scottish volunteer called Martin Messer who had been killed in the recent fighting at Boadilla del Monte. Kerrigan had known the 19-year-old Edinburgh University student personally, for he had been one of the hunger marchers accompanying him from Scotland just over a month previously. Kerrigan read the oration at his funeral, and the young Scot's death clearly had a profound effect on him, spurring Kerrigan to argue for the urgent repatriation of all British volunteers under 21 years of age.[44] The distressing funeral out of the way, Kerrigan paid a visit to the English-speaking Number One Company of the French 14th International Brigade, then fighting at Lopera, near Córdoba in Andalusia. Kerrigan found them occupying a poor position, scattered among olive trees, while enemy forces occupied a high ridge overlooking them and could draw on overwhelming air support.[45] Matters were made worse by the poor quality of the Republican volunteers' arms; many of the English-speaking volunteers were equipped with ancient Austrian Steyr rifles, which had to be loaded and fired one bullet at a time.[46]

Outnumbered and outgunned, Number One Company had little option but to make a difficult fighting retreat under heavy enemy fire. It was, Kerrigan came to realise, the final action of their catastrophic engagement with Franco's forces. The Company suffered very heavy losses, including Ralph Fox, the company commissar and a rising star in the British Communist Party, and Charles Darwin's great-grandson, the popular young Communist intellectual from Cambridge, John Cornford. An investigation into the debacle was held by senior International Brigade leaders, including Kerrigan and André Marty, who decided that the disaster could only be a result of deliberate sabotage. While Marty was notoriously paranoid, it was not a wholly unreasonable conclusion to draw, for many Spanish officers in the Republican Army undoubtedly had sympathies with the military uprising. However, the subject of Marty's intense suspicions, the French commander of the Marseillaise Battalion, Lieutenant-Colonel Delasalle, was almost certainly not a traitor, but rather a scapegoat for the disorganised and ineffective performance of the Internationals at Lopera.[47]

After the trial, Kerrigan returned to his work as base commissar, mainly at Albacete, but also at Madrigueras, home of the recently formed British Battalion. With new arrivals pouring into Spain, Kerrigan's job was not an easy one. His responsibilities included inducting the new arrivals, stressing the importance of their contribution to the Spanish Republican cause, while warning that the fight in Spain was a tough one, which would demand huge self-sacrifices. Unfortunately, not all were up to the job, many lacked military or political experience, others were physically weak, some were too young or old. Despite his well-earned reputation as a 'hard-line' Communist, Kerrigan was realistic enough to accept that recruiting unsuitable volunteers would cause serious problems of discipline and morale. Consequently, he wrote to Harry Pollitt in early January 1937 stressing that volunteers should be fully aware of the desperate situation they would be facing: 'this is war and many will be killed. They must understand this clearly and it should be put quite brutally.'[48]

Kerrigan's job of forging the volunteers into a cohesive unit was not helped by tensions between some of the Irish volunteers at Madrigueras and the mainly English battalion leadership. Several of the Irish, already unhappy with their officers' tendency not to make any distinction between British and Irish volunteers, had discovered that two senior figures in Spain had played a part in British covert activities in Ireland. At a stormy meeting on 12 January 1937, forty-five Irish volunteers voted to leave for the American Abraham Lincoln Battalion. While arguments persist over exactly why the schism developed and who was responsible, there is no doubt that it was extremely damaging for the leadership of the Battalion—and the International Brigades in general—who were loudly and proudly proclaiming the working-class solidarity and internationalism of the volunteers.[49] As the senior British Commissar in Spain, Peter Kerrigan certainly had knowledge of the crisis, yet he was always circumspect about it, admitting only that he had strongly resisted Marty's attempts to hold Frank Ryan, the leader of the Irish, responsible.[50]

Kerrigan found it rather harder to deny involvement in another disturbing incident that occurred the following month. As the British Battalion's commander, Wilf Macartney, was preparing to return home as part of his parole requirements following his release from Parkhurst prison for espionage, he was involved in a bizarre accident. On 6 February, a farewell supper was held at Albacete in Macartney's honour and, as the departing commander apparently didn't want to carry his large, heavy revolver home with him, it seems Kerrigan agreed to exchange it for his lighter Belgian pistol:

> I took the revolver in my hand and what I can't say for sure is whether or not I touched the catch or trigger, but suddenly there was a shot and he said, 'Oh, you've shot me in the arm!' We rushed him to hospital, got an anti-tetanus injection and he got patched up.[51]

There has long been a suspicion that the shooting was no accident, for a number of senior figures in the 15th Brigade and the British Communist Party—not least Kerrigan himself—had become increasingly disenchanted with Macartney's leadership:

> [Macartney] is far too irritable or querulous and I feel this has an effect on his ability to inspire the men with confidence in himself. I believe this querulousness is due in a measure to his anxiety to get the best possible results in a short time, but it makes him very critical of the Party . . . I do have the feeling

that there are signs that there is not the complete confidence there should be.[52]

However, this seems unlikely, for it would have been unnecessarily reckless for Kerrigan to have deliberately shot Macartney, who was anyway on his way home. Had senior Communist Party figures felt that the battalion would be better served without Macartney, there is little doubt that he could have been prevented from returning. Not surprisingly, in a letter to Harry Pollitt, Kerrigan insisted that the shooting had been entirely accidental:

The accident was the result of a stupid mistake for which I was responsible and it was just chance that the consequences were not a great deal more serious . . . it had bad effects politically . . . Mac is a well known figure in Britain being an author etc. and it would be impossible for the accident not to be known of there.[53]

Whatever the truth of the matter, Macartney never returned to Spain. When the British Battalion went into battle at Jarama later that month, he had been replaced by a long-standing Communist Party figure, the *Daily Worker*'s military correspondent, Tom Wintringham.[54] As Base Commissar, Kerrigan was kept out of the fighting, though when he heard of the dreadful slaughter during the Battalion's first day of action at Jarama—only half of the battalion were still standing by nightfall—he rushed off to visit the traumatised survivors:

I went to hospital and I saw one lad with a bullet wound in his stomach and they tell me that he's going to die and he couldn't get water and he's asking me to give him water. I came across [Doug] Springhall [the Battalion's Political Commissar]. He had a bullet wound in the cheek and it came out of the other side and by some miracle it didn't hit his eyes, it didn't go through his mouth and it didn't go into the brain. He was a lucky man.[55]

Despite the horrendous losses, Kerrigan always argued that

the sacrifice at Jarama had been unavoidable, for the battle had prevented Franco's forces from achieving their key objective of encircling the Spanish capital.[56] However, on a personal level, Kerrigan was worried that news of the bloodbath might have reached his wife, so he wrote to her on 26 February, reassuring her that, 'except for air raids [he] was as safe as anyone in Spain.'[57] He was very much looking forward to returning home to see her and his new daughter, who had been born on 24 January.[58]

Before leaving Spain, Kerrigan took the opportunity to visit the Jarama wounded who were scattered among hospitals across Republican Spain.[59] He also met with the poet Stephen Spender, who was in Spain hoping to secure the release of his ex-boyfriend, Tony Hyndman, who had been imprisoned after refusing an order while serving on the Jarama front. Kerrigan agreed to arrange Hyndman's release and, admitting to Spender that the young volunteer was unsuitable for front-line service, promised him that Hyndman would be allocated a job away from the front.[60] However, it was a promise that Kerrigan would be unable, or unwilling, to keep. In March 1937, Hyndman was informed that the military situation was now so desperate that every man was needed at the front and he was to be drafted. He promptly deserted again but was picked up in Valencia and thrown into jail.[61] Imprisoned for two months in a prison camp for malcontents, deserters and political dissenters, Hyndman was eventually released and invalided home in late July.[62]

Kerrigan returned to Britain with Doug Springhall, who was still convalescing from the wound sustained at Jarama. Special Branch carefully noted the pair's arrival at Dover from Calais at 5pm on 23 March 1937.[63] Both were expecting to return to Spain, though a confidential letter from 'The Old Man' (Harry Pollitt) to 'Robin' (Robert Page Arnot, the representative of the British Communist Party to the Comintern), admitted that neither would be allowed to go back; '[for] we have sent so many leading forces [that] it is now necessary to protect the Party here.'[64] After a visit home to see Rose and their new baby daughter, Sheila, Kerrigan took up campaigning for the Spanish Republic. On 4 April 1937, he spoke at a Party meeting in Battersea where he heaped praise on the British medical volunteers and enthused over the battalion's leader, Jock Cunningham, a veteran of the Argyll and Sutherland Highlanders, who had played a major part in maintaining the volunteers' nerve at Jarama. The following month, Kerrigan was one of many who turned up at Victoria Station to welcome home more than a dozen former members of the British Machine Gun Company who had endured three months as prisoners of war.[65] However, Spain was not Kerrigan's only concern; other matters could not be ignored. The summer saw Kerrigan elected to the Central Executive Committee of the Communist Party, just prior to leaving on a month-long visit to the Soviet Union.

Despite the Party's determination not to allow Kerrigan to return to Spain, his experience and authority were sorely missed. The near annihilation of the British Battalion during the Battle of Brunete in July 1937 caused a number of serious rows between a number of senior British figures in Spain, leading to five of them being recalled. Consequently, at a Communist Party Committee meeting in November, the decision was taken that Kerrigan would, after all be allowed to go back. When Bill Rust, the *Daily Worker* correspondent in Spain, returned to Britain in the summer of 1938, Kerrigan was sent out to replace him.[66]

Despite the appalling casualties at Brunete and a catastrophic drop in morale following the chaotic Republican retreats during the spring of 1938, when Kerrigan returned to Spain he found the British volunteers in surprisingly good spirits. 'They are great lads, all of them,' Kerrigan declared, 'and the folk at home should be proud of every member of our glorious British Battalion.'[67] Kerrigan's confidence and optimism would be sorely tested during the coming months, as Republican forces launched a huge, ambitious counter-attack across the River Ebro.

The offensive that began on 24 July 1938 initially caught Franco's forces unawares. Republican troops made swift progress and were able to regain some of the territory they had lost in the spring. 'Comrades, the British Battalion with the rest of the Spanish People's Army is writing a new page in history,' wrote Kerrigan triumphantly for the *Daily Worker*.[68] Kerrigan accompanied the British as they advanced; he and Joe North, the American *Daily Worker* correspondent, 'were the first newspaper correspondents to cross the Ebro.'[69] At first, however, Kerrigan was unable to cross the river, for the pontoon bridge was blocked by a broken down lorry. While he waited for a path to be cleared, Kerrigan, who was a strong swimmer, boldly decided to swim across the wide and fast-moving river.[70] It was a decision he soon came to regret when he was caught out in the middle of the river during an air attack. With bombs dropping all around him, he swam desperately for the shore, before taking cover in a railway tunnel, stark naked, until the Nationalist aeroplanes finally flew off.[71]

Reunited with the advancing Republican soldiers—and his clothes—Kerrigan watched as the battalion attacked the town of Gandesa, key to the entire offensive. Confident that the town was about to be overrun, Kerrigan filed a despatch to the *Daily Worker* reporting that 'Gandesa was in our hands and the troops who took it were driving south-west leaving some Battalions to mop up the hundreds of stragglers cut off by our smashing blows.'[72] However, when the town's defenders stubbornly refused to concede defeat, Kerrigan was forced to rewrite his presumptuous account. He returned to the Hotel Gran Vía in Barcelona, where he continued to file despatches and concluded his report of the previous twelve days' action with a passionate appeal:

> While these lads are resting and preparing to go into action once more, it is necessary to remind people in Britain of the importance of guaranteeing the best result from their magnificent work. Some have died, and many more have been wounded, though fortunately not very seriously, in this last great battle which is not yet ended. Please do not let us lose one little bit of what these men's effort and sacrifice have achieved for Spain and Britain.[73]

However, he wrote a rather more candid report for the Party leadership in Britain disclosing 'facts that I cannot write about in the *Daily [Worker]*,' including a revealing description of the pitiful condition of the British volunteers:

> From the 25th to the morning of the 30th they had nothing to drink but a little water, sometimes going for a day without this . . . They are fighting and marching over mountains, the rocks of which have cut their Spanish shoes to pieces. Many are literally barefoot as well as being in rags because of wear of clothes. Nobody has had a wash since the start of the offensive.[74]

Kerrigan's reports for the *Daily Worker* gradually lost the triumphalism of the summer, telling instead of a 'determined, valorous defence against massive over-whelming force.'[75] In the autumn, with the International Brigades debilitated by death, wounds and illness, Premier Negrín announced that they were to be withdrawn, vainly hoping to shame the western democracies into pressing Franco for a similar action. On 23 September, the British battalion went into action for the last time. Pounded by a terrifying Nationalist artillery barrage, they were completely overrun by Franco's troops. Several days later, a devastated Kerrigan wrote a letter to Harry Pollitt, 'the most difficult I have ever written in my life,' telling of his shock at the terrible outcome of their final battle:

> I could give dozens of individual acts of heroism but what is the use. The list of citations which I enclose, tells in brief official terms of the acts of deathless glory which were played out against a background of the cutting to pieces of our very bravest. I was at the beginning of the British Battalion. I saw what No. 1 Coy. came through at Córdoba and I will never forget when I was told what our casualties were in those first 3 days at Jarama. But nothing can compare with the end of our battalion.[76]

The surviving members of the British Battalion were withdrawn from the front on 24 September and repatriated just over two months later.[77] A disheartened Peter Kerrigan also prepared himself to return home. By mid-November 1938 he was back in Glasgow, picking up his old job as Scottish Organiser.[78]

For the veterans of the fighting in Spain, many of whom bore physical and mental scars, it was not always easy readjusting to 'normal' civilian life, assuming, of course, that they could find work. It was perhaps more straightforward for those like Kerrigan, whose function in Spain had essentially been a continuation of their work for the Party at home and were able to return to their previous jobs. However, as Kerrigan's wife discovered, while her husband might not have been directly involved in the fighting, it had still left an indelible mark:

> There was a terrible change in him, he was quite morose and he seemed very within himself. He was really going grey and this was because he'd seen all the people who had died in Spain.[79]

Kerrigan's state of mind might not have been helped by criticisms about the conduct of senior Communists in Spain. Kerrigan in particular was singled out by an Irish volunteer who complained that while the Party had provided Kerrigan with a safe job behind the line and he had been allowed to return home, the rank and file, who were being slaughtered on the battlefields, were prevented from doing so.[80] This was a popular complaint and was not without some basis.[81] Nevertheless, the Party leadership refused to accept the complaints, accusing the Irishman of being a 'lying, untrustworthy heavy drinker' and a deserter.[82] Another critic was the Glaswegian, Alec Marcovich, who had argued with Kerrigan several years earlier. Having arrived in Spain in October 1937, Marcovich had quickly gained a reputation as a troublemaker for repeatedly criticising the battalion command. When he rashly challenged the Scottish political commissar, Bob Cooney, in front of the battalion, Marcovich was accused of being 'a provocateur, a Trotskyist, and a generally pessimistic element.'[83] Hauled off to Brigade headquarters, Marcovich spent much of the war in jail and in a punishment battalion, an experience he was lucky to survive. He only managed to escape at the end of the war when the prison guards disappeared, allowing the inmates to break out. Marcovich eventually made it home in mid-February 1939, convinced that Kerrigan had been behind his ill-treatment.[84]

Yet while outspoken critics of the Communist Party's control of the Brigades were more numerous than Kerrigan and the Party leadership might be prepared to admit, they were nonetheless a minority. While it's impossible to quantify, given that some dissenters will have prudently kept quiet, most veterans appeared to feel a mixture of pride for what they'd achieved in Spain, together with sadness for the defeat and the death of so many comrades. Consequently, when the International Brigade Association (IBA) was formed in March 1939, several hundred veterans joined to 'carry on in Britain the spirit and tradition of the International Brigade as front-line fighters for the defence and advance of democracy against Fascism.' Inevitably, Kerrigan took a leading role, attending committee meetings, speaking at commemorations and ensuring that the association maintained a close relationship with the Communist Party.[85]

Following the tragic, though by this stage inevitable end of the civil war and Franco's triumphant proclamation of victory on 1 April 1939, campaigning and fund-raising for the exiled Spanish Republic continued, though many veterans' minds were increasingly preoccupied by the impending European war against fascism. However, on 23 August 1939 the signing of the infamous non-aggression pact between Hitler's Germany and Stalin's Soviet Union forced Communists around the world to discard anti-fascism in favour of 'anti-imperialism'. Kerrigan readily admitted that the pact presented members of the Communist Party with a powerful dilemma and he himself felt torn in two: 'Most of us were taken by surprise and there was an instinctive reaction against it . . . there was quite an argument on the executive committee on the question,' Kerrigan remarked with some understatement.[86] There was little time to adjust to the new Party line for one week later Hitler invaded Poland and Britain's declaration of war on Germany followed two days later.

Harry Pollitt immediately proclaimed it to be an anti-fascist war, just as the volunteers had been fighting in Spain. However, when news arrived that Stalin had declared this to be an imperialist war which must be opposed, there was another huge row among the Party leadership, leading to Pollitt being replaced. Despite initially having supported Pollitt, Kerrigan quickly dropped into line.[87] Many veterans and Party members did not; not least Kerrigan's wife Rose who, being Jewish, strongly disagreed with the Party's opposition to the war. However, as a loyal Party member—and wife—she kept her misgivings to herself.[88]

At the beginning of the war, Rose and the children—seven-year-old Rose and three-year-old Sheila—were evacuated to Ellon, 16 kilometres north of Aberdeen. However, when Kerrigan was transferred from Glasgow to London in November 1939, he pleaded with Rose to go with him and, apparently determined not to allow another woman the opportunity to make a play for her husband, she agreed.[89] With London in the midst of a massively ambitious evacuation programme, the children were unable to go with them, so they were evacuated to Dunoon, on the Cowal peninsula, but when Rose discovered to her horror that young Rose and Sheila had become infested with lice, the children were sent instead to stay with a large family in a crofter's cottage in Brodwick, on the Isle of Arran. Unfortunately, this arrangement proved no better, for the girls picked up ringworm, requiring treatment in Glasgow, which caused both of them to lose their hair. Finally, Rose found them a billet with the family who owned the butcher's shop in Brodick, where the girls remained for two and a half years.[90]

Though his younger brother, Herbert, who had also served in Spain, was drafted in to the British Army and another brother, John, served in the RAF, Peter Kerrigan, as a senior member of an organisation which was now officially opposed to prosecuting the war, was ineligible for British military service.[91] Furthermore, on 25 May 1940, Kerrigan's name was added to the list of political extremists who could potentially be interned under Defence Regulation 18B, part of the British Government's Emergency Powers (Defence) Act brought in at the beginning of the war. Consequently, the Party instructed Kerrigan to concentrate on his industrial organising work, so that if he were arrested, it could be portrayed as an undemocratic attack on trade unionism, rather than on the Communist Party.[92] With a wife and two children to support, Kerrigan needed a job, but his efforts met with strong disapproval from the Commissioner of Special Branch, who argued that 'there is no reason to believe that Kerrigan will further the war effort by entering factory employment.'[93]

In fact, the security services had long had very serious concerns about Kerrigan's activities beyond his overt work for the Communist Party, suspecting that he and other veterans of the Spanish war might be involved in espionage.[94] Their fears were stoked by reports that Kerrigan had been keeping watch on a small government building near Dartford, which Kerrigan (mistakenly) believed to be the base for British atomic research. MI5 had also discovered that Kerrigan was secretly using the home of two Communist associates to meet with a scientist who was suspected of passing on secrets to the Party.[95] However, as no firm evidence of spying could be found, the Security Services were restricted to keeping him under surveillance in the hope that he would give himself away. Consequently, Special Branch dutifully filed reports of Kerrigan's speeches, noting his wide-ranging attacks on the evils of 'capitalist imperialism' and demands for urgent wage increases in response to depressed living standards. Other targets included industrial conscription and the lack of air raid provision, and Kerrigan spoke of the importance of the People's Convention—for which he had been nominated as a potential delegate—the Communist Party's alternative to the current government, which was seen (or portrayed) as being in the pocket of the rich, appeasers and reactionaries.[96]

When the government banned the *Daily Worker* on 21 January 1941, accusing it of undermining national morale by its opposition to the war, campaigns for its restoration became a priority and Kerrigan's fear that he and other senior Communists might be interned was intensified. Rather than being interned, in April 1941, Kerrigan was required to register for employment, leading to him being allocated a job as a turner at D Napier & Son Ltd, an experimental aircraft factory in Acton.[97] A discreet word was had with the management, alerting them to Kerrigan's background and recommending that he 'ought not to be employed where he can have access to confidential information.'[98] In fact, banning the Communist Party and interning its leaders proved further than the government was prepared to go. The matter was anyway rendered irrelevant when Germany invaded the Soviet Union in June 1941 and the Communist Party performed a rapid about turn from bitter opponents of the war to its noisy cheerleaders. This brought to an end a difficult time for Kerrigan and other veterans of the Spanish war, for a return to the anti-fascist struggle meant that the lessons of Spain could now be applied to the war in Europe.[99] Despite having opposed the war for the last two years, Kerrigan brazenly explained that 'the policy of the CP in this war is to fight and kill as many German Nazis as possible.'[100] He justified the Party's dramatic shift by laying out what he saw as the differences between the current conflict and the imperialist war of 1914-1918:

> The alternatives before us are either a victory of the United Nations, the re-emergence of the working-class-movement in Europe, the preservation of the Socialist sixth of the world, and the establishment of a firm basis for going forward to Socialism in this country; or the triumph of Fascism, Lidices for South Wales, Durham, Yorkshire and Scotland, the destruction of the workers' movement in Britain, the destruction of the Socialist sixth of the world, and with that, the postponement of Socialism for generations.[101]

Not all were swayed by Kerrigan's rhetoric and his newfound enthusiasm for the war; as the chairman of the Home Defence (Security) Executive committee (established by the Prime Minister in May 1940 to tackle matters relating to the defence of Britain against a fifth column), elegantly put it: 'It is clear that the Communist game is still the same; but it is being played on a much better wicket.'[102] Consequently, despite the Party's dramatic reversal, Kerrigan remained ineligible for military service, restricting him to Party and Trade Union work. Denied an opportunity to return to the fight against fascism, Kerrigan continued his turning work at Napiers, where he was described by his superintendent as 'quiet and well behaved and an excellent worker', until 14 July 1941 when he quit to become the Communist Party's full time industrial organiser.[103]

A week later, Kerrigan spoke at a large IBA meeting at London's Red Lion Square. He argued forcefully that 'the Spanish people and the members of the International Brigade had started the war against Hitler five years ago. 'The present war is a continuation of the struggle. The only Government that comes out as having clean hands with regard to the Franco Spanish conflict is the Soviet Government.'[104] He urged that all possible assistance should be provided to the Soviet Union 'which was struggling heroically against the Germans', including the opening up of a second Allied front and increased levels of industrial production.[105] At a Party meeting in Motherwell in March 1942, Kerrigan lectured workers 'not to let Trade Union rules interfere with maximum production, for without that, the vital second front would not be possible.'[106]

The government's lifting of the ban on the *Daily Worker* in August 1942 meant that Kerrigan and other senior members of the Party could rest easier, freed from the prospect of internment.[107] At the end of October, Kerrigan replaced JR Campbell as Scottish Industrial Organiser which, though appearing to be a step down from his previous job, actually demonstrated the importance of Scotland to the Party (home, of course, to their solitary MP).[108] Consequently, though he moved to Glasgow, Kerrigan remained a member of the Party's Executive Committee, the Political Bureau, based in London.[109] Meanwhile, despite the lifting of the ban on the *Worker*, surveillance of the Party's senior figures continued. As a memorandum from the Chief Constable of Glasgow confirmed, '[Kerrigan's] future activities will receive the closest attention here and will be reported on.'[110] The efforts soon appeared to have paid off. During the spring of 1943, MI5 became aware that, with Harry Pollitt's full knowledge and permission, Kerrigan had met with a member of the Soviet Trade Delegation. However, what MI5 knew—and Pollitt didn't—was that Kerrigan had used the meeting to surreptitiously pass on secret information and photographs relating to British shipbuilding. When Pollitt found out, he was incensed. Fully alert to the potentially disastrous repercussions for the Party if a senior figure was caught passing documents to the Russians, he categorically forbade Kerrigan from holding any further meetings with the delegation.[111]

Despite his transgression, in the summer of 1943 Kerrigan returned to London and his job as the Party's National Organiser.[112] Charged with expanding Communist influence within the Trade Union movement, Kerrigan laid out his ambition to 'recruit millions of new members to the trade unions' at the Party's 16 National Congress in October.[113] It was not an easy task, not least because Kerrigan, in line with Party policy of working for maximum productivity in support of the war effort, was seen to have undermined shop stewards by actively working to prevent industrial action, such as during a strike at the Vickers Armstrong factory in Barrow-in-Furness the previous month.[114]

Throughout 1944, as Allied troops prepared to launch their assault on Nazi occupied Europe, Kerrigan continued his Party work, speaking at local meetings and contributing articles for the *Daily Worker* and other communist publications.[115] He was also put forward as the Communist parliamentary candidate for Shettleston in Glasgow, where the sitting MP, John McGovern (who had defeated Saklatvala in 1930 when Kerrigan had been his campaign manager), was a member of the Independent Labour Party and consequently bitterly anti-Communist.[116] The election was due to be held in July 1945, but preparations for the election were overshadowed by the defeat of Germany and the declaration of peace in Europe in May 1945.

The defeat of Hitler's Nazi regime offered the tantalising prospect that the Allies would be able to achieve what the veterans of the Spanish war had fought for: the removal of Hitler's ally, General Franco, and the return of democracy in Spain. After all, the Spanish dictator had clearly been a supporter of the Axis powers, even if Spain had never officially entered the war.[117] While the general election in July did not see great success for the Communist Party in general, nor for Kerrigan in particular (he finished in fourth place, with 7,000 fewer votes than McGovern), the new government did appear to offer further hope.[118] The new Prime Minister, Clement Attlee, had been deeply sympathetic to the Republican cause, and had even visited the British volunteers fighting in Spain who had the battalion's Number One Company in his honour. The Labour Party's chairman, Harold Laski, further inflamed the veterans' hopes when he declared that they 'were going to be in a position to do full justice to our Spanish comrades.'[119]

However, the new Foreign Secretary, Ernest Bevin, dashed the hopes of supporters of the defeated Spanish Republic when he declared that any form of military intervention was out of the question. Having seen six years of world war, Bevin argued vehemently that 'further civil war and bloodshed were too high a price for the disappearance of General Franco' and that, besides, foreign intervention might actually strengthen Franco's position.[120] It was a crushing disappointment, but Kerrigan and other supporters of Republican Spain did not give up hope, even if their efforts were limited to trying to restrain the excesses of the Franco dictatorship. At a large public meeting at Hyde Park on 11 September 1945, Kerrigan added his voice to a campaign which pressured Franco into commuting the death sentences on two Spanish Communists, Santiago Alvarez Gómez and Sebastián Zapirain.[121] The following March, he spoke at a demonstration organised by The Emergency Committee for Democratic Spain in favour of a boycott on supplying machinery to Franco's Spain.[122]

However, there was little appetite within the British government for serious action against the Franco dictatorship, not least because the dawning of the cold war meant a return to Stalin's position as the western democracies' *bête noire*. Consequently, Communist parties were regarded with the utmost suspicion by intelligence agencies, who suspected—sometimes with good reason—that Party members were involved in spying for the Soviet Union. In July 1947, the Security Services' suspicions that Kerrigan had been involved seemed to be confirmed when Alex Foote, a veteran of Spain who had been involved in a Soviet spy-ring during the Second World War (see Chapter Eight), named Kerrigan as a Russian agent. While Foote was unable to provide any evidence, the accusation very much coloured MI5's views of Kerrigan's trip to Budapest in June 1948 for the Communist Party's Unity Congress. They noted pointedly how Kerrigan appeared to be treated like royalty, accommodated in a luxury hotel with a swimming pool, while being plied with wine and given gifts, including a cigarette case and a bottle of expensive liqueur. Even more suspiciously, Kerrigan's finances appeared remarkably healthy, given the Communist Party's notoriously weak finances:

> KERRIGAN now lives in a state of comparative affluence, and though his wife has quite a good job as a tailoress in the West End earning about 5½ guineas a week, his general scale of living and expenditure seem to be in excess of his obvious means.[123]

A top-secret memo of 22 November 1949 confirmed that Foote's revelations had been taken seriously and that MI5 were convinced that Kerrigan had to be 'involved in the passing of some unspecified information to the Russians.'[124] Consequently, when surveillance revealed that there was regular contact between 'Russians employed at their 3 Rosary Gardens office (in South Kensington) and Kerrigan,' MI5 were cock-a-hoop that they might, finally, have got their man. However, it soon emerged that far from involving some form of skulduggery, the subject of the meetings was rather less sensational: the decline in circulation of *Soviet Weekly*, a turgid propaganda sheet providing 'news' from the Soviet Union.

Besides, as MI5 were aware, Kerrigan probably had plenty on his plate domestically. 1950 was a challenging year for the Spanish veteran, who found himself embroiled in damaging arguments involving both the IBA and the Communist Party. The first was very much self-inflicted, for Kerrigan had involved himself in a power struggle among the upper echelons of the Communist Party. Kerrigan had long been critical of Harry Pollitt's support for the election of a Labour Government, believing instead that efforts should instead be geared towards the Party's industrial policy and fomenting a revolutionary situation.[125] So, during the winter of 1949-50 when the latest of a number of periods of ill health forced Pollitt to take time off work, Kerrigan made a bid to take over as leader.[126] As a gleeful

MI5 report noted, when Pollitt got wind of Kerrigan's scheme, he was incensed:

> Behind the scenes, KERRIGAN is still fighting POLLITT . . .
> Both POLLITT and KERRIGAN try to give the impression that
> all is well, but really relations are very strained.[127]

However, Kerrigan's ambitions to replace the 'old man', as he was known within the Party, were unsuccessful, for Kerrigan did not command universal support. '[Pollitt's] corpse won't be cold before you'll be stepping in his shoes,' Herbert Matthews remarked, not entirely seriously.[128]

Kerrigan's second crisis, within the International Brigade Association was, perhaps, even more serious. A row had been building in the organisation ever since Tito's Yugoslavia had been expelled from the Cominform (the Comintern's successor) in 1948. Despite a powerful and heartfelt appeal from Yugoslav veterans of the International Brigades, Kerrigan and other Communists among the IBA's leadership had slavishly supported Stalin's action.[129] However, many British veterans sided with their former comrades-in-arms, causing a seismic rift in the organisation. For some veterans such as Julius 'Jud' Colman from Manchester, who had originally joined the YCL in 1933, it spurred them to split with Communism for good:

> Disillusionment set in . . . [with] . . . the attacks on Tito. Tito's
> government was composed mostly of Yugoslav brigaders.
> Stalin was accusing them of being anti-communist traitors . . .
> It didn't change my belief in Socialism and a better world, but I
> will no longer show blind loyalty to an ideology that will not
> allow another point of view.[130]

Others were similarly disgusted. The Scottish Secretary of the IBA, George Murray, who had served as a commissar in Spain, expressed his outrage at the Executive Committee's labelling of the former Yugoslav volunteers as 'liars and traitors'. This forced Kerrigan to make an emergency visit to Glasgow where he and Murray had a difficult meeting, for the pair were, MI5 noted, 'not at all on friendly terms.'[131] Unsurprisingly,

Kerrigan's seniority and authority in both the IBA and the Party held sway and having already been expelled from the Communist Party, Murray promptly resigned his IBA post.[132]

While Kerrigan, the IBA and the Communist Party managed to survive the two arguments, Kerrigan's woes were by no means over, for the Security Services had not given up trying to find evidence linking him to espionage. In December 1950, their hopes were raised when Kerrigan was spotted with Hilda Wright Forbes, the former secretary of London Communist MP, Phil Piratin, at a Royal Navy depot at Eaglescliffe, near Stockton-on-Tees.[133] Yet an investigation revealed that, rather than evidence of spying, the explanation was more prosaic: 'There is nothing of a secret or confidential nature kept by the Admiralty at Eaglescliffe . . . the interest shown by Peter KERRIGAN in the Naval Depot is in the possible formation of a Communist Industrial Group.'[134] The Security Services were not prepared to give up the chase, however, and several months later, Kerrigan was subjected to yet another detailed investigation. The fear on this occasion was that, as National Organiser, Kerrigan was 'in a good position to assist the Russian Intelligence Service by talent-spotting and making enquiries about potential agents,' giving a great significance to his recent trips to eastern Europe.[135] Consequently, he was placed under close surveillance once again and all his activities and meetings closely monitored and reported down to the finest detail. Yet, just as on previous occasions, the evidence suggested that MI5 were being overzealous; a dismissive report by the Chief Constable of Glasgow confirmed that Special Branch did not actually believe Kerrigan's contacts to be of any great significance.[136]

In fact, as MI5 knew, since 1951, Kerrigan's efforts had been directed mainly to his demanding work as National Industrial Organiser. Kerrigan believed it to be 'one of the most important posts in any Communist Party' and it certainly made him a powerful figure in both the Communist Party and the post war labour movement.[137] During the 1950s and 1960s, the Trade Union movement was the real centre of power and, as one historian shrewdly observed, 'King Street was far more likely to take orders from Communist union leaders than to give them.'[138]

Nevertheless, Kerrigan never achieved the prominence of another Trade Unionist and veteran of Spain, the General Secretary of the Transport and General Workers' Union and 'the most powerful man in Britain', Jack Jones.[139] On the contrary, Kerrigan's increasing age in the 1950s saw him approaching the end of his long career in the Trade Union movement. His final retirement was spurred by his involvement in a serious vote-rigging scandal at the end of the 1950s, which left his reputation badly tarnished. As 'the policeman for the Party', Kerrigan's history of arm-twisting was notorious.[140] However, this was something altogether more serious.[141]

In an election for the General Secretary of the Electrical Trades Union (ETU) in 1959, Frank Haxell, the official Communist Party candidate was initially declared the winner, but the result was overturned after a challenge in the High Court. Haxell was stripped of his title and a number of Party members were found guilty of conspiracy and fraud. A whistle-blower—a former member of the Party—admitted that for several years he had been involved in ballot-rigging with the ETU, and accused Kerrigan, who had acted as Returning Officer, of having orchestrated it.[142] While the Party always denied it, the High Court judgment which condemned the former Communist leadership of the ETU for ballot-rigging on a massive scale was hugely damaging and led to Kerrigan having to step down from the Communist Party Executive.

Five years later, Kerrigan turned 66 years of age. Having been a Trade Unionist for 50 years, during which time he had always held office, Kerrigan finally retired from his job as Industrial Organiser, handing it over to another veteran of the International Brigades, the Canadian born Bert Ramelson.[143] Despite his official retirement, Kerrigan remained determinedly politically active, working in the circulation office of the *Morning Star* and selling the paper on the streets of Sydenham every Saturday morning.[144] He continued to attend Party and Trade Union branch meetings and was a regular visitor to Scotland, where he helped organise overseas delegations.

He also continued to devote time to the IBA. In the summer of 1976, Kerrigan was one of over 100 veterans to participate in a conference organised by the association at Loughborough's Cooperative College, to mark 40 years since the outbreak of the civil war. Key to the event was the interviewing of veterans of the civil war for the Imperial War Museum's Sound Archive and the Manchester Studies Unit. Though he gave a detailed, highly informative interview, Kerrigan was evidently not an easy subject. In the recording held in the Imperial War Museum in London he can be heard interrupting and contradicting the interviewer and insistently slamming his hand down for emphasis.[145] Kerrigan stuck tenaciously to the line he had followed in Spain, that the war was an anti-fascist, rather than a civil war and he continued to hold the POUM responsible for the internecine fighting in Barcelona in May 1937. When asked about the scandalous kidnap and murder of the leader of the anti-Stalinist POUM, Andreu Nin, Kerrigan hedged: 'Well, I'm not sure of the facts and I wouldn't like to pass a judgement on the thing.'[146] Yet he could, on occasion, rise above his sectarianism, for instance applauding the work of reporters in Spain with whom he had profound political differences. He was particularly admiring of Henry Buckley, who wrote extremely fair-minded reports for the pro-Franco *Daily Telegraph* and the *Daily Express*'s Sefton Delmer, admiring the dedication and bravery that saw Delmer cross the River Ebro so he could see for himself what was happening on the front line.[147] Above all, though, what emerges from Kerrigan's interview (and those of many other veterans) is how genuinely proud he continued to be of his involvement—and that of his 2,500 comrades from Britain and Ireland—in the war in Spain: 'Looking back, in many ways it was a privilege to get the experience', he declared.[148]

The following year, less than twelve months after the IBA's anniversary conference, a relatively peaceful transition saw democratic elections in Spain. It was what the veterans had campaigned for ever since the end of the civil war. Kerrigan had refused to visit Spain while the dictatorship remained but insisted that 'if there was popular government there, I'd be straight away there with my wife for a visit.'[149] At long last he had the opportunity, yet he never did return, for just five months after the elections, on Thursday 5 December 1977 at the age of

78, Peter Kerrigan died. 'Big Peter,' mourned his old friend Manassah 'Sam' Lesser (still writing under his *nom de plume*, Sam Russell) 'is with us no more.'[150] In an obituary in the *Morning Star*, Lesser paid homage to Kerrigan's courage, arguing that the Scot was 'one of the most outstanding comrades in Spain . . . I can't think of any other comrade who was as successful as Peter Kerrigan.'[151]

Kerrigan and Lesser had long been close friends, so it would be surprising if he had said anything different, particularly within the pages of the Communist *Morning Star*. However, as the most senior political officer in Spain Kerrigan did command respect, among loyal Party members, at least.[152] And his authority was certainly not limited to his time in Spain. From the 1930s onwards, Kerrigan was one of the key Party members responsible for the tactics and policies adopted by the CPGB. The Security Services were certainly in no doubt of his importance: 'in any estimate of the Party's leadership, he would certainly be placed in the first half dozen,' claimed Sir David Petrie, the Director-General of MI5.[153] Having expended a huge amount of resources on keeping tabs on Kerrigan, they might be expected to stress his importance, but Kerrigan certainly also had admirers within the labour movement. In 1952, the AEU honoured Kerrigan's long period of service with the Order of Merit and, fourteen years later, he was honoured again having held office for more than 40 years. Unsurprisingly, Communists respected him, seeing him as 'a legendary force in the post-war labour movement.'[154] Finlay Hart, Kerrigan's predecessor as the Party's Scottish National Industrial Organiser, argued that 'even the most hostile anti-communist officials had a great respect for Peter's political and economic judgement.'[155]

To many, though, Kerrigan was seen as sectarian, inflexible and ruthless, a typical Communist Party apparatchik. In Spain, the London sculptor Jason Gurney had found Kerrigan as 'dour and ill-tempered as only a Scot can be, utterly devoid of any trace of humour.'[156] To one clearly unimpressed Socialist Labour League member, Kerrigan was simply 'a hard-core Stalinist.'[157] He could certainly be tough, disciplined and uncompromising; despite his personal admiration for the man, Sam Lesser acknowledged that Kerrigan could come across as 'a real typical Party bureaucrat.' Even Kerrigan's wife, Rose, admitted that the burly Communist was 'quite a disciplinarian.'[158] While other veterans of Spain gradually drifted away from the Party, appalled by the brutal excesses of the Soviet regime, Peter Kerrigan was not one of them. On the contrary, he never made any secret of his loyalty to the USSR and his great admiration of Stalin, despite the purges and regime of murderous terror.[159] Like Sam Lesser, (see Chapter Four) Peter Kerrigan supported the Soviet invasion of Hungary in 1956 even if he did oppose the later invasion of Czechoslovakia. While Kerrigan said that he condemned 'unequivocally' Stalin's murder of veterans of the Spanish war, he remained bitterly sectarian, or as he phrased it, 'hostile to Trotsky's theories.'[160]

Yet while Kerrigan was undoubtedly a determined advocate of Soviet Communism, there appears to be little evidence to justify the Security Services' fears that Kerrigan was a Soviet agent. While it is true that in 1943 he used a meeting with a Soviet Trade Delegation to surreptitiously pass on secret information and photographs relating to British shipbuilding, Kerrigan would no doubt have pointed out that the Soviet Union was then Britain's ally against the Axis powers. What the Security Service's file on Peter Kerrigan demonstrates more than anything else is how all of his activities, like those of the Communist Party itself, were always viewed as deeply suspicious.[161] Yet while a huge amount of time and effort was invested into keeping Kerrigan under surveillance and monitoring his telephone and post, the real Soviet fifth column, Philby, Burgess, Maclean and the other Cambridge spies, were overlooked and able to operate with impunity.[162] It was members of the British establishment itself, much more than working-class communists like Peter Kerrigan, who were able to do the real damage.

This is not to downplay either Kerrigan's importance in the Communist Party, nor his dedication to it. He was, after all, a member of the Party for the entirety of his adult life and a member of the Central Executive Committee for forty years. Never a womaniser or a hard drinker, Kerrigan's energies were always directed towards the ends of the Communist Party. Only his family occupied an equivalent standing. As a report in Kerrigan's MI5 file acknowledged, 'All the Kerrigans are greatly attached to each other.'[163] Certainly his relationship with his wife, Rose, was based on great affection and mutual respect. Kerrigan trusted Rose's judgement, admitting that, in general, 'her intuition proved to be correct', while she in turn was very supportive of his work, despite the impact on their social and family life.[164] He was undoubtedly proud of his daughters when they were admitted into a fiercely competitive north London girls' grammar school and perhaps even more so when they were accepted into Cambridge University.[165] However, the relative importance to Peter Kerrigan of his family and the Communist Party was revealed in a candid remark to a fellow Party member: 'If I ever had to choose one day, which I hope I will never have to—between my wife and my family and the Communist Party', Kerrigan confessed, 'I am a revolutionary—I must choose the Party.'[166]

Chapter Eight
The Red Musician: Alexander Allan Foote

On 10 November 1942, following the remarkable defeat of Rommel's forces at El Alamein in North Africa, a triumphant Winston Churchill famously announced that 'Now this is not the end. It is not even the beginning of the end, but it is, perhaps, the end of the beginning.' His words were to prove as prescient as they were erudite, for a year later the British Prime Minister was in a position to meet American President Franklin D Roosevelt and Russian Premier Joseph Stalin to agree on a date for a future invasion of occupied Europe. At the same time that this famous encounter between 'The Big Three' was underway in Tehran, though with rather less fanfare, police in neutral Switzerland were in the process of arresting a British national for being in possession of a clandestine, illegal wireless transmission set.[1] Set against El Alamein or Tehran, this was hardly big news. However, the importance of the work of this British national, and the team of spies of which he was part, should not be underestimated. Over the previous year and a half, the Swiss *Rote Drei* (Red Three) spy ring provided the Soviet Red Army with a mass of hugely important intelligence about the Wehrmacht. So highly did the Russians value the material that the British wireless operator, known by the code name 'Jim', was decorated four times and claimed to have been honoured with the rank of Major in the Red Army.[2]

The real name of 'Jim' was Alexander Allan Foote. Born on 13 April 1905 at 7 Rockley Street, Kirkdale, Liverpool, Foote was the eldest son of comfortably middle-class parents, Mary Florence and William Foote.[3] While Foote saw his father as 'a bit of a square peg' with a 'single-minded passion for chicken farming', Foote seems to have been given an upbringing typical of a child of the time, attending a local Yorkshire village school until the age of fourteen.[4] He initially found work as an apprentice and packer in a Manchester firm, though things clearly didn't work out, for by 1927, he was back living with his parents in Northenden, where he found temporary work as a coal merchant. By his own admission, bored and lacking direction, Foote struggled to settle into any form of career. Consequently, seeking adventure, on 26 July 1935, Foote enlisted for a six-year tour as an aircraft fitter in the Royal Air Force.[5] Posted to Gosport Fleet Air Arm, in Hampshire for training, 522151 First Class Aircraftman Foote struck up a friendship with a Corporal whose wife, he was to discover, was a member of the local Communist Party. Through them he met another member of the local Party, called Archie Williams. Known to friends and family as 'AC', Williams had migrated to Canada in 1923, but had been arrested for agitating against the infamous labour camps. Convicted of 'unlawful assembly and rioting', he was sentenced to two years' imprisonment, and had just been deported to the UK.[6] The pair became firm friends and Foote regularly visited AC and his wife Jane at their home in Gosport.[7]

When the Spanish Civil war broke out in the summer of 1936, both Foote and Williams were outraged that a democratically elected government should be attacked by a right-wing military uprising; Foote felt that it 'seemed to show everything up in black and white'. He watched on in horror as Nazi Germany and fascist Italy supplied Franco's forces with masses of aircraft, troops and weaponry, while Britain and France did very little to stop them. When news of the Communist Party's efforts to raise British volunteers for the Republic reached the local branch and fearing that he was about to be discharged for having made an invalid attestation in his original application, Foote promptly deserted. He was reported as illegally absent from his station on 23 December 1936.[8]

Both Foote and Williams resolved to volunteer for Spain. While Foote admitted that 'a love of adventure' played a part in his decision, he also insisted that 'I felt the cause was right.'[9] While, unlike the vast majority of volunteers for the International Brigades, Foote was not a Communist Party member, Williams was a trusted member of the Portsmouth branch and vouched for him.[10] Having both been accepted, they departed from Dover with a large group of volunteers.[11] They followed the route that most British followed; a weekend train ticket to Paris, then on to Perpignan by coach or train, then across the frontier into Spain. Foote and Williams arrived at the main International Brigade base at Albacete, roughly 150km south-east of Valencia, shortly after Christmas 1936. From there, the pair were sent for training at the embryonic British Battalion's base in the small village of Madrigueras, just north of Albacete.

While Williams joined the Machine-Gun Company of the British Battalion, Foote was posted to Brigade transport, where he worked as driver.[12] Promoted to Sergeant in charge of battalion transport, he took on the responsibility for chauffeuring battalion commanders including Jock Cunningham and Fred Copeman. By all accounts, Foote was well-thought of and popular, seen as a 'well-disciplined [and] responsible comrade.'[13] However, by the autumn of 1938, having been seriously injured in a vehicle accident, Foote was suffering from serious health problems. Consequently, he was sent home, arriving in Britain on 16 September.[14] Initially, Foote's period of leave was intended to be temporary, for the senior British Political Commissar in Spain, Peter Kerrigan, had earmarked Foote as a potential courier between London and Spain. While he would officially be transporting Red Cross supplies into Spain, in reality he would be carrying secret documents between the Communist Party headquarters in London and the Battalion command in Spain.[15] However, when Foote reported to the Party's head office in King Street to discuss the courier job, his former commander in Spain, Fred Copeman, informed him that the British Battalion's impending departure from Spain had made the courier job obsolete. However, over dinner, Copeman casually mentioned that a senior British Party figure in Spain, Doug Springhall, had asked whether Foote might still be interested in a job for the movement. 'I know nothing about the assignment,' Copeman told him, 'save that it will be abroad and very dangerous.'[16] Curious and with nothing else to occupy him, Foote agreed to discuss it further.

Consequently, Foote presented himself at the Belsize Park address given to him by Springhall. There, the door was opened by a 'respectable housewife with a slight foreign accent' who

Foote had been told was called Brigitte Lewis. After asking Foote a number of detailed questions, which he must have answered to her satisfaction, the enigmatic woman issued Foote with instructions. They were, Foote noted, suitably 'cloak and dagger': he was to go to Geneva, wearing a white scarf and holding a red belt in his right hand and wait outside the Post Office. At noon he would be approached by a woman carrying a green parcel, holding an orange in her hand. He was given no further information, not even who he would be working for: 'I knew that I was a spy and against whom I was supposed to be spying, but at first had no idea of the why and the wherefore or the directing hand.'[17] In fact, Springhall had recruited Foote for Red Army intelligence, the GRU.[18] He was a strange choice for an agent; as Foote candidly admitted, 'no one could have been more of an innocent in espionage than I was.' He didn't know how to operate a radio, he didn't know any secret codes and he was no linguist: he spoke French poorly, Spanish dreadfully and German hardly at all.

Nevertheless, Foote left for Switzerland on 20 October 1938 and at noon he was, as instructed, waiting outside the Geneva Post Office when he was approached by a smartly dressed woman, carrying a green parcel and an orange. She informed Foote, or 'Jim' as she instructed him to call himself, that he should call her 'Sonya'. From her accent, Foote guessed she was from Eastern Europe, perhaps Poland or Russia. She later told Foote that her real name was Maria Shultz, but this was not true. In fact 'Sonya' was a German born Jew called Ursula Hamburger (originally *Kuczyński*) and she was the sister of 'Brigitte Lewis', the mysterious woman who had interviewed Foote in Belsize Park. They were daughters of Robert René Kuczyński, a German-born Professor of Economics at London University, and they had four other siblings: Jürgen, Barbara, Sabine and Renate. All were involved in the Communist movement.[19] 'Sonya', allegedly a Colonel in the Red Army, would later become infamous as the handler for the German theoretical physicist Klaus Fuchs, who worked at the UK's Atomic Research Centre in Oxford. 'Sonya' passed vital secrets to the Russians enabling them to test their own nuclear device sooner than had been expected.[20]

Just as her sister had done before her, Ursula questioned Foote carefully, trying to ascertain whether he would be suitable for dangerous espionage work:

> He did not know that his mission would take him to fascist Germany. He had merely been sounded out on his readiness for international work under conditions as dangerous as the war in Spain . . . we spoke for several hours. Intensive conversations like this were important. I took note of everything, every word, cadence, gesture, every facial expression; and I pondered his reactions for a long time after we had parted.[21]

While she thought him 'a bit overweight', she concluded that 'his appearance was very acceptable and he knew how to behave.'[22] He would have to do.

As instructed by 'Sonya', Foote arrived in Munich on 10 November 1938, where he attempted to establish himself in the city, posing as a tourist who was looking to learn the language. He worked hard to be sociable and seems to have particularly sought out and enjoyed female company. At a dance held in the spring, he met a tall, twenty-six-year-old woman called Agnes Zimmermann, who was working in a Munich fashion bureau as a model. The pair fell in love and, following Foote's introduction to her family, became engaged to be married. However, when he realised that Agnes was the daughter of an ex-Nazi who had worked as a secret German agent in Switzerland, Foote took a chance and revealed to her that he was a spy. Fortunately, she was not frightened off and willingly became involved in his espionage activities, visiting him regularly in Switzerland until the outbreak of war, after which they kept in touch by letter. When not socialising, Foote spent his time learning how to become a radio operator, a 'musician' in intelligence jargon. In addition to learning the principles of radio-telegraphy and photography, Foote learnt how to build a short-wave transmitter, or 'music box'.

In a rare free moment, Foote was walking along Munich's Schellingstrasse one afternoon, whose restaurants were patronised by writers and artists such as Bertolt Brecht, Thomas Mann and Paul Klee. Tempted by the cheap tourist menu, he stopped for lunch at a typical local restaurant called the Osteria Bavaria.[23] Having taken a seat inside, Foote's eye was taken by two attractive young women seated at a nearby table.[24] However, Foote's casual interest in the pair was dramatically altered by the arrival of their lunch guest. Astonished, Foote realised that the two young women must be the English socialite and Nazi, Unity Mitford and Eva Braun, the girlfriend of Adolf Hitler. The women's lunch guest was none other than the German Führer himself.

As Foote had discovered, Hitler was in the habit of taking lunch in the Osteria and had been doing so for nearly fifteen years. The German leader felt not only at home in the restaurant, but safe, and therefore, as Foote noted with great interest, was often accompanied by only one or two adjutants. More surprising still, there was no SS presence at all in the restaurant. Foote excitedly reported his findings to 'Sonya' who immediately passed the information on to Moscow. News soon came back that Moscow was extremely interested in Foote's discovery and would be sending someone to help with surveillance. Assuming that they would be a long-standing operative, well-versed in the dark arts, Foote was taken aback to find one of his friends standing on the doorstep. The man, who had been instructed to use the code name 'John', was Leon Beurton, whom Foote had met in Spain when they were serving in the International Brigades' transport unit. Like Foote, Beurton was not a member of the Communist Party but had an outstanding record in Spain—an 'excellent comrade, always on the job'.[25] And he had also been recruited by Brigitte Kuczyński, before being passed on to her sister.

Beurton's orders were to reconnoitre the huge IG Farben chemical plant in Frankfurt, while helping Foote assess whether an assassination attempt on the German Führer might have a realistic chance of success. They began to keep watch on the Osteria, noting that while Hitler always dined in a private room, he was only separated from the main part of the restaurant by a thin wooden partition on which customers hung their coats. Foote was convinced that a bomb hidden among the coats, or left underneath them in an attaché case, would have a very good chance of eliminating the German leader. Furthermore, the lax security suggested that, as a backup, it might even be possible to smuggle in a pistol and shoot the Nazi leader. To test the theory, Beurton came up with an audacious plan:

> One day Bill [Beurton] stationed himself at the table next to the gangway, and as Hitler approached put his hand rapidly and furtively into his pocket—and drew out a cigarette case. I on the other side of the room watched the reactions of Hitler's entourage and the rest of the lunchers—among whom one imagined there must have been a fair sprinkling of trigger-happy Gestapo agents.[26]

To Foote's astonishment, 'nothing whatever happened.' The pair duly reported their findings to 'Sonya', who confirmed that Moscow was still considering their plan. With their hearts in their mouths, Foote and Beurton continued to keep watch on the Osteria, waiting for the go-ahead. However, days passed with no news, then weeks, until mid-August 1939 when Foote was abruptly ordered to stand down and return to Munich. Nothing more was said about the plan. Only on 23 August 1939, with the announcement of the Hitler-Stalin pact, did Foote understand why.

When Poland was invaded a week later, plunging Europe into war, 'Sonya' ordered Foote and Beurton to lay low in neutral Switzerland. Consequently, Foote spent the following nine months cooped up in a small pension in Montreux learning the principles of short-wave wireless transmission. Little was heard from Moscow until the capitulation of France in the summer of 1940, when Foote was ordered to return to work by improving his German and building up a ring of informants. Meanwhile, Kuczyński was ordered to incorporate Foote and her other agents into an existing Soviet spy network in Switzerland, run by a Hungarian cartographer called Alexander (Sándor) Radó.[27] Radó worked as a partner in a respectable Geneva cartographic firm and both he and his wife Helene were Soviet operatives. Radó was always careful to use the codename 'Albert' when dealing with fellow agents, though his coded signature in transmissions to Moscow, 'DORA' was hardly cryptic, as it was simply an anagram of his name.

Now freed of her responsibilities and terrified that if she were caught she could be expelled into Germany, 'Sonya' fled to England in December 1940 using a British passport that she had obtained by what was (initially at least) a marriage of convenience with Beurton.[28] Her new husband remained behind in Switzerland to help train up new radio operators, before following her to Britain in July 1942.[29] Foote, however, remained to begin work under his new chief, on whom he initially seems to have made a good impression:

Foote was undoubtedly an intelligent and determined man. He had a sense of humour, even inclining towards irony on occasion. Tall, broad-shouldered and powerfully built, he had blue eyes set in a permanently clean-shaven face . . . Jim was a talented student of Sonya's and became an outstanding radio operator. He had an extraordinary capacity for work.'[30]

However, Radó soon realised that while talented and hard-working, Foote was neither an ideological Marxist nor a disciplined Communist: 'What most surprised me about him', wrote Radó later, 'was his total lack of political education.'[31] Nevertheless, Radó trusted him to supervise two new recruits who used the codenames 'Edward' and 'Maude' (a local radio dealer called Édouard Hamel and his wife Olga) and train them up in the techniques of radio transmission. Once they were sufficiently proficient, Foote moved to Lausanne to set up his own transmitter.

Foote set up his 'music box' in the top floor apartment of a block in Chemin de Longeraie, just north of Lake Geneva.[32] Operating the transmitter in his kitchen, Foote set about contacting Moscow, but his transmissions initially went unanswered. Meanwhile, to help build up his 'cover', Foote did his best to integrate himself into the local Lausanne community, deliberately cultivating the impression of 'a mildly eccentric English millionaire who had managed to salt away a portion of his fortune abroad and who shunned the company of his fellow men.'[33] This wasn't always an easy fiction to maintain, for Moscow was notoriously reluctant to hand over money. Fortunately, Foote's efforts were helped considerably by his quiet demeanour and laconic humour. While he drank a lot, he never appeared to get drunk and was a very good listener. Bemused by Foote's apparent indolence and limited access to funds, neighbours joked that he might be a spy:

Stout and placid, with small porcelain-like eyes and thin blond hair, he once made an appearance in our group—and nobody gave him a second thought! He was the least mysterious fellow in the world! His face was so completely unexpressive that he never aroused curiosity on the part of his friends. Foote pretended to be in Switzerland for reasons of health. We made fun of his imaginary ills, which we suspected were a cover for his innate laziness. However, his paleness and slight cough, which he exhibited at the right moment, made these reasons plausible.[34]

Finally, on 12 March 1941, Foote's transmissions to Moscow were answered.[35] Initially at least, the demands of 'The Centre', as it was known by operatives, were not onerous: Foote was instructed to make contact twice a week and to prepare an economic analysis of Switzerland. However, as summer approached, the by now proficient radio operator took on some of Radó's work, transmitting intelligence received from the Hungarian's highly industrious sources. Of all of Radó's sources, by far the most productive and important was known by the codename 'LUCY'.

'Lucy' (or 'Lucie') was a German refugee publisher living in Lucerne called Rudolf Rössler (or Roessler).[36] He came from a middle-class Bavarian family, who were conservative, anti-Nazi and patriotic and Rössler had left Germany when Hitler came to power to become a naturalised Swiss citizen.[37] When Foote met him, he was surprised to find 'a quiet, nondescript little man . . . anyone less like the spy of fiction it would be hard to imagine . . . undistinguished looking, of medium height, aged about fifty, with his [mild] eyes blinking behind glasses, he looked exactly like almost anyone to be found in any suburban train anywhere in the world.'[38] However, Rössler's nondescript exterior disguised a prodigious memory, which contemporaries likened to a huge record card index. Rössler had been providing information to the Swiss intelligence agency known as Büro Ha since the start of the war, but was only prepared to pass on information to Radó's Soviet network if his identity and the source of his intelligence were both kept absolutely secret.[39]

Consequently, a number of intermediaries between Radó and Rössler, known as 'cut-outs', were put in place, in order to limit what could be revealed in the event of capture and interrogation. Rössler's contact was Christian Schneider, a German Jewish translator at the International Labour Office, part of the League of Nations, who used the codename 'TAYLOR' (an English translation of his name). Schneider's contact, known as 'SISSY', was a Polish Jew called Rachel Dübendorfer, who also worked in the International Labour Office as a stenographer.[40] She had previously worked with Radó's wife in the German Communist Party's Agitprop department and had herself been running a spy ring, which had been incorporated into Radó's network at the outset of the war.[41] She in turn passed on Rössler's intelligence to Foote ('Jim'), who transmitted it to Moscow.

Foote and Radó soon realised that 'Lucy' could supply an astonishing amount of detailed, up-to-date, high-level intelligence.[42] Initially, however, Moscow suspected that it was disinformation planted by the Abwehr and refused to believe it. As Foote later recalled, Radó also had his suspicions, but the Hungarian was quickly convinced:

One morning towards the middle of June my telephone rang and a voice which I recognised as Radó's bade me, in the usual veiled phraseology, to come to a rendezvous. When I saw Radó he was obviously worried and upset. He handed me a message that he had received . . . it stated that a general German attack on Russia would take place at dawn on June 22.[43]

According to Foote, Rössler warned about the forthcoming

launch of Operation Barbarossa, supplying precise information on the 148 German divisions massed on the Russian border.[44] Finally, on 22 June, with the Luftwaffe destroying Russian planes on the ground and Wehrmacht forces overwhelming the Russian defensives, Moscow's doubts were swept aside.[45] An abrupt message arrived for Foote and his fellow agents: 'Fascist beasts have invaded the Motherland of the working class. You are called upon to carry out your tasks in Germany to the best of your ability.'[46] As Wehrmacht troops advanced deep into the Soviet Union, intelligence obviously became of paramount importance. Foote's time as a socialite and gentleman spy had very much come to an end.

Radó later claimed that the intelligence provided by 'Lucy' included precise details of the location and makeup of German forces on the eastern front. It also, he said, included information obtained from the Japanese ambassador in Berne, confirming that Japan would not join the attack on the Soviet Union until Germany had scored a decisive victory. This helped formulate the Soviet Union's entire defensive strategy, enabling Stalin to transfer several divisions from the Far East to help repulse the German attack on Moscow.[47] Consequently, Moscow's demands became insatiable and Foote later claimed (with some exaggeration) to have been sending over 3,000 transmissions every month, all of which he had personally cyphered.[48] Foote's long sessions, often working through the night, were certainly extremely dangerous and laid him open to discovery by the Swiss authorities, but such was the urgency that Moscow deemed the risk justified. However, during September and early October 1941, Foote's contact became intermittent, as German bombing raids on Moscow forced 'The Centre' to go off air for increasingly long periods. Finally, on 19 October 1941, Moscow's transmissions ceased altogether. Fearing the worst, Foote continued to transmit until, six weeks later, his call sign was finally answered. As Foote discovered, the Soviet transmissions team had been forced to flee from Moscow to Kuibyshev (now Samara), 850km southeast of Moscow, following the rapid advance of German forces on the Russian capital.[49]

As Foote and his fellow agents were well aware, up to this

point the war had been going badly for the Allies. Triumphant Wehrmacht forces had advanced as far as the English Channel in the west and almost as far as Moscow in the east. However, the Americans' entry into the war at the end of the year, alongside the Red Army's astonishing efforts in containing the German offensive on the Russian capital, provided a huge fillip to anti-Nazis across the world. For Foote, though, it meant even more demands and pressure, so a new radio operator was taken on to help with the increasing workload. The new agent was a twenty-two-year-old Swiss dancer called Margrit Bolli, who had been working as a waitress when Radó met her.[50] The young anti-Nazi was given the code name 'Rosy' and, once trained up by Foote, was quickly able to take up her work.[51] This meant that by 1942 there were a trio of transmitters in operation—Foote's in Lausanne, plus the Hamels' and Bolli's in Geneva—making up what German Intelligence referred to as *Rote Drei*, or 'Red Three'.

All members of the network worked under the constant terror of being discovered, fully aware that the Germans would be making desperate attempts to track down their transmitters. German Intelligence had already closed down a network operating out of occupied Europe, known as the *Rote Kapelle*, or the 'Red Orchestra'. As Radó was aware, information taken from captured agents and intercepted messages had brought Foote's network to their attention: 'German counter-intelligence chiefs were dismayed and appalled to learn what high-quality information the 'Red Troika' was collecting and passing on to Moscow.'[52] The Nazi commander of foreign intelligence operations put pressure on the Swiss to close down the spy ring, hinting that invasion might be an option if the Swiss refused to cooperate. Clearly, it was only a matter of time before Foote's network was uncovered.

When the Hamels' home was raided by Swiss police on 27 October 1942, it appeared that the Swiss authorities had finally managed to break the ring. Edouard was arrested for illegal possession of a wireless transmitter, though his wife managed to hide the operative set and any incriminating evidence.[53] To everyone's great relief, it transpired that the police had not actually been looking for a transmitter but had arrested Hammel's brother the previous day for distributing left-wing literature and had assumed that Edouard must also be involved. Hamel was let off with a suspended sentence of ten days' imprisonment and the spy ring's transmissions were able to continue apace.

While Foote claimed that the information provided to Red Three by 'Lucy' had proven crucial during the invasion of Russia in 1941, it was as nothing to the quantity and quality provided from the spring of 1942 onwards. It included the outline of Hitler's plan to attack the southern sector of the eastern front, advancing towards Stalingrad and the oilfields in the Caucasus. In October, 'Lucy' provided key intelligence on German strategy and tactics during the siege of Stalingrad, to the extent of being able to respond to specific questions from Moscow. This gave the Soviets a huge advantage when they launched Operation Uranus in November, which eventually surrounded the entire German sixth army of nearly a quarter of a million soldiers.

The supply of information continued into 1943, unabated in quantity and quality. Foote's claim that, 'Moscow very largely fought the war on Lucy's messages', may be an exaggeration, but the information was so detailed and precise that it was able to provide details on key aspects of the German war effort, including the battle order of Wehrmacht forces on the Eastern front. This intelligence included the entire military plans for the German *Zitadelle* (Citadel) offensive at Kursk in the summer of 1943.[54] The defeat of the Wehrmacht at Kursk virtually guaranteed that Germany could no longer win the war. It was, by any measure, a huge triumph for 'Lucy' and the members of the Red Three spy ring.[55]

For Foote, however, any satisfaction he might have had at news of Soviet military successes on the eastern front was diminished by heightened fears of detection caused by news of his fiancée, Agnes Zimmerman. Since the beginning of the war, Agnes had been involved in anti-Nazi resistance and was a contact for Soviet spies dropped into Germany. Inevitably, a Russian agent had been captured and ended up in the hands of the Gestapo where he was tortured into revealing details of their contacts. In the ensuing round-up, both Agnes and her mother were arrested and badly tortured. Incredibly bravely, neither talked, but Agnes's mother is suspected to have died in prison, while Agnes lost her mind and never recovered. [56] Foote never saw her again.

News of Agnes's arrest had only added to Foote's existing terror that German intelligence might have penetrated his cell. He had good reason to be anxious, for by now German intelligence knew a great deal of the 'Rot Drei' spy ring, much of it obtained from information picked up by Bolli's boyfriend, a handsome young German called Hans Peters. Unfortunately, Peters turned out to be a Nazi agent and passed on any information he managed to weasel out of Bolli to his contact in the Abwehr. The Germans had discovered that the Hammels, Foote and Bolli were the operators of the three transmitters and it was actually German agents who had tipped off the Swiss authorities the previous October.[57] However, many Swiss were sympathetic to the Allies and not overly concerned with making great efforts to break up a spy ring that was working against Nazi Germany. Both Radó and Foote were believed to be involved, but the authorities were reluctant to move against two respectable residents, not least because they suspected that Foote might be a British agent.

However, the Italian surrender in September 1943 and the consequent Nazi occupation of the formerly fascist country reawakened the Swiss authorities' fears of a German invasion. Consequently, following a complaint from the German Consul, they stepped up their listening facilities. Having identified the existence of illegal transmitters in Geneva and Lausanne, specialised direction-finding equipment was used to identify the general location of the signal. Bolli's and the Hammels' sets were then pinpointed by the simple but effective method of systematically cutting off the electricity to any likely buildings one at a time during transmissions. When the signal disappeared, the police had their address. Among the haul captured during Bolli and the Hammels's arrests were detailed reports of the network's financial activities and a copy of Radó's codebook. Radó was himself almost caught when he went to find out what had happened to the Hammels and saw a policeman in their flat. Realising that he had been compromised and terrified of being deported to Germany if he were arrested, a panicked Radó proposed to Moscow that he take refuge in the British consulate and continue to work from there. Unsurprisingly, this idea was immediately dismissed by Moscow as 'completely unacceptable', so Radó prudently went into hiding.[58]

With Radó gone to ground, Rachel Dübendorfer ('Sissy') was forced to contact Foote directly. Both continued working, but much of their time and energy now had to be devoted to camouflage and security. Foote had been tipped off by Radó that the Swiss police were actively searching for his transmitter in Lausanne, but Moscow were so desperate for intelligence that he was ordered to continue transmitting, despite the risk. But having already shut down two of the three transmitters, it wasn't difficult for the Swiss authorities to track the third. By September 1943, they were confident that it was in Lausanne. Within days, they had pinpointed it on the fourth floor of number 2, chaussée de Longeraie. At 00:45 in the morning of 20 November 1943, moments after Foote had completed his transmission, police smashed through his front door and arrested him. Two army technicians accompanying the police attempted to continue the transmission but were thwarted by Foote having the presence of mind to put the set out of action.[59]

Under questioning, Foote, much more terrified of what the Russians would do to him if he talked than of what the Swiss could do if he didn't, said nothing. However, as the Swiss police revealed to Foote, the Russians were not his only worries: 'Inspector Knecht told me that the Gestapo knew a great deal about our organisation in Switzerland and that by arresting me the Swiss police had quite possibly saved my life.' The police were, in fact, telling the truth, for German agents had planned to kidnap Foote on 23 November and smuggle him out of Switzerland. He had had a lucky escape.[60]

Foote's arrest immediately shut down the network's ability to communicate with Moscow. In a panic, Dübendorfer ('Sissy') sent a telegram to a contact in Canada, asking them to contact the Soviet authorities and beg them for $15,000. Unfortunately, her message was intercepted and alerted the Canadian authorities to the existence of a Soviet spy ring operating in North America.[61] 'Sissy' was herself arrested by the Swiss police on 19 April 1944 and documents found in her flat led the police first to Schneider and then to Rössler, both of whom were picked up the following month.[62]

Assuming he would spend the rest of the war in prison, Foote set about making his life as comfortable as possible. This was helped considerably by the leniency of his Swiss jailors, who allowed him to order plenty of supplies, including three cases of Scotch whisky, his favourite sticky preserves and enough tinned food to last a year. Friends supplied him with cigarettes and he spent much of his time working his way through the prison library while trying to improve his Spanish. Frustratingly for the Swiss authorities, however, he gave little in exchange for his indulgent treatment. In line with the strict instructions given to all Soviet agents, he continued to deny that he had been a Russian spy, rendering him ineligible for legal aid, or parole. However, an agreement was eventually reached that he would admit to having spied 'for one of the united nations' and after ten months in prison, on 8 September 1944, Foote was released on bail of 2,000 Swiss francs.[63]

Soon after his release, 'Sissy', who had also been released on bail, got in contact with Foote to confirm that 'Lucy' wanted to continue passing on intelligence. The three agreed to finally meet in person, at which point Rössler handed over all the intelligence he had obtained while Foote had been in prison. None of it had yet been passed to Moscow, but as he no longer had a transmitter, Foote decided to take it personally to the Soviet Embassy in Paris. So, having made his way to the French capital, in early November 1944, Foote presented himself at the Embassy building in Rue de Grenelle. There, Foote submitted a report, which was ciphered and forwarded to the Centre.[64] He was then put through a long, thorough interrogation, before being informed that he was to be sent to 'The Centre' for a full debrief. Consequently, on 6 January 1945, Foote boarded a plane to Moscow. To his great surprise, sitting among his fellow passengers was his former superior, Sandór Radó, who had come out of hiding and also made his way to Paris.

The Russian intelligence services urgently wanted to interrogate the two agents: Radó relating to reports surrounding the embezzlement of funds and the loss of [his] codebook and Foote concerning suspicions that he might be a British agent. At a stop-off in Cairo, the pair shared a hotel room and during their conversation Radó came to the realisation that he could not rely on Foote's support.[65] In fact, as Foote would later admit, he had a very low opinion of his former superior and was 'constantly stressing the superiority of his judgement and integrity compared to Radó's.'[66]

Understandably, Radó concluded that returning to Russia might not be such a good idea and promptly disappeared. The Hungarian tried, in vain, to persuade the British to grant him political asylum and, having failed in an attempt to take his own life, Radó was released from hospital and extradited to the Soviet Union. In December 1946, he was sentenced without trial to 10 years on charges of espionage and the misappropriation of money.[67] Radó's good friend Arthur Koestler believed for years that he had been liquidated—which was what Foote was informed in Moscow—but later discovered to his relief that Radó had survived, was 'rehabilitated, and even lived to publish his autobiography.'[68]

Foote, however, continued on to Moscow, arriving on 16 January 1945, where he was met by a Red Army major who would be in charge of his debriefing. She introduced herself as 'Vera', though her real name was Maria Iosifovna Poliakova. She had been Radó's predecessor as the main (G)RU illegal resident in Switzerland between 1936 and 1937.[69] Foote was understandably wary: 'It became obvious to me, after the first few days in Moscow, that I was considered to be either a conscious or unconscious agent of the British.'[70] However, when a series of forensic interrogations failed to uncover anything at all to suggest that he was a double-agent, a very relieved Foote was informed that he had no case to answer. Nevertheless, despite his official exoneration, Foote was informed that he must remain in Moscow for the foreseeable future.

Accommodated in a flat in a newly constructed block in

Moscow, Foote discovered that life as a Red Army employee of the special reserve was far more comfortable than that experienced by most Muscovites. While he always had to be accompanied by his 'interpreter', Foote was allowed to use shops reserved for the Soviet military elite, which were stocked with a wide variety of goods at subsidised prices. And while his two-bedroom flat was anything but luxurious compared to Western standards of accommodation, it was sufficiently comfortable and with all necessary facilities like the indoor water supply, toilet and bathroom. However, with coal restricted to heating public buildings, and no available supply of wood in Moscow, Foote found it to be absolutely freezing in winter and often without any hot water.[71]

In addition, Foote had a problem that native Muscovites did not: he possessed no official papers or form of identification. Wartime Moscow was rife with criminality and black-market profiteering, so police spot checks were a regular inconvenience. Consequently, Foote was advised to always use quiet back streets, where he was less likely to attract the attention of militia patrols. However, Foote soon grew bored of 'prowling around the purlieus of Moscow' and, dragging his protesting minder behind him, marched impulsively onto the Mozhaiskoye Shosse in southwest Moscow.[72] He was, of course, quickly identified as a foreigner, detained and dragged off to the local militia station. There, Foote was interrogated by an NKGB officer who demanded his name and registered Moscow address. Having been warned by his GRU masters never to give away his name, Foote refused to do so. According to Foote, the outraged officer repeated his demand with increasing fury until Foote himself lost his temper and swore at the interrogators in English. Apparently relieved to have finally secured some sort of answer, the officer calmed down, wrote down Foote's words carefully and released him. Foote was never again asked to produce his papers and for his remaining time in Moscow the local militia patrols would greet him with a polite, 'Good day, Comrade Fuckoff.'[73]

Foote remained in Moscow until May 1945, when the defeat of Nazi Germany brought an end to the European war. For many soldiers this offered the happy prospect of returning home to be reunited with their families. For Foote, however, it offered nothing of the kind, instead signalling a return to active service. Foote was informed that he was to be posted to Mexico where he would be running Soviet espionage operations within the United States. Hiding his disquiet, Foote wisely declared great interest and enthusiasm for his new posting:

> In fact my first six weeks in Moscow had convinced me that Nazi Germany as I had known it was a paradise of freedom as compared with Soviet Russia. I was determined to get out of it as soon as possible and return to a world where freedom was more than a propaganda phrase.[74]

However, the Mexico operation had to be put on hold when Foote was taken seriously ill in November suffering from a duodenal ulcer. By the time he had recovered, disastrous consequences in Canada caused by 'Sissy's' earlier indiscretion had necessitated a massive reorganisation of the Soviet intelligence organisation, including the cancellation of Foote's mission to Mexico. Instead, in February 1947, armed with a new identity as a repatriated German prisoner of war captured during the battle for Stalingrad, 'Albert Mueller' was flown to Berlin. There, as he had done before, Foote lay low and set about establishing his German identity in preparation for his transfer to Argentina to work against the United States.[75]

However, having spent four months in Berlin, on 2 July 1947 Foote abruptly walked out of the Soviet sector and into the British zone. The following day, to their astonishment, 'FOOTE presented himself to the British Intelligence authorities in Berlin, claiming that he wished to take refuge from the Russians.'[76] He casually informed them that he no longer wanted to work for the Russians and wanted to work for the British instead. The officer interviewing Foote didn't believe a word of it, judging Foote to be, 'on the face of it, a very sick man, tired of playing for the Russians, wanting to go home to England.'[77] Despite the reservations, it was appreciated that Foote might still make an important asset, so on 7 August 1947, the former Soviet agent was flown to London for an extensive debriefing by officers from

MI6.[78]

Foote was interviewed by Joan Paine, one of MI6's most experienced interrogators.[79] At a safe house at 19 Rugby Mansions in Bishops' Bridge Road, Paddington, Foote was interrogated exhaustively for six weeks, while every piece of information he provided was cross and double-checked.[80] Eventually, MI6 were convinced that 'FOOTE appeared genuinely concerned to tell the truth and showed no reluctance to answer questions.'[81] However, the interrogators were fully aware that Foote had already been subjected to interrogation in Switzerland and Russia, so was likely to be adept at withholding key information.

Records of Foote's interrogation confirm that he undoubtedly gave up a wealth of information, revealing how he was recruited, his training and his role in the Swiss spy ring. However, attempts to get Foote to name names met with little success. He could not, or would not, reveal the names of former International Brigaders working as Soviet agents, with the exception of Doug Springhall, who was already in jail having been convicted for spying for Russia.[82] Foote also claimed to be unable to identify anyone from the *Rote Drei* spy ring, apart from his former chief, Sandór Radó, who Foote believed to be dead. Nonetheless, Foote did provide some helpful information about Russian intelligence operations in Switzerland. He also revealed useful details on the techniques of Soviet ciphers and spy craft, confirming British suspicions that Moscow was able to supply good quality false passports.[83] One nugget of information was greeted with considerably less enthusiasm, however. He revealed that when his potential posting to Mexico had been discussed in Moscow, Foote had been assured that he could rely on at least 1,000 contacts in the US alone. While undoubtedly an exaggeration, his remark nevertheless caused panic in American security circles and increasingly frantic requests were made to be allowed to interview Foote.[84] However, when Foote was pressed about the claim, he blithely admitted that this was only what he had been told and he was unable to provide any actual details.[85]

What the questioning did reveal to the interrogators was that Foote believed his work in Switzerland had demonstrated that he was 'a first-class operative' who would make a great asset. As Major Ronald 'Ronnie' Reed, who headed the Russian Desk of MI5 dealing with Cambridge spies remarked, Foote 'spends half his time asking us if we can find him a job in the Secret Service.'[86] Unfortunately, as an increasingly resentful Foote was coming to realise, while he might have been decorated by the Soviets, the British Security Services regarded him with much less enthusiasm:

> On all of his interrogations FOOTE left an impression of remarkable simplicity, and to such an extent did this characteristic affect his career that the present article might be subtitled 'an innocent abroad'.[87]

MI6 had in fact concluded that Foote's memory was 'by no means first-class,' and that anyway, 'it is now several years since he was actively engaged in operating.'[88] Nonetheless, while Foote may not have been potential MI6 material, that did not mean that he could not be of some use.

During his debrief Foote had admitted that although in the past he had possessed 'a moderately ideological belief in Communism' he was now 'thoroughly disgusted with Communism and the Soviet system.'[89] He was very enthusiastic about wanting to write a book about his experiences as a Soviet agent and had proposed it to his interrogators. The British security services were interested, hoping that the book could make some useful anti-Communist propaganda. Consequently, Foote was asked to put together a synopsis.

Unfortunately, when it was presented, Michael Serpell of MI5 (who later interviewed 'Sonya' during the Fuchs investigation) thought it 'a very unsatisfactory effort' and that Foote was 'well-nigh illiterate'. Therefore, the manuscript was actually ghostwritten by Courtenay Young of MI5.[90]

Foote was penniless, the Swiss having confiscated the 3,000 francs he earned during the war, so he was desperate for the book to succeed. MI5 also wanted it to sell, partly for the propaganda value but also because Foote had 'stated bluntly that he does not like work and that he has no intention of taking regular employment . . . and told me he only got into this work (i.e. espionage) because he did not fit into a normal job.'[91] Aware that Foote would need to be handled carefully to prevent him '[hawking] his wares on the international market,' Foote was reassured that he would be provided with a small advance and [urged] to be patient, for they were in the process of negotiating film rights.[92]

Handbook for Spies was published simultaneously in Britain and America in 1949.[93] The former Communist, Charlotte Haldane, enthused about it, arguing that it was 'the most extraordinary and impressive of all the anti-Soviet individual stories' that had been published in English.[94] However, Foote was disappointed, feeling that it had been 'mutilated' by MI5, accusing them of making cuts and adding passages that were simply untrue. In fact, Courtney Young had deliberately laced it full of subtle disinformation to discredit and embarrass Soviet intelligence. As MI5 head, Sir Percy Sillitoe, confessed: 'I think FOOTE's book should not be taken too literally, as questions of detail are not necessarily accurately presented.'[95]

If Foote was disappointed with his book, it was as nothing to his indignation when he realised that British Intelligence had no interest in making use of him as a double agent. Aggrieved, Foote forever nursed a bitter antagonism towards them.[96] Struggling to find a decent job—eventually accepting a low-ranking position in the Ministry of Agriculture and Fisheries—Foote sought solace from his disillusionment in drinking. The former Moscow correspondent for the *Manchester Guardian* (and an MI6 officer during the war) Malcolm Muggeridge, who knew Foote at the time, thought him 'a broken man.'[97] The possibility of a lecture tour to America talking about espionage raised his spirits briefly during the mid-1950s, but a reoccurrence of the duodenal ulcer that he had suffered from in Moscow scuppered the opportunity. Following an unsuccessful operation which resulted in the removal of half of his stomach, Foote's health deteriorated and he remained in hospital, reliant on tubes connected to his abdomen. On 1 August 1956, having deliberately ripped out the tubes and torn off his dressings, Foote died of acute peritonitis resulting from a perforated duodenum. He was fifty-one years old.

Twenty years after Foote's premature death, two of his fellow agents from the Red Three spy ring, Sandór Radó ('Dora') and Ursula Kuczyński ('Sonya'), released their own (Moscow-sponsored) accounts of the Swiss operation. As should have been expected, both strongly disputed Foote's version of events and Radó, in particular, went to great lengths to rubbish Foote's account, pointedly quoting critical reviews that had poured scorn on Foote's reliability as a witness, and which had accused *Handbook for Spies* of being 'a mixture of reality and imagination.'[98] Kuczyński was equally dismissive, acidly pointing out that 'some of the things described so cynically in *Handbook for Spies*, he saw differently at the time they happened.'[99] Much of their ire was due to Foote's sudden decision to switch sides; Radó, rehabilitated after his time in a Soviet prison and now living in Hungary, was scathing:

> But worse than all Foote's sensation-seeking was his political *volte-face* and his utter repudiation of the work he had done during the war. He sunk back into the swamp of petty-bourgeois existence from which, freed by a momentous task, he had for a while been able to free himself. His character was marked by an inner contradiction that his betrayal finally sealed.[100]

Kuczyński was similarly contemptuous:

> In running away, Jim [Foote] showed that his ties to the revolutionary movement were superficial; what was so abominable was that he went on to become a complete traitor. The final step must have been studied calculation. Merely to abandon his work for the Soviet Union would have meant an uncertain future, but by telling everything to British counter-intelligence he obliged them to take him in and offer him a good job. That is what happened. In addition, the publication of his lurid spy-thriller memoirs assured his prosperity.[101]

Any idea that Foote could have been an MI6 agent all along was abruptly dismissed. Kuczyński was in no doubt that Foote decided to turn either when he was in prison in Switzerland or, more likely, when he was in the Soviet Union after the end of the war: 'I do not think that he played a double game from the beginning,' she argued, 'he was far from the superior he made himself out to be.'[102]

However, three years after the publication of Radó and Kuczyński's memoirs, a new study of the Swiss spy ring was published. Written by two screen-writers, Anthony Read and David Fisher's *Operation Lucy* returned once again to the idea that Foote had been a British agent.[103] Their theory was that Foote had been recruited to work for British Intelligence in 1936 while working as a fitter at RAF Manston. They questioned why, when Foote abruptly resigned from the air force in the autumn of 1936, no attempt had been made to pursue him, that he was never arrested for desertion and had apparently been free to move around and travel at liberty.[104] The answer, they suggested, was that Foote had been recruited into a highly secretive unit called the Z Organisation, run by Lieutenant-Colonel Claude Dancey, the former Assistant Chief of MI6.[105] According to the authors of *Operation Lucy*, the target of Dancey's outfit was principally Stalin's Soviet Union, so Foote's sojourn in Spain was fundamentally a means of establishing his left-wing credentials. When the Second World War broke out, they argued, Winston Churchill ordered Dancey to use the Lucy network to provide Stalin with top-secret intelligence. This was obtained through the decryption work Bletchley Park passed on via Foote and Rachel Dübendorfer ('Sissy'), both of whom, they insisted, were British double agents.

Over the years, their theory has drawn much attention, most of it overwhelmingly critical. In F H Hinsley's seminal history of British Intelligence during the Second World War, published a year after *Operation Lucy*, the historian and former crypto-analyst at Bletchley Park gave their theory short shrift:

> There is no truth in the much-publicised claim that the British authorities made use of the 'Lucy' ring, a Soviet espionage organisation which operated in Switzerland, to forward intelligence to Moscow.[106]

Hinsley was by no means the only doubter. In his history of Soviet spy rings during the Second World War, *The Red Orchestra*, the military historian V E Tarrant dismisses Read and Fisher's theory about Bletchley Park intelligence being channelled through Foote's network as 'a complex conspiracy theory which is not only fantastic but totally untrue.'[107] Tarrant points out that even if Dancey had been able to access top-secret material from Bletchley Park, there was no way that he would have had regular access to it in the way that he would have needed to be the source of Lucy's intelligence. Furthermore, he points out, Bletchley Park prioritised material relating to the western front, so material relating to the Russian front was often vague, incomplete and delayed. Everything, in fact, that Rudolf Rössler's information wasn't.

Since the publication of Read and Fisher's book, considerable research has been undertaken into the Red Three networks, narrowing down the identities of who, if not the code-breakers of Bletchley Park, provided the game-changing intelligence. Despite never having met 'Lucy', Radó always insisted that 'Rössler's intelligence material came from members of the resistance movement, some of whom held high public office in Germany and others of whom had migrated to Switzerland.'[108] In fact, Rössler had actually divulged the identity of his sources, or at least of some of them, three and a half years before his death in 1958.[109] Rather than British agents, all the evidence suggests that most of the information came, as Rössler, Radó and others have stated, from disaffected high-ranking members of the German military and political class. [110] They apparently provided Rössler with an enigma machine and a radio transmitter which was used to feed him up-to-date secret intelligence that Foote transmitted to Moscow.

Since the fall of the Soviet Union, more information about Soviet spy networks and the activities of Alexander Foote has gradually emerged. Some of it is held in the Russian State Archive of Socio-Political History in Moscow, which fills out Foote's record with the International Brigades in Spain. However, it is the MI5 files released in 2003 and 2004 to the British National Archives which have been most revealing. They contain detailed files compiled on the members of the 'Lucy' network: Schneider, Dübendorfer and Rössler and there are several relating to Foote.[111] The latter contain a great deal of information relating to his work in Switzerland and meticulous reports of his debriefing by the British Security Services, in 1947. Those secret files reveal that, though the interrogators were fully aware of Foote's unreliability, they were confident that during the six weeks the spy was held, every piece of information he held was systematically uncovered.[112] There is nothing in them to suggest that Foote was in any way connected to British intelligence; rather that, as the Swiss who had investigated Foote during the Second World War were convinced, the International Brigade veteran was a genuine Soviet agent.[113]

Kuczyński's belief that Foote decided to leave Russian Intelligence while he was in Moscow is probably accurate, for Foote admitted to his interviewer that 'he had made up his mind to desert not long after his arrival in the USSR.'[114] Foote remarked pointedly on the lack of personal freedom he had witnessed in Moscow and his disillusionment following his realisation that Stalin's Russia was a nationalist, not an internationalist regime.[115] Likewise, Kuczyński's belief that Foote 'did not have a firm ideological grasp' is probably also fair.[116] Foote doesn't give the impression of ever really being a dedicated follower of Communism; apart from anything else, he appears to have considered it to be too much like hard work:

> You cannot join the Communist Party by just signing on the dotted line; you have to pass a period of probation and intellectuals especially are made to do all sorts of dirty work like carrying banners and selling newspapers. [117]

This is not to say that *Handbook for Spies* should not be taken with a pinch of salt. Given that Foote spent many years of his adult life working in the murky world of espionage, where misinformation and disinformation are currency, it should come as no surprise that Foote's account is neither wholly reliable, nor accurate. As he admitted to MI5, 'he spent ten days writing an autobiography in which he held nothing back, but to which he added a certain amount of ornament.'[118] And clearly, the contribution by Courtenay Young, MI5's ghost-writer, ensures that the book can hardly be seen as reliable. Yet, despite the propaganda, the errors and the outright lies, it would be a mistake to assume that there is no truth wrapped up within it. There is no doubt that Foote served in the International Brigades and that he was a key agent with the Red Three spy network, responsible for transmitting key intelligence to the Soviet Union. After all, if Foote had really been a British agent, it would have made no sense to risk going to Moscow in 1945. The war was almost over and he could have returned to Britain to collect the pat on the back to which he surely would have been due. The likelihood is that a recent assessment of Foote is a fair one: 'it is most plausible that the Englishman was what he seemed—a communist adventurer who enjoyed the game for its own sake.[119]

Chapter Nine
The Painter with Words: Clive Branson

Sitting in London's Tate Britain Gallery are five pictures representing the city's life in the period just before the Second World War.[1] Painted in a deliberately proletarian style, they reflect the artist's enthusiastic involvement in British working-class politics and his lifelong membership of the British Communist Party.[2] The artist was Clive Branson, a name unfamiliar to most present-day audiences. If he is known at all it is perhaps as the distant cousin of entrepreneur Sir Richard Branson, or as the husband of Noreen Branson, historian of the Communist Party and long-time editor of the *Labour Research Journal*. Yet, in addition to being a fine artist, Clive Branson was an accomplished poet and talented public speaker and deserves to be better known. Were it not for his misfortune to be born into an era of fascism and war, he might well have been.

Branson was one of approximately 2,500 British and Irish men and women to volunteer for the International Brigades during the Spanish Civil War. Most of these volunteers were working-class men and women from areas of severe economic deprivation, such as the Rhondda in South Wales, London's East End, Cheetham in Manchester and the Gorbals in Glasgow. Branson, however, came from a very different background. Clive Ali Chimmo Branson was born in Ahmednagar, India, in 1907. His grandfather was a notable High Court Judge and Privy Councillor. His father, Major Lionel Hugh Branson, was a British Indian Army officer and a famous magician and his mother, Emily Winifred Chimmo, was the daughter of a Hong-Kong banker.[3] Both of Clive's brothers followed in their father's footsteps and grew up to be conjurers: Cyril was a submariner in the British Navy during the Second World War, remembered for coolly performing magic tricks to keep up morale during a depth charge attack by a German destroyer. Clive's brother Tony later became the Mayor of Sevenoaks, reaching notoriety for being the only councillor not to support the banning of Sam Peckinpah's controversial 1971 film, *Straw Dogs.*[4] Clive's godfather was a cousin of King Alfonso XIII of Spain, the grandly named Prince Alfonso de Orleans y Borbón, Infante de España, who had studied at Heidelberg University with Branson's father.[5] In private, the Bransons called him 'Arly' and Clive was actually named after him.

Like many other sons of good bourgeois stock, Branson was first educated at preparatory school, before being sent off to public school, in Clive's case Bedford, in September 1921.[6] The school had been founded in 1552 during the reign of Edward VI and Branson followed in the footsteps of his father and illuminous alumni such as the Parliamentarian Thomas Erskine May. Branson was initially a boarder in Bedford's Talbot's House, until his parents returned from India, after which he became a day boy. At school, Clive showed an enthusiasm for sports, enjoying rugby, boxing, shooting and he was a 'very keen' and 'useful' cricketer, becoming captain of the 2nd XI. In 1922, he joined the Officer Training Corps, rising swiftly through the ranks; Lance Corporal in 1923, Corporal in 1924 and Sergeant in 1925. While achieving top marks in English and Maths, Branson finished sixth in his class in his final year, let down by his poor French. When he left Bedford in the summer of 1925, his parents recommended that he take up a sensible career in insurance or banking; Branson, however, had other ideas and was set upon becoming an artist. To his parents' credit, they supported his ambitions and Clive took up a place to study art at the Slade School in London.

In 1929, the young artist set off to Spain to paint the countryside, returning to Britain two years later. By this stage, his work was sufficiently accomplished for two paintings to be accepted for the Royal Academy's annual show in 1931, despite Branson being only 23 years of age. His precocious artistic talent was matched by a voracious appetite for serious reading, in particular non-fiction works of history, politics and economics. Genuinely appalled by the levels of poverty and unemployment that followed the Wall Street Crash, Branson began to involve himself in left-wing politics, joining the Independent Labour Party. Believing that, as he put it, 'to be able to paint, one must first learn about life', he vowed to take a break from painting to engage himself fully 'in the politics of the British working-class movement'.

Ironically, it was through his political activism that the well-connected young Branson met Noreen Browne, the daughter of Lord Alfred Browne, son of Henry Ulick Browne, the Fifth Marquess of Sligo. The former debutante's ancestry went as far back as the sixteenth century, to the infamous pirate from Clare Island, Grace O'Malley, whose son was knighted by Elizabeth I and made the 1st Viscount Mayo by Charles I.[7] The two met at an amateur dramatics society event and Noreen was immediately taken with the 'six foot tall, clean-shaven and rather good-looking' young man. They spent the remainder of the night in a Lyons' Tea House, discovering a shared passion for left-wing radical politics. Clearly enamoured, the two saw each other almost continuously over the following week, impetuously deciding that they should get married.[8] However, the young lovers' enthusiasm for an early wedding was not matched by that of Noreen's family, who refused to allow her to marry until at least the following year, when she would be 21. Gamely suppressing their impulsiveness, the determined couple waited dutifully for Noreen to come of age until, on 1 June 1931, the two were married. A daughter, Rosa, was born two years later.[9]

The couple would soon make clear that their enthusiasm for proletarian politics went beyond arcane, intellectual discussions. United by a philanthropic determination to move away from their moneyed and aristocratic origins, Clive and Noreen set about giving away their considerable inherited wealth. During the early 1930s, they donated over £100,000 to charity (equivalent to more than £6m today). Clive personally donated to and supervised a Labour Research Department fund, set up to commemorate the fiftieth anniversary of the death of Karl Marx by establishing 'a Marxist library, workers' school and educational centre.' When a building in London's Clerkenwell Green was acquired, Noreen's name was on the deeds as the purchaser. The building is now the Marx Memorial Library.[10]

However, the Independent Labour Party was not to be a beneficiary of the Bransons' largesse, nor their activist efforts, for in 1932 they left the organisation following Clive's decision to give a talk in favour of the Red Army, which explicitly rejected the ILP's pacifism. The pair decided, instead, to join the Communist Party, whose membership had been increasing rapidly over the previous two years.[11] They actively involved themselves in local political campaigns, leading a successful, if unglamorous fight to remove a malodorous public toilet from outside Sutton Dwellings in Chelsea.[12] The couple seem to have fully embraced the Communist Party's notorious sectarianism, a consequence of the official Moscow line of 'class-against-class', which dictated that the international Communist movement should treat other parties of the left as 'social fascists'. When Clive and Noreen helped establish a local news-sheet called *Revolt!*, the banner across the front page loudly proclaimed: 'The Labour Party and the TUC, are just the lackeys of the bourgeoisie.'[13]

However, much of their effort was directed towards the Party's most conspicuous political campaign of the 1930s: the struggle against fascism, particularly the home-grown version, Oswald Mosley's British Union of Fascists, formed in October 1932. The Bransons led the drive against local Blackshirts (as they were known), following the fascists' establishment of an unemployed centre at 263 Lavender Hill in Battersea. BUF meetings were disrupted, newspaper sellers chased off and the Blackshirts' divisive rhetoric was vigorously denounced at public meetings. They also found time and energy for other progressive causes. Clive joined the Transport and General Workers' Union and became a National Council of Labour Colleges tutor, giving talks to nearly every trade union branch in Battersea and at open-air meetings on Clapham Common. He quickly became an important and trusted member of the Communist Party; by 1935, he was acting as a courier, carrying secret documents between London and Moscow.[14] Meanwhile, Noreen took on the role of Secretary of the Battersea branch of the Party, which had a small but energetic membership of around fifty dedicated activists. 1930s Battersea was a highly industrialised and working-class district and had a reputation for militancy; the Indian Communist, Shapurji Dorabji Saklatvala, had been Battersea

North's popular MP up until 1929.[15] Most of the local Communist Party members knew each other and the Bransons were particularly good friends with a gifted young mathematician called David Guest. Noreen later described him as looking like a down-and-out, 'always untidy . . . a premature hippy,' much to Communist Party General Secretary Harry Pollitt's disapproval, but Guest was a brilliant mathematician and a tireless organiser and activist. Other close Party friends included Bert Sines, an engineer in whose lodgings Guest was then living, and a local carpenter called Tom Oldershaw. All would later volunteer to join the International Brigades.[16]

When a military coup was launched in July 1936 against the left-wing Republican government in Spain, the Bransons immediately involved themselves in efforts on behalf of the Spanish Republican cause, by giving speeches and helping to raise money. For Branson, the Spanish Republic's fight against the military rebels was exactly the same fight that anti-fascists were involved in in Germany, in Italy and in Britain. In one of his poems, Branson stressed the relevance of the war in far-away Spain to British workers:

You! English working men!
Can't you hear the barrage creeping
that levels the Pyrenees?[17]

Noreen was no less committed. Two weeks after the uprising, she called a meeting at the Railwaymen's Unity Hall on London's Euston Road to discuss the Iberian situation.[18] Much to her surprise, it was absolutely packed out; 'I've never seen so much support for any movement, ever since. It was most extraordinary . . . I mean that quite literally,' she recalled many years later.[19]

Later that year, when the Communist Party's call went out for volunteers to fight for the Spanish government, Branson immediately put himself forward, but his offer was refused; partly because he was married with a young child, but also because he had become a trusted Party cadre, for whom Harry Pollitt had other plans.[20] Instead, working alongside the senior

Scottish Communist R W Robson, known as 'Robbie', Branson spent a year interviewing potential volunteers, checking their medical records and backgrounds and making sure they were appropriately kitted out, before escorting groups from Victoria Station in London to the main recruiting centre in Paris's Place du Combat. As the British government had made volunteering illegal, everything had to be undertaken in the utmost secrecy. To evade Special Branch surveillance, Branson set himself up in a sandwich bar near the Communist Party's headquarters in London's Covent Garden, where covert messages could be left. However, the efforts at secrecy weren't always entirely effective: groups were always getting lost and Clive later confessed to being in a semi-permanent state of despair.[21] On one occasion, the driver of a train at Victoria Station, a fellow Communist, gave him a cheery Popular Front salute, right under the nose of a policeman.[22] It wasn't long before the police were knocking on Branson's front door, forcing him to make a hurried exit by climbing out of a back window.[23] By December 1937, with plain-clothes policemen permanently stationed outside the Bransons' house, Harry Pollitt finally accepted that Branson's cover was blown and that he could go to Spain. Like many other wives and girlfriends, Noreen didn't want him to volunteer, but she didn't think she should—or could—stop him.[24]

Branson set off for Spain in January 1938, just as Republican soldiers were fighting to hold on to the remote provincial capital of Teruel, set high in the mountains amidst deep snow and driving blizzards. Perhaps surprisingly, he was one of a large number to join the Spanish Republic's struggle at the time; while news of the appalling casualty rate experienced in Spain during 1937 had undoubtedly made its mark, fresh British volunteers were still arriving in Spain at the rate of nearly thirty a week. As Bill Rust brutally summarised in his 1939 account, *Britons in Spain*: 'the 1938 and late 1937 recruits had no illusions; they knew they had come to face death.'[25]

Branson re-trod his familiar route to the Communist Party offices in Paris, where he and the other British were united with volunteers from other countries. The multi-national group was then sent south by train, before undertaking an exhausting night-time climb over the Pyrenees conducted in silence to avoid police and border patrols. Strict warnings were given 'not to smoke, not to drop litter or leave any evidence of their passing.'[26] They were told to remove their footwear and instead given rope-soled *alpargatas* which were less likely to slip and made virtually no noise. For many of the British volunteers, the long, dangerous climb was the hardest physical task they had ever undertaken: 'It really was the worst experience ever I had in my life,' remembered one Scot.[27] Those who managed the gruelling sixteen-hour climb were rewarded by the sight of cheering Spanish Republican border guards.[28] Once across the frontier, fortified with a cup of '[coffee] substitute [and] a small hunk of white bread', the volunteers made their way slowly down into Spain, to be taken by lorries to the garrison town of Figueras in northern Catalonia, the mustering point for volunteers arriving from the north.[29]

Branson's group left Figueras on 16 January 1938, arriving at the main International Brigades' Headquarters in Albacete two days later.[30] Here, he and the other new arrivals were given a dire and graphic warning of what they would face in Spain and offered one final opportunity to change their minds and return home.[31] The volunteers were then officially enrolled into the Republic's International Brigades, before being sent off for military training at the British camp in Tarazona de la Mancha, 30km north of Albacete. Long-standing complaints about the poor quality and quantity of food persisted, as one of Branson's fellow trainees recalled:

We ate the old bean soup, with little bits of donkey meat, burro meat, dry bread. Although you weren't able to buy bread in the shops because it was rationed, if you were lucky you might be able to get into some Spanish house where they would serve you up a fried egg with some newer bread and a drink of wine. For that we used to pay ten pesetas.[32]

Nor had the military training greatly improved; even at this stage, some arrivals were only receiving two or three weeks' instruction. As they would discover, it was, quite simply, not enough.

Nonetheless, in early February 1938, armed with a rudimentary knowledge of soldiering, Branson left Tarazona de la Mancha to join up with the British Battalion, just as they were being sent into reserve at La Puebla de Valverde, a beautiful village surrounded by mountains, twenty kilometres to the south-east of Teruel. After a deceptively pleasant fortnight, Branson and the other British were then transferred to the Aragón village of Lécera. Here, Branson was placed in Number One 'Clement Attlee' Company, with the battalion still held in reserve. The conditions in Lécera were far removed from Valverde. Billeted 'in stone barns, [the volunteers] huddled together against the bitter cold' during one of the worst Spanish winters for 30 years.[33] In 1938, snow even fell in Valencia.

As the battalion shivered in Lécera, the depressing news arrived confirming that, on 21 February, the Republican Army had finally been forced out of Teruel, surrendering the ground over which they had fought so doggedly. The fall of Teruel marked the beginning of a disastrous period for the Republic. On 7 March 1938, Franco threw a colossal offensive against the Republican forces in Aragón. The 15th International Brigade, including the British, were rushed up to Belchite, about 50km south of Zaragoza, which Republican forces had captured the previous autumn. However, their position was quickly overwhelmed as the Nationalists swept forward, supported by a huge machine-gun, artillery and air barrage. Motorised units punched holes in the Republican lines, in a forerunner of the Blitzkreig tactics that would be used with devastating effect during the Second World War. So began what would become known as the great retreat.

Franco's offensive advanced at such as speed that many Republican soldiers had little option but to turn tail and run for their lives. It was a time of chaos, panic, and terror, as the survivors retreated past the evidence of what looked, to many, to be a complete collapse of the Republican lines. Bob Cooney, the tough political commissar from Aberdeen, vividly described the scene:

Once again we had an all-night march—this time across difficult country. None of us had slept since the morning of the ninth [March]—nearly seventy-two hours. We had been through an intense mental and physical strain. Little wonder that some of our lads collapsed on that gruelling trek over the hills. None of us who took part in that dreadful march will ever forget it . . . The heat was well-nigh unbearable. We were exhausted, foot-sore and our throats were parched. My boots were in tatters, my feet torn and bleeding. Many of the others were in similar shape. It was difficult to keep our column intact. We were in the middle of a rout. Thousands of men from other Brigades were also on the march and mixed with them went the fleeing civilian population. The scene beggared description. As the long black column climbed wearily up the steep rocky hillsides, enemy planes came swooping and machine-gunning their helpless victims. Franco had eight hundred planes on the Aragón front against the Republicans' sixty. I did not see a single Republican plane the whole of that dreadful week.[34]

It was only on 18 March that Republican forces, bolstered with reinforcements, were finally able to halt the Nationalist advance.[35] After ten days of essentially headlong retreat, all that was left of the battalion was a group of twenty men, the sorry remnant of what had once been a fighting battalion. As small groups of men drifted into the Catalan village of Batea, temporary headquarters of the 15th International Brigade, urgent efforts were made to return the handful of survivors to some sort of a meaningful fighting force. Promotions and commendations were awarded: for his courageous and level-headed actions during the retreats, Clive Branson was promoted to the rank of Sergeant. New arrivals brought the battalion number up to 650 men, the highest number ever, but by now the majority were Spaniards. By this point there were barely enough Britons in Spain left to form a company, let alone a battalion.

On 30 March 1938, Franco resumed his Aragón offensive. Thirteen divisions, plus a colossal number of tanks, artillery and more than 900 aircraft were massed for the final push through to the Mediterranean. The British were rushed to the front, where they moved forward cautiously towards the small village of Calaceite, which lay on the main road from Alcañiz to Gandesa and Tarragona. The volunteers spent the night billeted in the village and having woken before dawn on the last day of March 1938, made their way through the village.[36] As daybreak approached, Battalion commander George Fletcher ordered Clive Branson's Number One Company to an allotted position one kilometre beyond Calaceite, where they were to act as an advance guard for the battalion. Suddenly, as they advanced, a group of six tanks bore down on them from the trees alongside the road and opened fire.[37] Another group of tanks emerged from the woods on the right and a mass of Italian infantry appeared and opened fire.[38]

Having initially assumed that the tanks were Republican, the British were caught completely unawares. Eventually, a number of British machine-gunners did manage to return fire, forcing the tanks to withdraw, but by this stage the British had suffered numerous casualties, including a number of their most senior and experienced members. The battalion's senior political commissar, Walter Tapsell, was killed, and the commander, George Fletcher, was badly wounded in the shoulder by a burst of machine-gun fire from one of the tanks.[39] Many men were faced with little choice but to surrender, including Clive Branson.[40] Originally believed to have been killed, he was one of over a hundred British volunteers captured at Calaceite.

The prisoners were marched back into the village, which had already been captured by Franco's troops. Branson and the other captives were promptly lined up against a wall in front of machine-guns. All feared that they were about to be shot, until they were spotted by an American journalist, who was accompanying several Italian Army officers. Aware of the Internationals' value in an exchange for prisoners held by the Republicans, the Italians persuaded the *Guardia Civil* not to shoot them. Instead, the prisoners were locked up in a prison in nearby Alcañiz, before they were transported by train to Zaragoza, over 100km away.[41] In a foretaste of the appalling suffering that millions of men and women across Europe would endure, the prisoners were crammed into cattle trucks, 'packed in so close we had to stand for the whole 36 hours of the journey.'[42]

On their arrival at Zaragoza, the prisoners' heads were shaved in preparation for them to be presented to the world's press. Branson was interviewed by a Reuters journalist, who he persuaded to get a message to his wife, which confirmed the news of their capture that had appeared in the Sunday newspapers.[43] The prisoners were then interrogated by the English-educated Don Pablo Merry del Val (son of the Spanish Ambassador to London), whose aim was to identify officers and political commissars. During the questioning, Merry del Val recognised a young miller from Edinburgh called Jimmy Rutherford as one of the members of the British Machine-Gun Company who had been captured at the Battle of Jarama a year earlier. Rutherford was promptly taken away and executed for contravening the agreement he had signed on his release not to return to Spain.[44] Following their interrogation, Branson and the other prisoners were transferred to the Francoist prisoner-of-war camp of San Pedro de Cardeña, eight miles south-east of Burgos, built on the site of the first Benedictine monastery in Spain and allegedly the last resting place of El Cid. Their period of imprisonment at the camp was to be brutal and utterly miserable.

The International prisoners were kept in overcrowded dormitories, where 'the lavatories were open, of the crudest style, and were often blocked.'[45] Everyone was required to wait in line, sometimes for hours, to use them. One prisoner at San Pedro later remembered with disgust that there were piles of faeces almost a metre high. With only three taps divided between the prisoners, it was impossible to stay clean and Branson later recalled shivering under a blanket at night, 'kept awake by lice and a dry itching skin.'[46] Not surprisingly, most of the prisoners suffered from sickness in the camp.

A major contributor to the illnesses was the poor diet. Prisoners survived mainly on a thin soup—consisting of warm water flavoured with olive oil, garlic and breadcrumbs—and one small bread roll per day, roughly the size of a man's fist.[47] At lunchtime and in the evening the prisoners were also fed a spoonful of white beans which, on a few lucky occasions, contained a small piece of pork fat. However, appalling as the diet, sanitary and medical facilities undoubtedly were, it is the widespread brutality of the regime and the severe beatings meted out that many prisoners remembered.[48] They were treated with the utmost cruelty by the guards, 'belaboured with heavy bamboo staves and even rifle butts on the flimsiest pretext, or none at all.'[49] Inmates were warned that any unwillingness to obey regulations would result in them being 'shot like dogs'.

The authorities' agreement in April 1938 to a visit by the Red Cross did provide some relief, for it allowed prisoners the opportunity to send a message home, even if it was restricted to the brief phrase '*Notificándoles que me encuentro bien*' (Notifying you that I am well). For Branson, however, it offered additional benefits, for once his parents were informed that he was alive and a prisoner of war, they immediately contacted Branson's godfather, Prince Alfonso, for help.[50] Whether 'Arly' was able to achieve anything for Clive personally is not known, but conditions in the camp certainly began to improve. Permission was given for food parcels to be received and Branson was allowed to be sent money by his parents. And when, after a month in captivity, 100 British prisoners were selected for repatriation, Clive Branson was one of them. As a leaving present to those remaining at San Pedro, he left £100 that he had been sent by his parents to pay for chocolate, tobacco and cigarette papers.[51]

On Sunday 12 June 1938, Branson's group was transferred to an Italian-run camp in Palencia, 100km west of Burgos. To their relief, the prisoners quickly discovered that conditions in the camp were much less inhumane than at San Pedro. They were allowed to go swimming and were even fed spaghetti, one prisoner recalled in wonder. When Clive wrote home asking for books, two arrived from his brother Tony, along with news that a further 200 were on the way from the Society of Friends. Guessing that left-wing literature was highly unlikely to get through, Branson requested works on German philosophy and was soon immersing himself in Hegelian dialectics.[52]

Branson was, in fact, undoubtedly singled out for special

treatment at Palencia, for the Italian commandant had discovered that Branson was an accomplished artist.[53] He took Branson on a trip to Burgos to buy art supplies, even if war shortages meant that only yellow and blue paint was available. In a dramatic contrast to the brutality undergone at San Pedro, Branson was allowed outside the camp's confines to paint the local countryside. He was also instructed by the commandant to make six drawings of the camp. While the commandant kept the two largest for himself, the other four were sent home to Branson's wife, along with detailed sketches of many of the artist's fellow inmates.[54] Noreen later forwarded the sketches to the Communist member of the National Joint Committee for Spanish Relief, Isabel Brown, who passed them on to the prisoners' families. They were received with great relief by relatives, particularly one which showed a prisoner who had previously been believed to have been killed.[55]

Despite his preferential treatment, Clive wrote to Noreen at the end of August 1938 revealing that he had been taken ill with 'a chill in the kidneys'. Understandably, his physical malaise seems to have temporarily lowered his spirits and letters home reveal how desperately he missed his home and family. As Branson noted pointedly in a poem, while they were receiving better treatment, they were nonetheless still prisoners:

Here we can bask in the sun,
should our eyes have forgotten,
pointed at by the guard's bayonet.[56]

Yet apart from this brief period of despondency, Branson seems to have maintained a remarkably stoic attitude to his ordeal:

When I was taken prisoner in Spain I was very frightened because [I was] so helpless. We sat surrounded by barbed wire, on a dry river bed. And I watched two little clouds like pearls low and still settle above the horizon. Incredibly lovely and proof of the fact of history of life and of things worth living for no matter how difficult our act of living may be.[57]

Certainly, he provided support to many fellow prisoners, who were forever grateful to Branson and his ability to remain positive, even under extremely trying circumstances. One recounted that:

> In any difficult time, Clive was always cheery, putting forward what we should do, and helping to educate others in order to use the time usefully. He was one of the most popular and most respected among the British prisoners.[58]

David Lomon (originally Solomon), a young Jewish volunteer from London's East End, seems to have especially valued the emotional support that Branson had provided. He remembered one occasion when a number of starving prisoners were dwelling on the misery of the camp and their meagre rations, Branson asked them to describe what dish each of them missed most. He then sketched every item on the prison wall, conjuring up a huge imaginary banquet.[59] His ability to conjure images with paint and pen was both admired and appreciated; Branson, recalled a fellow POW admiringly, was 'a painter with words.'[60]

Despite his efforts, morale began to sag as the period of captivity in Palencia dragged on for months. Finally, on Saturday 22 October 1938, news arrived that Italians held by the Republicans had been released and that the British POWs prisoners were to be transferred to Ondarreta prison in San Sebastián in preparation for their repatriation.[61] Two days later, the first 40 British International Brigaders were released and taken to the French border at Irún. Chosen to lead them as they marched over the French border to freedom was Clive Ali Chimmo Branson.[62] Before they departed, Branson delivered a speech, reminding the former prisoners that they would be under the eyes of the world's Press, much of it deeply hostile:

> It's been rough. We're minutes away from freedom. Let's march like soldiers across this line. Get in lines of three, heads up, shoulders back and walk across in a disciplined manner.[63]

Branson and his 39 comrades finally crossed the border into France on 24 October 1938. Accompanied by French guards, the group then took a train north from Hendaye to Dieppe. Aboard the train Branson maintained his role as leader and successfully negotiated with the French authorities to secure food and drink for the long journey.[64] The former prisoners finally arrived at London's Victoria Station the following evening, under the watchful eyes of Special Branch.[65] Waiting to meet Clive at Victoria station was his wife, Noreen, and their now five-year-old daughter, Rosa.

Branson was obviously overjoyed to be home, but while the war in Spain dragged on, he could not give up on the cause for which so many of his comrades had died. So, after spending some time at home with Noreen and Rosa, Clive resumed campaigning for the Spanish Republic.[66] During December 1938 and January 1939, Branson helped organise the International Brigade Convoy, a nationwide tour of 20 British veterans—including himself, former battalion commanders Sam Wild and Fred Copeman, the political commissar Bob Cooney and 15th International Brigade Chief of Operations, Hugh Slater—which raised over £5,000 for the Spanish Republic (equivalent to over £400,000 today).[67] Branson also returned to selling the *Daily Worker*, and further honing his accomplished public speaking skills. 'Every Sunday afternoon, huge crowds would listen to him on Clapham Common,' his wife recalled, proudly.[68]

Meanwhile, in Spain, the situation facing the Republicans in early 1939 was becoming extremely perilous. Facing defeat on the battlefield and infighting between those who wanted to sue for surrender and those who were determined to fight on, the Spanish Republic essentially collapsed. Nationalist forces took full advantage and marched into Madrid virtually unopposed.[69] On 1 April 1939, a triumphant Franco proclaimed victory for the Nationalists and the end of the civil war. Those who had been part of the struggle to save the Spanish government were, understandably, utterly distraught: 'When Spain finally fell . . . Clive felt it to be the biggest blow of his life', Noreen recalled, admitting that he suffered from insomnia for a long time afterwards.[70] Yet along with a deep sense of sorrow at the

Republic's defeat, came a burning anger. For Branson, responsibility for the defeat lay squarely on the shoulders of the British Government. [71] Many former volunteers agreed, blaming British support for the policy of non-intervention in the war, which the permanent under-secretary at the Foreign Office Sir Robert Gilmour Vansittart later admitted, 'worked in an extremely one-sided manner.'[72] While campaigning for the exiled Spanish Republic carried on, many veterans' minds were becoming increasingly occupied by the obviously impending European war against fascism. Somehow, Branson found the time and energy to keep painting and the family managed to take a short holiday in Amsterdam in the summer, Clive having gloomily declared to Noreen that 'I must see Rembrandt's Night Watch before I die.' War was declared soon after their return.[73]

Branson was not immediately conscripted and finding himself short of funds, took a job as a painters' labourer, helping to renovate a hotel. After an initial misunderstanding—he was rebuked by his colleagues for 'working too hard and too fast' and thereby undermining trade union conditions—Branson quickly became popular with his colleagues. As Noreen stated proudly, despite his obviously privileged background and his intellectualism, 'Clive was very good with people, people couldn't help liking him.'[74] Branson joined a campaign at the hotel for air-raid shelters to be provided for the staff, in line with the Communist Party's wider campaign for air-raid provision. At a demonstration on Clapham Common Branson was arrested for blaming the Lord Privy Seal (later Home Secretary), Sir John Anderson, for the lack of shelters in London. He was charged with using 'insulting words and behaviour', fined £5 and bound over for 12 months.[75]

By the end of the year, with most of northern Europe under Nazi occupation and the Luftwaffe wreaking devastation on Britain's cities, Branson realised that he would soon be conscripted. He responded by painting furiously, depicting a number of scenes of Battersea during the Blitz and exhibiting them for an exhibition by the progressive Artists' International Association.[76] But just as he had feared, in early 1941 Branson's call-up letter arrived and he elected to join the infantry, modestly describing himself as a 'Painter's Labourer'. However, when the recruiting officer discovered that Branson had matriculated, he was instead put down for the tank corps, joining the 54th Training Regiment of the Royal Armoured Corps.

Like many Spanish veterans and Communists, Branson was wary of being discriminated against, so prudently made no mention of his time fighting with the International Brigades. However, he quickly discovered that concealing military experience is not a simple task. Soon after his admission, Branson and the other new arrivals were subjected to a kit inspection. When their commanding officer walked down the ranks, Branson sprang to attention, just as he had been trained to do in Spain. 'Have you been in the army before?' asked the officer, suspiciously. 'NO sir!', belted out Branson at full parade ground volume, not helping his case.[77] Besides, cooped up with other trainees, it was difficult to keep secrets and Clive soon let slip to a man in a neighbouring bunk that he had fought in Spain. And when the new recruits were issued with firearms, any last hope Branson may have had for secrecy vanished:

> During the first week all new recruits were taken for a trial to a rifle range and it immediately became apparent that Clive was a crack shot. This caused a stir and a rumour went round the camp that . . . an ex-International Brigader had arrived 'who had learnt to shoot sniping fascists in Spain.'[78]

Yet while some in the War Office and Security Services harboured suspicions and prejudices towards former members of the International Brigades, many veterans proved themselves to be highly effective soldiers.[79] Branson was no exception; scoring 96 per cent in his map-reading exam, he was rapidly promoted to corporal. His Regimental Sergeant Major actually wanted to promote him to sergeant, but was concerned, as indeed was Branson, that as Southern Military Command were probably aware of Branson's politics, it might be prudent for him to keep a low profile.

Unfortunately, with rumours concerning Branson's time in the International Brigades spreading beyond his barracks, fears of being victimised soon became realised. In February, he was identified as having been a Communist speaker on Clapham Common. Until this point, his local army educational committee had been happy for him to give talks on the Red Army and his experiences in Spain, but once the 'intelligence branch' became aware of his political background, orders were given that Branson should not be allowed to lecture again, on any subject, in any circumstances.[80] He later wrote to Noreen complaining bitterly that, 'I was fighting fascism *voluntarily* years before 1939—yet *I* am the one who is watched, who is not allowed promotion, simply because I demand an all-out effort against fascism by those who today pretend to be fighting for freedom.[81] In fact, the ban proved to be rather counter-productive:

> The above business came up today when we were put on re-volver [training]. We drew the revolvers—each one signed for. Then who to take the class? I was forbidden to do so by the SSM [Squadron Sergeant-Major], so I couldn't—ie, wasn't allowed to, so as no one else could, we returned the revolvers and did nothing. The sergeant in charge knows perfectly well I am well capable of instructing at this arm. But no! His attitude is: 'The SSM says Corporal Branson mustn't do the job; there's no one else who can, so ---- him, we won't do the revolver [training]'.[82]

Despite his determination to be a good soldier and a willingness to immerse himself in the proletarian culture of the lower ranks, Branson was honest enough to recognise that he loathed his military training. 'This army life is bloody in the extreme', he complained, sometimes finding the 'lumpen' attitudes of some of his fellow draftees dispiriting:

> God what a tedious life they lead! Eternally on the scrounge for petty gain; eternally feeling they are being swindled by the paymaster, by the canteen, the shopkeepers and therefore ready always to swindle someone else; disunited by the bitterness of life and, dialectically, united by their common fear of life and common hatred.[83]

He wasn't much keen on the enforced camaraderie in the barracks, either:

It's funny really. Some of the fellows said to me on going out, 'Why don't you come with us? Come on. Give yourself a break.' If they only knew that the real break I need is *to be alone* either painting and reading and above all *not* spending some three or four hours with them in a noisy room.[84]

During the spring of 1941, with the mindless kit inspections and parades getting on his nerves, Branson attempted to take refuge by painting local beauty spots around the military base at Perham Down, near Andover. A request to be allowed to paint within the camp area did little to raise his mood, when he was informed that if he was so keen to indulge his artistic talents, he could repaint the walls of the Squadron Office.[85]

The following March, with his period of training at an end, Branson was posted overseas to India. After a long and dangerous voyage evading U-boats, his ship docked at Bombay (now Mumbai) on 31 May 1942 and he was transferred to a camp just outside Poona (now Pune), south-west of Bombay. In addition to being taken aback by the overwhelming heat and noise, Branson was genuinely shocked by the appalling conditions in which much of the Indian population existed: 'Although I have only been in India a little time there is one problem which hits you in the face—the life of the peasantry; and, in Bombay, the housing.'[86] As Branson was acutely aware, the locals' conditions contrasted greatly with the lives of the British troops:

I cannot stress too much the appalling mass poverty, dirt, ignorance and backwardness of the people. Yet *we* travelled in modern lorries, went across railway lines and at times passed a factory with machinery. Past miles and miles of tilled soil with not a sign of a tractor (only a bullock with a single blade scraping the earth). Past village after village where human beings live in hovels; a bit of a roof resting against an old stone wall with mud floor; a shelter of matting laid over sticks (improved with bits of tin, old carpet, some tenting etc.) just high enough for the occupants to sit up on their haunches. This type of dwelling is the same as used by man 50,000 years ago.[87]

Branson was shocked by the callous attitude of many soldiers, and Anglo-Indians in general, towards the indigenous population of British India. In letters home he railed against 'the appalling conditions in which the people live' which, 'after 175 years of imperialism ... are a howling disgrace.'[88] Crucially, Branson was convinced that the high-handed attitudes of the British Raj were sabotaging the Allied war-effort:

Can you wonder that with their hatred of the British, some of the Indians, with their brains starved of anything practical, give way to rioting and listening to the practical voice from Tokyo and Berlin coming over the ether?[89]

Yet, despite the poverty, the misery and the appalling inequalities, Branson saw India as a country begging to be painted:

This country is giving me a new colour sense. The other evening, the sun was just setting making the whole sky a brilliant hard yellow. A labourer came past. His skin a brown black; round his head the folds of gleaming white cloth. The road, the dry earth, a pale mauve with strips of lemon-green sugar patches. No shadows, the light in the shaded part being too rich in colour to look different. [90]

However, his enthusiasm did not stretch to painting the dispiriting mundanities of army life: 'Of course I want to paint!!' he wrote in exasperation, '[but] I don't paint things I want to forget!'[91]

And there was much of army life that he did want to forget. Having served in the rather more informal and meritocratic International Brigades, Branson struggled to adapt to the more rigid life within the British army. In particular, he found the 'Blimpish' attitude of the army command and their expectation of unquestioning obedience to rules and regulations intensely frustrating. 'The Party must, must, must do something about the army,' he raged in a letter home to Noreen.[92] He held a particular loathing for the incessant and interminable kit inspections, which required hours and hours of preparation in the often vain anticipation of a visit by the 'top brass'. June 1942 found Branson fuming as he prepared his kit for a potential visit by the Duke of Gloucester:

> Nothing could help the enemy more by undermining morale, destroying enthusiasm and making us incompetent fighters than this kind of tomfoolery . . . Sevastapol is falling and our CO is disappointed at the lack of polish on the topee chin straps.[93]

His despair of army life and discipline was exacerbated by the feeling that it was not just unfair but, ultimately, self-defeating. In October, he wrote to Noreen complaining about what he felt was the particularly unjust treatment of a soldier under his command:

> Today a trooper got punished—given seven days CB [confined to barracks]—for obeying an order I gave him. I will not go into the whole story. But eventually he appears before his squadron leader on a charge of driving his vehicle along a wrong route. I appeared as a witness. I very plainly stated I told him to go that route. Result. Nothing happens to me—but *he* is punished. I have appealed to the officer in charge of the Gunnery wing to take it up. But I don't suppose anything will be done. Evidently an 'example' had to be made.[94]

Branson argued strongly that this kind of small-minded and unwarranted treatment was catastrophically damaging to morale: 'It makes one absolutely sick,' he wrote. In despair of the British Army mentality, he came to the conclusion that: 'There is only one way to make non-political men willing, of their own will, to fight and that is to get them 3,000% browned off; they will then do any madness.'

Yet, despite his frustration and anger and despite the War Office's distrust of former International Brigaders and Party members, Branson still managed to rise up the ranks. On 20 April 1943, he was promoted to 'made-up sergeant' and five months later he was declared a 'War Substantiated Sergeant', which meant that he could not lose his rank without an official court-martial. Nevertheless, like the former 15th International Brigade Chief of Staff, Malcom Dunbar (see Chapter One), Branson never rose higher than the rank of sergeant. This spurred Communist Party Secretary Harry Pollitt to complain that Branson was clearly being victimised:

> After he joined the Royal Armoured Corps, he proved himself a model of efficiency in mastering every aspect of armoured warfare. He was repeatedly recommended for promotion, which might have been quicker in coming had it not been for the political prejudices which die so hard in the War Office.[95]

However, Pollitt was mistaken. Again, like Dunbar, Branson was actually recommended for a commission, but he personally took the decision to reject it, following enquiries from a senior officer about the extent of his private income:

> I explained that among the rank and file there was much ill-feeling against the officers because of this business of money, school tie etc. I was still willing to become an officer on one condition, and only one—merit.[96]

In December 1943, Sergeant Branson's unit of the 25th Dragoons, comprising two squadrons of American M3 'Lee' tanks, finally prepared themselves to move up to the front at Sinzweya, in the Burmese province of Arakan, near the border with India.[97] Understandably apprehensive about returning into combat, Clive wrote an emotional letter home:

> It is December 4th and we are again on the move. It is nearing zero hour . . . Always remember that one is given by fate only one lifetime in which to work and live for humanity. There is no greater crime in my opinion than to renounce the world, no matter for what excuse. If anything should happen to either of us, never say, 'It is finished.' For we have both lived for one

purpose, the emancipation of the working people. If by chance one of us has to leave this work before it is done, then let the other go on and see it through—not in the spirit of holy self-sacrifice—as a monk or a nun—but even more in the fullness of human experience. What we miss we can only find in knowing humanity more deeply and not in the ever-narrowing circumference of private memories. Life for me has only been worthwhile in so far as I have been able to show, even a few people, the way to *forward* living. And above all, whatever happens, let us never for one instant, on the slightest excuse, forget we are human beings and belong to the brotherhood of man. Tyrants and hermits are tarred with the same brush. Whatever happens you must go on living—there are so many years of grand work ahead.[98]

In January 1944, Branson's tank group arrived at Sinzweya, where British and allied forces were occupying a defensive position, known as 'The Box', hemmed in by Japanese forces. To Branson's surprise and delight, he discovered that his friend Tony Gilbert, a fellow prisoner in San Pedro, had been posted to the same front. The war in Spain cast a long shadow, it seemed: 'One thought runs through my head continually—Spain! Here we have such a complete mastery in armaments of all kinds! . . . It may seem strange to you that in a sort of way I cannot help gloating over the affair—it is the reverse of Spain a hundred-fold.'[99] However, despite being equipped with the British Army's incomparably better *matériel*, Branson was only too aware that the defending Japanese forces had built numerous entrenchments and were preparing themselves to make whatever sacrifices were necessary to push back the Allies' advance. Every morning Branson's tank group would set off along the hazardous Ngakyedauk Pass, a small track running across the nearby hills, which was key to an advance into the Arakan province. Tony Gilbert remembered how he 'used to wave to him every morning as the tanks went forward to try to clear the pass, and wave joyfully when they came back.'[100] On 25 February 1944, Branson's tank set off as usual and he was 'trundling quite gaily along a sunny road north of Buthidaung', his head and shoulders jutting out of the tank's hatch for greater visibility, while cracking jokes to keep up the group's morale. A solitary Japanese 47mm anti-tank gun opened up from a hidden position and an armour-piercing shell penetrated the top of Branson's tank. He was killed instantly.[101]

Back home in England, Noreen was watching a newsreel with Rosa in a railway station café, which described serious fighting on the Arakan front in Burma and heavy Allied casualties. Noreen's face blanched, only too aware that this was where Clive was serving. Two weeks later, she received the terrible confirmation: Clive had been killed in action. A letter from a fellow member of Branson's tank regiment, Lance Corporal Bagshawr, filled in the awful details:

> If you have not received the telegram then I must tell you, me being his sparring partner, that Clive Branson was killed in action last Friday, Feb. 25th. It is a very short story and probably one of the unluckiest of this War. He was killed by a shot from a Japanese anti-tank gun, which pierced the tank's top armour at a weak point, where a periscope was mounted
> . . . It was as though one of our main nerve centres had gone.[102]

Branson was buried in the Taukkyan War Cemetery, just outside Rangoon. In a letter of condolence to Noreen, Branson's commanding officer mourned his death as a great loss to the tank unit, admitting that his 'rank of troop sergeant ... [was] nowhere near what he should have been.'[103] It was also a dreadful blow to the British Communist Party, whose General Secretary sent a personal telegram to Noreen: 'Please accept deepest sympathy with all your family in your sad bereavement— Harry Pollitt.' The Communist leader made a point of visiting Noreen and young Rosa, insisting that she call him 'Uncle Harry.'[104] Fellow International Brigade veterans were also devastated, particularly Clive's friend Tony Gilbert: 'It was a terribly sad loss', he recalled, 'because he was so very gifted.'[105] Even the local Labour Party managed to overcome their official distrust of Communists, setting up a children's crèche in Branson's name. Meanwhile letters poured into the Communist Party offices in London's King Street, expressing their sadness at

Clive's death and, despite any personal hardship, donating money to a 'fighting fund' in his honour:

I have already bought my monthly 'insurance' but this just HAD to be found, it's my tribute to Clive Branson's memory. No need to say more, but when such as Clive are lost, those of us left must work even harder.[106]

While the Security Services file on Branson noted only, 'Killed in Action. Communist',[107] the entire May 1944 issue of the British International Brigade veterans' newspaper, *Volunteer for Liberty*, was dedicated to his memory. The artist also received a heartfelt obituary, tucked away in a local Hampshire newspaper. It provides a fitting, final epitaph not just to Branson, but to the many, many others killed during the long war against fascism between 1936 and 1945:

His life and death prove once again what we have said so often: The first battles of this present war were fought in Spain . . . By his death on Feb. 25th last, one is reminded all too painfully of the appalling toll which war makes upon the youth of the nations, and, seemingly, upon the most promising of those who are blessed with the divine gifts of poetry, or artistic vision, or Christian statesmanship.[108]

Chapter Ten
The Brilliant Surgeon: Alexander Tudor Hart

For many years after the end of the Spanish Civil War, the role of the British medical services in the conflict was a rather overlooked subject. Yet British medics such as Len Crome, the Latvian-born commander of the 35th Division Medical Services and Reggie Saxton, the Reading GP who worked with the Canadian blood transfusion pioneer, Norman Bethune, played a vitally important role in Spain. Alongside others such as the Catalan surgeon Josep Trueta i Raspall and the New Zealander Douglas Jolly, as the historian Paul Preston has pointed out, they 'were of a colossal importance in the later development of traumatalogical medicine in both war and peacetime.'[1] Fortunately, the last fifteen years have seen this deficit substantially remedied, yet one influential British surgeon remains relatively unknown: his name was Alexander Ethan Tudor Hart.[2] Unlike some of his contemporaries who went on to have illustrious careers—for example, Len Crome later worked with Alexander Fleming at Paddington Hospital and Archie Cochrane became a pioneer in the field of epidemiology—Tudor Hart pursued a more modest vocation and left no published account of his life and work. Yet his story is important, not just because of his work in Spain and the war that followed, but also because of his personal connections to probably one of the most significant Soviet agents ever to operate in the United Kingdom.

Born on 3 September 1901 in Fiesole, Italy, Alexander Tudor Hart was the eldest of two children of 'conservative and bourgeois' parents. His father, Ernest Percival Tudor Hart, was a Canadian painter and sculptor who had exhibited internationally and was descended from Ephraim Hart, a Bavarian Jew and prominent merchant in New York.[3] His mother, Countess Éléonora Délia Julie Kleczkowska, was a descendent of a former King of Poland who also happened to be his father's Parisian cousin. Brought up in England, in 1915, Tudor Hart was sent to the prestigious Marlborough College, founded in the nineteenth century for the sons of Church of England clergy and whose former pupils included William Morris, Siegfried Sassoon and Anthony Blunt.[4] A junior scholar in Marlborough's Preshute House, Tudor Hart worked hard and made good progress, yet still found time to represent his house for rugby and join the school's Officer Training Corps.[5] Too young to serve in the First World War, he left Marlborough school in 1919, finding temporary work as a schoolteacher, despite not yet being 20 years of age.[6] Tudor Hart was also accepted to King's College, Cambridge where, from 1920 to 1924, he studied history and economics, the latter under the famous John Meynard Keynes, one of the most influential economists of the 20th century.[7] However, after graduation he had a change of heart and decided to pursue a career in medicine, studying at St Thomas's in London.[8] After graduating in August 1931, Tudor Hart was appointed house physician at Hampstead General and North West London Hospital, though the appointment was only for six months.[9] When the position terminated, with Britain in the depths of the economic depression, Tudor-Hart struggled to find another job.[10] Unable to secure even a temporary or part-time post, he decided to return to his studies, moving to Vienna to study under the world-famous Professor Lorenz Böhler, a surgeon who had developed a speciality in fractures during the Great War.[11] However, the illustrious surgeon's expertise was not Vienna's only appeal.

During his training at St Thomas's, the young medical student had become involved with a married doctor four years his senior called Alison Nicol Macbeth, and the couple had moved in together at Mecklenburgh Square in central London. Their son, Julian, had been born on 9 March 1927 and the couple were married three years later in St Giles' London.[12] However, it was not to be a long and happy marriage, for Alison soon came to the conclusion that Alex 'really wasn't a very effective husband [nor] a very useful person to live with.' While he could be extremely charming, Macbeth later confessed that Tudor Hart 'was like water, you couldn't really get a grip on him.'[13] However, rather more significant in the breakdown of the marriage than his enigmatic character was that Tudor Hart had become involved with somebody else.

His new love interest was a young Austrian woman called Edith Suschitzky, who he had met through his sister Beatrix. Born on 24 August 1908 in a secularised Jewish family in Vienna, Suschitzky was the daughter of a progressive bookshop owner and, later, publisher. Her father's socialist politics had a strong early influence on Edith, though it was actually more the Communist Party's radical youth movement that attracted her. She studied at the Montessori School in Vienna and in April 1925 went to England for an internship. Three years later she went to study photography at the famous Bauhaus in Dessau under Joseph Albers, Paul Klee and Vasily Kandinsky and was almost certainly a member of the student Communist faction there. She visited London again in October 1930 and when Alex met her, she was working as a student kindergarten teacher in a Montessori School in London.[14]

The two shared a similar political outlook for, like Suschitzky, Alex Tudor Hart had been drawn to the Communist Party; again like her, influenced by the appalling slaughter of the First World War. He was a very active member in Westminster and Paddington and a police report in 1929 identified him as one of two men arrested for distributing Communist literature to soldiers outside a barracks in Chelsea.[15] The arresting officers carefully noted down a description of the young activist: 'age 27, height 5'10½", complexion pale, hair light brown, eyes grey, long thin face, wears spectacles, shortened tendon on [the] index finger of [the] right hand; slim build, clean shaven.'[16] As an active Communist, Tudor Hart's activities soon came to the attention of the Metropolitan Police's Special Branch, who placed him under surveillance and intercepted his mail.

Suschitzky also came to the attention of the British police. In October 1930, the young Austrian teacher was observed with Tudor Hart, when the pair appeared to be taking a prominent role in a Workers' Charter demonstration in Trafalgar Square.[17] Suschitzky in particular gave every appearance of being 'on friendly terms with many of the Communist leaders.'[18] Concerned that her political activities might make her a danger to national security, on 4 December 1930 she was ordered to leave the country. Having been issued with a number of official warnings, the 'undesirable alien' reluctantly returned to Vienna on 15 January 1931.[19]

In April, Tudor Hart visited Suschitzky in Vienna and the pair kept in contact by letter, their correspondence monitored carefully by Special Branch.[20] The following August, Suschitzky wrote to him, admitting that he was '(as a friend) more and more to me,' thanking him for being kind to her and signing off 'with love, Edith.'[21] She wrote again the following month and in a heartfelt confession, confessed she found Alex to be an 'intelligent and loving comrade' one of 'few whom one can love,' nervously asking how he felt about her. She asked about his relationship with his ex-wife, exclaiming that 'they must both grasp the fact that marriage between them is impossible ... and that separation is natural.'[22]

Meanwhile, Suschitzky found work in Vienna as the photo correspondent for the Russian TASS news agency, capturing the 'horrifying misery' of poverty. She also worked for the Austrian Communist Party, a task which became considerably more dangerous when Engelbert Dolfuss was sworn in as Austrian Chancellor on 10 May 1932 and, supported by a coalition of right-wing and nationalist parties, set about dismantling the country's democracy and suppressing dissent. Within a year, the lower house of parliament was shut and Dolfuss was essentially ruling by decree. On 16 May 1933, Suschitzky was arrested while carrying documents for the Communist Party and a search of her parents' house produced further incriminating documents. She was promptly thrown in jail where she remained for a month, before being released, apparently for a lack of serious evidence, on 14 June. Her photographic material prepared for TASS was confiscated and never returned.[23]

Tudor Hart had only just taken up a residential position at the St Mary Abbotts Hospital in Kensington, but hearing of Suschitzky's arrest he flew to Vienna to help.[24] With Austria in political turmoil and terrified that she might be arrested again, Edith was desperate to get out of the country. Consequently, Tudor Hart and Suschitzky decided to get married, and the wedding was held in August 1933 in the British consulate in

Vienna. Two months later, the married couple left Vienna for London and set up home in Brixton, where Alex established a medical practice and Edith founded a photographic studio specialising in documentary photography, looking at issues of poverty, child welfare, unemployment and homelessness. Her photography business was supported by the modernist designer Jack Pritchard, who had just had a child with Alexander's sister, Beatrix.[25]

Tudor Hart moved to Wales in the latter part of 1934 and Edith joined him there, where she took a number of striking photographs that revealed in stark clarity the poverty-stricken existence of the local population.[26] For Edith Tudor Hart, 'photography was first and foremost a documentary means for conveying social and political concerns.'[27] As she later explained:

In the hands of the person who uses it with feeling and imagination, the camera becomes very much more than the means of earning a living, it becomes a vital factor in recording and influencing the life of the people and in promoting human understanding.[28]

While Edith was exposing the hardship facing many living in south Wales, her husband was helping alleviate it, by providing free medical treatment to Rhondda miners.[29]

When they returned to London, Alex continued working in his Brixton practice, while Edith moved her photography business to a studio in Haverstock Hill, in the wealthy bohemian area of Hampstead, in north London. There, as Special Branch were aware, the Tudor Harts were socialising with senior British Communists and hosted a number of German and Austrian refugees, most of whom were passionate anti-Nazis.[30] In fact, the Tudor Harts were committed antifascists and their efforts went a long way beyond simply hobnobbing with senior Party figures. Alex Tudor Hart was one of the protestors at the infamous rally of Sir Oswald Mosley's British Union of Fascists at Olympia in 1934 and he saw with his own eyes the violence inflicted by Blackshirt thugs on the anti-fascist demonstrators.[31] Meanwhile, Edith contributed work to the progressive Artists' International

Association's first major exhibition, 'Artists against Fascism and Against War', in 1935.

In April 1936, the Tudor Harts' attentions were taken by more happy matters, with the birth of their son, Tommy. However, their peaceful family existence was shattered by the arrival of news in July of the violent military coup against Spain's left-wing government. Despite the demands of parenthood, both were determined to do what they could to support the Spanish Republicans' cause. Alex became personally involved following an appeal by the Republican Government for medical assistance. This led to the creation of the Spanish Medical Aid Committee (known by the acronym SMAC), to raise money, supplies and medical volunteers for the Republic.[32] Despite having a wife and young baby to support, Tudor Hart threw himself into working with SMAC.[33] He spoke at meetings and demonstrations in support of the Spanish Republic and in August 1936, joined the Labour MP Ellen Wilkinson and the Communist Isabel Brown, the so-called 'Pasionaria of the Aid Spain movement', at a pro-Republican rally in Paris.[34]

The following month, Tudor Hart was approached by a Spanish doctor, who had come to Britain desperate to recruit medical staff. Surgeons were particularly badly needed and he pleaded with Tudor Hart for help. Reluctantly, the surgeon agreed to go to Spain, though insisting that he could only go for a short time, as he had only recently established his General Practice in Brixton and could not afford to leave it. Consequently, having said goodbye to his wife and child, on 28 December 1936 at 6.35pm, Alexander Tudor Hart joined a small band of medical volunteers en route to Spain.[35] Travelling by train down through France, they arrived in Albacete in Castile-La Mancha, the headquarters of the international volunteers, just before Christmas. There they were united with other English medical volunteers already in Spain. Marooned at Albacete for several days while awaiting orders, the reality of the situation they faced was made brutally clear, when Tudor Hart had to carry out an impromptu surgical operation in the middle of an air raid.[36]

As there was not yet an English-speaking Battalion or Brigade, Tudor Hart was posted instead to a French unit, the

14th International Brigade. Fortunately, having travelled widely, the surgeon spoke very good French as well as reasonable German and Italian.[37] So in the first days of January 1937, Tudor Hart set off to join the French at Las Rozas, some 15km to the north-west of Madrid where a hospital had been established behind the front, in a group of holiday villas in the nearby village of Torrelodones. When Tudor Hart arrived, a number of British medical workers were already there, under the command of a twenty-three-year-old Cambridge medical student called Kenneth Sinclair-Loutit. While the young medic was popular with his staff, doubts had been expressed about his leadership skills and experience.[38] As a qualified doctor with considerably greater surgical experience—not to mention long-standing membership of the Communist Party—Tudor Hart clearly outranked the young medical student. So, on 8 January 1937, the newly promoted Major Alexander Tudor Hart took up his post as commander of the small British medical unit. Sinclair-Loutit, to his chagrin, had to be satisfied with the rank of sub-lieutenant.[39]

Tudor Hart's team rushed to prepare the hospital for the forthcoming battle, and it was finally completed at two o'clock in the morning, only hours before the arrival of the first wounded. The trickle soon became a flood; in a masterly piece of understatement an official report later described that 'during the days of 11-15 January 1937, the hospital dealt with over 200 wounded, which rather over-taxed the capacities of the small staff.'[40] During the battle and throughout the Spanish Civil War, British medical units were frequently swamped by casualties. They ran out of the basic essentials, including anaesthetics. While sulphonamides were available, which had some effect against bacterial infections, there were no antibiotics, so there were many occasions where amputation was the only realistic option. On one occasion, Tudor Hart operated for nearly two hours trying to save the life of a Nationalist prisoner. Despite a number of blood transfusions, he died on the operating table.[41] While Tudor Hart raged at being unable to save the soldier, it was actually remarkable that more patients did not die, given the conditions under which he and his team were operating.[42] The mortality rate at the hospital in Las Rozas was five per cent, much the same as the British Royal Army Military Corps achieved at the end of the First World War, with considerably fewer resources.

Much of this was a result of good organisation. Before a casualty reached Tudor Hart, they would already have been assessed by a gifted medical student called Archie Cochrane. He was responsible for triage, a procedure which had been standard practice during the First World War. This involved separating the casualties into three broad categories: those with superficial injuries who could be quickly patched up, the more seriously though treatable wounded, and those who were unfortunately beyond help. 'I hated playing God,' Cochrane admitted, 'but I had to. I sought medical advice as far as it was available, but the doctors were far too busy.'[43] Any patient needing surgery would be marked up as 'flesh', 'orthopaedic', 'abdominal' as appropriate, following a scale of severity. However, given the impossible conditions, Cochrane could unfortunately often do no more than make the dying as comfortable as possible, an almost impossible task given the scarcity of effective painkillers.[44]

As Tudor Hart and other medics in Spain came to recognise, rapid casualty management was the key to reducing mortality rates. Tudor Hart never forgot how the victim of a minor road accident had died, because delays allowed the patient to go into medical shock, which prevented him from being anaesthetised.[45] He very much supported the view of Len Crome, the Latvian born British Commander of the 35th Division Medical Services, who argued that six hours was the maximum interval between being wounded and reaching surgery and that consequently more hospitals were needed closer to the front. Tudor Hart also pressed for first aiders to be made aware of the latest thinking on medical treatment, particularly relating to fractures, which required careful splinting and padding to minimise shock.[46]

Fractures comprised some seventy-five per cent of the injuries Tudor Hart treated, so he recommended that orthopaedic surgeons should be a standard fixture of front-line hospitals. Initially, when operating on fractures, Tudor Hart used the so-called 'open' or 'Böhler method' of splinting wounds involving fractures, which he had learned while studying under

Böhler in Vienna. This involved the removal of any foreign objects and any damaged tissue from the wound, which was then left open to limit the chance of infection. The damaged limb was then immobilised and elevated using wire splints. However, over the course his time in Spain, Tudor Hart came to recognise that the Böhler splints were impracticable during wartime. This led him to adopt the alternative Spanish or 'closed method', invented by the Canadian surgeon, Winnet Orr, during the First World War and developed in Spain by the distinguished Catalan physician, Josep Trueta.[47] This also required the removal of foreign matter and the cutting away of any damaged flesh, but instead of leaving the wound open, the entire damaged limb was encased in plaster, wound and all. This avoided the necessity of internal sutures and wound drainage and could save the patient a long, often extremely uncomfortable evacuation, allowing more time for rest and recovery. So successful was this procedure that, after the war, Tudor Hart was asked to explain it in a lecture to the British Postgraduate Medical School.

Tudor Hart remained at Torrelodones hospital until the beginning of February 1937 when, in preparation for a forthcoming Republican offensive at the Jarama river to the south-east of Madrid, Tudor Hart's unit was posted to the village of Villarejo de Salvanés on the main road linking the capital with Valencia. As there was no existing medical facility in the village, Tudor Hart was charged with locating a suitable building in which to establish a field hospital. Consequently, on 11 February 1937, accompanied by Reg Saxton, an 'open-hearted, friendly and kind' GP from Reading, and Aileen Palmer, a highly respected and experienced administrator, Tudor Hart arrived in the village looking for a suitable site.[48] It was not a straightforward task, as Saxton recounted:

It was after midnight . . . the early hours of the morning, complete darkness and . . . we were supposed to do something about starting up a hospital. It all seemed a bit difficult to know where to start.[49]

After stumbling around the village in the dark, they chanced upon 'a beautiful old hotel', which had once been owned by Don John of Austria, the illegitimate son of Charles V and the half-brother of King Philip II of Spain. Crucially, it was supplied with fresh water, so Tudor Hart believed it could serve very well. With no sign of life in the village, the trio hammered on the front door of the largest nearby building. When the door was eventually opened, Tudor Hart instructed Saxton (who spoke some Spanish) to tell the local that the International Brigades urgently needed the building as a hospital. Unimpressed, the local promptly refused to open up the hotel until daylight. An affronted Tudor Hart commanded Saxton to threaten him with arrest if he did not comply 'at once'. Unfortunately, the word for 'arrest' was not yet within Saxton's lexicon, so he used the only Spanish he knew: 'Listen here', Saxton improvised, 'if you don't open up, you're going to be shot.' At which point the already irritated Tudor Hart became utterly apoplectic, for while the surgeon didn't speak Spanish, his knowledge of French and Italian meant that he was certainly able to get the gist.[50] 'These are our friends and allies', Tudor Hart screamed, appalled. 'You can't threaten the locals with being shot!' As the two *extranjeros* yelled at each other on his doorstep, the terrified and bewildered local wisely retreated behind the door. The easy-going Saxton remained unfazed by the screaming argument with his superior officer: 'He's like that,' the Reading doctor shrugged, 'he makes a mountain out of a molehill.'[51]

In the morning, they located the local mayor who wisely granted them permission to use the building. Once they realised that they were not about to be shot, many locals proved sympathetic to the foreign medical volunteers, helping clear out and clean up the hospital and supplying the staff with food, despite the war shortages. The building possessed a big courtyard in the centre lined with benches, which were converted into serviceable beds and the former bar was converted into the operating theatre, to the disappointment of some thirsty locals.[52] Once converted, the building became 'a reasonably efficient hospital . . . [and] a reasonably happy one,' wrote Cochrane.[53] It was well situated for the forthcoming Jarama battle, lying less than twenty kilometres behind the line. 'A damn sight too near the front, if you ask me,' remarked Tudor Hart.[54]

Jarama was one of the bloodiest battles of the entire civil war and the sheer mass of casualties utterly overwhelmed the Republican medical services. Despite the careful preparations, the hospital was swamped, as more than 700 patients poured in over five days. One nurse was so exhausted, having not slept properly for three days, that she removed a dead soldier from a bed just so she could lie down for a few hours.[55] Overstretched, exhausted and lacking equipment and supplies, the medical volunteers—some of whom were students—were forced to take on responsibilities far beyond their training and experience. More than sixty surgical operations were carried out each night, with the medical staff like 'cogs in a machine, working in a frenzy, and dropping down to sleep whenever there was a chance'.[56] Tudor Hart operated for 14 hours straight, before repeating the feat the following day, having snatched only a few hours' sleep.[57] The surgeon frequently pushed himself to the edge of exhaustion, sometimes becoming so tired that he would fall asleep underneath the operating table. Unwilling to take breaks, he shocked the normally imperturbable Saxton by urinating into a bucket in the middle of an operation.

Unfortunately, Tudor Hart expected everyone else to push themselves just as hard, earning him a reputation as a perfectionist with little tolerance for others' weaknesses or failings. One unfortunate Irish volunteer's first experience of surgery involved assisting Tudor Hart during the height of the Jarama fighting:

Paddy [Cochrane] had been given the job of holding a bicycle lamp so that Hart could operate . . . Overcome by the sight of blood and froth coming from the lungs of the patient on the operating table, Paddy's resolve (and his legs) gave way. He was reprimanded by Hart for not holding the lamp steady.[58]

During the battle, an exhausted Saxton also experienced Tudor Hart's total lack of empathy:

I hadn't had any sleep for 48 hours and I was really feeling terrible, I just couldn't keep awake. You reach the stage when you feel, I don't mind what happens, I've got to sleep, I just can't stay awake any more. Not Hart, mind you, he was still rushing around, giving orders, making suggestions. I just couldn't stay awake any more. What could I do? . . . I thought of this pile of higgledy-piggledy benches on the balcony . . . and I crawled in under these benches and worked my way right to the back where no one could see me and I went to sleep. I didn't care what happened. I just couldn't stay awake. And after I'd slept for a couple of hours or so, I could hear a voice, 'Saxton? Saxton! Where the devil have you got to? Come along! Come at once! You're needed . . . Where *are* you Saxton?'[59]

As a consequence, while many of his staff respected him, few expressed great affection. An official report, while recognising the impossible conditions under which Tudor Hart was operating, was nonetheless very critical of the surgeon's imperious manner:

[Tudor Hart] provoked a considerable hostility towards himself by his love of absolute power, while often giving self-contradictory commands, his insistence on interfering with every phase of work, while leaving the spadework, both in organisational and medial work, to [Archie] COCHRANE, his incapacity to adhere to any plans (he would hold up the usual ward-round for hours to converse with a wounded commissar who stayed at the hospital for weeks), and his absolute imperviousness to advice and criticism.[60]

On 25 March, grievances about Tudor Hart were aired at a stormy general meeting, which resulted in the surgeon being relieved of administrative responsibilities. Nonetheless, he continued to interfere, attempting to transfer a nurse to a fever hospital in Valencia, despite her lack of training or experience. He also sent two of his chief critics, Kenneth Sinclair-Loutit and Thora Silverthorne, on leave and while they were away, replaced Silverthorne with another nurse. Unfortunately, the replacement soon declared that she did not want to work with Tudor Hart either, so had to be transferred to another surgical team.[61]

With the Jarama fighting finally at an end, Tudor Hart was briefly transferred to a hospital set in a former alpine club in the Guadarrama mountains.[62] Initially, he was the only surgeon in the facility, but he was eventually relieved at the end of the March by the arrival of three Spanish surgeons. When one of them—an experienced and highly skilled Catalan surgeon called Moisès Broggi—first set eyes on Tudor Hart, the English surgeon had been working for several days without proper sleep:

A somewhat picturesque figure appeared, like a spectre, carrying a tray with food on it which he offered us, in a friendly manner, whilst bidding us welcome. He was a tall, slim man, well-mannered and rather strangely dressed, in a sort of shirt down to his feet, and he expressed himself in very correct French. He was Commander Tudor Hart.[63]

While Tudor Hart himself might have cut an odd figure, Broggi—who Tudor Hart grew to like and respect—was highly impressed with the order and discipline of the hospital, which was in marked contrast to the disorganisation that he had witnessed elsewhere.[64] The operating theatre had been ingeniously set up with three operating tables set radially in a circle, 120 degrees apart. This enabled the anaesthetist Kenneth Sinclair-Loutit to stand in the centre and serve all three tables. 'We were running a surgical production line', Loutit explained with some pride.[65] His confidence was soon to be sorely tested.

As summer approached, the Republicans planned a new action at Brunete, to the west of Madrid, in another attempt to break the Rebels' stranglehold on the city. As preparations were finalised for what would be the largest Republican offensive of the war so far, a hospital was established in a former Catholic boys' school near San Lorenzo de El Escorial, site of the famous Renaissance monastery.[66] Almost all the English medical personnel working in Spain were concentrated in the hospital, the largest at which they had yet worked.[67] The building was spacious, with a large garden at the front, though the sanitation was poor and steep stairs made the transport of patients extremely difficult. There were five operating theatres, each with its own dedicated team under the command of a surgeon; Tudor Hart's team comprised three people, all working 16-hour shifts.[68] The surgical teams were supported by an array of other medical staff, with Archie Cochrane in charge of triage and Reg Saxton handling blood transfusions. Kenneth Sinclair-Loutit was responsible for evacuating patients, though he would also work in theatre when necessary. George Green, a musician from Stockport, was appointed orderly in Tudor Hart's theatre. He was initially taken aback to discover that the roles he would be expected to undertake included, 'anaesthetist, all-in wrestler, stage manager, settler of disputes between sister and surgeon, selector of raw material from the triage and secretary—and occasionally assistant surgeon in a consultative capacity when everyone else is too tired.'[69]

Despite the capacity of the hospital, it was just as overwhelmed as other facilities had been. Medical supplies quickly ran out, leading English nurse Penny Phelps to remember El Escorial with horror:

> The flow of casualties and the heat and the flies continued unremittingly . . . we became desperately short of supplies. Ether and chloroform ran out and Novocaine, Evipan or spinal anaesthesia were used. When we were without gowns, I draped the surgeon in sheets . . . three operations were in progress at the same time and the surgeons had to make do with the light of torches and the reflection from the fires burning in nearby Villanueva de la Cañada.[70]

Casualties were soon lined up on stretchers outside the hospital and any patients with head injuries, considered to be hopeless cases, 'were quite literally put in a shed to die.' Fully aware that there was no alternative, Tudor Hart was still thoroughly sickened: 'I still remain horrified at the triage system at El Escorial during the battle of Brunete. You don't treat human beings like that.'[71]

When the battle came to an end at the end of July, the shattered medical unit was withdrawn for some urgently needed rest. For a time, 'everything was very quiet,' Tudor Hart recalled.[72] A number of staff, including Archie Cochrane, Kenneth Sinclair-Loutit and (his now wife) Thora Silverthorne were sent home, while Tudor Hart was posted to the English-run hospital at Huete, 'a little village north-east of Barcelona.'[73] There he received a letter from Edith bemoaning the lack of information from Spain and the interminable unreliability of the postal service:

> I find it terribly difficult writing to you[,] it makes me very depressed and I have the feeling they don't arrive. I have not heard a word from you since your letter (which I think you wrote on June 15th).[74]

The letter, containing mainly domestic news of their son Tommy, was accompanied by a very welcome food parcel. Edith enquired about the possibility of visiting Alex in Spain, tentatively suggesting a rendezvous in Valencia. The letter was heart-rending, full of the unhappiness and yearning that must have been the daily experience of many partners left behind. 'It is altogether too much to be separated in such circumstances,' she wrote, 'I should have stayed with you and not had Tommy. It is no time for children.'[75] Given the difficulties of getting to Spain and the risk it entailed, Edith never managed to visit her husband. Perhaps it was just as well, for he would not have been able to give her much of his time. The demands of war during the spring and summer of 1937 meant he had little time for visitors. However, the situation would change dramatically for Tudor Hart in the autumn.

Tudor Hart's surgical work had earned much praise over the preceding months, though, as had been observed at Villarejo de Salvanés, his administration and management skills earned fewer plaudits. Consequently, it was an argument over patient administration and management that led to his downfall. During the fighting on the Aragón front in the autumn of 1937, the hospital's inexperienced Polish Political Commissar came to the conclusion that wounded patients were being transferred out of the hospital, 'without proper treatment or consideration.' He drew up a list of the doctors he believed to be responsible and

Tudor Hart, naively, endorsed the report. His colleagues were outraged and, following a number of furious complaints, Tudor Hart was summarily dismissed from the hospital.[76] Having been in Spain for eight months, in September, Tudor Hart wisely took the opportunity to return home.

When he returned, Tudor Hart intended to return to his Brixton practice, but his extended period in Spain had stymied any hope of that. So, with no other offer of employment on the horizon, he returned to Spain, arriving just as the battle of Teruel erupted. Fought in remote mountains in freezing conditions, Republican forces were desperately trying to hold on to the remote provincial capital against overwhelming odds. Tudor Hart, his earlier transgression apparently forgiven, was appointed Chief Surgeon at the University Hospital in Murcia, a convalescent hospital for badly injured International Brigaders. However, following Franco's recapture of Teruel in February 1938 and the subsequent offensive during the spring which threatened to cut the Republican zone in two, his hospital was urgently evacuated to the safety of Republican Catalonia. Set on a high hill overlooking the Mediterranean in the seaside town of Mataró, just north of Barcelona, the huge, spacious hospital could accommodate up to 14,000 patients.[77] The former Labour MP Leah Manning (see Chapter Two) visited the hospital in July and was much impressed with Tudor Hart, who she flatteringly described as 'the deluxe surgeon'. He was, she believed, doing 'marvellous work' and had 'won the respect of everyone' with his pioneering medical skills.[78] She also added pointedly that he had managed to avoid 'raising the ire' that had marred some of his earlier appointments. The hospital's director, Adrien Vogel, also praised Tudor Hart's work reporting that 'as a surgeon he works diligently without rest.'[79] However, he spoke disapprovingly of the surgeon's lack of organisation, his inability to know how to work well with colleagues and his lack of participation in the hospital's political life. Tudor Hart's political activities, complained Vogel, were always secondary to his surgical work.[80]

Criticisms of a 'lack of political development' and the accusation that he was a 'good doctor, but a hopeless organiser' dogged Tudor Hart during his time in Spain.[81] He was undoubtedly not always easy to work with: demanding, impatient and high-handed. Nevertheless, while he was not as prominent as pioneering contemporaries such as Len Crome, Josep Trueta, or Norman Bethune, the importance of Tudor Hart's contribution to the Republican medical services is undeniable and not just as a gifted orthopaedic surgeon. He was sufficiently well-regarded that he was sought out for advice on the provision and organisation of front-line medical services by no less than Oskar Telge, the Head of the International Brigades Medical Services in Spain.[82]

The assessment by his colleague, Reg Saxton, was probably a fair one. 'Tudor Hart', he said, 'had a lot of good ideas . . . [though] his head was mainly up in the clouds . . . nevertheless, he did think big and look ahead' and he contributed greatly to the setting up of hospitals and improving overall medical provision.[83] He acknowledged Tudor Hart's 'magnificent work' but felt that 'he was a very difficult person to work with, very difficult, very argumentative and dogmatic.'[84] However, Sinclair-Loutit, who had been so aggrieved when Tudor Hart was parachuted in as his superior, got over his irritation and happily admitted that he was a 'brilliant' traumatic surgeon: 'He saved hundreds of lives and thousands of limbs; I am proud to have worked as his anaesthetist.'[85] Mataró was to be Tudor Hart's last appointment in Spain. Before he left the hospital and handed over his responsibilities to a Spanish doctor, one of his final tasks was to accompany the British Communist leader, Harry Pollitt, on a tour around the hospital.[86] Tudor Hart was finally repatriated on 6 December 1938 and, as ever, a representative of Special Branch carefully recorded his arrival at Newhaven the following day.[87]

Having returned from Spain for good this time, Tudor Hart was determined to rekindle his medical career. However, as he had the previous year, the surgeon struggled to find work. His professional problems were also compounded by domestic woes. Even before he had gone to Spain, Alex's relationship with Edith had been stormy, leading to the couple temporarily living apart in April 1935.[88] During Tudor Hart's two years away, the two had drifted apart and by the time he returned, their marriage was effectively over. They would formally split in early 1940, and divorce in 1944. However, despite their estrangement, the pair still continued to meet fairly frequently, primarily due to the complex needs of their son, Tommy, who had severe developmental issues.[89]

Nevertheless, the specialist knowledge that the surgeon had gained in Spain was a sought-after commodity. *The Lancet* published several articles on medicine and surgery by Tudor Hart and other British medics. In mid-January 1939, the British Medical Association hosted a well-attended reception at its central London premises at which Douglas Jolly described the organisation of field hospitals, Reginald Saxton spoke on blood transfusion and Alex Tudor Hart on limb surgery.[90] The same month, Tudor Hart joined the Medical Sub-Committee of the China Campaign Committee, a *cause célèbre* of a number of veterans from Spain, which aimed to send doctors and medical supplies to Communist China, which had been invaded by Japan.[91]

In May 1939, Tudor Hart had two articles published in the *British Medical Journal* on 'War Surgery in Spain' and discussed the procedures he had refined for treating fractures at a conference of senior surgeons organised by the Emergency Medical Service.[92] Described as a 'Late Major, [in the] Spanish Republican Medical Services', Tudor Hart attempted to draw lessons from Spain that could be applied not just to the field in a forthcoming war, but to the home front. He concentrated on three main areas: excision of wounds, treatment of infected wounds, and 'conservative surgery of limbs'. Much was related to the prevention of infection that could develop into sepsis or gangrene, for though a research team at Oxford University was working on developing penicillin, antibiotics would not become available until the latter period of the Second World War. Tudor Hart continued to advocate the orthopaedic work of Franz Böhler, stressing that 'operative intervention is but an item of the treatment' and that good, post-operative care is essential for recovery. He also made the apparently simple, but ultimately very sensible suggestion that stretchers and fittings should be standardised, so that patients did not have to be transferred between stretchers *en route* to hospital.

Despite interest in the lessons from the Spanish war, Tudor Hart still continued to struggle to find work. In July 1939 he applied for a commission in the British Army, but was rejected: 'Obviously Tudor HART, who has been known to us as an active Communist since he was a boy . . . would be quite unsuitable as an officer in the TA [Territorial Army].'[93] As a note in Tudor Hart's file confirms, Sir Vernon Kell, the head of MI5, accepted that Tudor Hart was a British subject and technically eligible for a commission. However, Kell concluded, 'from a security point of view, and his character generally', Tudor Hart was believed to be 'an undesirable person to be in close contact with service personnel.'[94] Kell cited Tudor Hart's longstanding Party membership, his role as the head of the British Medical Unit in Spain, together with negative professional and personal reports from his time at the North West Hospital in Hampstead in the early 1930s.[95] The information provided by two former members of the Spanish Medical Aid Committee who had returned from Spain in June 1937, hinting at Tudor Hart's 'incompetency or immorality' also seem to have carried weight.[96] A short attachment to the report stated that:'

It is understood the Spanish Government was looking upon the members of the British Medical Services in Spain with disapproval owing to their loose morals. Tudor Hart was one of those in disfavour, but whether for incompetency or immorality it is not known.[97]

When the Second World War broke out in September, Tudor Hart continued to give lectures on the surgical lessons learned from the Spanish war, until he was quietly dropped in 1940. He was not disappointed by the rejection, believing that it should have been his colleague, the talented New Zealand surgeon, Douglas Jolly who was giving the lectures, rather than him. In fact, he long believed that the requests he had received to talk about Spain came about mainly because Jolly, who had returned home, wasn't available. 'I was treated as an expert,' he confessed, 'whilst Jolly did far more . . . He was the best surgeon we had.'

Tudor Hart awarded the New Zealander what might have been his highest accolade: 'Jolly was like me,' he said, 'only better.'[98]

In July 1940, with most of Western Europe in German hands and Britain steeling itself for the Nazi onslaught, Tudor Hart finally found work as a Temporary Medical Officer in an office in Birmingham. However, he was soon the victim of a vindictive anonymous tip-off by 'A. Warden', alerting the authorities to Tudor Hart's Communist background.[99] The informer identified Tudor Hart as 'a volunteer in that crowd of hooligans and Communists who went to assist Spain' and while admitting that 'excellent surgical work' had been done there by Tudor Hart, the complainant continued:

> It is a horrid thought that such rank COMMUNISTS whose every word was against this country and its Government, and who threw every missile at the small radio which played our own National Anthem on the radio and downed the Royal Family, can hold such responsible posts today . . . No man could have been a stronger communist, with hatred against this Government and its KING, than Dr. Tudor Hart and his other communist friends.[100]

In fact, the Security Services were already fully aware of Tudor Hart's politics. Several months earlier, the local Assistant Chief Constable had informed MI5 that Tudor Hart, who was using the pseudonym Harold White (to hide his political activities from his employer, the police believed) was holding Communist Party meetings every Thursday evening. Political meetings were being held in a flat in Edgbaston, where subversive literature such as Communist Party pamphlets lay all around and 'a photograph of Lenin, surrounded by red rosettes, was displayed.'[101] In slightly hysterical tones, the Birmingham Chief Constable revealed that the 'Red Flag' was sung at the conclusion of proceedings, together with 'another song which refers to the fall of Buckingham Palace and the conversion of it into a public lavatory.'[102] More significantly he alleged that, prior to going to Spain, Tudor Hart had studied at the Lenin School in Moscow, the secretive finishing school for Communist Party cadres from around the world.[103]

In a remarkably sanguine response, Vernon Kell confirmed that Tudor Hart was a person of interest to MI5 but reassured the Chief Constable that the medic 'is not a person who carries a great deal of weight [in the Communist Party].' He went on to tactfully point out that the Chief Constable was confusing Alex Tudor Hart with Alex Hart, a 22 year old Scottish Boilermaker, who had indeed attended the Lenin School between 1932 and 1934.[104] However, what were of serious concern, Kell confided, were the activities of his ex-wife, Edith.[105] As a foreign Communist, she had long been a person of interest to the British Security Services. As far back as the early 1930s, Special Branch had reported that Alex and Edith's flat in London's Westbourne Gardens was 'the resort of well-known persons connected with extremist propaganda.'[106] These suspicions had, of course, led to Edith being kicked out of the country in 1931 and they remained following her return in 1933. However, it was her potential connection to a Soviet spy ring in 1938 that had marked her as an individual of real interest.

In March of that year, a camera had been discovered in a police raid on the home of Percy Glading, one of the founders of the British Communist Party, who had been caught procuring secret material from the Royal Arsenal at Woolwich and was convicted of espionage.[107] Receipts showed that the Leica had been purchased by Edith Tudor Hart, using the address of her photographic studio.[108] As an MI5 report pointed out, 'GLADING used a Leica camera for his espionage work'. The conclusion that he deliberately used Edith, an established professional photographer, to procure his equipment for him, is almost irresistible.[109] However, when questioned by Special Branch, Edith flatly denied any involvement. As there was no other evidence, they reluctantly released her. It would not be until many years later that the Security Services realised how significant her role in Soviet espionage had really been. For Edith was, and had long been, a valuable Soviet agent and talent-spotter.[110]

At the age of seventeen, Edith had fallen in love with a good-looking Chemistry student called Arnold Deutsch, who was an open Communist, but was secretly working for the Comintern (the Communist International).[111] So when Deutsch—and his wife—were summoned to Moscow in January 1932, Edith was heart-broken. Her developing relationship with Alex Tudor Hart may have provided some consolation, as surely did her close friendship with a young Viennese Communist called Litzi Friedmann. Like Suschitzky, Freidmann had also become involved with an Englishman, a young man 'progressive, with leftist leanings' who she had met while working to help German refugees. A graduate of economics from Trinity College, Cambridge, the young Englishman had come to Vienna to learn German. His name was Harold Adrian Russell Philby, but he was better known by his nickname, 'Kim'.

When Edith and Alex got married in the summer of 1933, allowing Edith to escape to England, Freidmann and Philby had followed the same path, marrying soon after the Tudor Harts, and following them to London later in the year. In February, the following year, Edith's old flame, Arnold Deutsch, got back into contact with her in London. He had previously shown a talent for recruiting agents in Paris and had been sent to London in February 1934, under the cover of a postgraduate research appointment at University College.[112] Soon after Litzy Friedmann and Kim Philby had arrived in the UK, Philby had decided to join the British Communist Party and came into contact with one of its underground cells. This was promptly reported to Edith, who in turn informed Deutsch. On 1 July Edith accompanied Philby to a meeting in Regent's Park, where Deutsch introduced himself to Philby as 'Otto'. Deutsch shrewdly told Philby that he would be assisting the Comintern in its anti-fascist work, rather than, as is often suggested, that he would become a Soviet spy.[113] Consequently, Philby soon provided a list of his student friends many of whom would later be working for Soviet intelligence. As Nigel West has pointed out, Edith Tudor Hart could thus be seen as '[the] linchpin to the entire Cambridge five.'[114]

Yet though Edith Tudor Hart was on MI5's watch list, they never picked up on her contacts with Deutsch. What they did know was that in 1938 she had been in contact with Engelbert Broda, 'a well-known Austrian scientist and atomic physicist of communist leanings.'[115] Given this and her involvement in the Percy Glading spy ring, there was certainly plenty of evidence, if only circumstantial, to suspect Edith and, by association Alex.[116] A search through records at Somerset House confirmed that they were still married, even if they had officially separated. And Tudor Hart regularly visited his ex-wife, while providing financial support for their son Tommy. Clearly, the pair remained on good terms.[117]

Given MI5's concerns about Edith, it's hardly surprising that Sir Vernon Kell wanted Alex Tudor Hart to be restricted to a post where there were no security concerns. Unfortunately, as an interview with Tudor Hart's superior in the spring of 1940 revealed, this was exactly what his job at Birmingham entailed:

Dr. Hart was employed by the Ministry of Health as Deputy Hospital Officer for the No. 9 Region . . . His work is described as the control of all emergency hospital business in the region and, in this connection, he has access to all the secret information received at Regional Headquarters. He would know of all convoys of wounded arriving from abroad and would also be in a position to learn where the wounded had been in contact with the enemy. He is also in possession of information regarding munition factories, the number of employees at these places and of others now in course of erection.[118]

Consequently, on 13 May 1940, Tudor Hart was dismissed with a month's salary and care was taken to ensure there was no mention made of security concerns. During the remainder of the year and into 1941, Tudor Hart took a number of temporary appointments, travelling to wherever a vacancy had come available and leaving a paper trail of correspondence between MI5 and nervous local Chief Constables behind him. He took up a temporary locum post for a doctor in Cambridge in the summer of 1940, before being appointed Assistant Medical Officer at County Infirmary in Louth, Lincolnshire in September. This prompted the local Chief Constable to write a concerned memo to MI5 which, while remarking dryly that Tudor Hart would have 'little scope for his Communist activities in the Louth District', confirmed that the surgeon would be kept under close observation.[119]

In early 1941, Tudor Hart resigned from his post at Louth, initially to take up private practice in Wellington, Salop, before joining the Emergency Hospital in Winchester as temporary resident surgeon and medical officer in June. Despite the past criticisms of Tudor Hart, he seems to have been well thought of by colleagues and the hospital management.[120] However, his employers were rather less impressed with the behaviour of Tudor-Hart's current companion. In early 1940, Tudor Hart had struck up a relationship with Constance Swan, an artists' model and a member of the Communist Party.[121] Constance had been staying at the hospital, where local police claimed 'she has not acquired a very good reputation for herself. She is frequently seen in the public bars in the company of soldiers and she is a heavy drinker.'[122] Concerned that Constance might be attempting to inveigle military information from soldiers, Special Branch kept her under discreet surveillance. Nothing untoward was overheard, though it was observed with some disdain that 'Mrs Hart dresses in a most noticeable manner, at times wearing pink trousers . . . her general demeanour does not suggest she is the wife of a doctor.'[123]

When Hitler invaded the Soviet Union in June 1941, leading Communists around the world to become enthusiastic supporters of the war, the Security Service's concerns about the pair became less burning. It also allowed Tudor Hart, along with others who had previously been rejected, to join the British armed forces.[124] While MI5 still considered Tudor Hart to be 'a person of interest,' in September they confirmed that 'we raise no objection to his being granted a Commission in RAMC [the Royal Army Medical Corps].'[125] Consequently, on 17 November 1941, Tudor Hart was commissioned into the RAMC as a Lieutenant and sent for basic training at Aldershot. He was then posted to the Royal Army Medical Corps' training centre at Bulford in Salisbury, scathingly derided by the Spanish veteran as 'a safe but futile posting in a recruits' training camp.'[126]

However, in line with a memo issued by the War Office at the outset of the war that veterans of Spain should be kept under discreet surveillance, a request was made by MI5 to Tudor Hart's commanding officer to 'arrange for a quiet eye to be kept on him in case he should be making any attempts to carry on Communist propaganda.' Furthermore, as the War Office's instructions had dictated, care was taken to ensure that 'no action is taken which might lead TUDOR HART to suspect that he is viewed with some suspicion.'[127] An initial report in January 1942 on Tudor Hart's progress in the British army was not promising, describing the surgeon as having 'a non-military bearing coupled with a highly-pitched voice which would appear to reflect a negative personality.' However, Tudor Hart's superior did admit that the surgeon appeared keen and 'anxious not to do the wrong thing', even if 'he is also brainy but in a peculiar way, and he strikes him as one who might under certain circumstances over-balance.'[128] While Tudor Hart owned a number of left-wing books and made no secret of his 'admiration for the USSR', he generally kept his views to himself and made no effort to proselytise. In short, his commanding officer concluded that, 'I have not perceived any conduct calculated to undermine loyalty, morale or discipline and I consider Lt HART far removed from being a defeatist.'[129]

Nevertheless, despite the reassuring reports, MI5 considered it prudent to maintain surveillance as Tudor Hart was posted first to a military hospital in Tidworth (16 miles north of Salisbury), then to another hospital in Bracebridge, on the outskirts of Lincoln, before being posted overseas on 26 July 1942.[130] Posted initially to the RAMC's 82nd General Hospital, Tudor Hart worked as a surgeon in Egypt, Cyprus, Palestine and Syria.[131] While instructions remained in place that he should continue to be kept under observation, by the following year it was clear to his superiors that Tudor Hart was not engaging in any questionable behaviour. Consequently, on 30 March 1943 a note was sent to HQ Northern Command confirming that 'Tudor HART is cleared of suspicion of engaging in subversive activities or propaganda in the army' and his file was ordered to be destroyed.[132]

By 1944, Tudor Hart was working in a British Army Mission in Yugoslavia, where he was awarded a decoration, the 'Tilov Lik', for his work looking after the wounded.[133] Yet, despite the decoration, a superior officer's assessment was stinging in its criticisms:

[Tudor Hart was] sent home from the Mediterranean Theatre with a recommendation that he be called upon to resign his commission and be directed for employment with the Emergency Medical Service of the Ministry of Health. He was reported as being a misfit in Army Surgical practice, temperamentally unsuitable, and some doubt was expressed on his professional capabilities as a surgeon.[134]

Fortunately for Tudor Hart, not everyone agreed with the assessment nor, given the RAMC's great shortage of surgeons, the conclusion that he should be kicked out of the army. After consideration, Tudor Hart was posted instead to a military hospital back home, where he remained under the close supervision of the senior surgeon, until he was released from the British armed forces on 15 November 1945, with the rank of Captain.

After demobilisation, Tudor Hart fell back into the itinerant existence he had endured prior to the war, living first in Parkstone, near Poole in Dorset, before moving to Wakefield and finally ending up in Colliers Wood, South London, in 1948. There, having seen more than enough of trauma surgery and operating theatres during nearly ten years of war, Tudor Hart chose to move back into general medical practice.[135] Despite some domestic friction, he lived with Constance, who he married in 1947, and their two children, Judith who had been born in 1943 and George Henry, born four years later.[136] Both Tudor Hart and his wife continued to be active Communist Party members, while Tudor Hart was a member of the Socialist Medical Council.

In 1949, Tudor Hart was put forward by the Communist Party in the Surrey County Council elections to be held in April. Standing in the South Mitcham Division, which had been heavily bombed during the war but was still hardly a hotbed of revolutionary politics, he polled 142 votes, 2,650 fewer than the winning Conservative candidate.[137] Two years later, he tried again, standing in the Colliers Wood ward in the Mitcham Borough Council elections in May 1951. His election literature stressed his long medical career in Spain and the Second World War and membership of the BMA, and he promised to increase the building of houses, schools and health centres, while opposing cuts, cancelling arms spending and aimed to 'break loose from American domination.' Despite his ambitious and radical manifesto, Tudor Hart scored little better than he had in Mitcham, receiving a paltry 116 votes, compared to the Conservatives' 1,140, and Labour's 1,268.

While these fruitless attempts to gain office were hardly likely to be causing the Security Services to lose much sleep, his Party connections and past relationship with Edith meant that he remained a person of interest. In 1951, MI5's concerns were reawakened when Edith was interviewed in their attempts to find evidence that Kim Philby was a Soviet agent. On 10 December 1951, MI5 requested that a short-term telephone check be placed on Tudor Hart's phone:

Dr. Alexander TUDOR-HART, the subscriber to this number, is an active and long-standing member of the Communist Party. He is the divorced (and remarried) husband of Edith TUDOR-HART, the subject of H.O.W. No. 1281, who is at present being investigated on suspicion of espionage. The two persons are reported to have been in touch, sometimes at frequent intervals, since their divorce in 1944. It is desired to determine the nature of their association and to obtain further information on the husband's activities and contacts.[138]

In the interview conducted in Edith Tudor Hart's flat on 8 January 1952, she admitted to working for Russian Intelligence in Austria and Italy in the early 1930s but denied that she had ever worked for Soviet Intelligence in Britain, or that she had ever known Philby, pretending not to recognise him when shown a photograph. She was, reported William James Scardon, one of MI5's most experienced interrogators, 'a difficult person to interview', not least because she flatly refused to get out of bed: 'This woman steadily prevaricated from one end of the interview to the other . . . she was completely composed and answered questions in the manner of a person well trained to resist an interrogation.' She played Scardon well, for while admitting that it was almost impossible to come to a firm conclusion from the interview, he came away with the entirely erroneous impression that her knowledge of Philby was likely to be 'pretty limited'.[139]

It remains unclear how much Alex Tudor Hart was aware of his ex-wife's espionage activities and there have long been suspicions that he knew more than he was letting on. In his study of MI5's penetration of the CPGB, *Mask*, Nigel West asserted that Tudor Hart 'had been recruited by the NKVD *resident* in Barcelona, Alexander Orlov, during the Spanish Civil War.'[140] However, there is no evidence that Tudor Hart met Orlov in Spain, let alone was recruited by him.[141] In fact, Tudor Hart had been extremely critical of what he described as 'Stalinist' behaviour by some members of the British Battalion in Spain during April and May 1937, during the suppression and persecution of the POUM. Tudor Hart also hinted that he felt the GRU (Soviet military intelligence) had an undue and malign influence in Spain.[142] He was, of course, a firm believer in what MI5 termed 'theoretical Communism', but as he pointed out, in Spain 'most of the people in senior positions were Communists, or anxious to become Communists.'[143] Interviewed many years after war, Tudor Hart continued to see things the same way: 'Looking back on it now,' he reminisced, 'it seems to me that it was very difficult to be anything else but a Communist in that period.'[144]

Despite MI5's concern and Nigel West's assertion, it seems unlikely that Tudor Hart was involved in espionage. The Security Services' surveillance of the surgeon in the early 1930s had led them to believe that he was poorly thought of by his fellow Communist Party members: 'He is not taken seriously by educated persons . . . reliable persons who have had the opportunity of closely observing TUDOR-HART regard him as a crank, and say he has neither the character nor ability to become really important in the revolutionary movement.'[145] While they were wrong about a lot—not least missing Edith Tudor Hart's role as 'the grandmother of us all,' in Anthony Blunt's words—their withering assessment of Alex Tudor Hart's importance to the international Communist movement was probably fairly near the mark.[146]

Other questions remain, however. If he were not a Soviet agent himself, could he have been used by Edith, who certainly was? Did she really care for him or was their marriage one of convenience, primarily a means to allow her to escape from Austria and settle in England?[147] MI5 certainly fretted that it was a political convenience, given the timing and the apparent marital difficulties Alex and Edith experienced shortly into their marriage: 'Her marriage to TUDOR-HART appears to have been somewhat uneven.' They were also fully aware of the remarkable coincidence of the twin weddings of Alex Tudor Hart and Edith Suschitzky and Kim Philby and Litzy Friedmann:

> In both cases the husband, a British national, went to Vienna to marry a woman with a known, and possibly RIS or Comintern, background. These marriages were contracted at a time of political turmoil in Austria, when the RIS [Russian Intelligence Service] and Comintern might well have sought such means to protect their agents. [148]

However, as the report also acknowledged, letters from Edith to Alex in Spain intercepted by MI5 actually suggested that the marriage was based on genuine mutual attraction and affection.

Tudor Hart himself revealed little about his ex-wife when he was interviewed by the historian Jim Fyrth in 1983, beyond admitting that 'my former wife had been working for the Russians in Vienna. She was caught and imprisoned for a short time and then released with no charges.' Given that his ex-wife had died ten years earlier, there seems little reason to doubt that Tudor Hart was telling the truth when he continued, 'as far as I know, she was perfectly harmless.'[149] If she could deceive one of MI5's most experienced interrogators, his naivety can perhaps be forgiven.

In his latter years, Tudor Hart left behind much of his earlier life. In the early 1950s, he was divorced from his wife Connie following her decision to leave the Communist Party. Ten years later, the Communist Party decided to leave him, expelling him for 'Maoism'.[150] Yet, right up until his death in February 1992, Alexander Tudor Hart remained convinced that, despite any doubts he might have had in other areas of his life, he and the other volunteers had been right in their decision to go to Spain.[151] His colleague in Spain, Kenneth Sinclair-Loutit later wrote that 'sometimes the only thing to do is fight.'[152] Loutit and Tudor Hart certainly didn't agree on much, but on this they were as one. 'What could we do in 1936,' asked Tudor Hart, 'but resist?'[153]

Acknowledgements

I would like to thank the patient and helpful staff of the various archives I consulted, without whom these biographies could never have been written. All have been credited within the individual chapters, but I would like to express particular gratitude to Lynda Corey Classen and Matthew Peters of the Special Collections & Archives at UC San Diego, Matt Dunne and Meirian Jump of the Marx Memorial Library, Rafa Siodor at the Orwell Archive in University College London, Darren Treadwell at the People's History Museum and Stefan Vickers of the Bishopsgate Institute. My thanks also to Rosa Branson, Alan Cottman, Adrian Holme, Charlie Horner and Ken Loach for kindly allowing me access to their personal collections and recollections.

Many people generously took the time to read drafts and offer helpful advice, constructive criticism and invaluable corrections. I am extremely grateful to, among others, Chris Hall, Angela Jackson, Barry McLoughlin, Linda Palfreeman and Boris Volodarsky.

Finally, many thanks to my editors, Simon Deefholts and Kathryn Phillips-Miles and my tireless, patient and pedantic proof-readers (you know who you are).

Suggested further reading

For a good background to Britain during the period, see Juliet Gardiner's meticulous *The Thirties*. Noreen Branson's two volumes on the *History of the Communist Party* from 1927 to 1941 and from 1941 to 1951 offer a valuable insider's perspective on the Party. On British responses to the Spanish Civil War, see Tom Buchanan's *Britain and the Spanish Civil War*. For a longer and thematic perspective, his *The Impact of the Spanish Civil War on Britain* is very good. Adrian Bell's *Only for Three Months* evocatively recounts the story of the Basque refugee children in Britain.

Two helpful introductions to the Spanish Civil War are Helen Graham's *The Spanish Civil War: A Very Short Introduction* and Paul Preston's *A Concise History of the Spanish Civil War*. Preston's *We Saw Spain Die* is a fascinating account of the foreign correspondents.

On the role and contribution of the 35,000 international volunteers from around the world in the war, see Giles Tremlett's excellent *The International Brigades*. The most recent works on the involvement of British volunteers specifically are my *Unlikely Warriors: the British in the Spanish Civil War* and Charles Esdaile's *British Battles of the Spanish Civil War*. George Orwell's *Homage to Catalonia* and Chris Hall's *In Spain with Orwell* recount the experiences of the British fighting with the POUM militia. For the medics and nurses see Angela Jackson's *British Women and the Spanish Civil War* and Linda Palfreeman's *¡Salud!* Christopher Othen's *Franco's International Brigades* is the most recent work on the volunteers for Franco.

There is a huge literature on espionage, particularly during the Second World War. For an entertaining overview, see Max Hastings' *The Secret War*. Christopher Andrew's history of MI5, *Defence of the Realm* and Keith Jeffrey's *MI6* are both essential reference works. The list of books on the SOE is also daunting, but MRD Foot's *S.O.E.: An outline history of the special operations executive 1940–46* is an excellent place to start.

Notes

Note to Introduction

1 House of Commons debate on motion of 'No Confidence', 7 July 1942, cited in Churchill, *The Second World War, Volume IV: The Hinge of Fate*, p. 359.

Notes to Chapter One

1 An excerpt from this chapter appeared in *¡No Pasarán!*, 1:2023, pp. 9-10.

2 MML SC/VOL/MDU/1.

3 *The Times* Friday 26 July 1963, p. 9 from Marx Memorial Library (MML) SC/VOL/MDU/1.

4 Vincent Brome, *The International Brigades*, London: Heinemann, 1965, p. 281.

5 *The London Gazette*, 9 March, 1915, p. 2364.

6 Ronald Malcolm Loraine Dunbar's birth was registered in Totnes. His three older brothers were William Geddes Loraine, born in Calcutta in 1900, Edward Ughtred Loraine, born in Moray two years later and Archibald Loraine, born in Calcutta in 1906.

7 Dunbar was placed in Mitre House, Repton. I am very grateful to Jan Cobb of the Old Reptonian and Development Office, who confirmed details of Dunbar's attendance at the school.

8 'Territorial Army Record of Service Paper', 18 July 1940, Army Historical Disclosures, APA4/86/1, p. 1. In his brief autobiography, Dunbar gives a starting date of 1926, rather than 1925. See Russian State Archive of Socio-Political History (RGASPI), 545/6/126 p. 26.

9 Contrary to the claims by earlier studies, Dunbar studied at Christ's College, not Trinity.

10 Juliet Gardiner, *The Thirties: An Intimate History*, London: Harper Press, 2010, p. 184.

11 Morris Riley and Stephen Dorril, 'Rothschild, the right, the far-right and the Fifth Man.' *The Lobster*, 16.

12 Peter Stansky and Bill Abrahams, *Journey to the Frontier: Two Roads to the Spanish Civil War*, pp. 42 & 201; Carmel Haden Guest, *David Guest: A Scientist Fights for Freedom 1911-1938*, London: Lawrence and Wishart, 1939, p. 94.

13 Jason Gurney, *Crusade in Spain*, London: Faber and Faber, 1974, p. 67.

14 Gurney, p. 67.

15 'Autobiography of R.M.L. Dunbar', 17 April 1938, RGASPI 545/6/126, p. 38.

16 RGASPI 545/6/120 p. 35a.

17 *Ibid.*

18 *Ibid.*

19 Reports by Abe Lewis and by Jim Bourne, American Secretary of the Spanish Communist Party, 20 September 1938, RGASPI 545/6/126 pp. 33-34.

20 Gurney, pp. 67-8.

21 The MI5 list held in the National Archives in Kew reports that a Ronald Malcolm Loraine Dunbar 'left Dover for Dunkirk on 6 January 1937.' National Archives (NA), KV/5/112, p. 12.

22 After December 1936, each volunteer for the British Battalion was allocated a number. RM Dunbar was 145; John C Horner, 151. RGASPI 545/6/91, p. 53.

23 Interview with George Leeson, Imperial War Museum Sound Archive (IWMSA), interview 803, reel 2.

24 RGASPI 545/6/126 p. 41.

25 Gurney, p. 68.

26 Interview with Peter Kerrigan, IWMSA, 810, reel 3.

27 RGASPI 545/6/126 p. 43.

28 'Autobiography of R.M.L. Dunbar' RGASPI 545/6/126 pp. 38-9.

29 Dunbar's *Brigadas Internacionales* carnet remains among Malcolm Dunbar's papers, which have been carefully preserved by Thérèse Langfield and CJ Pearsall-Horner. I am extremely grateful to Charlie for allowing me access to Dunbar's papers, which have now been deposited in the Bishopsgate Institute in London.

30 'Chief of Operations', RGASPI 545/3/478, p. 47.

31 RGASPI 545/6/89.

32 Malcolm Dunbar papers, Bishopsgate Institute (MD papers).

33 Fred Thomas, *To Tilt at Windmills, A Memoir of the Spanish Civil War*, East Lansing: State University of Michigan Press, 1996, p. 18.

34 Interview with John Dunlop in MacDougall, *Voices from the Spanish Civil War: Personal Recollections of Scottish Volunteers in Republican Spain, 1936-1939*, Edinburgh: Polygon, 1986, p. 136.

35 RGASPI 545/2/262, p. 60.

36 MD papers.
37 MD papers. Fred Copeman later claimed responsibility for selecting the men for the unit, branding them 'the good-looking students'. This is unlikely to be the case. Fred Thomas, who served with the unit from May until the end of the war, recounted: 'Somebody chose the forty or so of us and omitted the known drunks and general nuisances, but not Fred Copeman.' Letter from Fred Thomas to James Hopkins, 8 June 1999 (courtesy of Fred Thomas).
38 Report on the formation of the British Anti-Tank Battery by Malcolm Dunbar. RGASPI 545/3/479, pp. 62–2.
39 A large number were Scots; one volunteer estimated that half of the men were from north of the border. Interview with Eddie Brown in MacDougall, p. 112.
40 Bill Alexander, *British Volunteers for Liberty*, London: Lawrence and Wishart, 1982, p. 219.
41 Interview with Jim Brewer, IWMSA, 9963, reel 3.
42 Interview with Jim Brewer, IWMSA, reel 7, cited in Peter Darman, *Heroic Voices of the Spanish Civil War*, London: New Holland, 2009, p. 160.
43 Fred Thomas, p. 30.
44 Interview with John Dunlop, IWMSA 11355, reel 4.
45 Letter from Jim Brewer to Bill Alexander, 3 December 1979, MML SC/VOL/JBE/1.
46 Interview with Fred Copeman, IWMSA, 794, reel 8.
47 See for example, the interview with Dr Frank Lesser: 'Malcom Dunbar impressed me at the time as a very considerable person and who was evidently highly regarded in the division.' Interview with Ephraim 'Frank' Lesser, IWMSA 9408, reel 7.
48 Interview with Hugh Sloan in MacDougall, pp. 202-3 & p. 234.
49 One exception was the Aberdeen volunteer, John Londragan, who described Dunbar as 'a very, very nice fellow'. Interview with John Londragan in MacDougall, p. 174.
50 Interview with Hugh Sloan in MacDougall, pp. 202-3.
51 Fred Thomas, p. 54.
52 Interview with Hugh Sloan in MacDougall, p. 235.
53 Julian Bell cited in James Hopkins, *Into the Heart of the Fire, The British in the Spanish Civil War,* California: Stanford, 1998, p. 181.
54 Brome pp. 279-281.
55 RGASPI 545/6/126 pp. 36 & 40 & MD papers.
56 1 January 1938, RGASPI545/6/126, p. 31.

57 Hopkins p. 227.

58 RGASPI, 545/6/126, p. 37.

59 Gurney, p. 67.

60 See Gardiner, pp. 577-582.

61 Lisa Kirschenbaum, *International Communism and the Spanish Civil War*, pp. 75-6.

62 James Jump, *The Fighter Fell in Love: A Spanish Civil War Memoir*, London: The Clapton Press, 2021, p. 92 and Robert Stradling, *History and Legend, Writing the International Brigades*, Cardiff: University of Wales Press, 2003, p. 28.

63 Interview with Fred Copeman, IWMSA, 794, reel 8.

64 Fred Thomas, p. 55.

65 Azaña cited in Anthony Beevor, *The Battle for Spain*, London: Weidenfeld and Nicholson, 2006, p. 278.

66 Fred Thomas, p. 33.

67 Fred Thomas, p. 36.

68 MD papers and interview with John Londragan in MacDougall, p. 176.

69 Interview with Bill Alexander, IWMSA, 802, reel 5. Slater was 'very brave, but extremely arrogant', according to the British research clerk and military censor in Spain, Tony McLean. Interview with Tony McLean, IWMSA 838, cited in Darman, p. 65.

70 MD papers.

71 Alexander, p. 151.

72 MD papers.

73 RGASPI 545/3/427, p. 163.

74 Report on British Political Commissars Conference, SC/IBA/5/3/1/16; Ivor Hickman in John L Wainwright, The Last of Fall, Southampton: Hatchet Green, p. 193.

75 Alexander, p. 159.

76 Fred Thomas, p. 65.

77 MD papers.

78 Alexander, pp. 169–70.

79 Sam Wild, 'Report by Battalion Commander on the last action', 23 May 1938. RGASPI 545/3/497, p. 23.

80 Alexander, p. 176 and MD papers.

81 Walter Gregory, *The Shallow Grave, A Memoir of the Spanish Civil War*, London: Victor Gollancz, 1986, p. 110.

82 Interview with Steve Fullarton in MacDougall, p. 294.

83 The former battery observer, John Dunlop, recounted how, 'in this happy existence, which was really enjoyable, we were out in the fresh air and we were sleeping under the open sky. The

weather was fairly good and we were getting plenty of exercise and plenty of food.' Interview with John Dunlop in MacDougall, p. 158.

84 RGASPI, 545/6/126 pp. 40-41. The award included an assessment of Dunbar in Spain, describing how he had been wounded on four separate occasions as he worked his way up steadily through the ranks: section commander, battery commander, 15th International Brigade Chief of Operations and now Commander of the *Estado Mayor*. Attached were four references from senior figures in the 15th International Brigade: its Spanish Commander, Major José Valledor, Brigade Commissar John Gates, the 35th Division political *responsable* Luis Sáez and Abe Lewis and Alonzo Elliott from the Brigade Political Cadres Commission. Also attached were *características definitivas* drawn up by the two most senior member of the International Brigades in Spain, the French Communist André Marty and 'L. Gallo' (the Italian, Luigi Longo).

85 Peter Kerrigan, 'Another Chapter in the Saga of the Sierras', 16 September 1938, MML SC/IND/PKE/1/47.

86 MD papers.

87 Bob Cooney, *Proud Journey*, London: Marx Memorial Library and Manifesto Press, 2015, p. 162.

88 Peter Carroll, *The Odyssey of the Abraham Lincoln Brigade*, California: Stanford Press, p. 162.

89 MD papers and Alexander, p. 239.

90 Interview with Bill Cranston in MacDougall, p. 190.

91 Interview with Sam Lesser, IWMSA, 9486, reel 6.

92 Interview with Jim Brewer, IWMSA, 9963, reel 4.

93 RGASPI, 545/6/126, p. 43. The other was the American volunteer, Joe Bianca, who was killed in the Sierra Pandols in August 1938. Milton Wolff, *Another Hill*, Champaign: University of Illinois Press, p. 358.

94 The other four were the political active Welsh Communist, Billy Griffiths, Mancunian Battalion Commander, Sam Wild, Anti-Tank Battery Political Commissar, Alan Gilchrist and Scottish Cadre, Alec Donaldson. RGASPI, 545/6/139, p. 61.

95 This number includes British volunteers with 15th Brigade staff and other units. Alexander, p. 241.

96 When the train stopped briefly at Versailles, Dunbar took the opportunity to disappear. Most assumed that the 'intensely private' Dunbar wished to avoid participating in any public ceremony upon their arrival in Britain; however, he later told a former comrade from the anti-tanks that, in fact, he returned to

Spain as a correspondent for the *Daily Worker*. Interview with Hugh Sloan in MacDougall, pp. 234, 349 fn 155; Alexander, p. 241.

97 Interview with Hugh Sloan in MacDougall, p. 234.

98 MML SC/IBA/5/4/2/6.

99 NA KV/5/120 47759 and MacDougall, *fn*. 155, p. 349.

100 Malcolm Dunbar to Harry Pollitt, 9 March 1939, MD papers.

101 NA KV/5/120 47759.

102 'The General Staff have of course issued no such order, and *for your own information* I may add that all that is done, is to make enquiries into the bona-fides of any would-be recruits, or men already serving in the forces, who are known to have served in the International brigade in Spain. Quite a number of men merely did so from a spirit of adventure and are now serving happily in H.M. Forces.' NA KV 2/609 37d.

103 'Territorial Army Record of Service Paper', p. 2 and Andy Croft, *Comrade Heart: A Life of Randall Swingler*, Manchester: Manchester UP, 2003, p. 112.

104 'Territorial Army Record of Service Paper' p. 2.

105 Interview with Sam Lesser, IWMSA, 9486, reel 6.

106 *Volunteer for Liberty*, No. 12, 12 May 1941, p. 5.

107 House of Commons debate on motion of 'No Confidence', 7 July 1942, cited in Winston Churchill, *The Second World War, Volume IV: The Hinge of Fate*, London: Cassells, 1951, p. 359.

108 *Hansard*, 1 October 1942. As recently as 1998, historians were still claiming that Dunbar had been denied a commission. See Alexander, p. 246 and Hopkins, p. 178.

109 NA WO/373/50.

110 Citation of 11 August 1944, announced in the *London Gazette* on 21 December 1944. NA WO 373/50.

111 'Notification of Impending Release', 5 January 1946.

112 NA KV/5/120 47759.

113 Nan Green to Hans Kaltschmidt, 17 September 1948. MML SC/IBA/3/3/1948/82.

114 MD papers.

115 MD papers.

116 Letter from Dunbar to DFJ Parsons, 16 April 1958, TUC archives, London Metropolitan University.

117 Brome, p. 279.

118 Brome, p. 280.

119 MacDougall, *fn*. 155, p. 349 and Morris Riley and Stephen Dorril, 'Rothschild, the right, the far-right and the Fifth Man', *The Lobster*, 16.

120 Interview with CJ Pearsall-Horner (widower of Thérèse Langfield), 18 September 2013.

121 https://api.parliament.uk/historic-hansard/commons/1964 /may15/woolf-inquiry-evidence, accessed 17 July 2018

122 See 'How to Become Dead', by Claud Cockburn, *Private Eye*, 9 August 1963.

123 'Although it is Government policy to neither confirm nor deny whether any individual or group has been subject to investigation by MI5, an exception to this policy allows us to release to The National Archive, files that are still in existence and at least 50 years old, if to do so would not damage national security.

We have researched our records and have to tell you that we hold no files relating to Ronald Malcolm Loraine Dunbar that fall within this category.'

124 For an account of the transformation of Dunbar, Nathan and others in Spain, see Hopkins, pp. 176-8. There is a brief obituary for Dunbar in the IBA Newsletter, August 1963, p. 3. MML SC/IBA/6/1/18.

Notes to Chapter Two

1 Adrian Bell, *Only for Three Months*, Norwich: Mousehold Press, 2007 p. 9. While nearly 10,000 children were rescued in the Kinder transport, the effort took place over several months, from December 1938 to September 1939.

2 Bell, p. 8.

3 Basque Children of '37 Association Newsletter, Aug 2003, p. 3.

4 https://www.yourharlow.com/2019/10/16/stan-newens-unveils-plaque-in-memory-of-leah-manning/ accessed on 7 March 2023.

5 Hull History Centre, U DX265/3 CM767 and Ron Bill and Stan Newens, *Leah Manning,* Harlow and Brentwood: Leah Manning Trust and Square One Books, 1991, pp. 10 & 13.

6 Bill and Newens, p. 15.

7 Hugh Dalton, *Call Back Yesterday*, London: Frederick Muller, 1953, p. 130.

8 Alison Oram, 'Manning, Dame (Elizabeth) Leah (1886-1977)', *Oxford Dictionary of National Biography*, Oxford University Press, 2004; online ed, May 2008. [http:// www.oxforddnb. com/view/article/45463, accessed 14 January 2016].

9 In her autobiography Leah states that she became engaged to Will 'at the beginning of 1914,' and that they married in July of the same year. However, the marriage certificate states that Leah and Will were married at the Holy Sepulchre Church in Cambridge on 26 July 1913.

10 Leah Manning, *A Life for Education*, London: Victor Gollancz, 1970, pp. 47-50.

11 Manning, 1970, p. 52.

12 Bill and Newens, p. 24.

13 Manning, 1970, p. 81.

14 Manning, 1970, p. 110.

15 Manning, 1970, p. 107.

16 See Paul Preston *Spanish Holocaust*, London Harper Press, 2013, pp. 84-5 and Leah Manning *What I Saw in Spain*, London: Victor Gollancz, 1935, p. 13.

17 Manning, 1970, p. 120.

18 Jim Fyrth, *The Signal was Spain*, London, Lawrence and Wishart, 1986, pp. 49-50.

19 Manning, 1970, pp. 114-5.

20 Manning, 1970, p. 117.

21 Manning, 1970, p. 119.

22 'British Policy and Bilbao', *The Times*, 13 April 1937, p. 17.

23 Tom Buchanan, *The Impact of the Spanish Civil War on Britain: War, Loss and Memory*, Eastbourne: Sussex Academic Press, 2007, p. 31.

24 Manning, 1970, p. 123.

25 Manning, 1970, p. 124. Churchill's nephews, Esmond and Giles Romilly, both fought in Spain.

26 Manning, 1970, p. 125.

27 Manning, 1970, p. 126.

28 See Steer's article in *The Times*, 28 April 1937, p. 17. Also available online: https://www.thetimes.co.uk/article/bombing-of-guernica-original-times-report-from-1937-5j7x3z2k5bv.

29 See, for example, Memorandum of interview, 3 May 1937, which shows Citrine's reluctance to accede to Leah's request: 'Matter already under discussion. Discussing matters direct with Basque Government representatives in London.' Warwick 292/946/16a/40.

30 Buchanan, *Impact,* p. 33.

31 'List of Personnel', Warwick 292/946/40/1.

32 Manning, 1970, p. 127.

33 Telegram from Leah Manning to Walter Citrine, 14 May 1937, Warwick 292/946/37/180(i).

34 Telegram from Leah Manning to Clement Attlee MP, 2 May 1937. Warwick 292/946/11/90.

35 Tom Buchanan, *Britain and the Spanish Civil War*, Cambridge: Cambridge UP, 1997 p. 110.

36 Manning, 1970, p. 131.

37 Manning, 1970, p. 129.

38 Manning, 1970, p. 131.

39 Interview with Dr Richard Ellis in Bell, p. 51.

40 Manning, 1970, p. 131.

41 '4,000 Children from Bilbao are Safe at Last,' *New Leader*, 28 May 1937.

42 Bell, p. 59.

43 Manning, 1970, p. 132.

44 Bell, p. 74.

45 Angela Jackson, *British Women and the Spanish Civil War*, 2nd ed., Barcelona: Warren and Pell, 2009, p. 106.

46 Interview with Flori Díaz Jiménez in Natalia Benjamin ed. *Recuerdos: Basque children refugees in Great Britain*, Oxford: Mousehold Press for Basque Children of '37 Association UK, 2007, p. 45.

47 One 15-year-old *niño* in the colony in Street wrote an impassioned article for the ILP paper, the *New Leader*, mourning the repatriation of his compatriots. 'What sort of country is that to which you will be returning? . . . You will find fascist regimentation, a regime based on war and exploitation, and mourning in your homes.' 'To the Basque children who are Returning,' *New Leader*, 24 December 1937, p. 8.

48 Leah Manning, 'Report to the National Joint Committee on the Refugee Problem in Catalunya', 2 October 1937, Warwick 292C/946/3/4.

49 *Ibid.*

50 Bill and Newens, p. 45.

51 'Report received from Mrs Leah Manning', 26 July 1938, Warwick 292/946/42/16iii.

52 *Ibid.*

53 List of people who have received passes for the front and have visited the Ebro sector. RGASPI 545/6/90 p. 24 and 'Report received from Mrs Leah Manning', 4 August 1938, Warwick 292/946/42/16iii.

54 'Report received from Mrs Leah Manning', 4 August 1938, Warwick 292/946/42/16iii.

55 *Ibid.*

56 As Angela Jackson suggests in *Beyond the Battlefield:*

Testimony, Memory and Remembrance of a Cave Hospital in the Spanish Civil War, Pontypool: Warren and Pell, 2005, p. 34, the English nurse 'Faith' was actually Patience Darton. Leah Manning identifies both Harry Dobson and Patience Darton by name in her report of 26 July 1938. See Warwick 946/42/16iii.

57 Manning, 1970, p. 136.

58 'Report received from Mrs Leah Manning', 26 July 1938, Warwick 292/946/42/16iii.

59 Bill and Newens, p. 45.

60 'Reports received from Mrs Leah Manning and circulated to the Committee in accordance with resolution 10th August 1938', Warwick 292/946/42/16.

61 For Saxton's transfusion work in Spain see Linda Palfreeman, *Spain Bleeds,* Eastbourne: Sussex Academic Press, 2015, pp. 86-117.

62 'Summary and critical survey of my work in Spain, since the outbreak of the war', Winifred Bates, Barcelona, September 1938, RGASPI 545/6/88.

63 Leah Manning, 'Report on Personnel in Spain', September 1938. Warwick, 292/946/43/52i.

64 *Ibid.*

65 Buchanan, *Impact,* p. 61.

66 'Report on Personnel in Spain', September 1938, Warwick 292/946/43/52, p.1.

67 Manning, 1970, p. 138.

68 *Ibid.*

69 *Ibid.*

70 Nan Green, *A Chronicle of Small Beer,* Nottingham: Trent Editions, 2004, p. 103.

71 Leah Manning, 'Report of Honorary Secretary', 8 May 1939. Warwick 292/946/43/22i.

72 Fyrth, p. 300 & Jackson, *British Women,* 2009, p. 257.

73 Chim's real name was David Seymour. With Robert Capa and Henri Cartier-Bresson, Seymour was a founder of Magnum Photos.

74 Leah Manning, 'Report on the International Emergency Conference for Spanish Refugees held in Paris', Warwick 292/946/43/3, p. 2.

75 Manning, 1970, p. 146.

76 Manning, 1970, p. 148-9.

77 Manning, 1970, p. 148.

78 Manning, 1970, pp. 148-9.

79 The seat of Epping was reorganised for the 1945 election.

Churchill's old seat was renamed Woodford and was uncontested by the Liberals and Labour in honour of the former Prime Minister's role during the war.

80 Hull History Centre, LM121, U DX/265/1 (i).

81 *Ibid.*

82 Manning, 1970, p. 164.

83 Leah obviously knew Nan Green well and there is record of an extensive correspondence between the two. Well enough, in fact, for Leah to write to Nan that 'she felt like wringing her neck' following a misunderstanding over travelling expenses for a political meeting in Bristol. That she signed the letter 'yours Leah', suggests that she probably wasn't overly offended. MML, SC/ORG/ECDS/3/1946.

84 Letter from Irene Falcón, *Unión de Mujeres Españolas*, to Miss E.A. Allen, International Women's Day Committee, 22 September 1946. MML, SC/ORG/ECDS/3/1946.

85 MML, SC/IBA/1/6/44.

86 MML, SC/IBA/3/1/1947/130.

87 Manning, 1970, p. 140.

88 *Daily Worker*, 15 November 1946.

89 Manning, 1970, p. 214.

90 Hugh Dalton, *High Tide and After,* London: Frederick Muller, 1962, p. 220.

91 Leah Manning, 'Growing Up', Labour Party, 1948.

92 Manning, 1970, p. 186.

93 *News Chronicle*, 23 March 1948, cited in Manning, 1970, p. 187.

94 Manning, 1970, p. 217.

95 Manning, 1970, p. 223.

96 Bill and Newens, p. 67.

97 Pat Gibberd, *Harlow News*, June 1991, p. 8.

98 Manning, 1970, p. 193.

99 Manning, 1970, pp. 195-6.

100 'A Tribute to Leah,' *Harlow News*, June 1991, p. 8.

101 'Leah Manning', Leah Manning Trust, Hull History Centre, LM127, U DX/265/2 (U)

102 Bill and Newens, p. 42.

103 Alison Oram, 'Manning , Dame (Elizabeth) Leah (1886–1977)', *Oxford Dictionary of National Biography*, Oxford University Press, 2004; online ed, May 2008 - [http://www.oxforddnb.com/view/]. article/45463, accessed 14 January 2016].

104 Bill and Newens, p. 68.

105 Manning, 1970, p. 155.
106 Bill and Newens, p. 68.
107 Walter Citrine, 'Spanish situation: evacuation of Basque children: memorandum of interview, with Jose I. de Lizaso', May 1937, Warwick 292/946/39/114(i).
108 Tom Buchanan, *Britain and the Spanish Civil War*, p. 110.
109 Letter from residents of North Stoneham camp to Leah Manning, [month unknown] 1937, in Manning, 1970, p. 133.

Notes to Chapter Three

1 Letter from Andrew White to The Communist Party, 4 January 1931. NA KV 2/4418.
2 Colonel Sir Vernon Kell to Lieut-Colonel GM Ormerod DSO, 12 January 1932. NA KV 2/4418.
3 Lieut-Colonel GM Ormerod to Colonel Sir Vernon Kell, 19 January 1932. NA KV 2/4418.
4 Peter Kemp is sometimes cited as having been born in 1913, but his birth certificate confirms his date and place of birth as 19 August 1915 in India.
5 I am extremely grateful to Caroline Jones, the archivist at Wellington College, for details of Kemp's time at the school.
6 Peter Kemp, *The Thorns of Memory*, London: Sinclair-Stevenson, 1990, p. 4
7 Judith Keene, *Fighting for Franco, International Volunteers in Nationalist Spain during the Civil War, 1936-1939,* Leicester: Leicester University Press, 2001, p. 110. Many thanks to Jane Murphy, Trinity College Alumni Administrator, for confirming Kemp's university record. Interestingly, in his application for a commission on 4 November 1939, Kemp claimed his degree had been a second, rather than third class.
8 Interview with Peter Kemp in Philip Toynbee, *The Distant Drum, Reflections on the Spanish Civil War,* London: Sidgwick and Jackson, 1976, p. 67.
9 The National Archive in Kew holds a list of 4000 men and women suspected to be on their way to Spain. Kemp's contacts enabled him to avoid such petty inconveniences and his name does not appear on the list. NA KV 5/112.
10 Peter Kemp, *Mine Were of Trouble*, London: Cassell, 1957, p. 48.
11 Kemp, *Mine Were of Trouble* p. 43; Judith Keene, p. 112.

12 Kemp, *Mine Were of Trouble*, p. 60.

13 Kemp, *Mine Were of Trouble*, pp. 78-9; *The Thorns of Memory*, p. 46.

14 Christopher Othen, *Franco's International Brigades, Foreign Volunteers and Fascist Dictators in the Spanish Civil War*, London: Reportage Press, 2008, pp. 159-60.

15 Kemp, *Mine Were of Trouble*, p. 86.

16 Kemp, *Mine Were of Trouble*, p. 46.

17 F.H. Thomas, diary in Robert Stradling ed. *Brother against Brother*, Stroud: Sutton, 1998, pp. 50-1.

18 Keene, p. 113.

19 Kemp, *Mine Were of Trouble*, p. 110 & p. 112.

20 Interview with Peter Kemp, IWMSA 9769, reel 3.

21 Kemp, *Mine Were of Trouble*, p. 164.

22 Kemp, *Mine Were of Trouble*, pp. 170-173. The date suggests that the executed brigader could have been Ben Murray, a Communist Party branch secretary born in County Tyrone. However, reports suggest that Murray was actually killed by a bomb during the retreat in March 1938. I am grateful to the late Jim Carmody for this information.

23 Kemp, *Mine Were of Trouble*, p. 184.

24 Priscilla Scott-Ellis, *The Chances of Death, A Diary of the Spanish Civil War*, Norwich: Michael Russell, 1995, pp. 90 & 232-233.

25 Kemp, *The Thorns of Memory*, p. 129.

26 Scott-Ellis, pp. 98-9.

27 Kemp, *Mine Were of Trouble*, p. 191.

28 Captain Tomás Zerolo had studied in London and the Irish-American plastic surgeon, Eastman Sheean, had carried out a number of facial reconstructive operations in the General Mola hospital in San Sebastián. Keene, p. 114.

29 Peter Day, *Franco's Friends*, London: Biteback, 2001, pp. 7-14 & 73-6 and Othen, p. 217.

30 Kemp *Mine Were of Trouble* pp. 200-1.

31 Kemp, *The Thorns of Memory*, p. 142.

32 Peter Kemp, *No Colours or Crest*, London: Cassell, 1950, p. 5.

33 Gubbins was often known simply by the initial 'M'. Kemp, *The Thorns of Memory*, p. 143

34 Letter William J. Sanderson, Barrister-at-Law [to War Office?], 16 November 1939. Historical Disclosures, Armoury Personnel Centre, Glasgow.

35 See the supplement to the *London Gazette*, 16 February 1940, p. 920 and Summary of Kemp's war record 14 April 1949,

Historical Disclosures, Armoury Personnel Centre, Glasgow.

36 Kemp, *No Colours or Crest*, pp. 10-11.

37 Summary of Kemp's war record 14 April 1949, Historical Disclosures, Armoury Personnel Centre, Glasgow.

38 Kemp, *No Colours or Crest*, p. 14.

39 Kemp, *The Thorns of Memory*, p. 46.

40 Kemp, *No Colours or Crest*, p. 21.

41 Memorandum to R Brooman-White, 28 December 1940. NA KV 2/4418.

42 Memorandum from R Brooman-White to P/O Park of SOE, 17 March 1942. NA KV 2/4418.

43 Kemp, *No Colours or Crest*, p. 46.

44 Kemp, *No Colours or Crest*, p. 42.

45 For an entertaining account of Anders Lassen and his legendary acts of derring-do, see Damien Lewis, *Churchill's Secret Warriors*, London: Quercus, 2015.

46 Kemp, *No Colours or Crest*, p. 46.

47 Lewis, p. 274.

48 Interview with Second Lieutenant Robert Marcellin Sheppard, IWMSA 10445, reel 3, cited in Roderick Bailey, *Forgotten Voices of the Secret War,* London: Ebury Press, 2008, p. 45.

49 Kemp married Hilda Elizabeth Phillips ('Libby'), the daughter of Captain Harold Lionel Phillips and Hilda Wildman Hills, on 4 October 1941, though they divorced in 1946.

50 Kemp, *No Colours or Crest*, p. 51.

51 Operation Dryad report by Major Gus March-Phillips, cited in Winston G. Ramsey, *The War in the Channel Islands,* Barnsley, South Yorkshire: After the Battle, 2023, p.143.

52 Kemp, *No Colours or Crest*, p. 58.

53 Peter Kemp to Marjorie March-Phillipps, 30 September 1942.

54 Kemp, *The Thorns of Memory*, pp. 174-5.

55 Now revered as one of the founding fathers of the SAS, there is a statue of Lassen at the Regiment's headquarters in Hereford and in Churchill Park, Copenhagen.

56 Kemp, *No Colours or Crest*, p. 72.

57 NA WO 373/100.

58 Kemp, *No Colours or Crest*, p. 91.

59 David Smiley was impressed with the 'unconventional and eccentric' Kemp, remarking on his bravery and combat experience and describing him as 'tall, fair, talkative, very entertaining, rather worried over his health, and he shared with me a liking for good food and drink.' David Smiley, *Albanian*

Assignment, London: Chatto and Windus, 1984, p. 64.'

60 Kemp, *No Colours or Crest*, p. 92.

61 Interview with Peter Kemp, IWMSA 12299, reel 1. Shehu had fought with the Italian Garibaldis in Spain, commanding the 4th battalion and awarded the honour of membership of the Spanish Communist Party. At the end of the civil war he was interned first in France and then in Italy, returning to Albania in 1942.

62 'Drawn by the Sound of Guns', *The Spectator*, 17 August 1985, p. 14.

63 Interview with Peter Kemp, IWMSA 12299, reel 1.

64 *Ibid.*

65 *Ibid.*

66 Interview with Peter Kemp, IWMSA 12299, reel 1.

67 Kemp, *No Colours or Crest*, p. 192.

68 Kemp, *No Colours or Crest*, p. 218.

69 All the members of the operation were allocated code names: Hudson was GIN, Solly-Flood MUR, Major Alan Morgan NAG, Kemp RUM, Cpt Anthony Currie (real name Anton Popieszalski) CUR and Captain P Galbraith was DON. Norman Davies *Rising '44: The Battle for Warsaw*, London: Pan, 2004, p. 449.

70 Kemp, *The Thorns of Memory*, p. 235.

71 Interview with Peter Kemp, IWMSA 12299, reel 2.

72 Kemp, *No Colours or Crest*, p. 251.

73 Kemp, *No Colours or Crest*, p. 278.

74 Interview with Peter Kemp, IWMSA 12299, reel 2.

75 MRD Foot, *SOE, 1940-1946*, London: Bodley Head, 2014, p. 222.

76 Kemp, *The Thorns of Memory*, p. 265.

77 Kemp, *The Thorns of Memory*, p. 269.

78 Kemp, *Alms for Oblivion*, p. 1.

79 Interview with David Smiley, IWMSA 10340, reel 5.

80 Kemp, *The Thorns of Memory*, pp. 298-9 and interview with David Smiley, IWMSA 10340, reel 5.

81 Kemp, *Alms for Oblivion*, p. 56.

82 Kemp, *Alms for Oblivion*, p. 81.

83 *Ibid.*

84 NA WO 373/100/420 and interview with Peter Kemp, IWMSA 12299, reel 2.

85 http://www.commandoveterans.org/PeterKemp. SSRF accessed 25 November 2018.

86 Kemp, *Alms for Oblivion*, p. 86.

87 Kemp, *Alms for Oblivion*, p. 85.

88 Kemp, *Alms for Oblivion*, p. 166.

89 NA KV 2/4418.

90 Kemp, *Alms for Oblivion*, p. 182.

91 Kemp was married to Cynthia Margaret Henry. He has little to say about his new wife beyond that she 'should have had a medal.' Kemp, *The Thorns of Memory*, p. 314.

92 Memorandum from Major PL Pearce-Gould, The War Office, to unknown, 22 November 1950, KV 2/4418.

93 Kemp, *The Thorns of Memory*, p. 315.

94 Kemp, *The Thorns of Memory*, p. 339.

95 Kemp, *The Thorns of Memory*, p. 341.

96 Kemp, *The Thorns of Memory*, p. 364.

97 'Drawn by the Sound of Guns', *The Spectator*, 17 August 1985, p. 14.

98 Kemp, *The Thorns of Memory*, p. 367.

99 Kemp, *The Thorns of Memory*, p. 369.

100 MRD Foot, obituary for Peter Mant MacIntyre Kemp, *Independent,* 4 November, 1993.

101 Kemp's three memoirs were *Mine Were of Trouble, No Colours or Crest* and *Alms for Oblivion* and his autobiography was entitled *The Thorns of Memory*..

102 Steve Hurst, *Famous Faces of the Spanish Civil War*, Barnsley: Pen and Sword Military, 2009, pp. 67-8.

103 Women rarely feature in Kemp's accounts as anything more than beautiful (and silent) objects to be admired. Unless, of course, one counts the regular soldiers' references to prostitutes and courtesans, or the occasional insults: 'the ugliest creatures in the East are water buffaloes and British officers' wives'. Just old-fashioned 'macho' attitudes perhaps, hardly unknown among certain 'army types', however, his analogy of the German occupation of Albania to rape—'if you know there's no avoiding it, it's best to relax and enjoy it'—suggests a level of misogyny that even his admirers might find discomfiting.

104 Kemp, *No Colours or Crest*, p. 2.

105 See Brian Crozier, *Franco: A Biographical History*. London: Eyre and Spottiswoode, 1967.

106 Kemp, *The Thorns of Memory*, p. 369.

107 NA KV 2/4418 p. 9a.

108 Kemp, *The Thorns of Memory*, p. 362.

Notes to Chapter Four

1 'Sam' the eldest, plus Frank, Syd, Queenie, Ruth, Ivor, Shirley and Miriam. Interview with 'Sam Russell', IWMSA, 9484, reel 1 and Roger Bagley, 'Obituary: Sam Lesser 1915-2010', *Morning Star*, 4 October 2010.

2 Interview with Sam Lesser by Harry Owens, 31 May 2010.

3 Interview with Sam Lesser in Max Arthur, *The Real Band of Brothers*, London: Collins, 2009, p. 213.

4 Interview with Sam Lesser in Arthur, p. 210.

5 RGASPI 545/6/162, p. 24.

6 Interview with Sam Lesser, IWMSA 9484, reel 1.

7 *Ibid.*

8 Interview with Sam Lesser in Arthur, p. 210.

9 RGASPI 545/6/162, p. 94.

10 Interview with Sam Lesser, IWMSA 9484, reel 2.

11 Interview with Sam Lesser in Arthur, pp. 214-5.

12 Interview with Sam Lesser in Arthur, pp. 216.

13 A list of the members of the 4th section resides in the Moscow RGASPI archives. While John Cornford is remarked upon as a 'good soldier', Edward Burke as 'brave' and Robert Symes as a 'good chap', Lesser does not fare so well, described as 'Student. Bad type socially'. RGASPI 545/6/1 p. 100.

14 Interview with Sam Lesser, IWMSA 9484, reel 2.

15 Interview with Sam Lesser in Arthur, p. 218.

16 John Sommerfield, *Volunteer in Spain*, London: Lawrence and Wishart, 1937, p. 92.

17 Interview with Sam Lesser, IWMSA 9484, reel 3.

18 Geoffrey Cox, *Defence of Madrid,* London: Gollancz, 1937, pp. 132-38.

19 Interview with Sam Lesser, IWMSA 9484, reel 6.

20 Interview with Sam Lesser, IWMSA 9484, reel 2.

21 Interview with Sam Lesser, IWMSA 9484, reel 3.

22 Interview with Sam Lesser in Arthur, p. 233.

23 There is an entry in MI5's list of volunteers, noting that an M. Lesser had returned wounded (though some details are mixed up with his brother's, who also fought in Spain). NA KV 5/112, p. 8.

24 RGASPI 545/6/162, p. 92 and NA KV 5/126.

25 Interview with Sam Lesser, IWMSA 9484, reel 4. The two remained in touch. Dora Levin (as she was later) returned to Poland after the Second World War, before she was thrown out during the anti-Semitic purges of 1968 and sought refuge in

Israel. In the late 1980s she visited Sam in London, attending the IBA's annual commemoration in Jubilee Gardens. I am grateful to Jim Jump for this information.

26 RGASPI 545/6/162, p. 95.

27 A letter by Frankford that initially appeared in the Treball of Barcelona was republished in the British Communist daily: 'They went to fight Fascism—were used to aid it', *Daily Worker*, 14 September 1937 p. 2. Frankford slightly rowed back from some of his accusations in a follow up two days later, admitting that some of the account was based on hearsay. However, he continued to claim that 'fraternisation that took place after May. Newspapers, drinks and smokes would be exchanged at night between the lines. These were fully known to everyone and never discouraged.' 'An ILP Member in Spain' *Daily Worker*, 16 September 1937, p. 6.

28 Gordon Bowker, *George Orwell*, London: Little, Brown, 2003, p. 218.

29 Interview with Sam Lesser, 5 June 2007. Frankford later stated that 'he didn't know if Lesser had published *The Daily Worker* story' which, unhelpfully, carries no by-line. See Jeffrey Myers, 'Repeating the old lies,' *The New Criterion*, April 1999.

30 Interview with Sam Lesser, IWMSA 9484, reel 5.

31 Myers, *op cit.*

32 In fairness to Lesser, I always found him to be an open and honest interviewee, even if there were some issues he was keener to talk about than others. This was more than seventy years after the event, so it's possible that he had forgotten. However, Georges Kopp stated that Frankford's letter had been dictated to the ILP volunteer, 'who has been weak enough to buy his freedom by signing it.' It's hard to see that would be something easily forgotten. See Kopp to ILP, 14 December 1938, PHM BE/5/4.

33 Interview with Sam Lesser, IWMSA 9484, reel 4.

34 Doubts have recently been raised about Ibárruri's speech, following the release in Spain of a new biography of Pasionara. See Mario Amorós, *¡No Pasarán!* Ediciones Akal, Madrid, 2021 and 'Great speech, but were the words ever spoken?' *¡No Pasarán!*, 3:2022, pp. 12-13. While Lesser refers to the dramatic speech, he makes no mention of hearing it at the 28 October farewell parade.

35 M. Lesser, 'Welcome Home Boys of the British Battalion', 6 December 1938. Box 19, Russell papers, Bishopsgate Institute.

36 M Lesser, 'The Army of the Ebro Concludes Four Heroic

Months', 11 November 1938. Box 19, Russell papers, Bishopsgate Institute.

37 M Lesser, 'The Invaders Take Revenge on Barcelona', 1 January 1939. Box 19, Russell papers, Bishopsgate Institute.

38 Interview with Sam Lesser in Arthur, p. 240.

39 M Lesser, 'The Invaders have Begun a New Campaign of Terror', 4 December 1938. Box 19, Russell papers, Bishopsgate Institute.

40 M Lesser, 'Barcelona Prepares to Meet The Enemy', *Daily Worker*, 23 January, 1939.

41 Interview with Sam Lesser by the author, 14 May 2001. The documents form the basis of the Russian State Archive of Socio-Political History.

42 M Lesser, 'The Army Sill Fights Back', undated, Box 19, Russell papers, Bishopsgate Institute.

43 M Lesser, 'Modesto's Army Withdraws into France', 10 February 1939. Box 19, Russell papers, Bishopsgate Institute.

44 M Lesser, 'Modesto's Army Withdraws into France', 10 February 1939. Box 19, Russell papers, Bishopsgate Institute.

45 Interview with Sam Lesser, IWMSA 9484, reel 6.

46 Colin Chambers and Sam Russell, *I Saw Democracy Murdered*, London: Routledge, 2022, p. 84.

47 NA KV 2/3741.

48 Interview with Sam Lesser, IWMSA 9484, reel 6.

49 Interview with Sam Lesser, IWMSA 9484, reel 6. A typescript of the interview, which was mailed from Belgium to the Communist Party offices in London and to Peter Kerrigan in Glasgow, was intercepted *en route* by the British Security Services and can be found within Lesser's file in the National Archives.

50 NA KV 2/3741, p. 34 and memorandum from unknown to Lt. Colonel V. Vivian of SIS, 16 February 1940. NA KV 2/3742, p. 40.

51 NA KV 5/126.

52 NA KV 2/3742, pp. 16-18.

53 NA KV 5/126.

54 NA KV 2/3743, p. 2 & memo 27 March 1940 from RHH/HW to Special Branch. KV2/3742. As Sir Denis Greenhill, Permanent Under-Secretary in the Foreign and Commonwealth Office, later admitted, MI5 also had concerns that Lesser might be a Soviet sleeper. Interview with Sam Lesser, 5 June 2007.

55 [?] July 1941, NA KV 2/1031.

56 Present were President of the Edinburgh Trades Council, Tom Murray, the President of the IBA, Sam Wild, and the

association's secretary, Jack Brent, plus veterans from America, Australia, Austria, Canada, Cyprus, Czechoslovakia, Germany, Greece, Poland and Yugoslavia.

57 *Report of the International Brigade Conference*, 3 April 1943, Box 26, Russell papers, Bishopsgate Institute.

58 The confession is part of short autobiography, signed under his pseudonym Sam Russell. Like pretty much everything else that passed across the desks at the Party's head office in King Street in London's Covent Garden, a copy of the document ended up within the files of the British Security Services and now resides in the National Archives. NA KV 2/3747, p. 344.

59 Chambers and Russell, p. 107 & NA KV 2/3747, p. 344.

60 Chambers and Russell, p. 112.

61 Sam Russell, 'The Angry Island', *Spotlight on the Channel Islands*, Daily Worker League, 1945, p. 4.

62 *Daily Worker*, 19 July 1945, p. 1.

63 Chambers and Russell, p. 115.

64 Memo 4 April 1951, NA KV 2/3745, p. 200a.

65 *Daily Worker*, 14 June 1950.

66 Ernest 'Frank' Lesser arrived in Spain in August 1937 and was sent to Officer Training School, where he learnt the skills of machine-gunning and sniping. He was trained as a lieutenant though the rank was never officially confirmed. He served at the front for three months and was wounded once by shrapnel, before returning home in October 1938. During the 1970s, then a senior lecturer in Chelsea College's department of pharmacology, (part of the University of London) he wrote three influential articles for *New Scientist* on the Thalidomide tragedy. See RGASPI 545/6/162 pp. 84-90 and Dr Ephraim Lesser, 'Thalidomide, drugs and society', *New Scientist*, 6 June 1974, p. 609.

67 Colin Chambers, 'Sam Russell obituary', *The Guardian*, 11 October 2010.

68 'Summary and critical survey of my work in Spain, since the outbreak of the war', Winifred Bates, Barcelona, September 1938, RGASPI 545/6/88 p. 11.

69 Ruth Muller, 'Remembering Margaret Powell', *IBMT Newsletter*, 36, 2014, p. 16.

70 Ruth Muller, 'Remembering Margaret Powell', *The Volunteer*, 22 March 2014.

71 'Extract from Special Branch report regarding a delegation of Soviet concert artists who arrived as guests of British-Soviet Friendship Society', 5 December 1952, NA KV 2/3746, p. 253.

72 Sam Russell, 'Moscow-Havana-Prague: recollections of communist foreign correspondent,' *Twentieth Century Communism*, 3, 2011, p. 163.

73 Russell, 'Moscow-Havana-Prague,' p. 154.

74 Lesser had to settle for reporting Krushchev's planned visit to Britain in April 1956. 'The Kremlin's Good Wishes: Friendship for Britain.' Lesser recounted that he had seen 'an amazing demonstration of the Soviet leaders' friendship for the people of Britain, France and the United States' at a reception for the Danish Prime Minister. *Daily Worker*, 7 March 1956, p. 1.

75 NA KV 2/3748, p. 370 a&b.

76 NA KV 2/3748 p. 374a.

77 Sam Russell, 'Moscow—City of Constant Surprises', 27 November 1957, p. 4. Box 31, Russell papers, Bishopsgate Institute.

78 Sam Russell, 'Man-made miracle of the new farms', *Daily Worker*, 10 September 1956.

79 Sam Russell, 'Forty Years On', 4 December [1957], Box 28, Russell papers, Bishopsgate Institute.

80 Sam Russell, '40 Years On—Backstage with a Bolshoi Ballerina', 8 November 1957, p. 2. Box 29, Russell papers, Bishopsgate Institute.

81 NA KV 2/3748 p. 376b.

82 Peter Matthews of the Foreign Office News Department, FO secret memorandum, 19 September 1957. NA KV 2/3748, p. 400a.

83 Estimates suggest that the British Communist Party lost over a quarter of its membership in response to the Soviets' brutal crushing of the Hungarian Revolution. See AJ Davies, *To Build A New Jerusalem*, London: Abacus, 1996, p. 179.

84 Interview with Sam Lesser, IWMSA 9484, reel 5.

85 Sam Russell, 'West Accused By Pravda of Subversion', *Daily Worker*, 29 October 1956, p. 1 & 'Kadar Reveals the Facts,' *Daily Worker*, 20 November 1956, p. 1.

86 Sam Russell, untitled typescript, 11 December 1956. Box 28, Russell papers, Bishopsgate Institute. The original quote includes a number of abbreviations, which have been expanded for the sake of clarity: 'In many plants, membrs of the Hungarian fascist Crossed Arrow organisation produced arms and forced workers to participate in the demonstrations.'

87 NA KV 2/3748, p. 389a.

88 Interview with George Leeson, IWMSA 803, reel 3.

89 NA KV 2/3749, p. 411z.

90 NA KV 2/3749, p. 413z.

91 NA KV 2/3749, p. 415a.

92 Conversation between Sam Lesser and Peter Kerrigan, 1 July 1959. NA KV 2/3749, p. 422b.

93 NA KV 2/3749, p. 403a.

94 Confidential memo of 30 October 1959 and Loose Minute, PF 47,183 'Sam Russell and the Russians'. NA KV 2/3749, p. 434a & p. 436.

95 Letter from Margaret Russell to Anna and Tim McWhinnie, 20 August 1958, NA KV 2/3749.

96 NA KV 2/3749, p. 417a.

97 Top-secret memo, 27 November 1959 NA KV 2/3749, p. 435a.

98 *Daily Worker*, 16 November, 1959.

99 'Close Thing Over Cuba' acknowledged the *Daily Worker*'s Peter Tempest from Moscow on 8 November 1962, p. 1.

100 'Why Kennedy Threatens Cuba—this little land offers peace but he plans war,' by Sam Russell, *Daily Worker,* 24 October 1962, p. 2.

101 'While discussions are continuing in New York between US, Cuban and Soviet representatives and between Mr Mikoyan and Premier Castro here, the people of Cuba are not relaxing their vigilance for a moment . . . [the revolution has] brought Cuba from being one of the most backward countries in the world in the educational field to one of the most advanced.' Sam Russell, Round-the-clock alert in Cuba,' *Daily Worker*, Saturday 17 November 1962, p. 2. The theme was picked up again on 26 November p. 2: Sam Russell: Cuba's other battle: against illiteracy.'

102 A report of the interview appeared in the British *Daily Worker* on 4 December. The report included a photograph of Sam Lesser and Che Guevara in deep conversation. 'For over two hours, until well past midnight, I discussed the situation with him in his office on Havana's Revolution Square, as he put Cuba's point of view with complete frankness and sincerity.' 'The Americans still want to Come Here,' *Daily Worker*, 4 December 1962, p. 2.

103 Russell, 'Moscow-Havana-Prague,' p. 160.

104 Russell, 'Moscow-Havana-Prague,' p. 164.

105 Russell, 'Moscow-Havana-Prague,' p. 169.

106 Francis Beckett, *Enemy Within; the Rise and Fall of the British Communist party,* London: John Murray, 1995, p. 165.

107 Russell, 'Moscow-Havana-Prague,' p. 165.

108 The fury and outrage in Lesser's article on the Chilean coup

is manifest: 'I saw democracy murdered in Chile by the rabble of Rip van Winkle generals and admirals recruited by the CIA to impose a savage military dictatorship on a people which had seen and welcomed the dawn of a new era.' Sam Russell, *Morning Star*, Tuesday 25 September 1973, p.1.

109 Bill Alexander, *No to Franco: The Struggle Never Stopped, 1939-1975!* London: Bill Alexander, 1992, p. 71.

110 Sam Russell, 'Taking exams at gunpoint in Spain', *Morning Star*, 17 July 1972, p. 2 and 'Spanish trade unionists jailed by Franco's thugs', *Morning Star*, 2 August 1972, p. 2.

111 Interview with Jack Jones in 'Voices from a Mountain'. Andrew Lee/David Leach, Narrative Productions, 2001.

112 Jackson, *British Women*, p. 346.

113 Jim Jump, 'Sam Lesser: Veteran communist journalist who served with the International Brigade during the Spanish Civil War,' *Independent*, 1 November 2010.

114 See Colin Chambers and Sam Russell, *I Saw Democracy Murdered*, London: Routledge, 2022.

115 Conversation with the author, May 2010.

116 Russell, 'Moscow-Havana-Prague', p. 171.

Notes to Chapter Five

1 Adam Hochschild, *Spain in our Hearts,* London: Macmillan, 2016.

2 Little has been written on Winifred Bates, though for Ralph see Mike Yates, *Ralph Bates, Swindon's 'Unknown' Author,* Bradford on Avon: ELSP, 2014. For Nan and George Green see Nan Green, *A Chronicle of Small Beer.* Nottingham: Trent Editions, 2004 and Paul Preston, *Doves of War: four women of Spain*, London: Harper Collins, 2002 pp. 121-201.

3 Samanth Subramanian, *A Dominant Character,* New York: Norton, 2020, p. 216.

4 Perhaps surprisingly, there is no file for Charlotte Haldane within the MI5 files at the National Archives. An enquiry to MI5 itself met with their standard, carefully worded reply: 'it is Government policy to neither confirm nor deny whether any individual or group has been subject to investigation by MI5. An exception to this policy allows us to release to TNA files that are still in existence and at least 50 years old, if to do so would not damage national security. We have researched our records and

have to tell you that we hold no files relating to Charlotte Haldane/Burghes/Franken that fall within this category.'

5 Charlotte Haldane, *Truth Will Out,* London: George Weidenfeld and Nicolson, 1949, p. 4.

6 Judith Adamson, *Charlotte Haldane. Woman Writer in a Man's World,* Basingstoke: Macmillan, 1998, p. 6.

7 Charlotte Haldane, p. 5.

8 Charlotte Haldane, p. 9.

9 Haldane's 1929 publication *The Origin of Life* which discussed the idea of progressive evolution 'was one of the most emblematic of the interwar period.' Stéphane Tirard, 'JBS Haldane and the origin of life,' *Genet,* 2017, 5, p. 735. Online at: https://pubmed.ncbi.nlm.nih.gov/2923 7880/.

10 Haldane Papers, UCL Archives, HALDANE/2/1/8 & 'Why I am a Cooperator', HALDANE/1/2/ 63, p. 4.

11 Krishna Dronamraju, *Popularising Science. The Life and Work of JBS Haldane,* New York: Oxford University Press, 2017, p. 6.

12 UCL HALDANE/2/1/8

13 Ronald Clark, *JBS. The Life and Work of JBS Haldane,* London: Hodder and Stoughton, 1968, p. 34.

14 'Why I am a Cooperator', HALDANE/1/2/63, p. 16.

15 *Ibid.*

16 Clark, p. 199.

17 Stephen Spender in *The God that Failed,* Richard Crossman ed., Washington: Regnery Gateway, c. 1983, p. 258.

18 Charlotte Haldane, p. 19.

19 'Why I am a Cooperator', HALDANE/1/2/63, p. 78.

20 Obituary for JBS Haldane, *The New York Times,* 12 December 1964, p. 1.

21 See Allegra Hartley, 'Sex and Suffrage in Charlotte Haldane's Man's World,' *The Modernist Review,* 30 September 2021 [available online at https://modernistreviewcouk.wordpress. com/2021/09/30/sex-and-suffrage-in-charlotte-haldanes-mans-world-1926/]

22 Dronamraju, p. 33.

23 Dronamraju, p. 40.

24 Charlotte Haldane, p. 38.

25 From JBS's brief hand-written autobiography in UCL HALDANE/2/1/8 [undated, but probably written in 1939-1940]

26 Charlotte Haldane, p. 68.

27 Charlotte Haldane, pp. 72-3.

28 Charlotte Haldane, p. 83.

29 Adamson, p. 115.

30 Charlotte Haldane, p. 92.

31 NA KV/5/112, p. 7. Ronnie Burghes is also listed as 'Haldane, son of JBS 24.12.36 Fighting with the International Brigade in Spain.' There is a hand-written addition cross-referencing his real name, albeit misspelled: 'See under Ronald Burgess'.

32 RGASPI 545/6/91. In fact, the unit included volunteers from other nations, including Ireland. The tendency to refer to all volunteers from Britain, Ireland and the former Empire has been the cause of much bad feeling.

33 Many who fought with No. 1 Company at Lopera believed that Delasalle was made a scapegoat: 'He may have been a coward . . . but it was manifestly absurd to maintain that he was in the pay of Franco.' Gurney, p. 82.

34 Tom Wintringham, *English Captain*, London: Faber and Faber, 1939, p. 166.

35 Charlotte Haldane p. 123

36 JBS was reported as 'going to Spain as adviser to Int. Legion.' NA KV 5/112, p. 7.

37 Cochrane later dismissed what he saw as Haldane's naïve and dogmatic view of the relation between politics and human psychology, though this was probably as much a reaction to Haldane's devout Communism as anything else. Archibald L. Cochrane, *One Man's Medicine,* London: BMJ, 1989, p. 33.

38 RGASPI 545/6/145, p. 23.

39 Letter from Harry Pollitt to Rose Kerrigan, undated [though probably January 1937]. NA KV 2/1832, p. 26.

40 Interview with Vera Elken, IWMSA 16900, reel 3.

41 Virginia Cowles, *Looking for Trouble,* London: Hamish Hamilton, 194, pp. 21-5, cited in Gavan Tredoux, *Comrade Haldane Is Too Busy To Go On Holiday*, New York: Encounter, 2018, p. 49.

42 Interview with Vera Elken, IWMSA 16900, reel 3 and NA KV 5/112, p. 7.

43 NA KV 2/1832

44 Special Branch report on Professor JBS Haldane, 27 February 1941. NA KV 2/1832 p. 143a.

45 JBS Haldane, 'A Tourist in Loyal Spain', RGASPI 545/3/478, p. 127.

46 RGASPI 545/6/145, p. 22.

47 Charlotte Haldane, p. 127.

48 Interview with Walter Greenhalgh, IWMSA 11187, reel 5.

49 Charlotte Haldane, p. 128.

50 Interview with Charles Bloom, IWMSA 992, reel 2.

51 Interview with Hugh Sloan in MacDougall, p. 203.

52 Interview with Fred Copeman, IWMSA 794, reel 3.

53 *Ibid.*

54 Haldane's arrival at Folkestone on 16 April 1937 was noted by Special Branch. NA KV 2/1832 p. 42.

55 Charlotte Haldane, p. 98-99.

56 Adamson, p. 114.

57 *Daily Worker,* 24 December 1936.

58 Interview with Frank Graham, IWMSA 11877 reel 3.

59 Charlotte Haldane, pp. 112-13.

60 Interview with Bill Cranston in Ian MacDougall, p. 187.

61 Charlotte Haldane, p. 114.

62 Charlotte Haldane, p. 102. Haldane's memoir is dedicated to 'Jack' from 'Rita' but his real name was Arnold Reid. He was the former editor of the American Communist journal, *New Masses.*

63 Interview with Tony McLean, IWMSA 838, reel 1.

64 Interview with George Murray in MacDougall, p. 101 and Charlotte Haldane, p. 117.

65 See correspondence between the Maskey family and the IBD & WAC, MML SC/ORG/DWAC/3/1937/4.

66 Alexander, *British Volunteers*, p. 243.

67 'One Year's Fight for Democracy in Spain', Warwick, 292/946/16b/80 and NA KV 2/1832, p. 54b.

68 Clark, pp.149-150.

69 NA KV/5/112, p. 7 and interview with John Dunlop in MacDougall, p. 149 & Charlotte Haldane, p. 127

70 Interview with John Dunlop in MacDougall, p. 149.

71 Ivor Hickman cited in Wainwright, p. 117.

72 'Nobody wanted to hear it, but Harry Pollitt insisted I had a democratic right to sing,' Norman remarked. Joe Norman memoir, p. 2. MML SC/VOL/JNO.

73 PHM, Manchester, CP/IND/POLL/2/5 and RGASPI, 545/6/212 pp. 53-4.

74 Harry Pollitt, *Pollitt visits Spain*, London: International Brigade Wounded and Dependents' Aid Fund, February 1938, p. 7.

75 Foreword by Professor JBS Haldane in *Pollitt visits Spain*, p. 3.

76 *Pollitt visits Spain*, p. 27.

77 NA KV 2/1832 p. 71a.

78 JBS in *Pollitt visits Spain*, p. 4.

79 JBS in *Pollitt visits Spain*, p. 6.

80 Letter from Sam Wild Commander British Battalion and Bob Cooney Battalion Commissar, to undisclosed recipients, 25 April 1938. UCL HALDANE/4/21/1/1.

81 Clark, p.153.

82 NA KV/5/112, p. 13.

83 Charlotte was informed that he had been killed, not while fighting with the American Lincoln Battalion, but with 'an obscure Spanish infantry Regiment'. Bill Rust, a senior British Communist in Spain, hinted to Charlotte that Jack had been 'sold down the river by his own Party', accusing a member of the American Politburo as being responsible. Charlotte forever harboured resentment over his death, 'I am convinced that Jack was not a war casualty, but a victim of political bigotry, envy, malice and intrigue. And in this young man of many aliases, of fanatical idealism, of absolute goodness and devotion to his cause, there perished one of the finest spirits it has been my proud privilege to know. For me he can never die.' Whether Rust was correct, is impossible to know. Charlotte soon came to realise that Rust was utterly unscrupulous and not always to be trusted. Charlotte Haldane, pp. 127 & pp. 132-3.

84 Charlotte Haldane, p. 128.

85 Letter from Bill Rust supporting request for repatriation on the grounds of illness, 6 April 1938. RGASPI 545/6/118 p. 63

86 An account of their visit to the British Battalion positions appears in Bill Rust, *Britons in Spain*, London: Lawrence and Wishart, 1939, pp. 114-5 and in Jim Fyrth and Sally Alexander eds., *Women's Voices from the Spanish Civil War*, London: Lawrence and Wishart, 1991, pp. 306-8.

87 Adamson, p. 121.

88 JBS Haldane, *A.R.P.* London: Victor Gollancz, 1938, p. 9.

89 *A.R.P.* p. 11 and, for example, NA KV 2/1832, p. 97a.

90 Ministry of Supply Report, 203/GEN/55, 4 December 1939, NA KV 2/1832, p. 15.

91 Charlotte Haldane, pp. 145-6.

92 Others included the former Political Commissar, Doug Springhall, the hospital administrator, Nan Green, and the English nurse, Patience Darton.

93 See Tom Buchanan, 'Shanghai-Madrid Axis? Comparing British Responses to the Conflicts in Spain and China, 1936-1939', *Contemporary European History*, 2012, p. 539.

94 Charlotte Haldane, p. 152.

95 Charlotte Haldane, p. 176.

96 Charlotte Haldane, p. 180.

97 As a letter from the AEU's solicitors confirms, though JBS was working for the Admiralty he was actually employed by the AEU. Letter from Evill and Coleman to JBS 28 May 1940. UCL HALDANE/1/5/2/10.

98 Letter from JBS to Fred A Smith, General Secretary of AEU, 12 March 1942. UCL HALDANE/1/5/2/17.

99 Clark, pp. 169 and Gabriel Jackson, *Juan Negrín: physiologist, socialist and Spanish Republican war leader*, Brighton: Sussex Academic, 2010 p. 309; NA HW17/20.

100 John Scott Haldane's highly important research led to the use of canaries in mines and diving decompression tables still in use in the 1950s.

101 *Yorkshire Observer,* Friday 21 July 1939, p. 1. I am grateful to Tam Watters for bringing the interview with George Ives to my attention.

102 Duff, a member of the TGWU from Ireland, was wounded four times in Spain, including being badly hurt in both arms in the Republican Ebro offensive which caused him to miss the dramatic farewell parade in Barcelona in October 1938.

103 Clark, pp. 172-3.

104 JBS Haldane, 'Life at High Pressures', *Science News*, 4, London: Penguin 1947, pp. 9-29, cited in Angus Calder, *The People's War,* London: Jonathan Cape, 1969, p. 465.

105 Dronamraju, p. 122

106 Clark, p. 169. Haldane later published a research paper on the experiments and sent a copy of it to all the volunteers involved. See JBS Haldane, 'After Effects of Exposure of Men to Carbon Dioxide', *The Lancet,* 19 August 1939, pp. 419-22.

107 'Scientist "Suffocates" in 14-Hour Thetis Test', *Daily Sketch,* 21 July 1939, p. 6.

108 Charlotte Haldane, p. 186.

109 See letter to *Saothar,* journal of the Irish Labour History Society, 18, 1993, and replies. Available online at http://irelandscw.com/ibvol-EDThetis.htm.

110 NA FO 371/49553-49558 and Clark, p. 174. The involvement of the German national, Hans Kahle, on the project was raised in a report by the Security Intelligence Centre Liaison Officers' Conference. NA CAB 93/4. Kahle was later deported and interned in Canada. Tredoux, p. 112.

111 Clark, p. 181.

112 Charlotte Haldane, p. 216.

113 Vavilov had crossed swords with Trofim Lysenco on a

number of occasions, though Simon Ings argues that it was Vavilov's plethora of international contacts that sealed his fate. He was denounced, sentenced to 20 years imprisonment and died of starvation in prison. See Simon Ings, *Stalin and the Scientists*, London: Faber and Faber, 2016, pp. 297-302.

114 Charlotte Haldane, p. 219.

115 Charlotte Haldane, p. 233.

116 C.C. Hertford report, 12 September 1941, NA KV 2/1832.

117 Dronamraju, p. 41.

118 Charlotte Haldane p. 263. Special Branch reported that Charlotte resigned from the Party on 30 April 1942, though they continued to view her as a 'suspected communist' into the late 1940s and she remained under surveillance. Special Branch reports, 29 January 1943 and 15 September 1947, NA KV 2/1832 p. 156a & NA KV 2/1832, p. 224a.

119 Charlotte Haldane pp. 267-8.

120 'Famous Scientist Joins Communists,' *Reynolds News,* 24 May 1942. However, Boris Volodarsky has suggested that JBS Haldane may have been recruited secretly in 1928 during his visit to Moscow with Charlotte. Boris Volodarsky, 'Soviet Intelligence Services in the Spanish Civil War, 1936-1939,' PhD thesis, London School of Economics, 2010, p. 314. If so, the British Party were unaware, for in July 1939 they were still trying to persuade JBS to declare himself a Party member, but he was not prepared to do so. Special Branch report, 27 July 1939, NA KV 2/1832 p. 125a.

121 Special Branch report of 9 February 1941 and CC Manchester report, 23 November 1942, NA KV 2/1832.

122 SB Report PF 45762 156a, 29 January 1943, NA KV s/1832. On 21 January 1943 a letter to MI5 from Lt. Anderson at the Admiralty asked for several of Haldane's assistants to be vetted. NA KV 2/1832.

123 Clark, p. 163.

124 Tredoux, p. 319. JBS has been identified by, among others, Nigel West (*Venona: the Greatest Secret of the Cold War*, London: Harper Collins, 1999, pp. 60-78.) as INTELLIGENTSIA, the leader of a Soviet spy ring called X Group. However, though Haldane may well have been part of the ring, INTELLIGENTSIA was more likely to have been Ivor Montagu, the Cambridge educated son of Lord Montagu, who gained fame as a filmmaker and critic and champion table-tennis player. See NA HW15/43 and Tredoux pp. 104-106.

125 NA KV 2/1832.

126 Thursday 18 November 1943, NA ADM 178/313.

127 From telephone check on Mountview 4212—James Klugman, 13 October 1947. NA KV 2/1832 p. 226a.

128 From telephone check [on King St.] on 2 December 1948, NA KV 2/1832 p. 254c.

129 NA KV 2/1832, p. 261a.

130 He probably left the Party at the end of the year, though MI5 believed he had still not broken with the Party as late as April 1951. Letter from JH Marriott to J Cimperman in the American Embassy, 7 April 1951. NA KV 2/1832 p. 309a.

131 Clark, p. 267.

132 Adamson, p. 189.

133 JBS Haldane, *Daedalus or Science in the Future,* London: Turner and Co., 1923.

134 Adamson, p. 198.

135 Interview with Tony McLean IWMSA 19991, reel 1.

136 Interview with Fred Copeman, IWMSA 794, reel 10.

137 NA KV 5/118 PF. 46229.

138 British Army Disclosures, Glasgow and Supplement to the London Gazette, 5 July 1940, p. 4085.

139 Letter from Betty Burghes to Bill Alexander, 19 May 1997, MML SC/VOL/WAL2/69.

140 International Brigade Association Newsletter, January 1998. MML SC/IBA/6/1/62.

Notes to Chapter Six

1 Interview with Stafford Cottman, IWMSA 9278, reel 7. This is clearly not just Cottman's opinion, for a 2009 account of the ILP volunteers in Spain was titled *Not Just Orwell.* Christopher Hall argues that 'the shadow of George Orwell has in some ways hindered research into the ILP volunteers.' *'Not Just Orwell': The Independent Labour Party Volunteers and the Spanish Civil War*, Barcelona: Warren and Pell, 2009, p. 241.

2 For a wider discussion of the value of Orwell's memoir, see Paul Preston, 'Lights and Shadows in Orwell's *Homage to Catalonia', Bulletin of Spanish Studies,* 2018.

3 See, for example, Chris Hall, *In Spain with Orwell*, Perth: Tippermuir, 2013 and Peter Thwaites, 'The Independent Labour Party Contingent in the Spanish Civil War,' *Imperial War Museum Review*, 1987.

4 Cottman is one of four volunteers featured in Chris Hall's *Disciplina Camaradas*, Pontefract: Gosling Press, 1994 and there is a brief, though useful biography of him in *Not Just Orwell*, pp. 176-184.

5 David Keys, 'Obituary: Stafford Cottman.' *Independent*, 3 November 1999.

6 Interview with Frank Frankford, IWMSA 9308, reel 1.

7 Don Bateman, 'Staff Cottman, Spanish Civil War warrior who fought on for socialism', The Guardian, 29 September, 1999.

8 Interview with Frank Frankford, IWMSA 9308, reel 1.

9 Interview with Stafford Cottman, IWMSA 9278, reel 1.

10 Interview with Stafford Cottman, IWMSA 9278, reel 2.

11 Stafford Cottman, cited in Hall, *Disciplina Camaradas*, p. 23.

12 'A volunteer in Spain', *The People's Chronicle*, 8, 1987, p. 5. Many thanks to Mike Eaude for bringing this to my attention.

13 Don Bateman, Introduction to John McNair's *Spanish Diary*, ILP, Undated. p. 5.

14 John McNair, *In Spain Now: a first-hand story of the fight against fascism and of the use of workers' power for socialism.* ILP, September 1936.

15 McNair, *In Spain Now*, p. 8.

16 Interview with Bob Edwards, IWMSA 4669, reel 2.

17 McNair, *Spanish Diary*, p. 8.

18 For the reaction of the ILP leadership to the Spanish war, see Gidon Cohen, *The Failure of a Dream: The Independent Labour Party from Disaffiliation to World War II*, London: Taurus Academic Studies, 2007.

19 Interview with Bob Edwards, IWMSA 4669, reel 2.

20 Despite Cottman's young age, his mother seems to have put up no objection to him going to Spain.

21 Interview with Stafford Cottman, IWMSA 9278, reel 2.

22 Interview with Stafford Cottman, IWMSA 9278, reel 4.

23 Interview with Stafford Cottman, IWMSA 9278, reel 3.

24 *Ibid.*

25 Report by Harry P. Thomas, MML SC/IBA/5/3/1/21. In fairness to Edwards, this report was clearly written to conform to Communist Party sensibilities.

26 'How I.L.P. Spanish Contingent Got Away—An Exciting Race with Scotland Yard,' *The New Leader*, 15 January 1937, p. 3.

27 NA KV 5/112.

28 *Ibid.*

29 'In Spain—Volunteers Arrive at Barcelona,' *The New Leader*, 15 January 1937, p. 1.

30 Interview with Frank Frankford, IWMSA 9308, reel 1.

31 *The New Leader* 15 January 1937, cited in Hall, *In Spain with Orwell,* p. 106.

32 George Orwell, *Homage to Catalonia,* London: Secker and Warburg, 1938, p. 4.

33 Interview with Stafford Cottman, IWMSA 9278, reel 3.

34 *Ibid.*

35 *Ibid.* Bob Edwards had claimed that 'the first instalment of our contingent is composed of twenty-five good fighters.' This can safely be viewed as propaganda. Bob Edwards, 'Why We Go,' *The New Leader*, 15 January 1937, p. 3.

36 Thwaites, p. 54.

37 Cottman, cited in Hall, *Disciplina Camaradas*, pp. 33-4.

38 Orwell, p. 19.

39 Born in St Petersburg of Belgian parents, Kopp had grown up and been educated in Belgium, training as an engineer. See Don Bateman, 'George Kopp and the POUM militia', in Al Richardson, ed., *The Spanish Civil War: the View from the Left,* London: Merlin, 1992 and Andy Durgan, 'With the POUM. International volunteers on the Aragon Front (1936-1937)', *Ebre 38*, 8:2018.

40 Stafford Cottman and Bob Smillie later described the organisation of the unit: 'We have a military leader, a political leader, four officers and a political committee, all elected by ourselves.' *The New Leader,* 25 June 1937, cited in Hall, *In Spain with Orwell*, p. 112.

41 Report by Harry P. Thomas, MML, SC/IBA/5/3/1/21.

42 Bob Edwards, 'Trenches on the Black Mountain,' *The New Leader*, 19 February 1937, p. 3.

43 Stafford Cottman, 'In the Spanish Trenches', *Orwell Remembered*, London: Penguin, 1984, p. 150.

44 Cottman, 'In the Spanish Trenches', p. 155.

45 Interview with Frank Frankford, IWMSA 9308, reel 2.

46 Cottman, 'In the Spanish Trenches', p. 151.

47 Cottman, 'In the Spanish Trenches', p. 150.

48 Cottman, 'In the Spanish Trenches', p. 152.

49 Interview with Frank Frankford, IWMSA 9308, reel 2.

50 Durgan, p. 147.

51 Cottman, cited in Hall, *Disciplina Camaradas*, p. 71.

52 Orwell, *Homage*, pp. 43–4.

53 Cottman, cited in Hall, *Disciplina Camaradas*, p. 81.

54 Interview with Frank Frankford, IWMSA 9308, reel 3; Thwaites, p. 55.

55 John Cornford, 'A letter from Aragon,' taken from *Collected Writings,* Manchester: Carcanet, 1986, p. 41.

56 Interview with Stafford Cottman, IWMSA 9278, reel 7.

57 Cottman, cited in Hall, *Disciplina Camaradas,* p. 47.

58 Interview with Stafford Cottman, IWMSA 9278, reel 3.

59 Bob Edwards, 'On the Aragon Front,' *The New Leader,* 5 March 1937, p. 2; Durgan p. 149.

60 An account of the action also appears in the ILP newspaper: 'Night Attack on the Aragon Front,' *The New Leader,* 30 April 1937, p. 3.

61 Cottman, cited in Hall, *Disciplina Camaradas,* p. 47.

62 Interview with Stafford Cottman, IWMSA 9278, reel 5.

63 *Ibid.*

64 Probably Hugh O'Donnell, who was working in a clandestine capacity for the PSUC, the Communist-dominated Socialist Party of Catalonia.

65 Angel Viñas, 'September 1936: Stalin's Decision to Support the Spanish Republic', in Jim Jump ed., *Looking Back at the Spanish Civil War*, London: Lawrence and Wishart, 2010, pp. 133, 149. Suspicion of the POUM actually existed in Spain before Russian involvement in the civil war. As the Communist dissident Franz Borkenau pointed out, 'It is difficult to say whether it [the POUM] was more hateful to the PSUC on account of its anti-Stalinism in Russian affairs or its extreme Leftist tendencies in Spanish questions.' Franz Borkenau, *The Spanish Cockpit*, London: Phoenix, 2000, p. 182.

66 Cottman, cited in Hall, *Disciplina Camaradas,* p. 94.

67 'Report on the position with regard to the ILP Group', 28 May 1937, MML SC/IBA/5/3/1/14.

68 Interview with Stafford Cottman, IWMSA 9278, reel 6 and Orwell, *Homage* p. 269.

69 Orwell, *Homage*, p. 295.

70 Having been arrested at the French border on 10 May 1937 for not possessing a military pass, Smillie was thrown into a Republican prison in Valencia, where he died on 12 June 1937. His death was clearly deeply mourned: 'It is an utter impossibility for us to express what we feel. His loss will cause the deepest grief and distress to every member of the Independent Labour Party.' Tribute to Bob Smillie by John McNair, *The New Leader*, 18 June 1937, p. 2. Although many suspected that Smillie was murdered by Russian agents, illness—albeit the result of official neglect—was almost certainly the cause of his death. An investigation by the ILP concluded

that, 'Bob Smillie's death was due to great carelessness on the part of the responsible authorities, which amounted to criminal negligence.' 'How Bob Smillie died' *The New Leader*, 11 March 1938, p. 7. For the most recent analysis of Smillie's death, see Buchanan, *Impact of the Spanish Civil War*, pp. 98-121.

71 McNair, *Spanish Diary*, p. 24.

72 Orwell, *Homage*, p. 263.

73 Orwell, *Homage*, p. 304.

74 Michael Shelden, *Orwell*, London: Minerva, 1992, p. 301.

75 George Orwell, 'Eye-witness in Barcelona', *Controversy*, August 1937, pp. 85–8.

76 John McNair, 'These children are being saved from Franco's bombers,' *The New Leader,* Friday 1 April 1938, p. 5. Cottman's visits continued until the colony was finally closed in June 1939. By this time all the children with living parents had returned to Spain. The remaining 15 or so were adopted by British families. See John McNair, 'A Great Task Accomplished,' *The New Leader*, Friday 2 June 1939, p. 6.

77 Interview with Stafford Cottman, IWMSA 9278, reel 4.

78 NA KV 5/112 and interview with Stafford Cottman, IWMSA 9278, reel 7.

79 For the ILP denials see, for example, Fenner Brockway, 'What I Saw in Spain,' *New Leader*, 16 July 1937, p.3: 'We met no one in Spain outside the Communist Party who believed that the POUM leaders have been acting as fascist agents, or that the POUM as an organisation has been directed to assist the fascists . . . the suppression of the POUM is the work of the Communist controlled police force, and that the Communist Party is almost exclusively responsible.'

80 David Keys, 'Obituary: Stafford Cottman.' *Independent*, 3 November 1999. Cottman also joined the ILP, seeing Attlee's Labour Party as tainted by their support for the British Government's policy of non-intervention in Spain (though he believed that both George Lansbury and Arthur Greenwood were sympathetic to the Spanish Republicans). Interview with Stafford Cottman, IWMSA 9278, reel 7.

81 George Orwell to Charles Doran, 2 August 1937, from *George Orwell: A Life in Letters* by George Orwell and Peter Davison, Penguin, 2011.

82 An alternative photograph, including European members of the International Bureau attending the summer school, appeared in *The New Leader*. 'Socialist Issues Discussed at the Summer School,' 13 August 1937, p. 3.

83 *Ibid.*

84 George Orwell, 'That Mysterious Cart,' *The New Leader*, 24 September 1937, p. 3.

85 Though there was clearly a sense of vindication at the rejection of the spurious charges of espionage, the article raged against the 15-year sentences imposed for rebelling against government authority, for which 'protest must be voiced immediately.' 'All Charges of Espionage and Desertion WITHDRAWN' and 'POUM Leaders Were Not Traitors,' *The New Leader*, 4 November 1938, p. 4 & p. 6.

86 This position was clearly laid out by the ILP's National Council during the Czech crisis of September 1938: 'Resist War! Would not be fought for Czechs but for Capitalist profits,' *The New Leader*, 30 September 1938, p. 1.

87 An article by John McGovern, the ILP's MP for Glasgow Shettleston, maintained that the Party 'would not support Capitalists even against dictators.' *The New Leader*, Friday 1 April 1938, p. 3.

88 Brockway argued that, 'I believe the ruling classes of all the Powers are responsible for the war. I believe the working classes are mere pawns in their hands. I believe the time will come when the worker will consent to be pawns no longer, and I hope the action I am taking now will do a little at least to hasten the coming of that time.' 'When Fenner Brockway Faced a Tribunal,' *The New Leader*, Friday 9 June 1939, p. 5.

89 RAF historical disclosures, 5829—Cottman, p. 1.

90 David Keys, 'Obituary: Stafford Cottman.' *Independent*, 3 November 1999.

91 RAF historical disclosures, 5829-Cottman, p. 2.

92 David Keys, 'Obituary: Stafford Cottman.' *Independent*, 3 November 1999.

93 *Ibid.*

94 RAF historical disclosures, 5829—Cottman, p. 1.

95 Interview with Stafford Cottman, IWMSA 9278, reel 7.

96 Eric Blair to Stafford Cottman, 25 April 1946. George Orwell, *Collected Essays, Volume 4, In Front of Your Nose, 1945-1950*, Sonia Orwell and Ian Angus eds., London: Secker and Warburg, 1968, pp. 148-9.

97 Available online at :https://www.youtube.com/watch?v=u9XA5OOoVA.

98 Cottman cited in Nick Lloyd, *Forgotten Places: Barcelona and the Spanish Civil War*, Barcelona: Privately published, 2015, p. 212.

99 Bateman, *op cit.*

100 Mike Eaude, 'The ILP and the Spanish Civil War', *Somerset Clarion*, August-September 1987.

101 Interview with Stafford Cottman, IWMSA 9278, reel 7.

102 Eaude, *op cit.*

103 Interview with Ken Loach, 3 February 2021.

104 David Keys, 'Obituary: Stafford Cottman.' *Independent*, 3 November 1999.

105 Email correspondence, Ken Loach to Alan Cottman, 23 May 2020 (courtesy of Ken Loach and Alan Cottman).

106 Bateman, Cottman, *op cit.*

107 Cottman cited in Hall, *In Spain with Orwell*, p. 188.

108 George Orwell, 'Looking Back on the Spanish Civil War', *New Road*, June 1943. Available online at: https://www.orwell foundation.com/the-orwell-foundation/orwell/essays-and-other-works/looking-back-on-the-spanish-war/.

109 Interview with Adrian Holme, 1 August 2021.

110 https://www.independentlabour.org.uk/2013/05/21/ilp120-stafford-cottman-%e2%80%93-%e2%80%98a-warm-and-generous-man%e2%80%99/ accessed on 25 February 2021.

111 Bateman, Cottman, *op cit.*

112 Hall, *Not Just Orwell*, p. 241.

113 https://elpais.com/espana/comunidad-valenciana/2021-05-25/ mue re-josep-almudever-brigadista-internacional-a-los-101-anos.html accessed on 25 May 2021. The story was picked up by media outlets around the world, including in the UK. See, for example, https://www.theguardian.com/world/2021/may/25/last-international-brigader-survivor-of-spanish-civil-war-dies-aged-101.

Notes to Chapter Seven

1 Interview with Dolores Long, June 2009, https://radical manchester/wordpress.com/2009/07/09/sam-wild-and-bessie-berry/ accessed 2 January 2023.

2 See NA KV 2/1030-1032 and John McIlroy & Alan Campbell, 'The 'core' leaders of the Communist Party of Great Britain, 1923–1928: their past, present and future,' *Labour History*, June 2021, p. 25.

3 NA KV 2/1030-1032. There was also, famously, a telecheck

placed on Temple Bar 2151, the telephone at the Communist Party's headquarters in King Street, Covent Garden. Much of the surveillance material reveals little about Kerrigan's covert activities, but reports in excruciating detail his daily comings and goings. They do, however, reveal the remarkable tenacity and patience shown by those responsible for keeping him under observation.

4 MI5 report September 1946. See NA KV 2/1031 p. 179a.

5 NA KV 2/1032. Kerrigan was well aware that he was a matter of interest for the British Security Services. Consequently he used the alias 'James' for his more sensitive Party work and took care never to discuss delicate matters over the telephone.

6 Peter had four brothers: Herbert, John, George and Thomas and a sister, Helen. PHM Manchester, CP/IND/MISC/7/3 & 'The Kerrigan Family,' 22 June 1948, NA KV 2/1031, p. 221G.

7 'Peter Kerrigan' in *World News and Views,* 23, 6 June 1942, p. 263 and interview with Peter Kerrigan, IWMSA 810, reel 1. The union was later amalgamated into the Amalgamated Engineers' Union.

8 Interview with Peter Kerrigan, IWMSA, 810, reel 1.

9 'Peter Kerrigan' in *World News and Views,* 23, 6 June 1942, p. 263 and interview with Peter Kerrigan in D. Corkhill, and S. Rawnsley eds. *The Road to Spain: Anti Fascists at War 1936-1939,* Fife: Borderline, 1981, p. 55.

10 PHM, Manchester, CP/IND/MISC/7/3.

11 'Peter Kerrigan—Biography' 2 July 1946, NA KV 2/1031 p. 191b.

12 'Peter Kerrigan' NA KV 2/1030 p. 4a

13 Interview with Rose Kerrigan, IWMSA 9903, reel 5.

14 NA KV 2/1030, 4 May 1932.

15 Unsigned memo, 3 March 1950, NA KV 2/1032 p. 259a.

16 Noreen Branson, *History of the Communist Party 1927-1941,* London: Lawrence and Wishart, 1985, pp. 9-10.

17 John McIlroy, Barry McLoughlin, Alan Campbell and John Halstead, 'Forging the faithful: the British at the International Lenin School,' *Labour History Review,* 68:1, April 2003, p. 113.

18 PHM, Manchester, CP/IND/MISC/7/3.

19 Assessment by Clemens Palme Dutt, NA KV 2/1030.

20 NA KV 2/1031.

21 Such was the extent of Special Branch surveillance that they were able to ascertain the serial numbers of the £10 notes sent to Kerrigan from the Communist Party headquarters in London's King St.

22 NA KV 2/1030, 13 February 1934.

23 Interview with Rose Kerrigan, IWMSA 796, reel 5.

24 City of Glasgow Police to MI5, 2 May 1935. NA KV 2/1030 p. 52a.

25 Interview with Rose Kerrigan, Manchester Studies Tape 197, Tameside Local Studies and Archives (TLSA).

26 City of Glasgow Police to MI5, 9 November 1935. NA KV 2/1030 p. 54.

27 Kerrigan later stated that, in fact, it was the youth vote which had made the difference, who had chosen the radical Communism of Gallagher over the more traditional Labour candidate. Peter Kerrigan in the *Daily Worker*, 5 February 1936, cited in Branson, p. 149.

28 Interview with Bob Cooney, IWMSA 804, reel 3.

29 NA KV 2/1030.

30 Interview with Alec Marcovich, 182, reel 2, side 1, TLSA.

31 *Ibid.*

32 For details of Marcovich's experiences in Spain see interview with Alec Marcovich, 182, TLSA and Hopkins, pp. 258-270.

33 Interview with Rose Kerrigan, 197, TLSA.

34 Interview with Peter Kerrigan, IWMSA, 810, reel 1.

35 NA KV 2/1030 November 1936.

36 Rose had been born in April 1932 and Sheila was born in January 1937. 'If I'd said no, I don't suppose he would have gone, but I didn't.' Interview with Rose Kerrigan, 197, TLSA.

37 Interview with Rose Kerrigan, 197, TLSA.

38 Interview with Peter Kerrigan in Corkhill and Rawnsley, p. 58. A Special Branch report from 21 December put the numbers rather lower: 'KERRIGAN left Dover for Dunkirk at 12.35am today with 65 poorly dressed young men, having a one-day excursion to Paris'. NA KV 2/1030, 20 December 1936.

39 RGASPI 545/2/262, pp. 107, 109.

40 Senior British commissars who had attended the Lenin School included George Aitken, Bob Cooney, George Coyle, Thomas Degnan, Harry Dobson, Peter Kerrigan, Will Paynter and Walter Tapsell. McIlroy et al, p. 113.

41 RGASPI 545/3/479, p. 22.

42 Interview with Thomas Glyndwr Evans, in M.J. Hynes, 'The British Battalion of the XVth International Brigade,' BA dissertation, Manchester, 1986, p. 58.

43 RGASPI 545/3/438, p. 52.

44 Interview with Peter Kerrigan, IWMSA, 810, reel 2.

45 Peter Kerrigan to Harry Pollitt, 30 December 1936 to 1

January 1937, MML SC/IBA/5/2/1937/5.

46 Interview with Peter Kerrigan, IWMSA, 810, reel 2.

47 Many volunteers who fought with No. 1 Company at Lopera believed that Delasalle had been made a scapegoat: 'He may have been a coward, he was certainly dandified and pretentious with an exaggerated idea of his military capacities, but it was manifestly absurd to maintain that he was in the pay of Franco.' Gurney, p. 82.

48 Letter from Peter Kerrigan to Harry Pollitt, 6 January 1937, MML SC/IBA/5/2/1937/5.

49 See Barry McLoughlin and Emmet O'Connor, *In Spanish Trenches,* Dublin: Dublin University Press, 2020, pp. 123-129.

50 Interview with Peter Kerrigan, 196 reel 1, side 1, TLSA.

51 Interview with Peter Kerrigan in Corkhill and Rawnsley, p. 59.

52 Letter from Peter Kerrigan to Harry Pollitt, 19 January 1937, MML SC/IBA/5/2/1937/6.

53 Letter from Peter Kerrigan to Harry Pollitt, 10 February 1937, MML SC/IBA/5/2/1937/17. See also interview with Peter Kerrigan, IWMSA, 810, reel 3.

54 Interview with Peter Kerrigan, 196 reel 1, side 1, TLSA.

55 *Ibid.*

56 Interview with Peter Kerrigan, IWMSA, 810, reel 3.

57 NA KV 2/1030 26 February 1937.

58 Interview with Rose Kerrigan, 197, TLSA.

59 Interview with Peter Kerrigan, 196 reel 1, side 1, TLSA.

60 Stephen Spender, *World Within World*, London: Hamish Hamilton, 1951, p. 213 & p. 222.

61 Account by Tony Hyndman in Toynbee, p. 127.

62 John Sutherland, *Stephen Spender: The Authorised Biography*, London: Viking, 2004, p. 224

63 NA KV 5/112.

64 Harry Pollitt to Robert 'Robin' Page Arnot, 24 March 1937, RGASPI 495/14/243 p. 85.

65 NA KV 2/1030, 31 May 1937. One of these was AC Williams, the Communist from Portsmouth, who had persuaded Alex Foote to volunteer. See Chapter Eight and Willy Maley, ed., *Our Fathers Fought Franco,* Edinburgh: Luath Press, 2023.

66 Kerrigan was observed leaving for Boulogne on 10 June 1938, using a weekend return ticket to Paris. NA KV 2/1030, p. 79a.

67 4 July 1938. MML SC/IND/PKE/1/7.

68 25 July 1938, MML SC/IND/PKE/1/14.

69 MML SC/IND/PKE/3/9.

70 Interview with Hugh Sloan in MacDougall, p. 227.

71 Interview with Peter Kerrigan, IWMSA, 810, reel 3 and MML SC/IND/PKE/3/9.

72 Peter Kerrigan, 'We Have Passed at Gandesa', 27 July 1938, MML SC/IND/PKE/1/16 & SC/IND/PKE/1/16

73 Peter Kerrigan, 'The British Battalion at Best', 8 August 1938. MML SC/IND/PKE/1/22.

74 MML SC/IBA/5/2/1938/17, p. 2.

75 16 September, MML SC/IND/PKE/1/47.

76 Letter from Peter Kerrigan to Harry Pollitt, 27 September 1938, MML SC/IBA/5/2/1938/27.

77 Kerrigan's younger brother Herbert, who had arrived in August and had been working as a chemist in the Pharmaceutical Department of the 15th International Brigade, returned home the following month. According to his file held in Moscow, Herbert Kerrigan 'was a good technician and worked with interest and enthusiasm' and was a 'good comrade'. See interview with Rose Kerrigan, 197, TLSA and RGASPI 545/6/158 pp. 95-8.

78 By 14 November, Kerrigan was back in Glasgow. Memorandum from Glasgow Police to MI5, 17 November 1938. NA KV 2/1030 p. 84a.

79 Interview with Rose Kerrigan, IWMSA 796, reel 1.

80 NA KV 2/1030.

81 For example, when the old Etonian, Olympic rower and Labour Councillor Lewis Clive was killed during the Ebro offensive, Kerrigan recommended repatriating the remaining three councillors in the battalion, a privilege certainly not extended to everyone in the unit. See letter from Peter Kerrigan to Harry Pollitt, 13 August 1938, MML SC/IBA/5/2/1938/22. Two Labour Councillors (and clandestine Communists) Jack Jones and Tom Murray, were both later safely repatriated. The third, Clem Broadbent 1938, was killed in September, probably by accidental friendly fire.

82 'Mentiroso, bebe mucho y no digno de confianza.' RGASPI 545/6/132 pp. 24-5.

83 RGASPI 545/6/99, p. 11.

84 Interview with Alec Marcovich, 182, reel 1, side 2, TLSA.

85 Bill Alexander, No to Franco: The Struggle Never Stopped, 1939–1975! London: Privately published, 1992, p. 19 and Tom Buchanan, 'Holding the Line: The Political Strategy of the International Brigade Association, 1939-1977,' Labour History Review, 66:3, Winter 2001, p. 296.

86 Interview with Peter Kerrigan, 196 reel 2, side 1, TLSA.

87 Branson, History of the Communist Party of Great Britain,

1927-1941, p. 273 and Kevin Morgan, *Harry Pollitt*, Manchester: Manchester University Press, 1993, p. 105.

88 Interview with Rose Kerrigan, IWMSA 9903, reel 6.

89 Interview with Rose Kerrigan, IWMSA 9903, reel 8.

90 PHM, Manchester, CP/IND/MISC/7/3 and interview with Rose Kerrigan, IWMSA 9903, reels 7 & 8.

91 *Volunteer for Liberty*, No. 14, Aug–Sept 1941, p. 16, 'The Kerrigan Family,' 22 June 1948, KV 2/1031, p. 221G and Interview with Rose Kerrigan, 197, TLSA.

92 Kevin Morgan, *Against Fascism and War: Ruptures and Continuities in British Communist Politics 1935-1941*, Manchester: Manchester University Press, 1989, p. 241 and Juliet Gardiner, *Wartime: Britain 1939-1945*, London: Headline, 2004, p. 295.

93 Letter from [unknown] to Deputy Assistant Commissioner, Special Branch, 30 March 1941. NA KV 2/1031/127a.

94 NA KV2/1596 and 2073. The Security Services were particularly worried about 'two CPGB political commissars in Spain, Bill Rust and Dave Springhall.' See Richard C. Thurlow, "A very clever capitalist class". British communism and state surveillance 1939-45, *Intelligence and National Security*, 12:2, 1997, p. 15.

95 The scientist 'as eminent as Professor Haldane' was not named. MI5 memorandum, 10 February 1940. NA KV 2/1030/98a.

96 Special Branch Report, 8 January 1941, NA KV 2/1031.

97 Special Branch report, 7 April 1941. KV 2/1031.

98 Letter [from MI5?] to Sir Frederick Laggett, Ministry of Labour, 2 April 1941. NA KV 2/1031/128a and NA KV 2/1031/131a.

99 'In these grave days of the present let us profit from Spain's experience. 'Root out every element that would impede the fullest co-operation of the British and Soviet peoples. Suffering Spain, first among nations to defy the Fascist murders, is with us today in the common struggle.' Peter Kerrigan, 'The Lessons of Spain,' *World News and Views*, 29, July 1941, p. 461.

100 Report of Communist meeting held the Co-Operative Building, Stockton-on-Tees, 12 October 1941. NA KV 2/1031.

101 'Trade Union Policy' Report by Peter Kerrigan, *Report of the 16th Congress of the Communist Party*, London, Communist Party, 1943, pp. 19-20.

102 Letter from Viscount Swinton, 2 October 1941, NA PREM 4/64/5B.

103 Report 9 July 1941, NA KV 2/1031.

104 Special Branch report, 20 July 1941, NA KV 2/1031.

105 Special Branch report, 23 November 1941, NA KV 2/1031.

106 Report by Motherwell Chief Constable, 17 March 1942. NA KV 2/1031.

107 NA KV 2/1031 p. 21.

108 In a letter from the Assistant Chief Constable, Glasgow to Sir Davie Petrie, he expressed surprise at Kerrigan's taking over the job of Industrial Organiser from JR Campbell, though went on to note that 'Glasgow and Clydeside generally have always received the greatest attention in the Communist Party and no doubt KERRIGAN, by reason of his previous association with this area, was an outstanding choice. 1 October 1942, NA KV 1031, p. 148a.

109 Brigadier Sir David Petrie to D Warnock, Asst Chief Constable Glasgow, 22 September 1942. NA KV 2/1031.

110 D. Warnock, Asst. Chief Constable of Glasgow to Sir David Petrie of MI5, 1 October 1942. NA KV 2/1031/148a.

111 NA KV 2/1031 PF 38389, p. 5. Pollitt had every reason to worry, for a few months later Doug Springhall was caught red-handed inveigling secret documents from a clerk in the Air Ministry. He was subsequently found guilty under the Official Secrets Act and sentenced to seven years' imprisonment.

112 PHM, Manchester, CP/IND/MISC/7/3.

113 NA KV 2/1031.

114 Special Branch report, 6 October 1941, NA KV 2/1031. For the Barrow strike see Branson, *History of the Communist Party, 1941-1951,* pp. 32-33.

115 At home there was a new addition to the family when his third daughter, Jean, was born on 3 February 1944.

116 NA KV 2/1031, 3 April 1944.

117 Report of the [United Nations] Sub-Committee on the Spanish Question, cited in K.W. Watkins, *Britain Divided: The Effect of the Spanish Civil War on British Political Opinion,* London: Nelson, 1963, pp. 197-201.

118 Kerrigan would try again in the Glasgow Gorbals by-election in September 1948. Though he was congratulated for his efforts by Isabel Brown, John Gollan and Harry Pollitt, Kerrigan finished last and Labour held the seat, albeit with a reduced majority. In three further elections during the 1950s Kerrigan finished last on each occasion, never scoring more than seven percent of the vote. NA KV 2/1032, p. 230.

119 Watkins, p. 205.

120 Watkins, p. 212.

121 Special Branch report, 20 September 1945. NA KV 2/1031, p. 166a. The IBA's efforts undoubtedly helped save the lives of the two Spaniards. See MML SC/IBA/3/2/22 and SC/IBA/3/1/1946 /57.

122 Special Branch report, 11 March 1946, NA KV 2/1031.

123 NA KV 2/1031/226w.

124 NA KV 2/1032/248b.

125 NA KV 2/1032, p. 254ab & 252a.

126 Morgan, *Harry Pollitt*, pp. 156-7.

127 Memo to Mr Oughton, B.1.A., 6 September 1950, NA KV 2/1032, p. 288.

128 Extract from telephone surveillance, 23 February 1951, NA KV 2/1032, p. 335.

129 Buchanan, 'Holding the Line', p. 304.

130 Jud Colman, *Memories of Spain, 1936–1938,* Manchester: Privately printed, date unknown, p. 17.

131 NA KV 2/1031/206a, 1 August 1947.

132 Report on Scottish District of the IBA, NA KV 5/54.

133 NA KV 2/1032, p. 8.

134 Letter from Sir Percy Sillitoe to A A Muir, Chief Constable County Constabulary, Durham, 3 January 1951. KV 2/1032, p. 318 and Report re. Hilda Forbes by Durham County Constabulary CID, 7 February 1951, NA KV 2/1032, p. 327z.

135 KV 2/1032, p. 328. Kerrigan visited Prague and Budapest in June 1948. Special Branch report, 20 June 1948, KV 2/1031, p. 222.

136 Letter from M. McCulloch, Chief Constable of City of Glasgow police, to Director General of MI5 Sir Percy Sillitoe, 19 January 1951. NA KV 2/1032.

137 'Ever since the party came into existence, the workplace had been regarded as the most important area of activity.' Branson, *History of the Communist Party of Great Britain, 1927-1941*, p. 26.

138 Francis Beckett, p. 152.

139 Andy Beckett, 'The most powerful man in 70s Britain', *The Guardian*, 23 April 2009.

140 A Special Branch Report of the annual conference of the IBA in London in July 1947 remarked on Kerrigan 'playing his usual role of policeman for the Party.' It recounted how: 'On one occasion when JACOBS from the London Trades Council was saying the wrong thing, KERRIGAN rose from his seat, walked across the hall to him and put him in his place.' Special Branch report, 1 August 1947, NA KV 2/1031, p. 205a.

141 During the election of the Executive Committee at the Nineteenth National Congress of the CPGB in London, Party members present were given lists of recommended and non-recommended candidates. Delegates were assured by Kerrigan that 'they could vote for whomever they pleased', though his assurances were rather undermined when he went on to state that as 'the qualifications of each individual had been thoroughly considered . . . all good comrades ought to vote for the "recommended" candidates'. Kerrigan got his own way for no recommended candidate received less than 500 votes, while no non-recognised candidate polled more than 90. Special Branch report, 21 May 1947, NA KV 2/1031/184d.

142 Beckett, pp. 149-50.

143 Roger Seifert and Tom Sibley, *Revolutionary Communist at Work: A Political Biography of Bert Ramelson,* London: Lawrence and Wishart, 2012, p. 72.

144 Sam Russell, 'Great-hearted Kerrigan, the workers' leader into battle', *Morning Star*, 17 December 1977.

145 For example, Interview with Peter Kerrigan, IWMSA, 810, reel 2.

146 Interview with Peter Kerrigan, IWMSA, 810, reel 4.

147 Interview with Peter Kerrigan, TLSA, 196, reel 3.

148 Interview with Peter Kerrigan, IWMSA, 810, reel 6.

149 Interview with Peter Kerrigan, TLSA, 196, reel 3.

150 Sam Russell, *op cit.*

151 Interview with Sam Russell, IWMSA 9484 reel 5.

152 See, for example, Walter Gregory, *The Shallow Grave,* London: Victor Gollancz, 1986, p. 29 and interview with David Anderson in MacDougall, p. 89.

153 Sir David Petrie to D Warnock, Assistant Chief Constable of Glasgow, 22 September 1942. NA KV 2/1031, p. 147a.

154 https://grahamstevenson.me.uk/2008/09/19/peter-kerrigan/ accessed on 13 September 2022.

155 Finlay Hart cited in https://graham stevenson. me.uk/2008 /09/19/peter-kerrigan/ accessed on 13 September 2022.

156 Gurney, p. 63.

157 Sean Matgamna: Finding my way to Trotskyism, part 2: from 'communism' to 'orthodox Trotskyism', Workers Liberty. Online at https://www.workersliberty.org/story/2009/12/18/sean-matgamna-finding-my-way-trotskyism-part-2-communism-orthodox-trotskyism, accessed on 13 September 2022.

158 Interview with Sam Russell, IWMSA 9484 reel 5 and interview with Rose Kerrigan, IWMSA 9903, reel 5.

159 See, for example, an article by Kerrigan in the Communist *World News and Views* that enthusiastically celebrated the Soviet leader's birthday: 'The period of the joyful celebration of Joseph Stalin's 70th birthday is an appropriate time for Communists to strive to understand something of the tremendous contribution he has made to human progress in building the Communist Party of the Soviet Union.' *World News and Views,* 29 October 1949.

160 Interview with Peter Kerrigan, IWMSA, 810, reel 5.

161 Thurlow, p. 19.

162 Ironically, some of the reports of Kerrigan's comings and goings, including overseas trips, ended up on the desk of Kim Philby. See, for example, confidential memo of 5 February 1946, NA KV 2/1031.

163 'The Kerrigan Family,' 22 June 1948, NA KV 2/1031, p. 221G.

164 Unsigned memo, 3 March 1950, NA KV 2/1032 p. 259a.

165 Interview with Rose Kerrigan, IWMSA 9903, reel 8 and NA KV 2/1032.

166 Kerrigan to Kearney, 15 December 1949, KV 2/1032, p. 253d.

Notes to Chapter Eight

1 Report 23 February, 1945, NA KV 2/1611.

2 Alex Foote, *Handbook for Spies*, Landisville: Coachwhip, 2011, pp. 58-9.

3 NA KV 2/1611, p. 49a.

4 'S's interview with F – MONDAY MORNING', NA KV 2/1611 p. 70.

5 NA KV 2/1611.

6 Maley, pp. 114-148.

7 NA KV 2/1611.

8 NA KV 2/1611, p. 76a. PF/66965 and 'Royal Air Force Certificate of the Service and Discharge of FOOTE Alexander Allan', NA KV 2/1613.

9 Foote, p. 194.

10 NA KV 2/1611.

11 NA KV 5/122 and Special Branch Report of 23 December 1936, NA KV 2/1611.

12 NA KV 2/1612.

13 RGASPI 545/6/135 p. 8 and NA KV 2/1612, p. 95a.

14 RGASPI 545/6/135 p. 7 and NA KV 2/11611 pp. 48a & 59a.

15 Foote, pp. 8-9.

16 Foote, p. 20.

17 Foote, p. 14.

18 Report 3 July 1947, NA KV 2/1611.

19 NA KV 2/1611.

20 Like many Soviet agents, she used a number of aliases and codenames and later published her autobiography under a *nom de plume*: Ruth Werner, *Sonya's Report*, London: Chattus and Windus, 1991 (it was first published in German in 1977 as *Sonyas Rapport*). For the most recent account of her life see Ben Macintyre's *Agent Sonya*, London: Viking, 2020.

21 Werner, p. 193.

22 Werner, p. 194.

23 Foote, p. 27.

24 The famous Munich restaurant, now called the Osteria Italiana, exists to this day.

25 Peter Kerrigan, the senior British commissar at the International Brigades headquarters at Albacete, described Beurton's politics as 'undeveloped'. RGASPI 545/6/105 p. 138.

26 Foote, p. 33. Foote's version told to his MI5 interrogators in 1947, was rather different, suggesting that he and Beurton only went to the restaurant to spy on Hitler. It was Sonya who suggested an assassination attempt, but Foote and Beurton wouldn't go along with it. 'S's Second Interview with F. SUNDAY MORNING', NA KV 2/1611, p.63a.

27 Sandor Radó, *Codename Dora*, London: Abelard, 1977, p. 45.

28 'Len agreed to the "marriage". I assured him that he could trust me to divorce him again as soon as he required. I did not grasp why he retorted with such uncustomary belligerence that he understood the meaning of a paper marriage perfectly well without further explanations from me.' Werner, pp. 209-221. The pair were married on 23 February 1940. NA KV 6/41.

29 'Alexander Allan FOOTE', NA KV 2/1613.

30 Radó, pp. 45-6.

31 Radó, p. 46.

32 'Interim Notes on Foote's Information about RIS in Switzerland', NA KV 2/1612.

33 Foote, p. 87.

34 Interview with Mme Colette Nuraille in the *Gazette de Lausanne*, 2 March 1949, cited in David J Dallin, *Soviet Espionage*, Newhaven: Yale University Press, 1955, p. 200.

35 Foote, p. 53.

36 V E Tarrant, *The Red Orchestra: The Soviet Spy Network*

Inside Nazi Europe. London: Arms and Armour, 1995, pp. 156-7.
37 NA KV 2/1612 and Radó, p. 132.
38 Foote, p. 144.
39 NA KV 2/1612 and Radó, p. 130.
40 Tarrant, p. 156.
41 NA KV 2/1612, Foote, pp. 72-3 and Radó, p. 86.
42 Foote (p. 94) suggested that information sometimes arrived in 24 hours, but this is likely to be an exaggeration.
43 Foote, p. 96.
44 However, Mark Tittenhofer argued that 'Lucy' did not actually start supplying Red Three with intelligence until the later summer of 1942. See Mark A Tittenhofer, 'The Rote Drei: Getting Behind the "Lucy" Myth', *Studies in Intelligence* 13:3, Summer 1969 pp. 51-90.
45 NA KV 2/1619.
46 Radó, p. 63.
47 Radó, p. 68.
48 'Alexander Allan FOOTE. Notes on Second Interview by 309 F.S.S.' NA KV 2/1611 p. 51a.
49 Foote, p. 106.
50 NA KV 2/1404.
51 Radó refers to her as ROSA.
52 WF Licke, *Agenten funken nach Moskau*, p. 21 cited in Radó, p. 148.
53 NA KV 2/1625 and Radó, p. 119.
54 Foote, p. 81 and Tarrant, pp. 174-5.
55 For a discussion of the relative importance of the 'Lucy' intelligence on the battle of Kursk, see Timothy P Mulligan, 'Spies, Ciphers and 'Zitadelle': Intelligence and the Battle of Kursk, 1943', *Journal of Contemporary History,* 22. 1987, pp. 235-260.
56 NA KV 2/1612.
57 Radó, p. 216.
58 Radó, pp. 254 & 263.
59 'Transmitters', NA KV 2/1612/784 p.4.
60 Report by Alexander Allan Foote, 'JIM', 1945, cited in Radó, p. 274.
61 Foote, p. 144.
62 NA KV 2/1619 and Tarrant, pp. 187-8.
63 Foote, p. 141.
64 'The re-establishment of communication in Paris', NA KV 2/1612.
65 According to Arthur Koestler, who knew them both, Foote

bore a great dislike for Radó. Arthur Koestler, *The Invisible Writing*, London: Collins, 1954, p. 305.

66 NA KV 2/1611 & 1612.

67 Tarrant, p. 198.

68 Koestler, p. 309.

69 See Valery Kochik and Vyacheslav Lurie, *GRU: Dela i Lydi*, Moscow: OLMA Media Group, 2002, pp. 452-3. I am grateful to Boris Volodarsky for identifying this reference.

70 'Outline of period in Moscow', NA KV 2/1612.

71 Foote, pp.172-3.

72 Foote, p. 176.

73 Foote, pp. 177-8.

74 Foote, p. 180.

75 Koestler, p. 307; Report 3 July 1947, NA KV 2/1611.

76 NA KV 2/1612.

77 Report 8 July 1947, NA KV 2/1611.

78 NA KV 2/1611.

79 Paine was assisted by Robert Hemblys-Scales (who would later be a British adviser to the Australian Government on the creation of their Security Intelligence Organisation), who acted as Administrative Officer in charge. NA KV 2/1611-1612 and Christopher Andrew, *The Defence of the Realm*, London, Allen Lane, 2009, p. 370.

80 NA KV 2/1613.

81 'Alexander Allan FOOTE. Notes on Second Interview by 309 F.S.S.' NA KV 2/1611 p. 51a.

82 'Foote believes that in every country there is a Comintern agent whose function is liaison with the resident Red Army agent; in England he believes SPRINGHALL held the post.' Joan Paine to the Deputy Commander, Special Branch, 8 July 1947. NA KV 2/1611, p. 48a and NA KV 2/1612.

83 'Conspirative Technique', NA KV 2/1612, pp. 4-5 and NA KV 2/1615.

84 See, for example, letter from J.A. Cimperman of the American Embassy in London to Arthur S. Martin, Leaconsfield House, Curzon St. 29 March 1950. NA KV 2/1616.

85 NA KV 2/1616 p. 316a.

86 R.T. Reed to G.T.D. Patterson, British Embassy, Washington D.C. 28 April 1942. NA KV 2/1615 p. 370a.

87 'Alexander Allan FOOTE', NA KV 2/1613.

88 P. Frawley, S54, 'Interrogation of Foote', 25 August 1947. NA KV 2/1612, p. 112a.

89 NA KV/ 2/1614.

90 NA KV/ 2/1614 and Tarrant, p. 198.

91 RV Hemblys Scales, 8 September 1947. NA KV 2/1612.

92 'Foote's Book', NA KV 2/1612.

93 NA KV 2/1616.

94 Haldane knew Foote well and clearly admired him, describing him as 'a hard-headed matter-of-fact North Countryman in his middle forties; with an odd steak of restless romanticism in his veins.' Haldane, *Truth Will Out,* p. 288.

95 Sir Percy Sillitoe to R Thistlethwaite, British Embassy, Washington D.C., 13 April 1949. NA KV 2/1616 p. 283a.

96 'S's interview with F – MONDAY MORNING', NA KV 2/1611 p. 70.

97 Malcolm Muggeridge, 'The Lucy Mystery', *The Observer Review*, London, 8 January 1967.

98 Radó, p. 295.

99 Werner, p. 229.

100 Radó, p. 295.

101 Werner. p. 230.

102 Werner, p. 229.

103 Anthony Read and David Fisher, *Operation Lucy*, Hodder and Staunton, 1980.

104 Read and Fisher, *Operation Lucy*, p. 21.

105 Anthony Read and David Fisher, *Colonel Z: The Life and Times of a Master of Spies*. London: Hodder and Staunton, 1984. See also Keith Jeffery, *The Secret History of MI6*, New York: The Penguin Press, 2010, pp. 314 & 343.

106 F H Hinsley, *British Intelligence in the Second World War*, vol. 2, p. 60, cited in Tarrant, p. 170.

107 Tarrant, p. 169.

108 Radó, p. 133.

109 https://www.cia.gov/library/center-for-the-study-of-intelligence/kent-csi/vol13no3/html/v13i3a05p_0001.htm Accessed on 8 April 2020.

110 Radó, p. 144.

111 For Foote (Jim) see NA KV 2/1611-1616; Margarite Bolli (Rosy) NA KV 2/1404; Schneider (Taylor) KV 2/1406; Rachel Dübendorfer (Sissy) NA KV 2/1620; Rössler (Lucy) KV 2/1627.

112 NA KV 2/1613.

113 Dallin, pp. 202-3.

114 'S First Interview with 'F' – Saturday', NA KV 2/1611 p. 61a.

115 'S's interview with F – MONDAY MORNING', NA KV 2/1611 p. 70.

116 Werner, p. 229.

117 'S's interview with F – MONDAY MORNING', NA KV 2/1611 p. 70.

118 *Ibid.*

119 Max Hastings, *The Secret War*, London: William Collins, 2015, p. 542.

Notes to Chapter Nine

1 This chapter is an extended version of a talk given at the Pallant House Gallery, Chichester, on 14 February 2015 to mark the opening of the exhibition, 'Conscience and Conflict: British Artists and the Spanish Civil War.'

2 'Portrait of a Worker' (1930), 'Selling the *Daily Worker* outside Projectile Engineering Works' (1937), 'Blitz: Plane Flying, 'Bombed Women and Searchlights' and 'Still Life' (all from 1940).

3 Lionel Hugh Branson, *A Lifetime of Deception: Reminiscences of a Magician*, 1953. An important member of the magic circle, Lionel Branson wrote several books on magic under the pen name of Elbiquet. See Lee Siegel, *Not of Magic: Wonders and Deceptions in India*, University Of Chicago Press, 1991, p. 201.

4 http://www.thisiskent.co.uk/Councillors-grilled-ban-movie/story-18491803-detail/story.html#axzz2sZRWnzdR accessed on 7 Sept 2014.

5 Conversation with Rosa Branson, 28 July 2014.

6 I am extremely grateful to Gina Worboys, Assistant Director of the Old Bedfordians Club, for providing details of Clive Branson's time at Bedford.

7 Quote taken from Harry Pollitt's introduction to Clive Branson, *British Soldier in India, The Letters of Clive Branson*, London: The Communist Party, 1944, p. 7.

8 Interview with Noreen Branson, IWMSA 9212, reel 1.

9 Rosa followed in her father's footsteps, studying art at Camberwell and the Slade and has received an MBE for her work with numerous charitable organisations.

10 Rosa Branson papers. In addition to its collection of books, pamphlets and newspapers connected with Marxism, the MML holds the archives of the International Brigade Association and is the head office of the International Brigade Memorial Trust.

11 Communist Party membership in 1930: 2555; 1931: 6279;

1932: 9000. Branson, *History of the Communist Party 1927-1941*, p. 188.

12 Interview with Noreen Branson, IWMSA 9212, reel 1.

13 *Ibid.*

14 He left London on the Russian Ship SMOLNY on 13 July 1935, remaining in the Soviet Union for a month. Nigel West, *Mask*, London: Routledge, 2005, p. 114.

15 Mike Squires, *the Aid to Spain Movement in Battersea, 1936-1939*, London: Elmfield Publications, 1994, pp. 3-4.

16 Herbert J Sines, a veteran of the First World War and an experienced engineer, left for Spain in December 1936. Having been wounded at the Battle of Jarama on 15 February 1937, he was invalided home in July, but returned on 29 March 1938. After fighting on the Battle of the Ebro, he was repatriated on 19 October 1938. David (Haden) Guest joined No 2 Company of the British Battalion in May 1938. He was killed on Hill 481 at Gandesa, on 26 July 1938. Tom Oldershaw arrived in Spain on 1 September 1937. He was wounded in the retreat from Caspe in the spring of 1938 and disappeared on 16 March after being left in a doorway. He was probably captured and executed. RGASPI 545/6/200, pp. 71-8, 545/6/144, pp. 17-23 and 545/6/181 p. 28. Branson recommended another Battersea Communist, Alex Watts, for Spain. However, Watts deserted and ended up being incarcerated in the Republican prison at Castelldefels, 545/6/212 p. 96.

17 Clive Branson, 'December 1936, Spain,' in Jim Jump ed., *Poems from Spain*, London: Lawrence and Wishart, 2006, p. 31.

18 Squires, pp. 8-9.

19 Interview with Noreen Branson, IWMSA 9212, reel 2.

20 Clive also returned to his painting; his 'Selling the Daily Worker outside Projectile Engineering Works', was completed during 1937, in between selling the paper himself and speaking on behalf of the Spanish Republic.

21 The Security Services were clearly on to Branson's covert activities. MI5's record card for a twenty-one-year-old YCL member from Battersea, who volunteered in December 1937, reads, 'Clive Branson, Communist, said to be responsible for the departure of Jack Tompkins to Spain.' NA KV 5/131/C.C.220,792.

22 Interview with Noreen Branson, IWMSA 9212, reel 3.

23 Conversation with Rosa Branson, 6 February, 2015.

24 Interview with Noreen Branson, IWMSA 9212, reel 3.

25 Rust, p. 104.

26 Interview with Arthur Nicoll, IWMSA 817, reel 2.
27 Interview with Frank McCusker in MacDougall, p. 42.
28 Interview with Garry McCartney in MacDougall, p. 243.
29 Gregory, p. 25.
30 RGASPI 545/6/91.
31 RGASPI 545/2/303. British volunteers were usually allocated an ID number: Branson was number 1572.
32 Interview with George Drever, in MacDougall, p. 280.
33 Edwin Greening, *From Aberdare to Albacete*, Pontypool: Warren and Pell, 2006, p. 71.
34 Cooney, p. 60.
35 Rust, p. 148.
36 Bob Cooney, 'Report by Battalion Commissar on the action commencing at Calaceite, 31.3.38,' RGASPI 545/3/497, p. 17.
37 Report by George Fletcher, 5 May 1938, RGASPI 545/3/497 p. 30.
38 Cooney, p. 66.
39 Report by George Fletcher, 5 May 1938, RGASPI 545/3/497 p.33.
40 Letter from Will Paynter to Harry Pollitt, 8 April 1938, MML SC/IBA/5/2/1938/4.
41 Anon., *They Fought in Franco's Jails,* London: CPGB, 1939 pp. 3-4.
42 Cyril Kent, 'I Was in a Franco Prison', *Challenge,* 5 January 1939, pp. 10-11.
43 Interview with Noreen Branson, IWMSA 9212, reel 3.
44 Interview with James Maley, IWMSA 11947, reel 2.
45 Cyril Kent, 'I Was in a Franco Prison', *Challenge* 5 January 1939 pp. 10-11; Alexander, *British Volunteers for Liberty*, p. 188.
46 Clive Branson, 'To the German Anti-Fascists in San Pedro,' from Jon Clark, Margot Heinemann, David Margolies and Carole Snee eds., *Culture and Crisis in Britain in the Thirties*, London: Lawrence and Wishart, 1979, p. 127.
47 Carl Geiser, *Prisoner of the Good Fight*, Connecticut: Lawrence Hill, 1986, pp. 102-103.
48 Interview with Tony Gilbert, IWMSA 9157, reel 7.
49 John Anthony Myers, 'Franco's Prisoner', *West London Observer*, 24 February 1939, p. 5.
50 Conversation with Rosa Branson, 28 July 2014.
51 Interview with Morien Morgan, IWMSA 9856, reel 3; Geiser, p. 128.
52 Noreen Branson papers, Bishopsgate Institute, p. 25.
53 Noreen states that Branson was identified from his passport.

This seems unlikely, given that passports were usually confiscated when men joined the International Brigade, supposedly to protect them. A number of passports ended up in the Soviet Union, where they were used for espionage.

54 Interview with Tony Gilbert, IWMSA 9157, reel 8 and Noreen Branson papers, p. 25.

55 Many years later Noreen bequeathed the sketches to the International Brigade Archive in the Marx Memorial Library. See MML SC/VOL/CBR/2.

56 Clive Branson, 'In the Camp,' *Culture and Crisis,* p. 128.

57 Noreen Branson papers, letter 28, p. 8.

58 Quote from Harry Pollitt's introduction to *British Soldier in India*, p. 9.

59 Interview with David Lomon, 16 February 2011.

60 Interview with Tony Gilbert, IWMSA 9157, reel 5.

61 Geiser, p. 174.

62 MML SC/IBA/1/8/3/32.

63 Interview with Tony Gilbert, IWMSA 9157, reel 8.

64 List of prisoners returning from Palencia with Branson included Tony Gilbert, David Lomon and Alfred Sherman. MML SC/IBA/1/8/3/16.

65 A brief note in Branson's MI5 file remarked only: '38 Returned.' NA KV 5/112 p. 18.

66 The brief period between Spain and the Second World War allowed the young Rosa time to establish a very close relationship with her father. She later remembered him as a man with a large personality and an even bigger laugh. During Christmas 1938, Clive caused much family amusement by allowing their pet parrot to inspect his teeth by placing the bird's head in his mouth. Conversation with Rosa Branson, 27 February 2014.

67 MML SC/IBA/5/3.

68 Branson papers, p. 28.

69 Helen Graham, *The Spanish Civil War*, Oxford: Oxford University Press, 2005, pp. 111–13.

70 Branson papers, p. 26.

71 Interview with Noreen Branson, IWMSA 9212, reel 3.

72 NA FO 371/2415-W973/5/41, Vansittart to Halifax, 16th January 1939, cited in Edwards, p. 212.

73 Branson papers, p. 27.

74 Interview with Noreen Branson, IWMSA 9212, reel 2.

75 Report from *South London Press*, cutting held in Noreen Branson papers.

76 Founded in 1933, the AIA was a left-wing organisation that espoused 'Unity of Artists for Peace, Democracy and Cultural Development.'

77 Letter from Clive to Noreen Branson, 11 January 1941.

78 Branson papers, pp. 31-2.

79 A number of veterans were decorated during the Second World War and the former battalion commander Bill Alexander was awarded the Sword of Honour for finishing top of his intake at Sandhurst.

80 Branson papers, p. 32.

81 Letter from Clive to Noreen Branson, 25 July 1943 from Clive Branson, *British Soldier in India*, p. 87.

82 Letter from Clive to Noreen Branson, 19 September 1942 from Branson, p. 33.

83 Letter from Clive to Noreen Branson from Poona, undated (probably June 1942).

84 Letter from Clive to Noreen Branson, 13 March 1941.

85 Letter from Clive to Noreen Branson, 22 May 1941.

86 Branson, p. 11.

87 Branson, p. 9.

88 Branson, p. 11.

89 Letter dated September 1942, Branson, p. 27.

90 Branson, p. 13.

91 Noreen Branson papers, letter 30, p. 2.

92 Letter from Clive Branson to Noreen, 13 March 1942. From Rosa Branson's personal collection.

93 Branson, p. 18.

94 Noreen Branson papers, letter 31, pp. 1-2.

95 From Harry Pollitt's introduction to Branson, p. 9.

96 Letter from Clive to Noreen Branson, 17 May 1943 from Branson, pp. 65 & 68.

97 For a good account of Branson's period of service in Arakan, see Edith Mirante, 'A Death in Arakan,' *Mekong Review*, March 2023. Online at https://mekongreview.com/a-death-in-arakan-part-2-tanks-and-poets/.

98 Letter from Clive to Noreen Branson, 2 December 1943 from Branson, p. 115.

99 Letter from Clive to Noreen Branson, 26 January 1944 from Branson, pp. 122-3.

100 Interview with Tony Gilbert, IWMSA 9157, reel 5.

101 John Leyin, *Tell Them of Us*, Standford-le-Hope: Lejins, 2000, p. 183 and Tony Grounds, *Some Letters from Burma*, Tunbridge Wells: Parapress, 1994, p. 151.

102 Noreen Branson papers.

103 Letter from Major LV Johnstone, Squadron Leader, 25th Dragoons, March 5th 1944.

104 Conversation with Rosa Branson, 27 February 2014.

105 Interview with Tony Gilbert, IWMSA 9157, reel 5.

106 Presumably wary that his details might be intercepted by Special Branch, the writer added, 'Don't send a receipt as address is fictitious.'

107 NA KV 5/118 40176.

108 *Hampshire Chronicle*, 28 October 1944.

Notes to Chapter Ten

1 Paul Preston, 'Two doctors and one cause: Len Crome and Reginald Saxton in the International Brigades,' *International Journal of Iberian Studies*, 19:1, 2006, p. 5.

2 See, for example, Nick Coni, *Medicine and War*, New York: Routledge, 2008, Linda Palfreeman, *¡Salud!*, Eastbourne: Sussex, 2012 and Sebastian Browne, *Medicine and Conflict*, Oxford: Routledge, 2019.

3 RGASPI 545/6/146, p. 64.

4 I am very grateful to the staff of Marlborough College for providing details of Tudor Hart's record.

5 RGASPI 545/6/146, p. 64 and extract from FO file P/87592/1 re. A.E. Tudor Hart, NA KV 2/1603/99a.

6 NA KV 2/1603.

7 I am very grateful to the archivists at King's College Cambridge for this information.

8 RGASPI 545/6/146, p. 64.

9 Palfreeman, p. 186.

10 Sergeant W. Delaney of Special Branch to MI5, 21 February 1934, NA KV 2/1603.

11 RGASPI 545/6/146, p. 84

12 Special Branch report, 2 August 1929, NA KV 2/1603. Julian later followed his parents into medicine, working as a GP in West Glamorgan, Wales. President of the Socialist Health Association, he published a number of books, including a passionate defence of the egalitarian ethos of the NHS: *A New Kind of Doctor: the general practitioner's part in the health of the community*, London: Merlin, 1988.

13 Interview with Julian Tudor Hart in 'Tracking Edith', directed

by Peter Stephan Jungk, Peartree Entertainment, 2016.

14 Special Branch to SIS, 3 January 1931, NA KV 2/1603 p. 29b and Special Branch report, 21 February 1934, NA KV 2/1012/16a.

15 Interview with Alexander Tudor Hart, IWMSA 13771, reel 1 and RGASPI 545/6/146 pp. 65-6.

16 Undated extract [probably 1929], NA KV 2/1603.

17 Suschitzky was described as '5'6", slim build, pale complexion, blue grey eyes and blond, bobbed hair.' [Special Branch?] report 31 October, 1930, NA KV 2/1012 p. 2a.

18 Special Branch to MI5, 23 February 1934. NA KV 2/1012 p. 16a and report of 16 August 1935, NA KV 2/1012/21a.

19 Special Branch report, 16 August 1935. KV 2/1012, p. 21a & Foreign Office memo of 24 February 1947, KV 2/1014 p. 112a.

20 NA KV 2/1604.

21 'Edith' to Dr A E T Hart, 14 April 1931, NA KV 2/1603.

22 Letter from Edit Sushitzky to Alexander Tudor Hart, 22 June 1931, NA KV 2/1603.

23 Duncan Forbes, Anton Holzer and Roberta McGrath, *Edith Tudor Hart: Im Schatten der Diktaturen*, Berlin: Hatje Cantz Verlag, 2013, pp. 11-18. I am grateful to Boris Volodarsky for this information.

24 Special Branch report, 21 February 1934, NA KV 2/1603

25 Duncan Forbes, 'Edith Tudor-Hart in London', *In the Shadow of Tyranny*, Hatje Cantz Verlag, 2013, p. 65. Special Branch were also interested in Tudor Hart's younger sister, Beatrix, who was a pioneering educationalist. She had been taken to court in 1933 to prevent her from running a nursery school in Hampstead's select Fitzjohn's Avenue, allegedly due to inconvenient 'noise on the part of the pupils'. Special Branch believed her to be 'a known sympathiser with the Soviet Union,' who was using the premises for 'gatherings of extremists' and this may have played a part in the action. She was also recorded as giving generous subscriptions to the King Alfred School in Hampstead, whose head teacher was a member of the World league for Sexual reform and the Federation of Progressive Societies and Individuals. Beatrix later set up her own school for children aged 4-11 in Muswell Hill, in north London. 'It was a co-operative non-profit-making co-educational school owned and democratically controlled by a society of parents, teachers and educationalists.' For Beatrix Tudor Hart see Deborah Gorham, 'Dora and Bertrand Russell and Beacon Hill School', *Russell: the Journal of Bertrand Russell Studies*, 25, 2005.

26 Special Branch report, 21 February 1934, NA KV 2/1603.

27 Anton Holzer, 'Activist with a Camera: Edith Suschitzky in the Context of the Viennese Photo Scene around 1930', in *Edith Tudor-Hart: In the Shadow of Tyranny*, p. 44.

28 Edith Tudor Hart, *Housewife Magazine*, June 1945, cited in https://spartacus-educational.com/Edith_Tudor_Hart.htm accessed 17 February 2021.

29 Alex Tudor Hart cited in Hynes, p. 31.

30 Special Branch report, 20 April 1935, NA KV 2/1603.

31 *Daily Mail*, 7 February 1936 cited in NA KV 2/1603/126a.

32 Drawing from a wide political background, SMAC was characterised by one medical volunteer as 'a concerned group of kindly British progressives.' Kenneth Sinclair-Loutit, *Very Little Luggage*, Privately published, 2021, p. 83.

33 Interview with Alexander Tudor Hart, IWMSA 13771, reel 1.

34 Special Branch reports, 14 & 17 August 1936, NA KV 2/1603 & Loutit, p. 48.

35 NA KV 5/112, p. 6 and Special Branch report, 28 December 1936, KV 2/1603.

36 Interview with Alexander Tudor Hart, IWMSA 13771, reel 1.

37 RGASPI 545/6/146 p. 65.

38 Archie Cochrane described Loutit as 'a likeable medical student and an obvious secret party member,' but qualified his assessment by arguing that 'I did not think he would be a good leader. He had a weak streak.' Cochrane, p. 22.

39 Interview with Reginald Saxton, IWMSA 8735, reel 3; Fyrth, p. 63 and Palfreeman, p. 70. While Nicholas Coni stated that Sinclair Loutit 'accepted it philosophically', in an interview in the Imperial War Museum, Tudor Hart alluded to friction between the two, albeit mitigated by a certain amount of professional respect: 'Kenneth Sinclair-Loutit is the man. He will give you his version, which will probably be violently anti-Hart, as you can imagine, but it's not likely to be invented.' Fyrth, advised Tudor Hart, should 'make allowances for natural indignation.' Coni, p. 124 and interview with Alexander Tudor Hart, IWMSA 13771, reel 2.

40 K.S. Loutit and Aileen Palmer, 'Survey of a year's work with the British Medical Unit in Spain.' RGASPI 545/6/88 p. 35.

41 Aileen Palmer's diary, cited in Fyrth, p. 65.

42 Fyrth, p. 65.

43 Cochrane, p. 32.

44 *Ibid.*

45 Cited in Fyrth, p. 145. While he was in Spain Tudor Hart wrote a series of articles for *Ayuda Médica Internacional*, the

journal of the medical services in Spain, arguing for full and detailed investigations to establish best practice.

46 Dr Hardt (Alexander Tudor Hart), 'The treatment of fractures at front-hospitals,' undated, courtesy of the IBMT.

47 Palfreeman, pp. 187-8.

48 Esther Silverstein, cited in Jim Fyrth and Sally Alexander, p. 150 and Sinclair-Loutit cited in Sylvia Martin, *Ink in her Veins: the troubled life of Aileen Palmer*, Crawley: UWA Press, 2016, p. 140.

49 Interview with Reginald Saxton, IWMSA 8735, reel 4.

50 Letter from Reg Saxton to Alex Tudor Hart, 28 September 1988. Courtesy of the IBMT.

51 Interview with Reginald Saxton, IWMSA 8735, reel 4.

52 Fyrth, p. 66.

53 Cochrane, p. 35.

54 Interview with Alexander Tudor Hart, IWMSA 13771, reel 1.

55 Fyrth, p. 77.

56 Wogan Philipps, 'An Ambulance Man in Spain', in Valentine Cunningham ed., *Spanish Front: writers on the civil war*, Oxford: Oxford University Press, 1986, p. 45.

57 Fyrth, p. 66; Coni, p. 157.

58 Max Colin, cited in Palfreeman, p. 210.

59 Interview with Reginald Saxton, IWMSA 8735, reel 4.

60 KS Loutit and Aileen Palmer, 'Survey of a year's work with the British Medical Unit in Spain.' RGASPI 545/6/88 pp. 38-39.

61 Loutit and Palmer, *op cit*, pp. 40-41.

62 Palfreeman, p. 91.

63 Moisès Broggi, *Memorias de un cirujano*, 2001, cited in Palfreeman, p. 91.

64 *Ibid.*

65 Loutit, p. 99.

66 Cochrane, p. 40.

67 Loutit and Palmer, *op cit*, p. 46.

68 *Ibid.*

69 George Green, cited in Fyrth, p. 90.

70 Fyvel, p. 29.

71 Interview with Alexander Tudor Hart, IWMSA 13771, reel 3.

72 *Ibid.*

73 Interview with Annie Murray in MacDougall, p. 69.

74 Edith Tudor Hart to Alex, 22 July 1937. NA KV 5/1603.

75 *Ibid.*

76 Interview with Alexander Tudor Hart, IWMSA 13771, reel 2.

77 RGASPI 545/6/146, p. 61.

78 'Report received from Mrs Leah Manning', 4 August 1938, Warwick 292/946/42/16iii.

79 'Como cirugano trabaja asidumente sin descanso' [*sic*]. Assessment by Adrien Vogel, 10 October 1938. RGASPI 545/6/146, p. 70.

80 RGASPI 545/6/146 p. 78.

81 The British nurse Ethel 'Molly' Murphy described Tudor Hart as 'the worst of all' the Party members in the medical unit: 'He is both small-minded opportunist [sic] not the slightest idea of organization and generally disorganizes everybody else. As far as I'm concerned, he has only one qualification, i.e. setting fractures and for that reason at the moment must be tolerated.' Molly Murphy to 'Bill and Gordon', 13 April 1937, British Online Archives at https://microform.digital/boa /collections/ 95/ debate-and-division-on-the-british-left-1917-1964.

82 Palfreeman, p. 188.

83 Interview with Reginald Saxton, IWMSA 8735, reel 3.

84 Interview with Reginald Saxton, IWMSA 8735, reels 3-4.

85 Loutit, p. 86

86 *Daily Worker*, 1 September 1938.

87 NA KV 5/112, p. 6.

88 NA KV 2/1604.

89 Tommy developed relatively satisfactorily until he was about five years old. Edith always blamed the bombing in the Second World War for his issues; he could be very obsessive and wouldn't hold or make eye contact. MI5 unkindly referred to him as 'mentally defective', though it's more likely that Tommy was severely autistic. He was initially placed in Redhill hospital and later moved to a Steiner boarding school in Aberdeen.

90 *BMJ*, 28 January 1939, p. 168.

91 NA KV 2/1603/126a.

92 A. Tudor Hart, 'War Wounds and Air Raid Casualties', *BMJ*, 27 May 1939, pp. 1099-1101 and 3 June 1939, pp. 1146-1149.

93 B.1. note, 3 July 1939, NA KV 2/1603.

94 Note from HH Bacon, for Colonel Kell of MI5, 11 July 1939, NA KV 2/1603.

95 MI5 report on Alexander Ethan Tudor-Hart, 11 July 1939, NA KV 2/1603.

96 Robert Bowie Bernard and Alan Douglas Ware, an engineer and an accountant and members of the Spanish Medical Aid Committee, sailed for Dieppe on 13 March 1937 and both returned from Spain on 3 June. NA KV 5/112.

97 NA KV 2/1603/106.

98 Interview with Alex Tudor Hart, IWMSA 13771, reel 4.

99 Letter to the Inspector of Police, Birmingham, undated, NA KV 2/1603/119a.

100 *Ibid.*

101 CID report, 27 May 1940. NA KV 2/1603.

102 NA KV 2/1603/109a.

103 Most senior CPGB figures and British political commissars in Spain had studied at the Lenin School. See McIlroy et al, pp. 99-128.

104 Major General Sir Vernon Kell to Cecil C H Moriarty, Assistant Chief Constable of Birmingham, 9 May 1940, NA KV 2/1603.

105 Major General Sir Vernon Kell to Cecil C.H. Moriarty, Chief Constable Birmingham, 9 May 1940. NA KV 2/1603, p. 110.

106 One in particular MI5 would note with great interest: Rosa Shar, who married Percy Glading, a founder-member of the British Communist Party who was arrested for spying for Russia just before the Second World War and sentenced to six years hard labour. See [Unknown] October 1930, NA KV 2/1603.

107 Urgent and Personal report to Special Inspector T Thompson of Special Branch, 26 February 1938. NA KV 2/1603.

108 Letter to Major H. A. Golden, Chief Constable for Shropshire, 3 March 1941. NA KV 2/1603.

109 EDITH TUDOR-HART, 1 December, 1951, NA KV 2/1604.

110 Nigel West in 'Tracking Edith'.

111 Nigel West and Oleg Tsarev, *The Crown Jewels*. London: Harper Collins, 1998, p. 273. For Deutsch see Boris Volodarsky, *Stalin's Agent: The Life and Death of Alexander Orlov*, Oxford: OUP, 2014, pp. 477-491.

112 West and Tsarev, p. 106 and Forbes, p. 15.

113 I am very grateful to Boris Volodarsky for this information.

114 'Nigel West' in 'Tracking Edith'.

115 EDITH TUDOR-HART, 1 December, 1951, NA KV 2/1604.

116 NA KV 2 1603–4.

117 Special Branch report, 15 August 1940, NA KV 2/1603.

118 Report by CID, 14 May 1940. NA KV 2/1603/111a.

119 Chief Constable, Lincoln Constabulary to Brigadier O.A. Parker, Oxford, 12 November 1940. NA KV 5/1603.

120 A report from the local Chief Constable reassured the Security Services that 'the Master and Matron of the hospital are both very impressed with his work as a doctor.' NA KV 2/1604.

121 Special Branch assumed her to have married Tudor-Hart, as she had taken his surname. However, it was later discovered that

she had changed her name by deed poll and the pair were not actually wed until 6 November 1947. Special Branch Report, 29 June [year unknown], NA KV 2/1604/217a.

122 C.C Winchester, 16 June 1941, NA KV 2/1603.

123 Report by Det. Sergeant [unnamed], Winchester City Police to Head Constable, 16 June 1941, NA KV 2/1603.

124 A memo from Major W.A. Alexander [of MI5] on 25 September 1941 confirmed not only that 'we did not regard service in the Spanish Republican Army as necessarily affording grounds for objection from the Internal Security point of view,' but furthermore that Tudor Hart's 'special knowledge of war wounds rendered him desirable for the RAMC, and that . . . he ought to receive a Commission.' NA KV 5/1603.

125 WO to MI5 19 September 1941 and reply 26 September, NA KV 2/1603.

126 Alex Tudor Hart, in Hynes, p. 71.

127 Captain M. Johnstone to Major E. Bird, Southern Command, Salisbury, 21 November 1941. NA KV 2/1603/142a.

128 'Secret and Personal' report on Lieutenant P.T. Hart, 8 January 1942, NA KV 2/1603 and Report HQ Southern Command, Salisbury, 29 April 1942, NA KV 2/1603, p. 154a.

129 HQ Southern Command [undated] 1942, NA KV 2/1603.

130 Major E. Bird, to Captain M. Johnstone to, 29 April 1942. NA KV 2/1603/154a.

131 Letter from Alex Tudor Hart to Bill Rust, 1 June 1943. NA KV 5/1603.

132 Captain I. R. Deacon to Major J.P. McGeagh, Northern Command, York, 30 March 1943. NA KV 2/1603/168a.

133 *Volunteer for Liberty*, July 1944, p. 19.

134 DP Stevenson to MI5, 30 January 1945, NA KV 2/1604.

135 His reputation gained in Spain followed him to Colliers Wood, where other veterans such as John Longstaff and the former Head of Medical Services, Len Crome, took their children to Tudor Hart's surgery.

136 Extract from SB report 29 June 1949, NA KV 2/1014/123z.

137 Extract from SB report, 8 September 1949. NA KV 2/1604/213b.

138 NA KV 2/1604, p. 220, 10 December 1951.

139 Report by WJ Scardon, 9 January 1952, NA KV 2/4091 p.180b.

140 West, p. 202.

141 Volodarsky, p. 85.

142 Interview with Alexander Tudor Hart, IWMSA 13771, reel 4.

143 Interview with Alexander Tudor Hart, IWMSA 13771, reel 3.

144 Interview with Alexander Tudor Hart, IWMSA 13771, reel 4.

145 Special Branch report, [unknown] August 1931, NA KV 2/1603.

146 Duncan Forbes, '"Tracking" Edith Tudor-Hart', *History Workshop Journal*, 84, 2017, p. 239.

147 As Duncan Forbes points out, 'her few surviving letters to Alexander from the nineteen-thirties reveal a disarming mix of anxiety and passion quite beyond simulation.' Forbes, p. 65.

148 Report on Edith Tudor-Hart, 1 December 1951, NA KV 2/4091 p. 166a.

149 Interview with Alexander Tudor Hart, IWMSA 13771, reel 3.

150 Tudor Hart instead joined the Working People's Party of England (a Marxist-Leninist Party formed in the late 1960s) of which he became chairman. See John Moorhouse, *A Historical Glossary of British Marxism*, Paupers' Press, 1987.

151 Tudor Hart remained an active member of the International Brigade Association until his death, attending the annual commemoration in London and the unveiling of the national memorial in 1985. He also kept in regular contact with former comrades including Doctor Reg Saxton, and IBA committee members John Longstaff and Bill Alexander.

152 Loutit, p. 105.

153 Interview with Alexander Tudor Hart, IWMSA 13771, reel 4.

Index

MEMORIES OF SPAIN SERIES
AVAILABLE FROM THE CLAPTON PRESS

Never More Alive: Inside the Spanish Republic – Kate Mangan

The Good Comrade: Memoirs of an International Brigader – Jan Kurzke

In Place of Splendour – Constancia de la Mora

Firing a Shot for Freedom – Frida Stewart & Angela Jackson

The Fighter Fell in Love: A Spanish Civil War Memoir – James R Jump

The Last Mile to Huesca – Judith Keene and Agnes Hodgson

Struggle for the Spanish Soul – Arturo & Ilsa Barea

Hotel in Spain – Nancy Johnstone

Hotel in Flight – Nancy Johnstone

Sombreros are Becoming – Nancy Johnstone

Behind the Spanish Barricades – John Langdon Davies

Single to Spain & Escape from Disaster – Keith Scott Watson

Spanish Portrait – Elizabeth Lake

British Women in the Spanish Civil War – Angela Jackson

Boadilla – Esmond Romilly

My House in Málaga – Sir Peter Chalmers Mitchell

The Tilting Planet – David Marshall

Hampshire Heroes: Volunteers in the Spanish Civil War – Alan Lloyd

Remembering Spain: Essays, Memoirs and Poems on the International
Brigades and the Spanish Civil War – edited by Joshua Newmark/IBMT

www.theclaptonpress.com

Milton Keynes UK
Ingram Content Group UK Ltd.
UKHW010256070224
437385UK00011B/509